SEATTLE

KOBE TERRACE PARK

KU ARCOLOGY

Map Legend

Medical
1. Seattle General Hospital
2. Harborview Hospital
3. U.S. Public Health Hospital

Body Shops
4. Nightingale's Body Parts
5. Health Maintenance Organization
6. Fast Freddie's Surgery

Hotels
7. The Mayflower Park Hotel
8. The Westin Hotel
9. Hotel Nikko
10. Wylie's Gala Inn
11. Laubenstein Plaza
12. Chez Ogino
13. Lucas Palace
14. The West Coast Hamlin Hotel
15. The Warwick Hotel
16. The Stouffer-Madison Hotel
17. The New Century Square Hotel
18. The Seattle Hilton

Restaurants & Bars
(Cultural bias in parentheses)
19. Cafe Sport
20. Ohgi-Ya (Chinese)
21. Lee Chee Garden
22. The Green Village (Chinese)
23. The Other Place
24. The Edge (Elven)
25. Damian's
26. You Should Not Eat So Much!
27. Run Run Shaw's (Chinese)
28. Takuri's (Japanese)
29. The Glass Onion (Japanese)
30. Ling Ho (Japanese)
31. The Big Rhino (Orkish-Underground)
32. Purple Haze
33. Icarus Descending (Elven)
34. Bosco's (Elven)
35. The Gravity Bar
36. The Pink Door
37. A Little Bit O' Saigon
38. Marcus' Hovel
39. THE Sports Bar
40. Nyen Lang's (Chinese)
41. Tam's Under The Needle
42. Murphy's Law
43. Reno's
44. Knutson's Country Home
45. Elliot's
46. Miner's Landing
47. The Grey Line
48. Maximillion's
49. Gracie's for Ribs

Tourist Attractions
50. Seattle Aquarium
51. The Omnidome
52. Seattle Library
53. The County Courthouse
54. U.C.A.S. Post Office
55. Y.M.C.A.
57. Pacific Science Center
58. Seattle Repertory Theatre

TABLE OF CONTENTS

CONTENTS

CONTENTS

Designers
Bob Charrette
Paul Hume
Tom Dowd

Concept
Jordan Weisman
L. Ross Babcock III
Dave Wylie
Bob Charrette
Sam Lewis

Additional Fiction
Dave Wylie
Jordan Weisman

Playtesters

Bob Willis	John Saughnan
Carl Burke	Jeff Jarka
Chris Loew	Mike Knorr
Tom Ray	Caroline Maher
Tony Davrio	Mike Petrucci
Rex AKA Javis	

Editorial Staff
Senior Editor
Donna Ippolito
Editor
Jim Musser
Editorial Assistants
C. R. Green
Kent Stolt

Special Thanks
Ed Andrews
Steve Kramarsky

Production Staff
Production Manager
Sam Lewis
Art Director
Dana Knutson
Project Directors
Jim Nelson
Jeff Laubenstein
Cover Illustration
Larry Elmore
Shadowrun Logo and Cover Design
Jeff Laubenstein
Jim Nelson
Dana Knutson
Color Plates
Jeff Laubenstein
Jim Nelson
Illustration
Dana Knutson
Jeff Laubenstein
Jim Nelson
Joel Biske
Steve Venters
Dwane Loose
Alex Ross
Tim Bradstreet
Rick Harris
Earl Geier
Layout
Tara Gallagher
Jeff Laubenstein
Jim Nelson

SHADOWRUN and MATRIX
are trademarks of FASA Corporation
Copyright © 1989 FASA Corporation. All Rights Reserved.
Printed in the United States of America.
Corrected Second Printing

Published by
FASA Corporation
P. O. Box 6930
Chicago, IL 60680

THE YEAR IS 2050

*"Watch your back. Shoot straight. Conserve ammo.
And never, ever, cut a deal with a dragon."*
—Street Proverb

he blending of technology and human flesh began in the late 20th century. Interfacing the human mind with computers was just the first step. Implants that "jack up" reflexes and cybernetic replacements followed quickly. Then came the Awakening. A three-thousand-year lull in the flow of mystical energies subsided, and Magic returned to the world. Elves, Dwarfs, Orcs, and Trolls assumed their true form, throwing off their human guise.

The decades that followed the Awakening were years of turmoil, panic, and chaos, as the Horsemen of the Apocalypse raced across the Earth. Primitive cultures that had never lost touch with their mystical past began to utilize magic against the great nations that had suppressed them for so long. The vast, global telecommunications network collapsed under an assault by a mysterious computer virus. Nuclear missiles were launched, but failed to detonate. Dragons soared in the skies. Epidemics and famine ravaged the face of the Earth. Clashes between newly Awakened races and the rest of humanity became common. All central authority crumbled and the world began to spiral down into an abyss.

But man and his kin are hearty animals. Out of the devastation and anarchy, order slowly reemerged. Cybertechnology eradicated the last vestiges of the computer virus and replaced the old telecommunications network with what became known as the Matrix. New nation-states of Amerindians, Elves, Orks, and Dwarfs were formed. Megaplexes, vast city-states, sprawled over the landscape. Central governments were replaced by Mega-Corporations, which were a law unto themselves. People who accepted their sovereignty were protected. The outcasts, dissidents, and rebels were exploited and abused, as it had always been between the weak and the powerful since time began.

In the world of 2050, the megaplexes are monsters casting long shadows. As shadowrunners, that's where you live, in the cracks between the giant corporate structures. When the megacorps want something done but they don't want to dirty their hands, it's a Shadowrun they need, and they come to you. Though your existence is not acknowledged by any governmental or corporate database, the demand for your services is high. You might be a Technomancer, sliding like a whisper through the databases of giant corporations, spiriting away the only thing of real value–information. Or perhaps you are a Street Samurai, an enforcer for hire whose combat skills and reflexes make you the ultimate urban predator. Or perhaps a Mage, one with an ancient gift, the ability to wield and shape the magical energies that now surround the Earth. And that's exactly the kind of firepower you'll need if you get hired to make a Shadowrun…

NIGHT ON THE TOWN

Shadowrun **n. Any movement, action, or series of such made in carrying out plans which are illegal or quasilegal.**
—WorldWide WorldWatch, 2050 update

host walked into Club Penumbra and let the beat fill him. His head began to bob with the cardiac pulse, and he felt the feathers tucked into his hachimaki slide across his rain-slick neck. He wished he wasn't hunting business. Drops of water flew from the rampant ends of his frizz as he shook himself free of the music's spell.

The entryway was dark after the glow of the city streets, even with the shine of the wall-sized trid screen. A figure, full and feminine, shifted into his way. He tensed, then caught the gleam of the fiber-optic line running from the box on her belt to her head, and suppressed the urge to reach for his weapon. No danger here. She was a deckhead, her eyes turned inward to the simsense world filling her skull through the porcelain-lipped jack behind her ear. Lost in her head, she never felt the brush of his casual caress as he stepped past her onto the floor.

The Penumbra was crowded for so early in the night. Ghost threaded his way between the gyrating bodies on the dance floor, avoiding all contact with the frenetic revelers. His warpaint hardly looked out of place, but his broad Amerindian features marked him as an outsider among the mostly Anglo and Asian crowd. It didn't bother him. Those few who met his eyes returned wary, almost fearful stares. That was fine. He felt tough and ready. Their reactions only confirmed it.

He found her sitting in the back of the room, her stool rocked up onto its hind legs. The angle made her fringed, deer-leather duster, unfastened in the close heat of the club, fall away from her shoulders to reveal an expanse of fair flesh. Her fine, regular features were relaxed, green eyes hooded under languid lids. One leg rested on the table edge, and she toyed with the feathers decorating the top of her knee-high boot. She made an inviting picture, all allure, until you saw the weapon belts crossing her cut-off jeans, just above the crotch. The sculpted grip of her Remington Roomsweeper, snugged into the holster on her right hip, was barely visible in the shadows. Her intricately hilted magesword hung scabbarded on her left, nestled into a fold in her coat. A sharp edge to the image.

A dark-haired stranger eclipsed his view. Ghost had seen the type before. A line and a fast smile showing perfect corporate teeth to hide the tension in his body as he tried to hustle what he thought was a pretty piece of rough streetmeat. The suit had his courage up. With another glass of it in his hand, he was making his move, secure in the knowledge that his corp would protect a good little sarariman like himself.

A shift in the suit's stance let Ghost catch a glimpse of the woman's face. Her eyes now sparkled coldly behind a rigid, indifferent mask. The slumming sarariman was looking for a dangeroso thrill, and he blathered on, unaware how close he was to an unexpected return on his investment.

Her slim fingers twisted in a negligent gesture, chromed nails glinting in a flash of neon from the stage. Then she whispered something that Ghost doubted he would have heard even if the room were silent. Blinded to her actions by his own desires, the suit never saw the liquid rise from his glass and fling itself onto the pale gray denim of his Jeddi Kal jeans.

Smiling, Ghost stepped up behind the sputtering sarariman.

"Buzz, chummer."

The man spun, eyes widening with fear and showing Ghost his own reflection in the man's gold-irised Zeiss eyes. Though Ghost's ragged street grin was distorted by the curve of the lens, it carried his feral mood anyway. The man backed away, wet spot growing on his jeans. He stumbled into a passing reveler, who shoved him hard but without real rancor. Rubbing a bruised arm, the man disappeared into the crowd. Ghost turned his attention to the woman he had come to see.

"Hoi, Sally. Whuzappening?"

She gave him the knowing little smile that always annoyed Ghost and tapped the stool at her side. "You've heard or you wouldn't have come uptown. Any trouble crossing Ancient's territory?"

He shrugged as he sat. "Naw. Them Elves is still lying low after their last tumble with the Tigers." He waved off the approaching barmaid, who favored him with a sour look. "I heard you had a shadowrun cooking. Ain't heard anything about how hot the oven is."

"If it were easy, I wouldn't need you."

Her compliment pleased him, but Ghost kept his face straight. This was still business. "Tricky, is it?"

"Not really, but I want a good gun at my back."

That lit a warning light. When Sally wanted muscle and guns, she was expecting trouble. "Who's the mark?"

"Mitsuhama," she whispered.

"MCT? No wonder you want a good gun."

She gave him a nod, looking slightly apologetic. "I owe somebody. This is the way they want to be repaid."

"You must have a hell of a debt."

"Not really. This run's a simple snatch and grab on some data. My somebody is just a little short on allocable resources at the moment."

"If that's all, what do you need a samurai for?"

"I suppose I don't," she said softly, reaching across to rest a hand on his arm. "But I'm feeling something odd about this one. It's making me nervous, so I want some quality back-up, Ghost-Who-Walks-Inside."

He snorted. She always knew how to get to him. "You'll still need a good decker."

"Got one." To his raised eyebrow, she continued, "Dodger."

That was a surprise. "If the Dodger's in, the haul must be worthwhile. But even he's not gonna get through their Ice."

"Says who?"

Ghost turned casually, recognizing the voice. The booming bass drum impression that the band's sasquatch was belting out had drowned the approach of the tall, slim man in black leathers. No, not man—Elf. The new arrival's delicately pointed ears showed plainly against the depilated side of his head, and his datajack ports gleamed a bright silver in the flashes of strobe from the dance floor.

"Sneaking up like that ain't healthy, Dodger," Ghost warned.

The Elf shrugged away the implied threat. "The Ice will not concern us, Sweet Lady Tsung. I have the key that will unlock the castle gates."

He held up a slim plastic rod for her to see.

"Where'd you get that?"

"Conjured it?" he suggested. To her disbelieving face, he added, "A cautious person takes care of his sources, Lady Fair."

Ghost was surprised at Sally's breach of business etiquette in inquiring after Dodger's source. She must be worried. He wanted to know, too, but he had his own standards to live up to. Still, he needed to know what was going on. "'Scuse me, you two. What's the stick, and how's it going to help us?"

Dodger gave Ghost a look that left no doubt that the Elf considered him a moron. "Very simple, Sir Razorguy. This is the security key to a Mitsuhama monitor station. With this, we can open the can and get at the station. From there, I can jack directly into their mainframe, safely inside their Intrusion Counter-measures."

"They've still got to have protection."

"Of course. But that will be no problem. I am the Dodger, after all."

Ghost and Sally exchanged knowing glances. Dodger was good, all right, but only a decker would be so sure of himself.

"Have faith, my companions. We shall run through the shadows unseen by the corporate guard dogs and escape with the swag." The Elf leaned forward in a conspiratorial fashion. "But we must be quick, for my magic key fades to dross at midnight."

Ghost called the time function to his retinal display. 10:42:33 PST. That didn't leave much time. "Who else we waitin' on, Sally?"

"Who else do we need?" she said with a grin, shoving away from the wall. "Let's do 'em."

Ghost matched her grin. He liked her style.

The rain had stopped, and the streets were filling up as the trio left Club Penumbra. Dodger had put his Yamaha Rapier in the rack next to Ghost's own Harley. The Elf's bike looked slim and fragile next to the big combat hog. Despite Dodger's objections, Ghost insisted on checking out the bike and fiddling with its systems. By the time he was satisfied with its response, Sally had pulled up on her red and silver custom-fitted Rapier and the Elf shut up. They roared away from the club in a cloud of petrochem smoke.

They had a few tense moments when they ran into some toughs on Trog turf, but the Orks didn't push it. Just outside the part of town the big corps called their own, they found a nice quiet alley. A certified credstick with a 200-nuyen balance and bottle of Old Redeye bought a squatter's assurance that he'd hit

the PANICBUTTON if anybody molested the bikes. The promise wasn't worth much, but the bribe would likely keep the alley's residents away from the machines.

Then they were off, moving through the shadows of the corporate streets. There were no crowds here, just empty, clean streets. Full of corporate pride and roving corporate security patrols. The big boys didn't like trouble on their turf.

It took them a cautious hour to reach the goal, a dark, dank alley in back of Mitsuhama's downtown offices. Halfway down the puddled lane, flanked by hollows in the smooth concrete, was the black macroplast tower that shielded the station they sought. The monitor station, back out of sight of the upper-class types, was for the convenience of Mitsuhama's security goons, letting them report to their bosses or check out any data or system updates. A key was the only way past the casing that protected the terminal. The black macroplast was proof against anything short of an anti-tank warhead, and anybody trying that way in would destroy the terminal beneath the armor.

Dodger produced the keystick and held it poised above the slot. "Your assessment, Lady Fair?"

Sally closed her eyes and rocked her head back, turning it slowly from side to side. Ghost knew what she was doing, but his shoulder muscles still twitched. No matter how many times he saw her do it, Sally's astral scanning still rattled him.

"All clear," she announced. "Do it."

Dodger slipped the black rod into the station's key slot. For a few long seconds, nothing happened. Ghost wondered if Dodger's source had sold him a dud, or worse, a screamer that would call down the corporate heat while they waited. His eyes roved the alley, which seemed to contain no one else but his companions and the local rats. Sally was nervous, too. She slid her Remington out of its holster and ran the tip of her tongue tentatively along her upper lip. A soft hum rose from behind the macroplast, bringing a smile to Dodger's lips. As the panel slid up, Ghost felt Sally relax.

A soft pop caught Ghost's attention. He snatched a glance at the source of the sound. Three shiny prongs stretched clawlike out of the back of Dodger's hand. The Elf snugged them into slots in the Mitsuhama monitor station, then rocked his hand back. The silvered cones remained in the terminal, but cables as fine as fairy thread ran from them to the receptacles in Dodger's hand. "So ka," Ghost whispered to himself in understanding.

The prongs were program carriers. The chips the Elf had inserted into the station would allow him to run the Matrix as soon as he jacked in through his datajack. It wasn't as safe as using a proper cyberdeck, but carrying one here wouldn't have been safe, either. There was no way to explain to a corpcop why you had a deck on their turf. Deckers that weren't corporate property were dead meat in this part of town.

Dodger flipped open a panel next to the keyboard. Pulling the cable free, he snapped the plug into his jack. As his fingers began to fly over the keys, his eyes rolled back in his head, focused inward as the vision of cyberspace filled his mind. The tap-tap of the keys floated out into the night.

Seconds stretched into minutes, and the minutes started piling up. It was taking too long. The corp patrols wouldn't leave them alone forever. Sally's chromed nails rang on the station's aluminum rim. "Hurry," she chanted. "Hurry, hurry."

Light flooded the alley.

Ghost almost breathed a sigh of relief as he snatched his twin Ingrams from their holsters. The tension of waiting was almost over. He held his eagerness in check, waiting for the guards he could hear moving toward them.

Dodger cursed as he jerked back from the terminal. The black shield whistled down, slicing his datajack cord and the prong lines as easily as it would have parted bone and flesh if his hand had been slower.

Getting dumped had left him disoriented. Sally propped him against the wall. Ghost could see that the Elf was still half-lost in cyberspace, but he had no time for concern. The running footsteps were closing.

Ghost smiled to himself as several dozen or so Orks rounded the corner of the warehouse. His reflexes were tuned so high that it almost seemed that Ghost fired at open air, the Orks somehow appearing just in time for the bullets to strike them. Screeching tires suddenly punctuated the scene as a security groundcar appeared at the end of the alley. It was a corporate vehicle, and obviously armored. Mystic energies crackled at Sally's fingertips, and a ball of energy leaped at the car, blowing it in two and igniting the fuel tank like a bomb. The corporate goons froze in the white flash of the flame, to which Ghost's Chiba eyes instantly compensated. Putting a fourth and fifth burst of 9mm slugs into a temporarily blinded Troll, he thanked himself for spending the extra bucks for flare compensators.

"Head for the bikes. I'll catch up." Ghost walked backward, scanning the area and engaging targets. Sally grabbed the Elf's arm and got him moving, while casting a look at Ghost as though about to speak.

"Beat feet, people!" Ghost hissed, cutting off any protest. They began to move faster as the Elf shook himself out of his stupor.

In moments, Sally and Dodger were legging it hard toward the alley where their bikes awaited. Ghost scanned the scene one last time before he too turned and ran. What had taken over an hour to cover in stealth, they now moved across in minutes.

Ghost knew it was inevitable that they would run into more trouble. When they were just a few hundred meters from their transportation, another security car appeared in front of them. Sally and the Elf halted, their breath coming in short gasps.

She began trying to put together another spell. "Save it," Ghost told her as he fished a grenade out of his pocket and yanked the pin.

The car doors were opening and the bad guys getting out. As they did, Ghost tossed the grenade. His wired body seemed to pick out every detail as the sphere crossed the distance to its target. The spoon made a tiny metallic popping sound as it sprang free. Pretty white sparks made a trail as the willie peter bounced under the car. When the White Phosphorus grenade blossomed into its full glory with a dull "whump," Ghost chuckled softly. The car disintegrated in a cloud of debris, and bits of Toyota flew through the air.

"See," Ghost said, smiling as he swung a leg over his bike, "you don't have to be a wizard to throw a fireball."

Sally laughed and shook her head. "That's why I like working with you, Casper. It's always a blast!"

Dodger's words were drowned out as Ghost started his engine, and the three sped off into the night.

AND SO IT CAME TO PASS...

"Walking the beat those first couple of months was bizarre. You never knew if your partner was going to suddenly grow fangs."
—Pat Mifflin, Retired Policeman

 oday, in 2050, our world is radically different from that our great-grandfathers knew. Where once superpower nations dominated the globe, threatening all with sudden nuclear annihilation, the superpowers have now broken up into many smaller, autonomous nations, and corporations have taken over their once-immense power. Our science and technology, too, set us apart, with current levels making previous advances look like a child's experiments with a science kit.

But that is not all that divides our age irrevocably from the past, for magic has emerged again on Earth and we live in an Awakened world.

RISE OF THE MEGACORPS

It all began in the late 1990s, as the civil unrest that marked the end of the millennium intensified even more. Alarmed at the state of things, the corporations feared to trust their interests to indifferent or, in their eyes, incompetent governments. Beginning with their holdings in the Third World countries, they armed their security personnel with the finest available equipment and hired professional mercenaries on both long- and short-term contracts. As the tide of civil disobedience and urban violence began to engulf every nation on the globe, the corporations began to transfer their paramilitary assets wherever needed. The stage was set.

In 1999, food riots in New York City created the flashpoint. Angered and frightened by a three-month truckers' strike that had stopped the flow of fresh foods into New York, the people took to the streets. Hundreds were killed and thousands injured as the violence spread through the city.

At one point, a Seretech Med-Research truck hauling wastes, including infectious materials, became the target of a mob. In what became a running gunfight, Seretech security came to the aid of the corporate truckers, withdrawing them to one of the firm's medical research facilities. More violence followed as the maddened crowd stormed the building. By dawn, 20 Seretech employees were dead, while 200 rioters lay lifeless on the grounds and in the street.

In a misguided attempt to crush the growing corporate armies, the city, then the state and federal governments, charged Seretech with criminal negligence. Seretech asserted that by defending its truck from the mob, it prevented the potentially lethal cargo from infecting the population at large. In a landmark decision, the Supreme Court upheld Seretech's right to maintain an armed force for the protection of its own personnel and property, and commended the corporation for protecting innocent citizens and honoring its trust to dispose of contaminated materials safely. The case set a precedent that led to the Shiawase Decision of 2001, firmly establishing the extra-territoriality of multinational corporations in international law.

More disasters followed. In 2004, Libya unleashed a chemical weapon against Israel. The Israelis responded by destroying half of Libya's cities with nuclear weapons. Then, in 2005, a major earthquake hit New York City, killing more than 200,000 people and leaving behind over 200 billion dollars worth of damage. It would be 40 years before the city was fully rebuilt. In the meantime, the United Nations moved to Geneva and the East Coast Stock Exchange to Boston.

RESOURCE RUSH

With their new freedom, the corporations of North America increased their exploitation of the continent's resources with a vengeance. In what the media dubbed "The Resource Rush," corporate coalitions demanded and were granted access to oil, mineral, and land resources on federal lands. Again and again, in the years 2002–8, the government invoked the right of eminent domain to bring property under its control, only to license its exploitation to a corporate sponsor. Taking the brunt of this landgrab were the Indian reservations and federal parklands.

Conservationists and Indian-rights groups expressed their shock and disgust, though corporate influence and paramilitary power made it dangerous to object. Angry and frustrated, the more radical elements founded the Sovereign American Indian Movement (SAIM), whose roots traced back to the Indian-rights struggles of the twentieth century.

The growing tension and hatreds finally erupted in 2009. On May 5, United Oil Industries announced that it had acquired the right to exploit the petrochemical resources in one-quarter of the remaining federal parks and one-tenth of the Indian lands, which the government had just confiscated. SAIM reacted immediately. A small band entered the Shiloh Launch Facility in northwest Montana, capturing a missile silo. To this day, no one knows how the raiders managed to bypass the security patrols, but once inside the missile silo, they met up with John Redbourne, a USAF major and a full-blood Dakota Sioux. After knocking his partner unconscious, Redbourne took the man's keys and codes to unlock the launch failsafes.

THE LONE EAGLE

Issuing a demand for the return of all Indian land, the Shiloh raiders threatened to launch the silo's missiles. Ten days of tense negotiations ended when a black-garbed delta team invaded the silo. During the struggle, which resulted in the death of all of the occupying Indians, a Lone Eagle missile was launched.

NORAD command in Cheyenne Mountain watched help-lessly as the missile headed for the Soviet Union. All their auto-destruct signals went unheeded, and the military had no interceptors in position to down the bird. Though denying responsibility for the launch, President Jesse Garrety informed Moscow of the targets of each of the missile's multiple warheads, hoping to avert a full-scale retaliation by giving the Soviets enough warning to use their semi-secret ballistic defenses to stop the missile.

Moscow was understandably skeptical of Washington's claims that the Lone Eagle was an isolated accident and not a ploy to make a surgical strike against selected Soviet targets. They put their forces on full alert. As tank divisions began preparations to invade Europe, all Soviet citizens were ordered to shelters. In the United States, however, the public was unaware that it was perilously close to nuclear war.

President Garrety waited anxiously, and as later revealed in the celebrated "Back-Room Tapes," alternately wept, ranted, and prayed. Two hours later, General Secretary Nikolai Chelenko tersely informed him that the warheads had been stopped. A privately conducted stress analysis of Chelenko's voice later indicated only a 79 percent probability that he spoke the truth, but neither seismic nor space-based sensors recorded any nuclear explosions at that time. Explosion or not, there was definitely fallout from the incident.

THE BLAME FALLS

When the American public learned of the Lone Eagle crisis, the outcry was enormous. Goaded by corporate propagandists, the people began to blame SAIM, and by implication, all Native Americans. This fit well with the larger plans of the megacorporations, principally United Oil Industries, which was not satisfied with their rate of acquisition. By 2010, they had applied enough pressure to pass the Re-Education and Relocation Act. This new law called for the confinement of anyone connected in any way to SAIM. Abuses of the law were rampant because of the general hatred of Indians. Thousands of innocent Native Americans were sent to concentration camps, euphemistically called "re-education centers." Among those shipped to the Abilene camp was Daniel Coleman, future Prophet of the Great Ghost Dance and the first war shaman of the Native American Nations. History knows him as Daniel Howling Coyote.

In a government economy measure, Congress soon contracted out management of the re-education camps to the corporations. As the camps dropped out of the media spotlight, overcrowding, poor sanitation, and insufficient medical care began to plague the inmates of the camps. Was this a deliberate plan of genocide, as Coleman would one day claim? In one of the great ironies of history, however, the isolation of many tribes in the re-education camps spared them from the scourge that hit the world in 2010.

TRIBULATIONS

Virally Induced Toxic Allergy Syndrome (VITAS) broke out first in New Delhi, but within weeks, cases were being reported all over the globe. In the worst epidemic since the Black Plague, an estimated 25 percent of the world's people were dead or dying by the end of 2010. Most fatalities were in outlying areas where medical care was unavailable or in high-population

THE SIXTH WORLD

What we know as the Year of Chaos was actually the end of the old age and the beginning of the new, the dawn of our Awakened World. Some mystics point to the Mayan calendar as an authority, noting that it predicts the start of a new cycle of humanity on December 24, 2011. They also say the appearance of the Dragon Ryumyo is the signpost marking what the Mayans called the Sixth World.

Had they done better research, these dreamers would have discovered that the Mayans also predicted a world-destroying calamity that would herald the birth of a new, improved race of humans. Where were these things? It is true that we faced trials, disasters, and great change, but we do not have a new world. It's still good, old Mother Earth, even if she has entered a new phase.

We get a better model of the change by looking at the historical shift from B.C. to A.D. No one at the time knew it had happened. Only hindsight reveals it. Even the calendar had to be backdated to take into account the change.

THE DANCE

For years after Daniel Coleman led his cadre of believers out from the Abilene REC compound, he dropped from public view. Knowledge of his activities during that period is minimal, but he was, most certainly, proselytizing. Among Native Americans—those still free as well as those incarcerated in camps or restricted to the ever-shrinking reservations—word spread of a new prophet, a great shaman to whom the spirits had taught a powerful dance.

This inspired Native Americans to resist the tyranny of their existence. Many more escaped the camps, eluding the federal

centers where the supplies of medicines and interim vaccines were insufficient. China, India, many African nations, and many densely populated Third World cities suffered disproportionately because their medical delivery systems could not provide adequate symptomatic relief.

Tragic as the VITAS plague was, it was only the beginning of unprecedented chaos. Beginning with the violent dissolution of the Mexican government in January 2011, more governments fell than in any other five-year span in history. Famine stalked the world, adding to the already-lengthy rolls of the dead. Massive civilian protests led to raids on European nuclear power plants, three of which suffered meltdowns. Radiation fallout was extensive and damaging.

On the heels of VITAS came the frightening phenomenon later named Unexplained Genetic Expression, or UGE. All over the world, mutant and changeling children were being born to "normal" parents. Newsweek dubbed these UGE children "elves," and it seemed that the horsemen of the Apocalypse had finally arrived. This year has become known as the Year of Chaos.

As miracles and calamities were reported from every nation, religions rose and died. Prophets appeared, proclaiming the end of the world. One of these emerged from the despair of a concentration camp. On December 24, at the same moment that hundreds of Japanese witnessed the first appearance of the great Dragon Ryumyo as they sped past Mount Fuji on a bullet train, the Prophet of the Great Ghost Dance, Daniel Howling Coyote, led his followers out of the Abilene Re-Education Center.

THE AWAKENING

"It was uncanny. They just ignored us, but it was more like they never heard a word we said. I thought it might have been the thunder that was drowning out the loudspeaker, but my boss didn't agree. He decided to make good his threat to fire if they didn't stop. I was scared, though, what with the spooky way them Injuns was acting. When the others started firing, I did, too.

"But the Injuns just kept walking. And that Coleman fella was kinda like glowing. I know the scientists say it was just a trick of the light, some kind of reflection from the lightning. I still swear I hit him clean two or three times, but he just kept on walking.

"When they got to the gate, which had come blown open in the wind, they just waltzed right on out. We didn't go after them that night 'cause of the storm. Next morning, we couldn't find a trace. It was really weird."
—Testimony given before the Abilene Official Investigating Commission by Harry Wood, a guard at the Abilene Re-education Center on December 24, 2011

---

and corporate hunters by fleeing into the wilderness. Like their ancestors, they began a guerrilla war against an army that wanted to destroy them. Unlike their ancestors, they had access to the same technology as their enemy.

In 2014, Daniel Coleman stepped out of the shadows. He called himself Howling Coyote and declared that he was a shaman of the Ghost Dance. Backed by an elite core of fanatics, he announced the formation of the Native American Nations, a coalition of tribes. They laid claim to all of North America and demanded the immediate withdrawal of all persons of European, African, and Asian ancestry, threatening dire magical retribution if the demand was not met. Of course, the media tried to make a laughingstock of Coleman and his followers. Though magical phenomena had become increasingly commonplace, no one believed any group of persons could enforce such a threat.

Insulting jokes were still making the talk-show circuit when Howling Coyote and his Ghost Dancers demonstrated their power. In 2014, Redondo Peak erupted, burying Los Alamos, New Mexico under a cloud of ash. Howling Coyote appeared in a vid-cast from a nearby Zuñi reservation. He claimed credit for invoking "our Mother Earth to punish the children who forsook Her."

Surviving documentation indicates that the U.S. government did not take the claim seriously, except to capitalize on an opportunity to capture the elusive resistance leader and smash his growing movement. Within an hour of Howling Coyote's broadcast, a federal reaction force, composed of the Sixth Air Cavalry Battalion from Fort Hood, Texas, was in the air. The helicopters and support aircraft never reached the Zuñi reservation. All were destroyed by the sudden appearance of violent tornadoes. When a second force arrived, the self-proclaimed shaman was long gone.

The guerrilla war went on, to the great embarrassment of the federal and corporate forces, who seemed unable to see or touch their prey. While frustration mounted in the government, it became harder to enforce news blackouts and official denials wore increasingly thin. Finally, someone leaked the whole story, and it rocked the government, with President Jesse Garrety forced to take the heat.

THE INDIAN QUESTION

Amid the storm of criticism, Garrety was assassinated in late-2016, followed shortly by the assassinations of General Secretary Nikolai Chelenko of the USSR, Prime Minister Lena Rodale of Great Britain, and Minister Chaim Schon of Israel. The assassins of Chelenko, Schon, and Rodale were ultimately killed in violent confrontations. William Springer, the man identified as Garrety's assassin, was never captured.

William Jarman, the new U.S. President, issued the now-infamous Executive Order 17-321 immediately upon taking office. One month later, Congress ratified it with the Resolution Act of 2016. The corrupt government had sanctioned Jarman's plan to resolve "the Indian question": total extermination of all Native American tribes.

While the government huddled with the megacorporations to plan their strategy, Howling Coyote's people had quietly begun their own solution to the "Indian Question." We now know that the Great Ghost Dance began in 2017, as men and women of the tribes all across the continent performed the ritual that Howling Coyote had taught them. They sang his songs and chanted his chants. Their power grew.

Early in the year, when the government moved to implement the Resolution Action of 2016, several months of freak weather and other uncanny disturbances disrupted military bases and supply dumps assigned to the plan. With each new delay, the President sacked another general, but he refused to commit his forces piecemeal. By August 17, the government had finally managed to assemble its troops, and the operation began to roll.

That morning, at 10:32 A.M, Mount Hood, Mount Rainier, Mount St. Helens, and Mount Adams all erupted in cataclysmic fury. Mother Earth had announced whose side she was on, and even the most skeptical became believers.

TREATY OF DENVER

Meanwhile, Native American tribesman and non-Indian sympathizers were occupying military bases in all three North American countries. Chastened and wary, the three governments sent representatives to Denver to negotiate with the Ghost Dancers in 2018. Three months later, they had hammered out the Treaty of Denver.

In the treaty, the federal governments of the United States, Canada, and Mexico acknowledged the sovereignty of the Native American Nations (NAN) over most of western North America. The document outlined a ten-year population adjustment plan that would relocate all non-Indians off lands belonging to NAN. Provisions included the establishment of reservations for non-tribal peoples and corporations, the maintenance of certain cities (such as Seattle) as extraterritorial extensions of the governments that had formerly claimed that land, and the retention of most of the state of California by the United States.

No one was happy with the Treaty of Denver, but no one had a better solution. The magical capacity of NAN offset the nuclear capacity of the three North American nations, which is why they agreed to give away large portions of their land and wealth. Though the Native Americans had not achieved their goal of removing all others from their homelands, they had regained control over much of it.

Howling Coyote was named the head of the Sovereign Tribal Council, the NAN governing body. Though he found it difficult to mediate among the bickering that now began to plague the various factions, Howling Coyote was probably the only man who could still rally the loyalty of all sides.

While the Tribal Council struggled with internecine problems, the people of the United States experienced a new shock of horror when the spaceplane *America* disintegrated in orbit. The wreckage landed in Australia, killing 300 in the small town of Longreach.

Also in 2018, the first-generation ASIST (Artificial Sensory Induction System) technology was created by Dr. Hosato Hikita of ESP Systems, Inc. in Chicago. While the entertainment industry was going wild exploiting the commercial aspects of "simsense," other researchers saw the technology as a key to containing the data explosion.

GOBLINIZATION

On April 30, 2021, a totally inexplicable phenomenon began. All over the world, one out of every ten men and women suddenly metamorphosed into hideous humanoid shapes. For some, the process was short and mild. Others spent days or weeks in the hospital. Some recovered, while others died screaming in agony. In those horrible weeks, two new races of man were emerging like strange spring flowers under the Awakened sun.

"Goblinization" was the name the media gave to this seemingly catastrophic process which was but another threshold point in the reemergence of magic. Researchers had their own names for it, mostly polysyllabic mouthfuls or strings of consonants standing in for strings of seemingly unconnected words. Whatever the name, the result was the same. No race or ethnic group was spared as 10 percent of the world population became what were soon dubbed "orks" and "trolls," projecting dark dreams of goblins onto the unsightly physical modification of the victims.

Most of these unfortunates were traumatized by the experience. And if they were not, their loved ones were. Some accepted the media's name for them as license to act like the ghouls and goblins of legend, making incidents of violence common.

Had it ended there, surely the psychological wounds would have healed in time. But some "normal" children changed as they grew older, joining the ranks of the so-called Orks and Trolls. These either grouped with their own kind or mated with great-hearted souls who could see past the physical shells. The offspring of such unions were sometimes normal and sometimes produced the new racial types. Not all the "normal" children remained that way, however. Many suddenly underwent goblinization at puberty, and the trauma and its associated maladjustments cycled again through the community.

> "The Matrix is a computer-generated, symbolic representation of the Grid, the world information network. Instead of dealing with messy manual commands and procedures, the cyberdeck lets the user perform apparently real actions in cyberspace and translates these into system operations. A person in the Matrix reaches out and touches the symbol representing a file. The deck's software knows that the user wants to open that file. The machine performs all of the complicated microtronic operations, freeing the user from the tedious task of having to enter those commands manually. Matrix imagery is imposed on the user by the Grid in a "consensual hallucination," to use Dr. Hikita's term. It's no more an ultimate reality than an animated vid-chip. It's computer-generated graphic images. The systems and the functions those images represent are real, but the images are just that. There is no reality."
>
> —Dr. William Spheris, interviewed on the trid show, *People to People*, broadcast June 12, 2049

UGE, Goblinization, and the violence it spawned consumed the people of Earth for much of the next year. Where the color of men's skins had once been the great barrier, the people of Earth now began to hate and fear the new "races," the emerging Elves, Dwarfs, Orks, and Trolls. In the year 2022, race riots wracked the globe on a scale never seen. In the turmoil, new nations emerged when states split from parent countries or coalesced from two or more units. In the North American sphere, the most important of these were an independent Quebec and the newly formed Caribbean League.

The U.S. government declared martial law for several months in a futile attempt at control, while reports trickling out of the Soviet Union told of deaths on a mass scale. In fear for their lives, many of the changed beings went into hiding, whether underground, into the wilderness, or in communities of their own kind.

As the year drew to a close, however, another specter more gruesome than any Ork or Troll raised its head as a new wave of the VITAS plague swept the planet. While another 10 percent of the world's population fell before the onslaught, racial violence flickered out, leaving both human and metahuman reunited in fear.

It was in this grim year that *Data*, an electronic news magazine, first coined the term "Awakened" for the metahumans and other lifeforms recently come into being.

MAGIC AND THE MATRIX

Though humanity suffered through another devastating crisis, science and technology marched on. In 2024, the first simsense entertainment unit (a kind of sensory VCR) became available. The unit offered the user rudimentary sense impressions, with full awareness that the experience was a simulation. Also in this year, the experimental "remote-vote" system was used in the U.S. presidential election for the first time. President Jarman was reelected by landslide victories in urban centers, though the opposition claimed fraud. Meanwhile, the NAN relocations continued relatively peacefully despite continued provocation by the hostile Jarman White House.

In 2025, magic joined the ranks of science at last, when UCLA gave the discipline academic recognition by establishing the first undergraduate program in occult studies. Fine programs at the University of Southern California, Brown, and Yale soon followed. Within two years, technical magic programs and magical research facilities were established at Texas A & M and MIT, with the latter adding "& M" to its name (for "and Magic").

In 2027, science tapped another source of power, this time in the sunlit world. After years of pursuing the dream of tabletop cold fusion power, the first powerplant went on-line. The dream of tiny generators had not been fulfilled, but the research led to breakthroughs that made possible the construction of large power plants.

The other breakthrough of this year was the development of cyberterminals. As computer systems became increasingly complex during the late 20th century, many programs replaced lengthy strings of commands with simple pictures, or icons, that symbolized specific commands or programs. You picked the icon you wanted, and the computer would do whatever the picture meant. By the late 1990s, however, a typical user was dealing with so many thousands of icons that data-processing systems were breaking down under their own complexity.

By 2029, Sony Cybersystems, Fuchi Industrial Electronics, and RCA-Unisys had all developed prototype cyberterminals that allowed a user to interface with the world data network via his nervous systems, which translated the data and issued the commands. Instead of typing in commands or clicking a mouse at an icon, operations were carried out literally at the speed of thought. These early cyberterminals were massive, requiring that the user be in a sensory-deprivation tank. Largely funded by various intelligence agencies, the goal of the research was to allow agents to raid data systems, creating strike teams of "super-hackers."

In the United States, the CIA, NSA, and IRS pooled their resources to exploit this development. Under the code name of Echo Mirage, they recruited and trained a team of "cyber-commandoes." Fighting balky equipment and the psychoses in-

---

Sometime during the big troubles in the 'teens, people started doing magic. It's possible that magic existed before then, but it was unreliable. Now it worked every time you did it right. During those years of chaos, magic and magicians became part of modern life.

Some scientists have trouble dealing with the fact of magic. On one hand, they can't deny that there is something that does all these things, but they are unwilling to believe it's "magic." No matter how they try to fit magic into their scientific model of reality, magic seems to break most of the laws of physics, as they apply to observed phenomena in the normal continuum. In other words, what you and I call "the real world." Other scientists posit that magic uses a form of energy simply not relevant to the physical laws of our universe, and thus the descriptive mathematics of the theoretical physicist do not apply.

Magic has been defined as the art and science of causing change in conformity with the will. The keywords are "art and science." Magic operates by strict laws within its own frame of reference, and therefore may be considered a science. Yet, it is also an art because only a living mind can make it work. Like all arts, magic uses emotion and willpower to open the doors of consciousness. Thus, one must be a poet as well as a mathematician to deal with theoretical thaumaturgy. A touch of sheer insanity seems to help, too.

This may be a bitter pill for the more materialistic researchers to swallow, but it is also why our laboratories have no "magicometers." It is why no spell-casting programs run on our most sophisticated computers, and why no batteries of magical energy power our cars or appliances. The only machine able to wield magic remains the living mind of a magician.

—From "Observations Toward a Theory of Somatic Mutation and Psionic Developments," paper presented by Dr. Randall Grant, AAAS Conference, 2038

---

duced by the overwhelming sensory signals generated by the primitive cyberterminals, Echo Mirage was advancing toward a workable technology when disaster struck.

CRASH OF '29

On February 8, 2029, computer systems across the world were attacked, apparently at random, by a virus program of unprecedented power. Systems crashed, their data wiped clean and even their hardware burned out by the effects of the virus. As the killer program spread, governments toppled and the world economy neared collapse.

During the first quarter of the year, the virus shattered the data network that held the world together. By presidential order, Echo Mirage was activated to counteract the virus, but the "straight-arrow" agents of Echo Mirage were overwhelmed by the psychological demands of combat in cyberspace.

Echo Mirage's masters responded by recruiting the most brilliant, if erratic, data-processing mavericks from industry and the universities. Their choices were drafted under a presidential emergency order and rammed through a brutal training program. A cadre of 32 men and women graduated with their sanity intact.

It was not until August 2029, however, that the new cadre, armed with improved cybertechnology, could mount a coordinated attack on the killer program.

Eighteen minutes after engaging the virus, four members of Echo Mirage were dead. When the data logs were analyzed,

two things became apparent. First, the virus program could induce lethal biofeedback in humans accessing the Matrix. Second, no existing computer security could even slow down someone using a cyberterminal.

The corporations involved in the effort were horrified at the ease with which Echo Mirage penetrated their most secure data systems. In reaction, secret corporate research was begun to develop new security software that could repel intruders in the Matrix. This included research to duplicate the lethal effects generated by the virus. The resulting software was the first generation of Intrusion Countermeasures, or IC, known worldwide as "Ice".

Echo Mirage learned techniques to isolate and contain the virus. Equipped with new combat programs and beefed-up cyberterminals, they began the lengthy task of purging the Grid of infection. By late 2031, they had wiped out the last-known concentration of the virus code.

These second-generation terminals used desk-sized hardware and needed no sensory deprivation tank. Shortly after the final purge of the virus, four of the surviving seven members of Echo Mirage decamped into the private sector, taking with them the secrets of the new technology.

In May 2034, Matrix Systems of Boston came out with the first "gray-market" cyberterminal. Six weeks later, Matrix Systems' main computer crashed and its two founders died in apparently unrelated accidents.

From the perspective of the military-industrial complex, the damage had already been done. Matrix technology was loose. Fuchi Industrial was the first major corporation to break ranks against the invasion of the deckers when, in 2036, it marketed its own third-generation cyberdeck, the desktop CDT-1000.

The majority of cyberdecks sold today are licensed machines that inject a unique signature into the logs of any systems they access, thus recording all legitimate activity in the Matrix. For years, however, pirate users, or deckers, have been acquiring decks and modifying them. Deckers suppress their system's signature and add capabilities that are of little use to an honest cyberterminal operator. That's the way of the world in 2050.

THE SUPERPOWERS

The Computer Crash was the death knell of the world dominators. Already weakened by the catastrophes of the first three decades of the century and exhausted by the trials of the Awakened World, they reeled under the new assault.

For twelve years, beginning in 2030, the people of Europe and Asia underwent a series of conflicts now known as the Euro-Wars. With their communication and surveillance systems disrupted, the old men in Moscow found their subjects making a long-overdue bid for a home-rule. The separation was difficult and prolonged. Also during this period, the Awakened came to dominate the Western Siberian Lowland, Yukut ASSR, and all other USSR lands to the west of the lowlands. Like the U.S. and Canada, the Soviets lost their wilderness areas to the newcomers.

The Crash was a gut punch to the United States of America. In a country that was increasingly dependent on information technologies, the virus was more devastating to the economy than VITAS had been to the population. Canada was even worse

off. In 2030, what was left of the United States merged with what was left of Canada, including her major industrial centers and important natural resource areas. The new government was called the United Canadian and American States, though there were protests on both sides of the border.

Almost four years later, a coalition of ten southern states seceded from the union to form the Confederated American States. The CAS was instantly recognized by Aztlan, itself recently separated from the NAN. Sentiment ran high, and fears of a second civil war were rampant. Nevertheless, the transition was relatively orderly. Military units, divided in loyalties, split up and moved to their preferred countries with few incidents of violence.

Europe was not so lucky. In 2031, a desperate Moscow launched an invasion of western Europe to secure vital industrial and agricultural resources. Soviet and Warsaw Pact forces met unexpectedly tough opposition from NATO, even though the European forces fought without their American allies. In a fit of isolationism, the UCAS Congress recalled American troops from Europe.

Within a year, the European conflict slowed to a deadlock as attrition took its toll. Though the losses in men and materiel had been high for both sides, little territory had actually changed hands. Then, in late 2032, forces of the Republic of Moscow renewed the war in a surprise attack on Hamburg. Their mechanized forces, carefully husbanded while the other republics and their Warsaw allies had taken the brunt of the fighting, initially made great gains. The allies were thrown into confusion, but managed to slow the offensive. Previously uncommitted, Britain stepped in by sending troops into the Low Countries "to protect British interests." Further escalation seemed inevitable.

Then on the frigid night of January 23, 3033, Swedish airspace monitors detected several flights of British aerospace FA-38 *Nightwraith* fighter-bombers streaking across northern Europe. In short order, the aircraft obliterated key communications and command centers belonging to both sides. With all their offensive plans crippled beyond repair, both sides announced a cease-fire the next day. No one knows who was responsible for the strike.

The end of Euro-War was not the end of problems. Unable to stabilize their economies, the European Economic Community, the Warsaw Pact, and what remained of the USSR fragmented. The Germanies reunited, becoming one of the stronger states in the new Europe. Italy, southern France, and southeastern Europe shattered into hundreds of tiny states and returned to the city-state politics that have plagued so much of their history. Lost in impotent dreams of empire, the Republic of Moscow continued to attempt self-aggrandizement, but was repulsed on all fronts by neighboring states, corporate pressure, and Awakened activity.

INDEPENDENCE FEVER

As the fighting died in Europe, the specter of violence flared again in the Americas when a force of Awakened beings and metahumans led by three great dragons descended on the Amazon basin. In a short but extremely bloody conflict, the Brazilian forces had to cede most of the Amazon basin to the invaders. The Brazilian government fell, and two days later, most of their territory was claimed by the newly declared nation of Amazonia, self-acclaimed savior of the eco-sphere.

All was not quiet north of the equator, either. With Aztlan, the NAN member that had taken over the southwestern portions of Texas, now independent and no longer under the Sovereign Tribal Council's protection, the Texas state legislature agitated for a military venture to recover those lost lands. In 2035, the CAS government refused, however, suspecting that NAN would defend its former member anyway. No one in Atlanta wished to risk the power of the Great Ghost Dance. The angry Texans declared their own independence and launched an invasion. Four months later, a frustrated and embarrassed Texas applied for re-admittance to the CAS.

CAS fears of the NAN were groundless. The Sovereign Tribal Council had its own problems. Having opened its arms to the various metahuman races, NAN was finding that these new children of Mother Earth had their own ideas. A powerful group of Awakened beings and metahumans, mostly Elves, were in the process of doing to NAN what they had done to the United States. In an unprecedented interruption of worldwide broadcasting, the Elves of the Northwest announced the birth of Tir Tairngire (the land of promise) and seceded from NAN in 2037.

Unwilling or unable to resist the move, the Native American Nations did nothing to stop the formation of this new state in the region of former Oregon. Emboldened, The Tsimshian also declared their separation from the organization. In the wake of these defections and renewed internal dissent, Howling Coyote resigned. The shaman of the Great Ghost Dance withdrew into isolation.

Independence fever was contagious. Long isolated from its parent, California declared itself a sovereign nation. After immediately recognizing the nation, the powerful Japanese Imperial State followed up by landing its troops to protect Imperial interests from any possible disturbances. Within five years, San Francisco was almost totally controlled by the Japanese corporations.

NEW VIOLENCE

In 2036, the napalm fire-bombing of a small community in rural Ohio announced the arrival of the New Terrorism. Twenty people, most of them metahumans, died in the flames on that Sunday morning. A group calling itself Alamos 20,000 claimed responsibility. Over the next 15 years, this terrorist group was positively linked to the deaths of more than a thousand metahumans and publicly sympathetic normals.

Three years later, metahuman hatred peaked in the Night of Rage. Worldwide riots resulted in the deaths of thousands of metahumans and others cosmetically altered to appear metahuman. In New York City alone, 836 such persons perished. There were backlashes and incidents of counter-violence.

Retaliation came in 2041, when EuroAir flight 329 was destroyed with no survivors. While en route from London to Atlanta, the aircraft was attacked over the Atlantic by a great dragon identified by some as Sirrurg. A garbled last transmission from the doomed craft seems to indicate that one heroic passenger held the beast off for several minutes with sorcery before both passengers and crew were destroyed by the terrorist's fiery breath.

Another important development of 2041 was the birth of Policlubs in Europe. These youth-oriented associations were dedicated to promoting a particular philosophy. Each policlub proclaimed its intention to impose its viewpoint on the general public by taking the lead in the so-called European Restoration.

In 2044, Aztlan nationalized all foreign-owned businesses, under heavy pressure from Aztechnology Corporation. Semi-open warfare broke out as some corporations attempted to hold onto their properties. Using the confusion as a screen, Aztlan annexed most of what was left of Mexico. The exception was the Yucatan, where Awakened forces halted all take-over attempts.

By 2046, the Policlub idea had spread to North America. The movement spread quickly, but violence followed in its wake. Humanis Policlub, in particular, has built a major following that cuts across economic, social, and political divisions. Terry Smith, a metahuman rights activist and head of Mothers of Metahumans (MOM), has denounced Humanis as an arm of the shadowy Alamos 20,000 in a series of advertisements in major dailies.

In 2048, the Aztlan government negotiated the Veracruz Settlement with several megacorps in the wake of a combined corporate military strike on Ensanada. In that same year, Alan Adams, former CEO of the Colbert Group, an Illinois-based multinational corporation, was elected President of the UCAS. Edna Wallace, former governor of Louisiana, was elected President of the CAS.

This year, 2050, has seen the development of the 7th-generation cyberdeck, which is now keyboard size. Though the hatred between humans and metahumans still simmers, things are relatively quiet. But even in an Awakened World, how long can that last?

GAME CONCEPTS

"You wanna run the shadows? Then listen, chummer, learn everything you can, cuz ignorance will kill you faster than a fireball."
—Ess El El, Snake Shaman

 ere are a few concepts and key words that we use in **Shadowrun**. Some are general roleplaying slang, and others are peculiar to this game system. If you are familiar with them, the rules will make a lot more sense. If you forget, you can always come back here and check them out again. The first time a term appears in this orientation section, it is set in **bold** type.

ROLLING THE DICE

In **Shadowrun**, your character will run into situations where the game-master will ask you to roll dice. These dice rolls, known as **Tests**, gauge how well or poorly your character performs a required task, such as shooting an Ork security guard who disapproves of your face or persuading an employer that your services are worth a lot more than what he originally offered. Tests also determine how well a character resists damage and other unpleasant matters.

Shadowrun uses a number of six-sided dice to resolve any challenge for your character. The gamemaster will not ask you to make a roll to see if you open the door, but he will probably ask you to roll dice to see if you can somersault through the office door, land on your feet, and fire your AK-98 at the three Ork assassins who are standing behind the corporation's Chairman of the Board, without splattering yourself or the hostage all over the room.

Unlike most roleplaying games, you do not add up the dice that you roll, unless the rules specifically direct you to do so, or unless you see D6 preceded by a number or a **Skill** or **Attribute** name. In **Shadowrun,** each die result normally stands alone against the **Target Number**. There are two other rules that you should keep in mind when rolling the dice.

RULE OF ONE

This is the fumble rule, and it has two parts.

Any time a die comes up 1 in a Test, *the die* is an automatic failure, no matter what the Target Number.

In addition, if a character's dice roll ever consists totally of ones, the character has made a disastrous mistake. The result may be humorous, embarrassing, or deadly. The gamemaster determines whatever tone is appropriate for the situation, the players, and the dramatic or humorous needs of the moment.

RULE OF SIX

For every 6 a player rolls, he rolls that die again and adds the result to 6. The Rule of One does not apply to these secondary rolls. A second result of 6 adds to the first to become 12, plus the result of a third roll. Thus, a player who rolls three sixes in a row and then rolls a 4 has a result of 22.

SUCCESS TESTS

The rules frequently call for a **Success Test**. First, check the **Rating** of the Attribute or Skill named for the test. The Rating defines how many six-sided dice to roll for the test. For example, a Firearms Skill Test means you check the character's Firearms Skill Rating and roll that number of six-sided dice for the test. A Willpower Attribute Test means that you should use the character's Willpower Attribute Rating for the number of dice to roll.

The gamemaster provides a Target Number for the test. Each die result that equals or exceeds the Target Number is a **Success**. A single success indicates that the character has accomplished the task, but the more successes rolled, the better. In most situations, multiple successes mean that the character will receive more information, or do more damage, or make that bank shot off the Troll's head and into the side-corner pocket look so easy a child could do it.

RESISTANCE TESTS

Resistance Tests are the flip side of Success Tests. A character makes a Resistance Test when something bad has happened to him.

Like a Success Test, a Resistance Test uses an Attribute or Skill to determine the number of dice to roll. The gamemaster assigns a Target Number based on the circumstances. Successes reduce the effect of the calamity. For example, if that fireball got five successes, char-broiling your character, and you rolled four successes on the Resistance Test, then your character would still be pink in the center.

RESISTED/UNRESISTED TESTS

Some situations call for simple Success Tests. Determining if your character opens a lock would be a typical case. Sometimes only a Resistance Test is required, such as when a magician attempts to overcome the natural fatigue that results from casting powerful spells. Many times, a Resistance Test follows a Success Test.

The term **Unresisted Success Test** means there is no corresponding Resistance Test. The term **Resisted Success Test** indicates that a Resistance Test follows the Success Test, mitigating the effects of the action.

For example, a Resisted Firearms Skill Test means that the player should roll a number of dice equal to the character's Firearms Skill Rating. If any of the dice match or exceed the Target Number, the target can reduce, or totally offset, the number of successes, and therefore the damage, with a Resistance Test.

The gamemaster should use a Resisted Firearms Skill Test whenever a player character or non-player character fires at another character. He should use an Unresisted Firearms Skill Test only if the character is target-shooting. In this case, the number of successes would indicate how close the shot is to the bull's-eye.

OPPOSED SUCCESS TEST

An **Opposed Success Test** is a special type of Success Test, used when two characters are attempting to do exactly the same thing to one another and one person's success is the other person's failure. Examples might be hand-to-hand combat or negotiating new terms in your deal with the Rat Shaman. In this case, each character makes a Success Test, and the one with more successes wins.

DICE POOLS

When things are hot, and your basic skills and attributes are not enough to let you see the next morning, you will want some help. That's what **Dice Pools** are for.

A Dice Pool is a number of dice that you may add to those allowed for a Success or Resistance Test. The five possible pools come from different sources, usually Skills or Attributes. The Dodge Pool, for instance, is equal to the character's Quickness Attribute Rating, and it can be used only for a Resistance Test. Other Dice Pools can be used to supplement either a Resistance or Success Test.

The number of dice in a pool is equal to the character's rating in the Skill or Attribute that is the source of the pool. Each

die in a pool may be used once during an **Action**. A player's turn can consist of several Actions.

MODIFICATIONS

These rules often call for a +1 or –1 as a modifier. Unless otherwise stated, that modifier should be applied to the Target Number. Thus, a –3 modifier to a Target Number of 5 produces a Modified Target Number of 5 – 3, or 2. If the rules call for +2 dice or –1 dice, you should add or subtract that number of dice from your Success or Resistance Test. Thus, a Shaman who has a +2 dice for summoning certain nature spirits adds two dice to the normal number he would have for this Success Test.

OTHER CONVENTIONS

There is one other way **Shadowrun** treats dice. This convention usually applies only to the gamemaster, letting you know how many Orks appear or how much your character can lift.

When you see a number before D6, as in 3D6, it tells you to roll that many six-sided dice. It also tells you to add up the results into one number. If you roll 3D6 and get a 3, a 2, and a 5, your result would be 10.

A Skill Rating or an Attribute Rating might be used to determine the number of dice rolled. Examples of this might read (Strength)D6 or (Computer)D6. In this case, roll a number of dice equal to the Strength or Computer Rating and add up the results. Finally, some of these rolls use a multiple of a rating. This will be shown as, say, (Strength ÷ 2)D6 or (Computer x 4)D6. In this case, roll dice equal to the Strength or Computer Rating multiplied or divided by the number. Unless specifically directed otherwise, round fractions down to the nearest whole number.

DEFINITIONS

These are simplified definitions of common game terms to help acquaint you with the rules. The body of the rules contains complete definitions and examples in the appropriate sections.

CHARACTERS

Archetypes are pregenerated characters created from the main classes and races of **Shadowrun**. Players can use these with little other preparation. Attributes describe each character and give a general picture of his abilities. Skills and spells refine those abilities. A Character Record Sheet keeps track of each character: his belongings, abilities, appearance, and status. An important part of the Record Sheet is the **Condition Monitor**, consisting of three tracks. The **Physical Damage** Track displays Wound Damage and shows when the character dies. The **Mental Damage** Track shows Fatigue and Stun Damage and indicates when a character falls unconscious. If a character suffers additional damage after his Mental Damage Track is used up, he applies that damage, be it Fatigue or Stun, to the Physical Damage Track. There is also a track for recording damage to a character's **Cyberdeck**.

Weapons have a **Damage Code** that tells the player how much damage they do. The Code consists of a number, a letter, and another number. The first number is the **Power Level**, which indicates the difficulty of offsetting damage from such a weapon. The letter indicates the **Wound Category** (Light (L), Moderate

(M), Serious (S), or Deadly (D)) that the weapon inflicts. The other number is the **Staging Number**, or simply Staging, which indicates the number of successes needed to raise the Wound Category to the next more serious level. The Staging also indicates the number of successes needed in the Resistance Test to reduce the damage to the next lower Wound Category.

There is one other term **Shadowrun** uses to describe characters, though not those just starting out. That term is **Karma**, the numerical representation of a character's accomplishments. Later on, a character can use his Karma Level to improve his skills and even his attributes. He can also use Karma to do better in Success Tests or to get out of trouble.

SKILLS

Areas of knowledge or technique are known as Skills, which have ratings that are used to carry out Success Tests. A **Concentration** represents a focused field of training or education in one aspect of a general skill. For example, a character with Firearms Skill can concentrate on Rifles, improving his ability when firing rifles, but reducing his skill with other types of firearms. **Specialization** is a further narrowing of a focus in a skill that already has a Concentration. This increases a character's expertise in one specific area, but it lowers his ability in related subjects. The character with a Concentration in Rifles could then specialize in AK-98s, becoming more proficient with that weapon but less skilled with other weapons. A character need not concentrate or specialize.

MAGIC

Magicians, characters who can use magic, come in two types. **Hermetic** magicians believe that magic is a natural force that can be understood and controlled like any other physical force. Their magic comes from rigorously applied rules. **Shamanic** magicians believe in spirits that are a part of all things. Their magic involves making deals with those spirits. Each type of spell or spirit has a **Force**, chosen by the magician and limited by his abilities, time, and money. The Force acts like a Skill or Attribute Rating in Success Tests. Casting spells and conjuring spirits causes a magician Fatigue, called **Drain**. After casting a spell, the magician checks the spell's **Drain Code**, which works much like a weapon's Damage Code, except on its user instead of the target. The letter is the **Fatigue Category** (Light, Moderate, Serious, Deadly), just as with a weapon, and the Staging Number also works the same way. Instead of the weapon's Power Level, the spell's Force indicates the difficulty of avoiding Drain's Mental Damage. The magician makes a Resistance Test to keep from going down to Drain.

MATRIX

The **Matrix** is the cybernetic analog space inside the Grid, the worldwide computer network. Only a character equipped with a cyberdeck can enter this "cyberspace," which appears as a huge lattice. Jacking into the Matrix enhances the character's capabilities in a number of ways, but he only appears to be inside, leaving a zombie-like shell in the physical world for his companions to protect. A character inside the Matrix appears as a **Persona**, a stylized image of his personality. Software, electronic security systems, electronic addresses, other Persona, and everything else the character encounters in the Matrix appear as **Constructs**, other stylized images in the same motif.

METAHUMANITY

"My folks are human. They'll die out soon, like the dinosaurs did, and have no idea why."
—Jason Ironstone, Dwarf

ince the Awakening, five major subspecies of *Homo sapiens* have appeared throughout the world. They are evenly distributed geographically, racially, and ethnically.

DWARF

Homo sapiens pumilionis

Identification: The average Dwarf is 1.2 meters tall and weighs 72 kilograms. His coloration is usually pinkish white or light tan, but may be as dark as ebony. His skull has 32 teeth. Female dwarfs have two mammae. Dwarfs' legs are disproportionately short, making them poor runners. Their torsos are wide, with great breadth at the shoulders, endowing the subspecies with increased arm strength. Their body hair is well-developed and head hair profuse; males have extensive facial hair. The Dwarvish nose tends to be large and long, and the ears slightly pointed.

Habitat: This subspecies prefers artificial or natural caverns in wilderness areas. In urban environments, Dwarfs show a preference for dwelling in basements or sub-basements.

Habits: Dwarfs may be active by day or night. They are omnivorous. Populations form small family groups, and though they show isolationist tendencies, small enclaves are found in communities all over the world. Their life span is unverified, but predictions based on metabolic rates run to over a hundred years. Their breeding season is unrestricted. The gestation period is 284 days.

Young: One. Birth weight as a percentage of mother's weight is 5.6. Suckling time is more than 15 months.

Commentary: With eyes sensitive to the infrared spectrum, a Dwarf's activity is as unrestricted underground as above. Dwarf phenotypes show an increased resistance to pathogens.

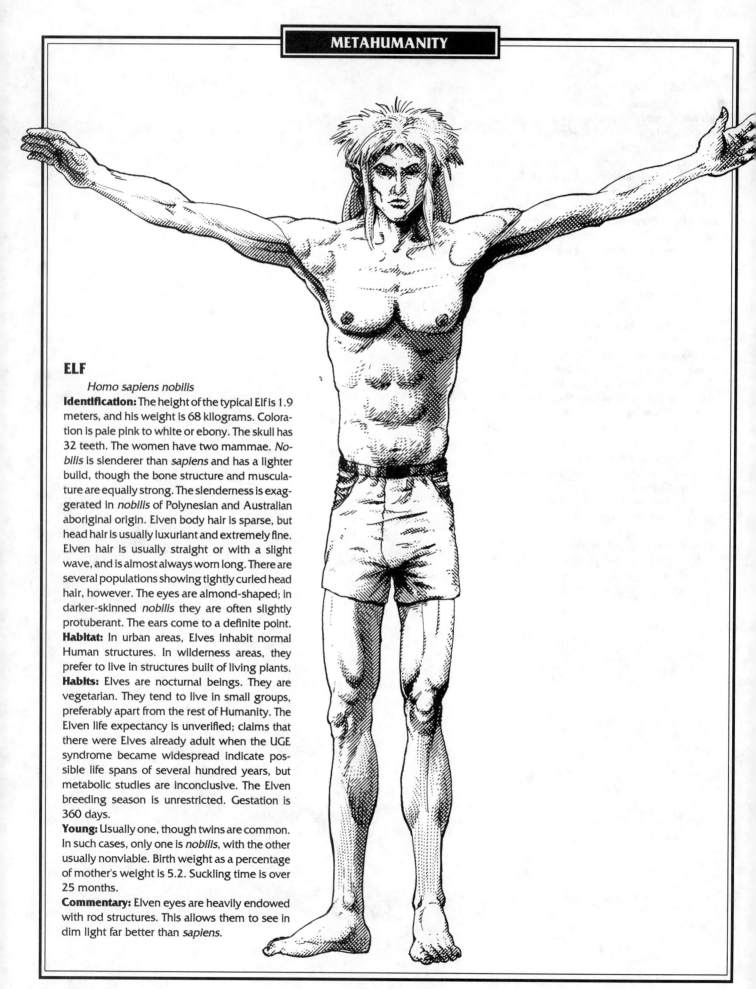

ELF

Homo sapiens nobilis

Identification: The height of the typical Elf is 1.9 meters, and his weight is 68 kilograms. Coloration is pale pink to white or ebony. The skull has 32 teeth. The women have two mammae. *Nobilis* is slenderer than *sapiens* and has a lighter build, though the bone structure and musculature are equally strong. The slenderness is exaggerated in *nobilis* of Polynesian and Australian aboriginal origin. Elven body hair is sparse, but head hair is usually luxuriant and extremely fine. Elven hair is usually straight or with a slight wave, and is almost always worn long. There are several populations showing tightly curled head hair, however. The eyes are almond-shaped; in darker-skinned *nobilis* they are often slightly protuberant. The ears come to a definite point.

Habitat: In urban areas, Elves inhabit normal Human structures. In wilderness areas, they prefer to live in structures built of living plants.

Habits: Elves are nocturnal beings. They are vegetarian. They tend to live in small groups, preferably apart from the rest of Humanity. The Elven life expectancy is unverified; claims that there were Elves already adult when the UGE syndrome became widespread indicate possible life spans of several hundred years, but metabolic studies are inconclusive. The Elven breeding season is unrestricted. Gestation is 360 days.

Young: Usually one, though twins are common. In such cases, only one is *nobilis*, with the other usually nonviable. Birth weight as a percentage of mother's weight is 5.2. Suckling time is over 25 months.

Commentary: Elven eyes are heavily endowed with rod structures. This allows them to see in dim light far better than *sapiens*.

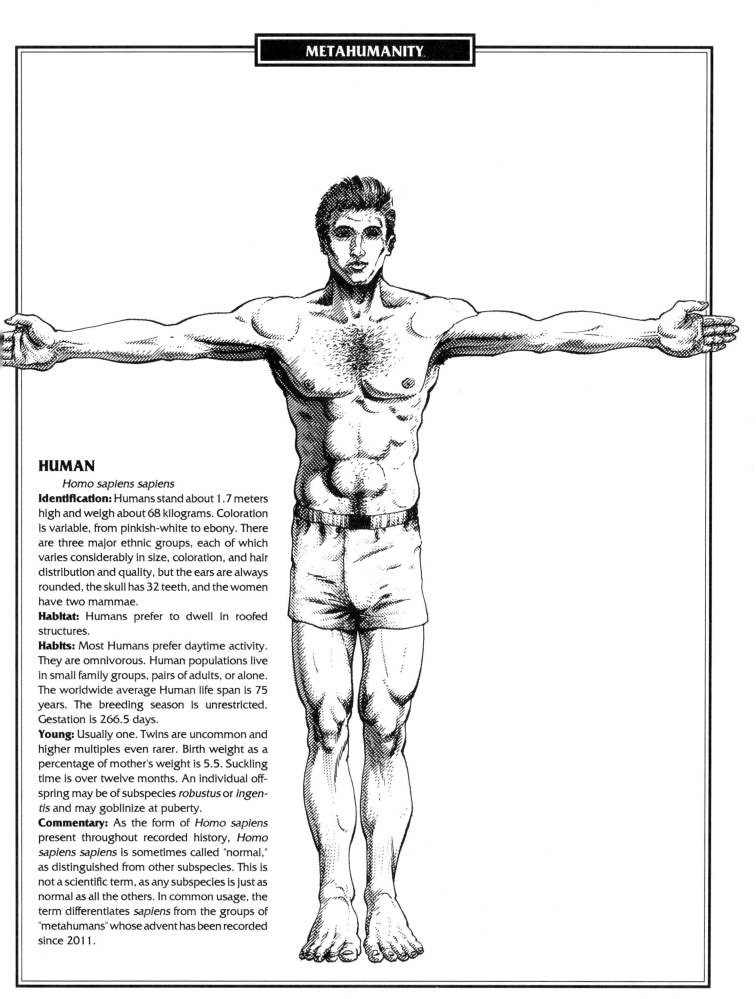

HUMAN

Homo sapiens sapiens

Identification: Humans stand about 1.7 meters high and weigh about 68 kilograms. Coloration is variable, from pinkish-white to ebony. There are three major ethnic groups, each of which varies considerably in size, coloration, and hair distribution and quality, but the ears are always rounded, the skull has 32 teeth, and the women have two mammae.

Habitat: Humans prefer to dwell in roofed structures.

Habits: Most Humans prefer daytime activity. They are omnivorous. Human populations live in small family groups, pairs of adults, or alone. The worldwide average Human life span is 75 years. The breeding season is unrestricted. Gestation is 266.5 days.

Young: Usually one. Twins are uncommon and higher multiples even rarer. Birth weight as a percentage of mother's weight is 5.5. Suckling time is over twelve months. An individual offspring may be of subspecies *robustus* or *ingentis* and may goblinize at puberty.

Commentary: As the form of *Homo sapiens* present throughout recorded history, *Homo sapiens sapiens* is sometimes called "normal," as distinguished from other subspecies. This is not a scientific term, as any subspecies is just as normal as all the others. In common usage, the term differentiates *sapiens* from the groups of "metahumans" whose advent has been recorded since 2011.

ORK

Homo sapiens robustus

Identification: Orks average 1.9 meters tall and 73 kilograms in weight. Their skin coloration varies from pale pink to ebony. When individuals undergo goblinization, their skin color usually remains unchanged. Ork bodies are proportioned similarly to those of *sapiens*, but *robustus* is more heavily built. Body hair is usually well-developed, but may sometimes be absent altogether. Head hair is usually more prominent than the *sapiens* ethnic group from which the individual *robustus* was derived. The Ork nose tends to be broad and the lips thin. The ears show definite points and are sometimes elongated as well. The Ork skull has 32 teeth, with greatly enlarged lower canines. Ork women have two mammae.

Similar Species: *Robustus*, like *ingentis*, is highly variable in appearance, leading investigators to theorize that certain individuals or small communities of them are, in fact, other subspecies or other species entirely. Such hypotheses are, at best, tentative. This variety of types continues to mislead unwary researchers.

Habitat: Usually in roofed buildings.

Habits: Orks are active day and night, but seem to prefer the night. They are omnivorous, but with a distinct preference for meat. Populations form large groups, often of a tribal structure. The typical life span appears to be between 35 and 40 years. Their breeding season is unrestricted. Gestation is 187 days.

Young: Ork mothers usually bear four children, but litters of six or eight are not uncommon. Birth weight as a percentage of mother's weight is 4.2. Suckling time is over seven months. Most newborns are obviously *robustus*, but may appear as *sapiens*; 95 percent of the latter will goblinize at puberty, which occurs at an average age of ten.

Commentary: The higher proportion of rod over cone structures in the Ork's eyes allows enhanced low-light vision. Individuals goblinizing into *robustus* usually evince negative psychological effects, with severe psychoses and aberrant behavioral patterns common. Individuals born *robustus* may be socialized normally.

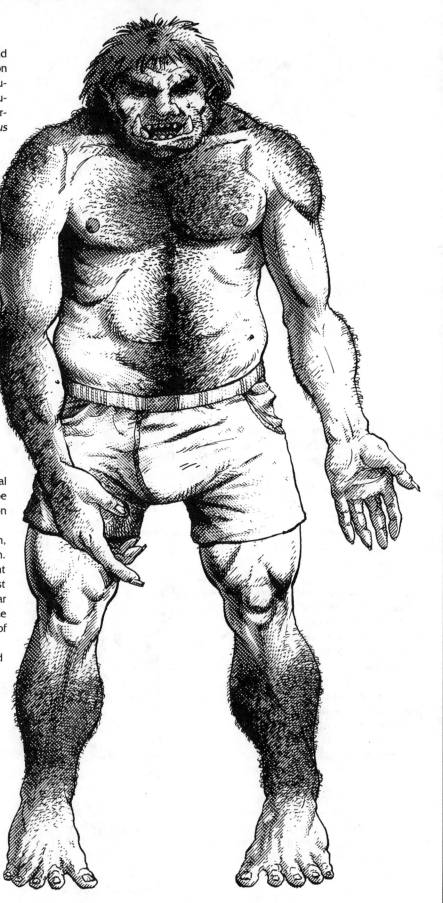

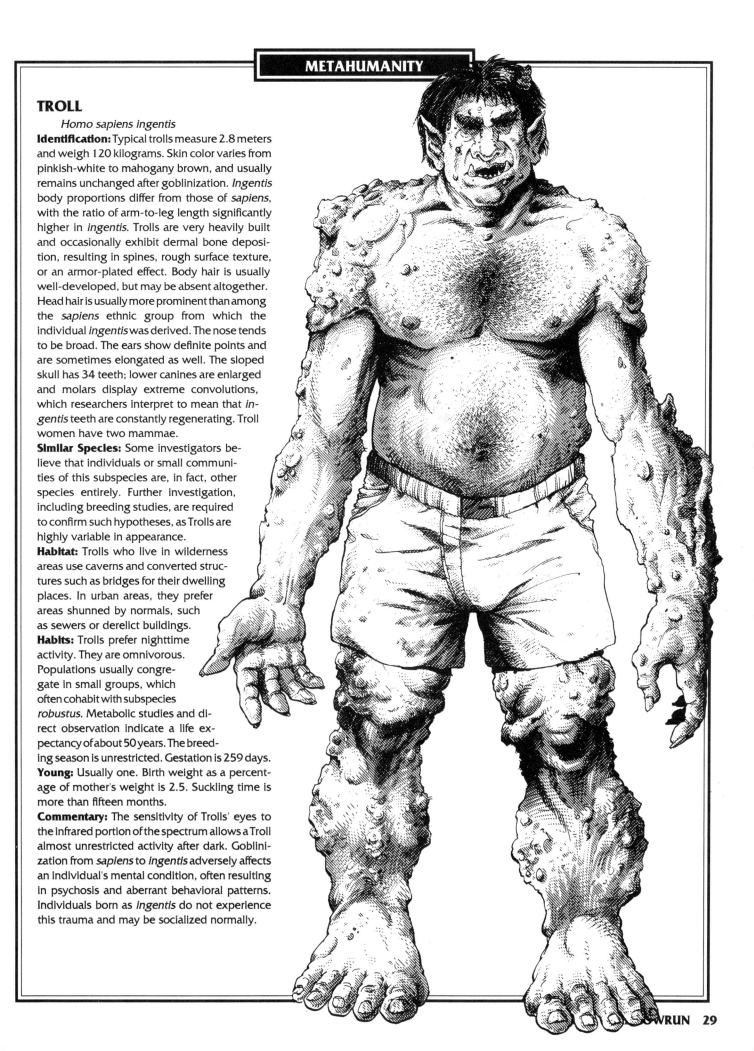

TROLL

Homo sapiens ingentis

Identification: Typical trolls measure 2.8 meters and weigh 120 kilograms. Skin color varies from pinkish-white to mahogany brown, and usually remains unchanged after goblinization. *Ingentis* body proportions differ from those of *sapiens*, with the ratio of arm-to-leg length significantly higher in *ingentis*. Trolls are very heavily built and occasionally exhibit dermal bone deposition, resulting in spines, rough surface texture, or an armor-plated effect. Body hair is usually well-developed, but may be absent altogether. Head hair is usually more prominent than among the *sapiens* ethnic group from which the individual *ingentis* was derived. The nose tends to be broad. The ears show definite points and are sometimes elongated as well. The sloped skull has 34 teeth; lower canines are enlarged and molars display extreme convolutions, which researchers interpret to mean that *ingentis* teeth are constantly regenerating. Troll women have two mammae.

Similar Species: Some investigators believe that individuals or small communities of this subspecies are, in fact, other species entirely. Further investigation, including breeding studies, are required to confirm such hypotheses, as Trolls are highly variable in appearance.

Habitat: Trolls who live in wilderness areas use caverns and converted structures such as bridges for their dwelling places. In urban areas, they prefer areas shunned by normals, such as sewers or derelict buildings.

Habits: Trolls prefer nighttime activity. They are omnivorous. Populations usually congregate in small groups, which often cohabit with subspecies *robustus*. Metabolic studies and direct observation indicate a life expectancy of about 50 years. The breeding season is unrestricted. Gestation is 259 days.

Young: Usually one. Birth weight as a percentage of mother's weight is 2.5. Suckling time is more than fifteen months.

Commentary: The sensitivity of Trolls' eyes to the infrared portion of the spectrum allows a Troll almost unrestricted activity after dark. Goblinization from *sapiens* to *ingentis* adversely affects an individual's mental condition, often resulting in psychosis and aberrant behavioral patterns. Individuals born as *ingentis* do not experience this trauma and may be socialized normally.

CHARACTER GENERATION

*"That which does not kill me
is dead when I'm through with it."*
—Joel Neechi, Merc

 our character in **Shadowrun** is your alter-ego in the world of 2050. Created from a collection of attributes and skills, he will have the personality only you can inject into him. The character need not be the same sex, weight, height, race, or any other thing that you are. This is a game of the imagination, which gives you a chance to try out what it feels like to be someone else.

Characters in **Shadowrun** possess various physical, mental, and magical Attributes, Skills, Spells, Gear, Contacts, and implanted Cyberware.

ATTRIBUTES

In **Shadowrun**, each character has eight attributes, or nine if he is a magician. There are three Physical Attributes, three Mental Attributes, and two or three Special Attributes. The following sections identify and describe them:

ATTRIBUTE TABLE		
Physical Attributes	**Mental Attributes**	**Special Attributes**
Body	Charisma	Essence
Quickness	Intelligence	Magic
Strength	Willpower	Reaction

Body represents general health and resistance to injury and pain.

Quickness represents overall speed, dexterity, and agility. The Quickness Rating equals the number of meters a character can move in a Combat Turn.

Strength represents the ability to lift, carry, and cause physical damage.

Charisma represents attractiveness (not necessarily physical beauty), persuasiveness, and general likability.

Intelligence represents overall quickness of mind, aptitude, and the ability to perceive surroundings.

Willpower represents determination and mental stability.

Essence is a measure of the soundness of the central nervous system and spirit. Invasive things, such as Cyberware, reduce Essence. When Essence declines, **Magic** declines by the same amount. If a character's Essence falls below 0, he dies.

Magic is a measure of magical energy. Serious damage to the body and invasive additions such as Cyberware reduce magical energy.

Reaction determines how quickly and how often a character can act under pressure.

ATTRIBUTE RATINGS

A normal Human character's physical and mental attributes are rated from 1 to 6. Humans with Cyberware, Elves, Dwarves, Dragons, and so on can have higher scores in one or more Attributes. Each species has its own maximums.

Determine a character's Physical and Mental Attributes by choosing an Archetype, which fixes all Attributes. Some Attributes have a number in parentheses. The first number is the character's real Attribute. The number in parentheses is the Attribute Rating plus the effect of any Cyberware the character has.

To get a character's Reaction, add his Quickness and Intelligence and divide by 2, dropping any fractions. Any effects of Cyberware also carry over to affect Reaction.

All characters have a starting Essence Rating of 6. Cyberware implants and improperly healed damage reduce this rating.

If the character can use magic, his Magic Rating starts at 6. The Magic Rating declines with the Essence Rating. A character who cannot use magic has no Magic Rating.

HUMAN ATTRIBUTE RATINGS
1 Weak
2 Underdeveloped
3 Typical
4 Improved
5 Superior
6 Maximum unmodified human

RACIAL MAXIMUM TABLE

	Human	Elf	Dwarf	Ork	Troll
Body	6	6	7	9	11
Quickness	6	7	5	6	5
Strength	6	6	8	8	10
Charisma	6	8	6	5	4
Intelligence	6	6	6	5	4
Willpower	6	6	7	6	5
Essence	6	6	6	6	6
Magic	6	6	6	6	6
Reaction	6	6	5	5	4

OTHER DISTINCTIONS

Besides Attributes, characters differ in training, equipment, and abilities.

SKILLS

Each character has his own set of knowledge and abilities, known as Skills. Like Attributes, skills have ratings. Unlike Attribute Ratings, Skill Ratings have no upper limit.

GEAR

All characters have some type of equipment, be it a Shaman's medicine bag or a Street Samurai's HK227.

CYBERWARE

This is high-tech gear implanted into the body. Some types of Cyberware artificially increase a character's attributes. Other types allow a character to interface directly with computer systems in the computer-generated environment of the Matrix. Still other types temporarily provide the character with skills and knowledge.

SPELLS

Magicians who use Cyberware lose the ability to manipulate magical energies to some degree or other. Their magical energies, however, can work spells that are sometimes better than technological devices. Like skills, each spell has a rating of its maximum strength. Spell Ratings have no upper limit, but casting a spell that is higher than the character's Magic Rating can cause him physical damage.

CONTACTS

These are the people that your character can call on for help, information, and jobs during the course of the game. Lone wolves do not last long in the urban wilderness of a place like Seattle.

GENERATING CHARACTERS

You can generate a character in two ways, by starting with a pre-generated Archetype or by creating your own. It might be a good idea to use an existing Archetype from those described in the next chapter until you've become more familiar with the game.

ARCHETYPES

To create a **Shadowrun** character, start with one of the classes presented in the **Archetypes** chapter. This lets you get started right away. No fuss. No muss. Right into the action.

If you don't like the gender of the published Archetype, change it. You are not required to play, say, a female Rocker if you would rather play a male one. There is no need to change the numbers, just the pronouns.

Eventually you may become dissatisfied with the limited choice of published Archetypes, and will want to try something different. Or you might not agree with the kind of priorities the descriptions give the character. Or maybe you just want to have a Decker who is a real weenie but has a top-of-the-line Cyberdeck. Check out the Archetype Creation rules on page 53. They tell how to go about it.

BURNED-OUT MAGE

"Don't listen to all that crap about a mage being on top of the world. It's a con, a slick, a come-on…a lie. Casting spells is surely a kick, but it doesn't last a lifetime. Even if you don't ever get hurt or run the shadows, you can't toss fireballs forever. Age'll get you if nothing else does. You'll be left howling for the touch of the power, knowing that to call it again will kill you.

"So what do you do? You take a good, long look at the writing on the wall, my friend. Like I have. The Magic may work well for a kid, but nobody stays young. Sooner or later, you have to face the fact that bodies wear out. But that's not the end, you know. Not anymore. They can rebuild you now. Make you stronger, faster, better. You may not be able to toss a fireball, but who needs a fireball when you can pack an HK227 SMG?

"I may not be throwing fireballs anymore, but me and my little HK familiar can conjure you quite a bit of effective magic."

Commentary: The Burned-Out Mage has become disillusioned with the path common to those capable of utilizing the magical energies. He has bartered his magical capability away in favor of technological enhancements. The trade has left him bitter and cynical, at least outwardly.

Attributes:
- Body: 3
- Quickness: 2 (3)
- Strength: 3 (4)
- Charisma: 1
- Intelligence: 4
- Willpower: 4
- Essence: 1.4
- Magic: 1
- Reaction: 3 (5)

Skills:
- Conjuring: 4
- Etiquette (Corporate): 2
- Etiquette (Street): 2
- Firearms: 2
- Magical Theory: 4
- Sorcery: 4
- Stealth: 2
- Unarmed Combat: 2

Cyberware:
- Cybereyes with Thermographic Imaging;
- Wired Reflexes: 1
- Muscle Replacement: 1
- Skillwires: 4
- Smartgun Link
- Skillsoft (Fichetti Pistol: 4)

Contacts:
- Bartender
- Mr. Johnson
- Street Doc
- Talismonger

Gear:
- Lined Coat
- DocWagon™ Contract (gold)
- Fichetti Pistol with Smartgun Adapter
- Two Specific Spell Focuses (1 point each, choose spell)
- 1 Trauma Patch (5)

Spells:
- Analyze Device: 5
- Analyze Truth: 5
- Armor: 4
- Clairvoyance: 5
- Heal Moderate Wounds: 5
- Hibernate: 4
- Invisibility: 4
- Mana Bolt: 5
- Mind Probe: 5
- Sleep: 5
- Telekinesis: 5

DECKER

"Technomancer, that's what I am. A wizard with technology, not that fuzzy mumbo-jumbo razz. The mighty computer is at my command, trembling to perform my least wish.

"You want some Ice cracked, I'm your girl. I've got programs to slide past the best. You got a shadowrun? No sweat. I've done 'em, and come away clean, too. Ain't no corp tracer or groundhound gonna pick up my trail. I hit 'em sharp and hard, then I'm away and running, a ghost in the Grid. The only touch they'll ever make is my street name, and I'll only let 'em have that if I feel like it.

"You'd better have plenty on your credstick, chummer. I ain't cheap. I'm a big leaguer, not some junkyen runner. I'm slick and I'm fast, the cutting edge. The Matrix is my home, and I wouldn't have it any other way. You ain't alive till you've jacked in and seen the electron horizon in Cyberspace. I'm going places.

"Maybe you've heard of Fastjack? Well, forget him! I'm the hot new decker on the Grid, and I'm gonna put him in the history banks."

Commentary: Decker is a console cowgirl, a descendent of the computer hacker of the latter part of the 20th century. She jacks into the Matrix to manipulate the dataflows to her own ends while seeking the big score or the trick that will snug her firmly into the annals of the technomancers. She skirts the edges of legality, overstepping them more than occasionally.

Attributes:
  Body: 2
  Quickness: 4
  Strength: 3
  Charisma: 1
  Intelligence: 6
  Willpower: 4
  Essence: 5.5
  Reaction: 5

Skills:
  Bike: 4
  Computer: 6
  Computer Theory: 6
  Computer (B/R): 6
  Electronics: 6
  Etiquette (Street): 5
  Firearms: 3
  Physical Sciences: 4

Cyberware:
  Datajack
  Headware Memory (30 Mp)

Contacts:
  Another Decker
  Fixer
  Media Producer
  Dwarven Technician

Gear:
  Fuchi Cyber-4 with Response Increase: 2
  Programs:
    Bod: 6
    Evasion: 6
    Masking: 6
    Sensors: 6
    Attack: 6
    Browse: 4
    Deception: 4
  Microtronics Workshop; Table-top Personal Computer (100 Mp)
  Yamaha Rapier
  Ruger Super Warhawk

DETECTIVE

"They told me you were looking for me. Well, you found me. So turn on the sob story. I got the time. But first, tickle my comp with your credstick. I may have the time, but I haven't got the interest until I know you've got the nuyen. Time takes money, chummer. Just flick the stick into the slot. The box will dump my rates and sheet onto your stick.

"The sheet will give you the highlights of my illustrious career: maidens rescued (extra charge for preserving original status), the lost found, the necessary lost, but I don't do erasures. No point in going on. I see by your eyes you've already scanned the sheet. Charlie at the precinct, or did Stevie the Snitch pass it on? Don't really matter. If somebody hadn't given you my name, you wouldn't be looking for me.

"Now before we go any further, let me check the cred balance. Whew! You got my interest, all right. What's the job?"

Commentary: The detective has led a hard life, balanced between the shadows of crime and the harsh glare of corporate and city life. Looking to keep his own code of honor and justice intact, he must make constant compromises to make it through the day, or the night. He won't touch magic, though his cases often involve it, and he won't augment his body, though sometimes his resolve puts him at a disadvantage. He'll tell you that a man has to stand on his own feet.

Attributes:
 Body: 4
 Quickness: 4
 Strength: 3
 Charisma: 3
 Intelligence: 6
 Willpower: 4
 Essence: 6
 Reaction: 5

Cyberware:
 None

Contacts:
 Bartender
 Bouncer
 City Official
 Fixer
 Gang Member
 Gang Boss
 Media Producer
 Any Street Type
 Another Street Type
 (The Detective may select three extra contacts, for a total of five.)

Gear:
 Ares Predator
 Armor Vest
 Investigator's License
 Micro-Recorder
 Sony Pocket Secretary
 Walther Palm Pistol

Skills:
 Biotech: 2
 Car: 4
 Computer: 4
 Etiquette (Corporate): 3
 Etiquette (Street): 4
 Firearms: 6
 Negotiation: 6
 Stealth: 5
 Unarmed Combat: 6

ELVEN DECKER

"They say the Awakened have no touch for technology. Well, short, squat, and ill-favored, don't believe everything you hear on the street. I am living proof that a metahuman, most especially an Elf, can ride the Matrix and bend it to his will.

"I am a technomancer, and there isn't a drop of the Rain Dance in the magic I do. My spells are programs, offering reliability no spellworm can boast. My wand is my datajack, portal to the glittering scenery of the Matrix. My conjurings are electrons slaved to my will under the drivers of my most elegant and sophisticated software. You will find no better.

"So, tell me what it is you wish me to do. If it piques my interest, I will essay the task and complete it to my satisfaction, which shall most certainly exceed your requirements.

"There will, of course, be a fee."

Commentary: The Elven Decker seems, at first, a contradiction in terms. He is living proof that metahumans cannot be stereotyped, and he will be the first to tell you that not all Elves live in the woods. Magic has no attraction to him, and though he has the superior attitude of his brethren in the wilderness, he has little use for their customs and practices. He is quite happy living in the modern technical world.

Attributes:
    Body: 2
    Quickness: 5
    Strength: 2
    Charisma: 3
    Intelligence: 5
    Willpower: 4
    Essence: 5.5
    Reaction: 5

Skills:
    Bike: 3
    Computer: 6
    Computer Theory: 6
    Etiquette (Elven): 2
    Etiquette (Street): 2
    Firearms: 3

Cyberware:
    Datajack
    Headware Memory (30 Mp)

Contacts:
    Decker
    Another Elven Archetype
    Fixer
    Dwarven Technician

Gear:
    Fuchi Cyber-4 with Response Increase: 2
    Microtronics Workshop
    Programs:
        Bod: 6
        Evasion: 6
        Masking: 6
        Sensors: 6
        Attack: 4
        Evaluate: 4
        Sleaze: 5
    Table-top Personal Computer (100 Mp)
    Yamaha Rapier

Notes: Natural low-light eyes. Check for allergic reaction.

FORMER COMPANY MAN

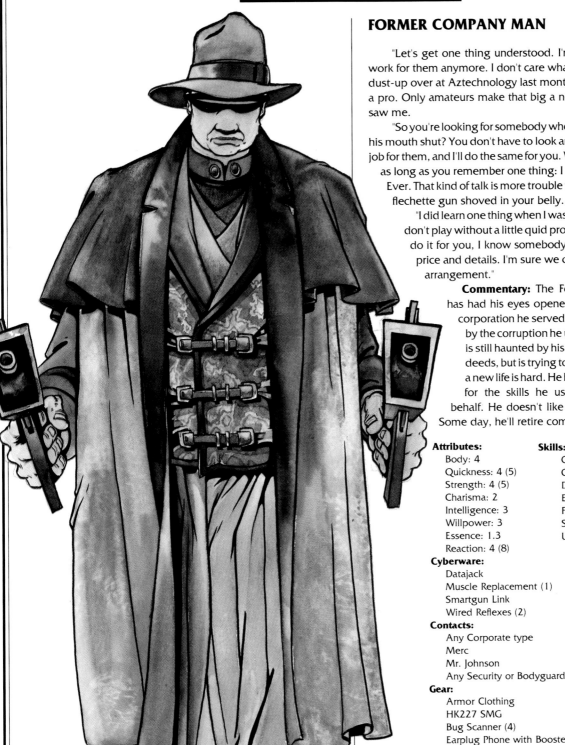

"Let's get one thing understood. I'm a freelancer. I don't work for them anymore. I don't care what you heard about the dust-up over at Aztechnology last month. That wasn't me. I'm a pro. Only amateurs make that big a noise. Besides, nobody saw me.

"So you're looking for somebody who can do a job and keep his mouth shut? You don't have to look any further. I did a good job for them, and I'll do the same for you. We'll get along just fine as long as you remember one thing: I don't talk about them. Ever. That kind of talk is more trouble than a Beretta full-auto flechette gun shoved in your belly.

"I did learn one thing when I was working the corp. You don't play without a little quid pro quo, ya know. If I can't do it for you, I know somebody who can. So let's talk price and details. I'm sure we can come to a working arrangement."

Commentary: The Former Company Man has had his eyes opened to the nature of the corporation he served for so long. Disgusted by the corruption he uncovered, he quit. He is still haunted by his former employers and deeds, but is trying to bury the past. Making a new life is hard. He has little to offer except for the skills he used in the company's behalf. He doesn't like it, but he uses them. Some day, he'll retire completely.

Attributes:
Body: 4
Quickness: 4 (5)
Strength: 4 (5)
Charisma: 2
Intelligence: 3
Willpower: 3
Essence: 1.3
Reaction: 4 (8)

Skills:
Car: 5
Computer: 2
Demolitions: 2
Etiquette: (Corporate): 4
Firearms: 6
Stealth: 4
Unarmed Combat: 5

Cyberware:
Datajack
Muscle Replacement (1)
Smartgun Link
Wired Reflexes (2)

Contacts:
Any Corporate type
Merc
Mr. Johnson
Any Security or Bodyguard type

Gear:
Armor Clothing
HK227 SMG
Bug Scanner (4)
Earplug Phone with Booster
Fichetti Pistol with Smartgun Adaptor
Jammer (4)
Low-Light Goggles
Medkit
Partial Heavy Armor
Survival Kit
Tranq Patch (5)
Trauma Patch (5)
White Noise Generator (6)

FORMER WAGE MAGE

"You would do well to withdraw your questions as to why I left my former employ. I will not satisfy your curiosity. Ask my old boss if you want to know.

"But let us not sour a mutually profitable arrangement over such trivia. While my refusal to speak of the past may seem inconvenient and perhaps a trifle disconcerting, I assure you that I bring no tail behind me. I am a free agent, and am quite capable of keeping any threads from my past from tangling your schemes further.

"We are all aware of the state of the world and the changes that are the legacy of our grandfathers' time. I assume that your concerns touch on, at least in part, some of these changes. You need a competent mage, well-versed in the fine points of Magic.

"Tell me your problem. Once I know what it is, I can begin to solve it."

Commentary: The Former Wage Mage has had her eyes opened to the nature of the corporation she served for so long. Disgusted by the corruption she uncovered, she quit. She is still haunted by her former employers and the perversion of the life energies of magic she performed for their benefit. She wants to forget the past and make a new life. She has the skills she used in the company's behalf and uses them, more positively she hopes, to do good. Some day, the scales will be balanced, and she will be able to rest.

Attributes:
Body: 2
Strength: 1
Quickness: 3
Charisma: 1
Intelligence: 5
Willpower: 3
Essence: 6
Magic: 6
Reaction: 4

Cyberware:
None

Contacts:
Any Corporate Type
Media Producer
Mr. Johnson
Talismonger

Gear:
Armor Clothing
Computer Media Hermetic Library
    Conjuring: 3
    Magical Theory: 3
    Sorcery: 3
Datareader with 60 Mp of Storage
Ruger Super Warhawk

Skills:
Conjuring: 6
Etiquette (Corporate): 4
Firearms: 2
Magical Theory: 6
Negotiation: 2
Psychology: 2
Sorcery: 6

Spells: Choose one orientation from the following:

Fighter:	Healer:	Prowler:
Heal Severe Wounds: 3	Cure: 4	Analyze Device: 5
Mana Bolt: 6	Detox: 3	Chaotic World: 5
Powerball: 6	Heal Deadly Wounds: 5	Clairvoyance: 4
Sleep: 5	Heal Moderate Wounds: 5	Entertainment: 3
	Hibernate: 3	Mask: 3

GANG MEMBER

"You don't look so tough to me, but that's okay. Whadd'ya expect from some liner who ain't run with my gang. You looking for tough? You got it right here.

"There's only one real power in this part of the 'plex. We know the streets, and the people know us. This is our turf. Gang turf! And we protect it. You want a piece of us, you know where to find us. That is, if you're stupid enough to try.

"Anything you need on the street, you come to me. Just remember, you burn me, the gang burns you. Simple law of the 'plex, chummer. We take care of our own."

Commentary: The Gang Member may be young, but he is old in the ways of life in the metroplex. He is a survivor, a predator of the concrete jungle. He is tough, smart, and more than a little confident.

Attributes:
Body: 5
Quickness: 6
Strength: 5
Charisma: 6
Intelligence: 5
Willpower: 4
Essence: 5.7
Reaction: 5

Skills:
Armed Combat: 5
Bike: 4
Etiquette (Street): 4
Firearms: 4
Projectile Weapons: 3
Stealth: 5
Unarmed Combat: 5

Cyberware:
Hand Razors
Retinal Modification: Low-
Light

Contacts:
Any Street Type
Any Other Street Type
Bouncer
Fixer

Gear:
Knife
Second-Hand Yamaha Rapier
Simsense Player and Half a Dozen Sense
Chips
Streetline Special Pistol
Synth-Leathers

Notes:
The Gang Member can call on 2D6 other members for help.

MERC

"We're all businessmen, right? We both work for a living, don't we? I got bills to pay, just like you. Only difference is you work with a cyberdeck. I work with an Uzi III.

"Look, my record's good. Three years in the corp's first-run circuit and a clean two with the Atzlan Third Legion. No demotions or discipline problems logged in my jacket. Huh? Don't give me that stuff about doctored records. I'm telling you my record's clean. I can do your job quiet, or I can do it loud. Either way, I'll get results, and that's what you want, isn't it? "Thought so. Now, let's talk price."

Commentary: The Merc is a tough veteran who has seen combat in every corner of the world. He'll work for the corp, the policlubs, a petty dictator, or a noble revolution. Just as long as he gets paid. The contract is all that matters. Receiving payment on a job has never been a problem for him. No employer would dare to renege on a Merc contract.

Attributes:
Body: 5
Quickness: 4
Strength: 5
Charisma: 3
Intelligence: 4
Willpower: 3
Essence: 5.4
Reaction: 4

Skills:
Armed Combat: 6
Car: 4
Demolitions: 3
Firearms: 6
Gunnery: 4
Military Theory: 2
Rotorcraft: 3
Stealth: 3
Throwing Weapons: 3
Unarmed Combat: 6

Cyberware:
Radio Receiver
Retinal Modification: Low Light

Contacts:
Former Company Man
Media Producer
Mr. Johnson
Rigger

Gear:
Ingram Lt. MG with Smartgun Adaptor
Ares Predator
Partial Heavy Armor
Knife
Smart Goggles
Throwing Knife

ORK MERCENARY

"What'cha staring at, chummer? Ain't ya never seen a live Ork before? Sure you have. Everyone's seen us. I guess you could say we sort of stand out in a crowd. Ease off on the baby talk, chummer. Just cause I'm Ork don't mean I'm an idiot. I got brains, and I use 'em, too. Wouldn't be here if I didn't.

"So don't ya go giving me none of your sorry eyes. It ain't been no easy life dodging the Badge, but I'm still here staring you in your pasty face. Like all Orks, I'm a survivor. Ain't nothin' or nobody too tough for me, chummer.

"So's you wanna hire me? Could be that I'm available. That is, if my services ain't in demand elsewhere. Slot your credstick in my box and let's see. If it shows enough zeroes in the right place, you got yourself some muscle."

Commentary: The Ork Mercenary is hardly an advertisement for the gentler side of his metahuman race. He is coarse and rough and of limited sensibilities, but he does function in society. He is not a psychotic killer as some Humanis cultists claim. He's just making a living doing what he does best.

Attributes:
  Body: 7
  Quickness: 4
  Strength: 6
  Charisma: 1
  Intelligence: 3
  Willpower: 2
  Essence: 6
  Reaction: 3
Skills:
  Any Ground Vehicle Skill: 3
  Armed Combat: 5
  Demolitions: 3
  Etiquette (Corporate): 2
  Etiquette (Street): 3
  Firearms: 5
  Stealth: 3
  Unarmed Combat: 5
Cyberware:
  None
Contacts:
  Bartender
  Gang Member
  Merc
  Rigger
Gear:
  Armor Jacket
  Big and Nasty Sword That He Calls a Knife
  AK-97 Assault Rifle
Notes:
  Low Light Eyes; Check for Allergic Reaction

RIGGER

"We were screaming down the dunes when Oldfield's panzer lifted skirts. Fool thought we had cleared the sight line for their AVMs. Paid for his stupidity. Cost the company two mil on that panzer. Oldfield never could slide her down the path the way a rigger's got to. We pulled it out, though. I canceled the rocket team with a twitch of the old trigger muscle and roared my turtle past their sec teams and scrambled the reins before they could hit the main force. Got a nice bonus for that scrap. Good ratings on the first-run circuit, too. Old EBM2 appreciates quality workmanship. Just wanted you to understand what kind of quality you're talking to here.

"Most people don't understand us riggers. Never will, I suppose. You just have to feel it, the adrenalin rush when you rev the old turbines, the air howling over your hull. Ain't nothing like it."

Commentary: The Rigger is a specialized breed of console cowgirl. She trades all normal sensations for the input of a cybernetic link-up, typically to a vehicle or a security system. Jacked into her vehicle, she feels the revving of the engine becomes her heartbeat, and the flow of fuel the adrenalin rush. Here she is as one with her machine. Yet, at the end of a run, she can separate her perceptions from the machine and walk away without giving it another thought.

Attributes:

Body: 5
Quickness: 6
Strength: 4
Charisma: 4
Intelligence: 6
Willpower: 5
Essence: 1.1
Reaction: 6

Skills:

Bike: 4
Car: 6
Computer: 3
Electronics: 3
Etiquette (Corporate): 1
Firearms: 2
Gunnery: 4

Cyberware:

Cybereyes with Thermographic Imaging, Low-Light and Flare Protection
Datajack
Radio
Smartgun Link
Vehicle Control Rig (2)

Contacts:

Fixer
Mechanic
Merc
Mr. Johnson

Gear:

2 Surveillance Drones
Ares Predator with Smartgun Adapter
Armor Jacket
DocWagon™ Contract (Platinum)
Hunter-Spotter Drone with 2 Lt. MGs and 1,000 Rounds of Belt-Fed Ammo
Patrol Vehicle with 2 MPMG and 1,000 Rounds of Belt-Fed Ammo
Remote Control Deck with Three Slave Ports
Rigged Eurocar Westwind with Concealed Lt MG (1,000 Rounds of Belt-Fed Ammo) and Two-Shot Missile Launcher (2 AVMs)
Rigged Harley Scorpion

ROCKER

"Look, this shadow business ain't really my scene. The spotlight's where it lives for me. Out in the glare and the heat and the roar of the crowd. It's the wiz, chummer. When I'm on stage no one can touch me or bring me down. No one. It's the best high. There ain't nothing else to live for.

"I may not be on the charts yet, but it's only a matter of time. Did you know Concrete Dreams played here before they were anybody? They didn't even headline. But now it's my turn. Top bill and screaming neon. Launch code for the ride to the stars, chummer. Launch code for the stars.

"Hey, I know the scene around here. I know the life. You only get one chance. So tell me your gig and let's see if we can jam. Shoot, chummer. If you sing it sweet enough, I might even play along for the kick."

Commentary: The Rocker is not a professional adventurer, but is always seeking a new thrill. Maybe she's looking for experiences to fuel her music or maybe she just wants an adrenalin rush. Though not a professional musician, she's got what it takes. She came up from the streets the hard way and is determined not to go back.

Attributes:
    Body: 5
    Quickness: 5
    Strength: 4
    Charisma: 6
    Intelligence: 4
    Willpower: 6
    Essence: 5.6
    Reaction: 4
Skills:
    Armed Combat: 3
    Bike: 2
    Etiquette (Media): 3
    Etiquette (Street): 5
    Firearms: 2
    Unarmed Combat: 2
Special skills:
    Instrumental Music: 6
    Musical Composition: 3
Cyberware:
    Datajack
    Synthesizer Link
Contacts:
    Any Street Type (Rocker may select one extra contact)
    Bouncer
    Media Producer
Gear:
    Favorite Instrument and Amps
    Knife
    Studded Synth-Leather Jacket
    Throwing Knife
    Yamaha Rapier
Notes:
    Cosmetic Surgery to suit chosen image

SHAMAN

"I am the one you seek. Step closer. Do not be afraid. My medicine is strong, but you will not be harmed if you have no evil intentions toward me.

"I knew you were coming. It is always the need that brings them to me. I knew you were coming. My totem whispered of it to me. Speak of your desire, that I may gauge your intent.

"If your desire is in accord with the land and the spirits, I can help you. Those who aid and guide me can then be called to come to your aid. There will be a price, but it shall be a just price suited to what is done and what you can pay."

Commentary: The Shaman treads the path of the spirits. Festooned with fetishes and the implements of his trade, he walks the land, in tune with its spirit and seeking to preserve its harmony. More than the ordinary mage, he abhors the encroachment of technology, especially that which invades the body.

Attributes:
Body: 3
Quickness: 3
Strength: 3
Charisma: 5
Intelligence: 4
Willpower: 6
Essence: 6
Magic: 6
Reaction: 3

Skills:
Armed Combat: 3
Conjuring: 6
Enchantment: 3
Etiquette (Tribal): 4
Magical Theory: 3
Sorcery: 5
Stealth: 3

Cyberware:
None

Contacts:
Another Magical Archetype
Any Tribal Type
Media Producer
Talismonger

Gear:
Knife
Medicine Lodge Materials (2)

Spells:
Choose one orientation from the following:
Fighter:
Mana Bolt: 4
Powerball: 6
Healer:
Heal Deadly Wounds: 4
Heal Moderate Wounds: 4
Hibernate: 2
Deceiver:
Chaos: 4
Entertainment: 3
Mask: 3
Detector:
Analyze Device: 4
Clairvoyance: 3
Detect Enemies: 3

Note:
A Shaman must select a wilderness totem. See the **Magic** chapter for details.

STREET MAGE

"The streets are where the life is. Life, ya know. The very stuff of magic.

"Those wage mages caught in the corporate rat race just don't understand. You got the power, you take it out and use it. For yourself. For the people. Slotting the clock to turn nuyen for the corp is like selling your body, chummer. You prostitute the Magic.

"I tried their way for a while, you know. But my eyes got opened when I saw the suits and the clock like a tombstone for the future. They didn't have anything to teach me, so I flew. Got out where the life is. They shook their wise old heads and invoked the mighty bottom line. What fossil brains!

"Look around you. It's life, you know. We're all a part of it, and it's the real power. I'm going to ride that power, chummer. All the way to the heavens."

Commentary: The Street Mage has left the path of rigorous magical study, seeking his own path of enlightenment and perfection at street level. He has all the heart and energy of youth, and its headstrong stubbornness as well. He knows his is the way that will change the world for the better even if he must take a circuitous route and engage in activities that seem to contradict his goals. He is sure that it will all work out in the end.

Attributes:
- Body: 3
- Quickness: 3
- Strength: 2
- Charisma: 3
- Intelligence: 4
- Willpower: 5
- Essence: 6
- Magic: 6
- Reaction: 3

Skills:
- Bike: 2
- Conjuring: 6
- Etiquette (Street): 4
- Firearms: 2
- Magical Theory: 5
- Sorcery: 6
- Stealth: 3
- Unarmed Combat: 2

Cyberware:
None

Contacts:
- Any Street Type
- Gang Member
- Street Samurai
- Talismonger

Gear:
- Armor Clothing
- Ritual Sorcery Materials (4 Points for Detect or Illusion Spells)
- Streetline Special Pistol

Spells:
Choose one orientation:
Fighter:
- Mana Bolt: 4
- Powerball: 6

Healer:
- Heal Deadly Wounds: 4
- Heal Moderate Wounds: 4
- Hibernate: 2

Deceiver:
- Chaos: 4
- Entertainment: 3
- Mask: 3

Detector:
- Analyze Device: 4
- Clairvoyance: 3
- Detect Enemies: 3

STREET SAMURAI

"The streets may look like a mess to you, chummer. Just shows that you ain't got eyes. Maybe you should take a trip to Chiba. I hear they got a pair for everybody, so they must have a set for you. Let you see it up close, real time. Like I do. I see the streets as the land of opportunity for a charger. Possibilities everywhere for a guy with an edge.

"What's my edge, you ask. Slot me if I'll spill to you just for the asking! Oh, I've my edge all right. I'm still blowing air past my teeth, ain't I? That's all the credentials a guy in my business needs.

"I've done shadowruns since...well, never mind since when. I may be a street samurai, but I've got enough experience to handle your work. What is it? Muscle down? Lift? Or just a straight-out raid? Hum, your turn to keep it close. That's okay. I can respect that. But you keep something from me that I need to know, and you'll find out just how sharp my edge is. Didn't think you'd like that."

Commentary: The Street Samurai can be male or female, but sex has nothing to do with how tough a Street Samurai is. Born to the metroplex, he's as tough as its alloy steel bones and as dangerous as ground glass. His augmentations are more than just tools to him, they are his style, his badge of commitment to the high-tech life of the city. He's chromed and proud of it. Bodyguard or strongarm man, hired muscle or street soldier, he's a lion of the plex, a hunter in the shadows.

Attributes:
Body: 6 (8)
Quickness: 4 (5)
Strength: 6 (7)
Charisma: 2
Intelligence: 5
Willpower: 5
Essence: .35
Reaction: 4 (8)

Skills:
Armed Combat: 4
Bike: 2
Etiquette (Street): 4
Firearms: 5
Stealth: 4
Unarmed Combat: 6

Cyberware:
Cybereyes with Low Light
Dermal Plating (2)
Muscle Replacement (1)
Retractable Hand Razors
Smartgun Link
Wired Reflexes (2)

Contacts:
Any Street Type
Fixer
Gang Member

Gear:
100 Mp Data Reader
Ares Predator With Smartgun Adapter
DocWagon™ Contract (platinum)
Harley Scorpion
Partial Heavy Armor
Signal Locator
Stun Baton
Tracking Signal (10)
Uzi III With Smartgun Adapter and Silencer
Wrist Phone with Vid Screen

STREET SHAMAN

"Others will tell you that only on the land may you find the spirits who guide and nurture. They are sadly wrong. They cling too fervently to the old ways, the old tales. The future calls to all of us, and we must walk new paths to reach it.

"I have found the spirits of the city, and they have power. They lend their power to me, that I can work to see the new paths, that I can walk strong and proud to meet the future.

"Talk to me of your problems. If there is a harmony with my path, I can help you. Those who aid and guide me can be called to your aid. There will be a price, but it shall be a just price suited to what is done as well as your ability to pay."

Commentary: The Street Shaman walks the path of the spirits. He haunts the metroplex, in tune with its spirit and seeking to preserve its harmony. Unlike the ordinary shaman, he does not abhor the encroachment of technology, though he finds no personal solace in the fruits of the manufactured world. Like all magicians, he avoids technology that invades the body.

Attributes:
  Body: 4
  Quickness: 3
  Strength: 2
  Charisma: 5
  Intelligence: 4
  Willpower: 6
  Essence: 6
  Magic: 6
  Reaction: 3

Skills:
  Conjuring: 5
  Etiquette (Street): 3
  Firearms: 3
  Magical Theory: 5
  Sorcery: 5
  Stealth: 3

Cyberware:
  None

Contacts:
  Any Street Type
  Gang Member
  Street Samurai
  Talismonger

Gear:
  Medicine Lodge Materials (1)
  Medkit
  Ruger Super Warhawk

Spells:
  Choose one orientation from the following:
  Fighter:
    Mana Bolt: 4
    Powerball: 6
  Healer:
    Heal Deadly Wounds: 4
    Heal Moderate Wounds: 4
    Hibernate: 2
  Deceiver:
    Entertainment: 3
    Chaos: 4
    Mask: 3
  Detector:
    Analyze Device: 4
    Clairvoyance: 3
    Detect Enemies: 3

Note:
  A Street Shaman must select an urban totem. See the **Magic** chapter for details.

TRIBESMAN

"The land is the life of the world. For too many years, we have forsaken our proper role, abandoned our task as guardians. To our shame. We must now take up the mantle again. The shamans understand this. They are wise men.

"Years ago, the Great Ghost Dance promised our fathers salvation. It was so, but not as our fathers foresaw it. The Great Spirit has a deeper plan. He has given us much to aid us in our work. We must provide the rest. We will only see the land prosper if we work to aid it. The old ways are forever gone, but that is not bad. There are new ways now, but that too is not bad. We walk a path between the old and the new. A path of our own choosing. One that will lead us to greatness and the fulfillment of our dreams as long as we do not neglect or forsake the land.

"I walk now in the shadows of the towers of steel and glass rather than the shadow of the trees. It is a stalker's path, sometimes a warrior's path. Always I strive to make it a path of honor and wisdom."

Commentary: The Tribesman is a member of one of the local Tribes, possibly metahuman, scattered throughout the wilderness. He is partisan of the sanctity of the land and of the body.

Attributes:
    Body: 5
    Quickness: 5
    Strength: 5
    Charisma: 5
    Intelligence: 5
    Willpower: 5
    Essence: 6
    Reaction: 5

Skills:
    Armed Combat: 5
    Biological Sciences: 3
    Biotech: 2
    Etiquette (Tribal): 4
    Horseback Riding: 3
    Projectile Weapons: 6
    Stealth: 6

Cyberware:
    None

Contacts:
    City Official
    Shaman
    Dwarven Technician
    Member of Another Tribe

Gear:
    3 Antidote (4) Patches
    3 Smoke Grenades
    Binoculars
    Bow and 20 Arrows
    Knife
    Low-Light Goggles
    Medkit
    Real Leathers
    Survival Kit
    Tranq Patch (5)
    Trauma Patch (5)

Notes:
    The Tribesman may call on 2D6 members of his tribe for help.

DEVELOPING THE CHARACTER

"We're in the minority; Runners who are not jacked, rigged, or wakened. We live by our guts and wits."
—Jazzman Harker, Shadowrunner

y now, you've chosen your Archetype, which is like your character's chassis. Next, you'll add the trim and hood ornament. As you do so, begin to fill out a Character Record Sheet from those supplied at the back of the book. First you'll fill in the pertinent information from the **Archetypes** chapter. Then fill out the other sections of the Character Record Sheet using the following rules.

SKILLS

The skills listed with the Archetypes contain no concentrations or specializations. They can be used that way, or a character can refine his skills by using the rules in the **Using Skills** chapter.

DICE POOLS

Each character has a number of Dice Pools, each representing his abilities in certain areas. There is the Astral Pool, Defense Pool, Dodge Pool, Hacking Pool, and Magic Pool.

ASTRAL POOL

The Astral Pool is equal to the sum of the character's Magic and Intelligence Attribute Ratings, plus his Sorcery Skill Rating. This pool is only available to magicians while in Astral Space, where it functions as a Magic Pool and a Defense Pool.

DEFENSE POOL

The Defense Pool is equal to the Armed or Unarmed Combat Skill, as you so choose. You can also choose any applicable concentration or specialization. Use this pool to counterattack in Melee Combat. If your character has no Armed or Unarmed Combat Skill Rating, the Defense Pool is equal to his Strength Attribute Rating minus 4, with a minimum of 1.

DODGE POOL

The Dodge Pool is equal to the character's Quickness Attribute Rating. It can be used to limit the damage done by firearms or projectile and throwing weapons.

HACKING POOL

The Hacking Pool is equal to your character's Computer Skill Rating plus his Reaction Rating. Only characters with Computer Skill have this pool, and only when in the Matrix. If the character has Software concentration or Decking specialization, substitute either of these ratings for Computer Skill.

MAGIC POOL

The Magic Pool is equal to your character's Sorcery Skill Rating, or the Spellcasting concentration, if he has one. Magicians use this pool to increase their effectiveness in casting and resisting spells.

MONEY

All Archetypes receive a credstick with a balance of 3D6 x 1,000¥, or nuyen, the worldwide standard currency. This balance has two uses, to determine a character's lifestyle and to provide money he can spend before play. You can spend it on "off-the-shelf" items listed in the **Equipment** chapter of the rules, but not for anything that must be custom-made or tailored or that requires surgery, like all Cyberware. Find the balance on the following table to determine a character's lifestyle. See the **After The Shadowrun** chapter to apply this information.

LIFESTYLE TABLE	
Balance	**Lifestyle**
3,000 to 8,000¥	Streets
9,000 to 15,000¥	Lower Class
16,000 to 18,000¥	Middle Class

LANGUAGES

Each character starts with a native language skill. Characters should normally choose a language commonly spoken in Seattle, such as English, Japanese, or City Speak. The languages are treated like a *specialization* in a skill. Because we haven't gotten to the specialization rules yet, simply add 2 to your Intelligence and that becomes the Skill Rating for your native language.

Your character may also choose secondary languages. Every point of Intelligence Rating earns the character 1 Rating Point in another language family. Or, you may spend Intelligence Rating Points to learn a language in your character's own language group, with a Language Rating equal to the character's Intelligence Rating plus the points applied. Note that your fluency in a second language cannot exceed your fluency in your native language. Street Archetypes and those with a Street Lifestyle may choose City Speak as their native language. Note that City Speak is one of several languages that are not part of any language group.

The **Using Skills** chapter lists many language groups and languages to get you started.

CONDITION MONITORS

The tracks for Physical and Mental Damage on the Character Record Sheet reflect the beginning status of an uninjured and rested character. Do nothing to these tracks at this time.

If a character has a Cyberdeck, see the Cyberdeck Table on page 139 in the **Equipment** section.

ALLERGIES

Each metahuman race, or subspecies of *Homo sapiens*, offers variations on the basic theme, advantages and disadvantages. You probably have noticed that only two of the Archetypes specify metahuman races. Any metahuman race can be any Archetype. Of course, some are better at certain things than others.

In any case, all members of the metahuman races are allergic to some substance. Remember that whenever you take a metahuman as your character, you must roll on the following tables.

ALLERGIC REACTION TABLE	
2D6	**Substance**
2	Silver
3 – 5	Plastic
6 – 8	Sunlight
9 – 11	Iron
12	Two Substances (Roll again, ignoring 12)

DEGREE OF SEVERITY	
2D6	**Effects of Contact**
2 – 6	Nuisance
7 – 8	Mild
9 – 10	Moderate
11 – 12	Severe

SUBSTANCES

Iron refers to any ferrous metal, such as steel or any variety of steel alloys. This makes the use of most weapons and firearms hazardous to the metahuman.

Plastic refers to all synthetic materials. A metahuman with such an allergy could not use most ballistic armor or Cyberware.

Silver is the mystic lunar metal. This allergy makes some jewelry hazardous.

Sunlight refers to natural light. Beings who are allergic to sunlight are also allergic to X-rays.

SEVERITY

Nuisance means that contact with the substance annoys the character.

A **Mild** reaction means the character is continually distracted when in contact with the substance (+1 to all Target Numbers).

A **Moderate** reaction means that the character is affected with a Mild reaction, and must make periodic checks to avoid a Severe reaction. Make a Resistance Test using the Body or Willpower Attribute, whichever is smaller. The frequency of the check is one hour times the Body Attribute. The Target Number is 6.

A **Severe** reaction means the character must add 1 to all Target Numbers whenever he is in contact with the substance. In addition, contact with the substance causes a Light wound. There is no roll to avoid this damage. Continued contact causes an additional Light wound periodically. The period before the next wound is a number of minutes equal to the character's Body Attribute. Thus, a character with a Body Attribute of 3 who has a Severe reaction to an item receives an additional Light wound every 3 minutes that he remains in contact with that item.

FINISHING TOUCHES

The remaining sections on the Character Record Sheet help you round out the character's personality. The Archetype's comments and descriptions should give you some ideas, but do not feel constrained by them.

Don't forget your street name. Everybody's got to have one who wants to do a shadowrun. Choose one now, in addition to your character's "real name."

The terms Dwarf, Elf, and Human are not descriptive enough to flesh out your character's physical description. Are you a tall, skinny Dwarf? Or a squat, fat Elf? Are you old or young? Is your shadowrun attire different from what you wear to the corporate meetings? If not, why does any rational security guard let you into the lobby, much less the board room, when you are carrying enough assault gear to invade a small island?

If you are a metahuman, do not forget to include your allergies and the degree of severity. Also, you should record any special racial advantages, such as Low-Light eyes.

What is your background? Your character had a life before he went running in the shadows. What happened? If he is an Awakened type (Elf, Dwarf, Troll, or Ork), what was his childhood like before he found out that he was not "normal"? Are you running the shadows for some higher purpose, or are you only there for the money?

Who do you know? A character may select two Contacts from among those listed with his Archetype. The **Contacts** chapter describes these in detail. Remember that you can choose either an Archetype or a non-player Contact. The guys you choose are your buddies, helpers, and confidants. They are unlikely to rip you off because you go way back. Still, do not abuse these Contacts. They have their own interests and lives to lead.

And while we're on it, why are you chumming around with these folks anyway? **Shadowrun** is designed for team play. It would be preposterous for a group of people to meet by chance in a bar, and, on the spur of the moment, to decide that knocking off a dragon would be a fun thing to do. Your character should have some connection with one or more of the other player characters. Talk it out and have some fun.

ARCHETYPE CREATION AND MODIFICATION

To create an Archetype, assign a priority from 0 to 4 to each of the five columns in the Master Character Table. All five Priority Levels (0, 1, 2, 3, 4) must be assigned.

The left-hand column is the priority you assign. Magic refers to the ability to use magic. Attributes is the number of points to divide among Physical and Mental Attributes, following the racial maximums, with none less than zero. Essence is always 6. Skills is the number of points to divide among skills. Tech is the amount of nuyen to spend on Cyberware or other equipment. If the character can use magic, he uses the number after the slash as his total Force points in spells. The final column indicates Race.

Decker was designed with these priorities: Magic: 1; Attributes: 2; Skills: 4; Tech: 3; Race: 0.

Elven Decker had these: Magic: 0; Attributes: 1; Skills: 2; Tech: 3; Race: 4.

METAHUMANS

If you choose a metahuman, roll for allergic reactions on the chart on page 52. In addition, apply the following modifiers.

RACIAL MODIFIERS TABLE

Elf: +1 Quickness, +2 Charisma, Low-Light Eyes
Dwarf: +1 Body, −1 Quickness, +2 Strength, +1 Willpower, Thermographic Eyes, Resistance (+2 Body) to Disease
Ork: +3 Body, +2 Strength, −1 Charisma, −1 Intelligence, Low-Light Eyes
Troll: +5 Body, −1 Quickness, +4 Strength, −2 Charisma, −2 Intelligence, −1 Willpower; +1 Reach for Armed/Unarmed Combat, Thermographic Eyes, Dermal Armor (1); +2 on severity roll for allergic reaction

---

BUYING FRIENDS

An Archetype may spend part of his Tech value on friends and acquaintances. Each Contact costs 5,000¥. You can buy any number of contacts, but you can buy only one Buddy, for 10,000¥. He is the same Archetype as you and more loyal than a contact. He has Attribute and Skill Ratings of 4.

A gang or tribe costs 15,000¥. Roll 2D6 to see how many people are available at any given time. They come when you call and are very loyal. They have Skill and Attribute Ratings of 3.

Followers cost 200,000¥. As many as five different Archetypes come when you call. Roll 1D6+1 to see how many are available at any time. They are willing to die for you. They have standard Archetype Ratings and Cyberware, but you supply the gear.

MODIFYING ARCHETYPES

Well, you may be thinking that you'd really rather make up your own character, but you don't want to go through the hassle of creating a new Archetype. No problem. The Archetypes are only there to give you a fast start on playing the game. For players too choosy to settle for one of the Archetypes provided and too impatient to create their own, here are some quick modification rules.

If you just want to tweak an Archetype a little to make it more comfortable, you can do it in two easy ways. You can juggle the Mental and Physical Attribute Ratings any way you like. Remember not to exceed racial maximums, to apply all Cyberware and racial modifications, and to recalculate your Reaction. You can also change your skills. The primary way to do this is by using the rules for Concentration and Specialization in the **Using Skills** chapter. In addition or instead, you can shift Skill Ratings around. Any changes are fine as long as the ratings total does not change and no skill is rated at more than 6.

Magicians get another option. They can swap spells around just like skills.

If you want to change your gear or Cyberware, you might as well make an Archetype from scratch.

METAHUMANS

If you want to use any regular Archetype as a metahuman, but you do not want to go through the full Archetype-creation procedure, try this. It takes a few liberties with rules, but it's fast. Make sure your gamemaster approves.

First, select an Archetype and the desired race of metahuman. If the Archetype is non-magical, subtract 6 points from his total Skill Ratings or 5 from his total Attribute Ratings. If the Archetype is magical, subtract 5 points from his total Skill Ratings or 3 from his total Attribute Ratings. Reduce his Spell Ratings so that their total is one-half the previous total.

Next, apply racial modifiers from the Racial Modifiers Table, and roll for allergies. If you get an allergy that would prevent the use of any listed Cyberware, keep the level of allergy and switch to a different substance. If the allergy means that you cannot use some of the equipment listed, tough luck. Maybe you have friends who would like it.

No Attribute may be less than 1 after modification. To prevent a lower rating, rate the attribute in question at 1 and shave the extra points from another Attribute. Suppose you wanted a Troll Decker. The Decker Archetype has a Charisma of 1, and Trolls get a −2 to Charisma. Because the Archetype's Charisma is already at the bottom, that −2 has to go somewhere else, either as two points from one Attribute or one point from each of two.

All set? Then it's time for a Shadowrun. Let's do it.

MASTER CHARACTER TABLE

Priority	Magic	Attributes	Skills	Tech	Race
0	None	15 Points	17 Points	100/5	Human
1	None	17 Points	20 Points	1,000/10	Human
2	None	20 Points	24 Points	20,000/20	Human
3	If Metahuman	24 Points	30 Points	400,000/50	Human
4	Yes	30 Points	40 Points	1,000,000−	Metahuman

USING SKILLS

"If you did it and lived, then you probably did it right."
—J.K.W., Freelancer

hen trying to accomplish something more refined than hefting a load, spotting an ambush, or running for cover, a character will normally use a skill. **Shadowrun** skills are groups of closely related techniques and knowledge, not narrow, limiting areas of function. The game takes this approach in an attempt to keep down the number of statistics. If a character does have concentrations and specializations, he has increased capability in that specialized area, but at the cost of reduced ability with the rest of the functions covered by the general skill.

SKILL RATINGS

Skill Ratings begin at 1. There is no maximum rating, but characters will find it increasingly difficult to raise their ratings as they get better in a particular skill. Beginning characters may not start with a skill rating higher than 6. A character with no rating in a skill is untrained. He may still attempt to perform a function covered by a skill in one of two ways: use a related skill or default to an Attribute. To do so, he must use the Skill Web, which appears later on page 57 of this chapter.

SUCCESS TESTS

The rules make frequent reference to Success Tests. To make a Success Test, first check the rating of the attribute or skill named for the test to determine how many six-sided dice to roll. Each die result that equals or exceeds the specified Target Number is a success. Usually one success is enough to indicate that the character has passed the test. A Resistance Test works the same way except the the character is trying to avoid something rather than accomplish something.

There are three kinds of Success Tests. In an **Unresisted Success Test** (or simply Success Test), the character is attempting to accomplish something without any interference. In a **Resisted Success Test**, the target or object makes a Resistance Test to offset the character's Successes. In an **Opposed Success Test**, two characters use the same skill or an opposing skill against one another, with only one of them actually able to succeed in the effort. Negotiation is an example of this.

Using the Skill Success Test Table as a guide, the gamemaster determines the Target Number necessary for success. In some cases, the rules specify a Target Number for specific skill uses. Circumstances and conditions (bad weather, stress, acting while moving, and so on) can change the Target Number.

SKILL SUCCESS TABLE

Difficulty	Target Number
Simple	2
Routine	3
Average	4
Challenging	5
Difficult	6
Strenuous	7
Arduous	8
Extreme	9
Nearly Impossible	10+

Once the Modified Target Number is determined, the player rolls the number of dice indicated by the character's Skill Rating. (Remember to re-roll with a 6.) If the situation calls for only a simple success, his character is successful if any of the dice rolled equals or exceeds the Modified Target Number. In more complicated situations, the *number* of successful dice is meaningful. In general, the number of successes is a guideline for the gamemaster to measure a character's level of achievement. The more the better.

LEVEL OF SUCCESS TABLE

Successes	Level
1–2	Barely Achieved
3–4	Noteworthy
5–6	Praiseworthy
7+	Exemplary

Neddy scribbled notes on the big old book, just as he had done dozens of times since he'd copped it off that Aztechnology wage mage on the last run. He spouted his usual cusses and was downright impolite to Iris when she tried to help. Suddenly, he sat up straight and shouted "Eureka!"

Neddy, with an Intelligence Attribute of 5, has been been looking for a particular bit of information in that book. Each time he gets a chance to study it, the gamemaster has been allowing him an Intelligence Success Test to find it. The gamemaster decided that it was an extreme task (Target Number 9) because the previous owner kept the notes in his own kind of shorthand. Neddy finally got a Success. It was an Unresisted Success Test, and so no further rolls were necessary.

In an Opposed Success Test, the gamemaster determines the Target Number for each of the characters involved. Each player rolls the appropriate dice for his character. The character with the most successes wins the test. If the players tie, no one wins. They can try again later.

For example, two characters engaged in a duel cross swords, each using his own Armed Combat Skill. The one who has more successes will pierce his opponent's guard, possibly wounding him. The Opposed Success Test applies in non-combat situations as well. Two characters might try to work out an agreement using their Negotiation Skills. Each has a Target Number of the other's Willpower Attribute. Whichever character gets more successes is able to talk the other into advantageous terms. As in any Success Test, a larger number of successes represents a greater achievement.

Neddy stood in the middle of the vacant lot. He had never liked being so out in the open, even in the dead of night, but Raul wanted it this way, and the customer is always right.

After a five-minute wait that lasted an eternity, a Mitsubishi Nightsky pulled up. Raul got out and walked across the tufts of grass and discarded plastic to Neddy.

"You finally figured out that Aztech's chicken-scratching. Three weeks ago, that information was worth 10,000 nuyen, but now it's old and dated," Raul sneered. "Best I can give you is 5,000."

Neddy glared at Raul. "Can the drek about the depreciating value of information. You know as well as I that no one at Aztechnology knew what that wage mage kept in his little book, or that we had got ahold of it. The price is still 10,000."

Raul nodded slightly and took out a certified credstick. He extended it to Neddy. "10,000 it is."

Neddy met his fence, Raul, and negotiated a price for the information that Neddy was able to decipher from the book. Neddy has a Negotiation Skill of 2 and a Willpower Attribute of 5, while Raul has a Negotiation Skill of 3 and a Willpower Attribute of 3. Neddy rolls two dice, resulting in a 4 and a 5, or two Successes. Raul rolls 3 dice, getting a 2, 2, and a 5, for only one Success. Neddy wins with one net success, enough to keep the price at the original level.

Remember that a Resisted Success Test is a simple Success Test by one player, followed by another player's Resistance Test to prevent or offset the success. That is, once a level of success is determined, the victim of a Resisted Success Test or the loser in an Opposed Test has a chance to mitigate the level of damage or otherwise reduce the size of the success by making a Resistance Test. This normally is done only in situations that would cause damage on the Condition Monitor. Rules for Resistance Tests for **Combat, Magic**, and **Matrix** operations can be found in the appropriate sections of the rules.

TAKING THE TIME

Characters sometimes use skills and attributes for activities that do not have immediate results. Examples would include fixing a car, building something, learning a new spell, and so on. The gamemaster determines how long a task should take. Extra successes divide the specified time with fractions rounded up or down to the nearest whole time unit (2 2/3 hours counts as 3 hours). Thus, if a job typically takes ten hours, and the character gets three extra successes (10 ÷ 3 = 3.3) he would do the job in 3 hours.

Fractions smaller than 1 round up, so even if you get twelve extra successes doing a 3-hour job, it takes you an hour to do it. You do it with style, but you still need an hour. If you want your extra successes to make the result more spectacular, you cannot use these same successes to cut the time.

Fastjack slipped the chip-puller back into its slot in his microtronics toolkit, gave it a pat, and smiled. He had just finished repairing the telecom for Lady Tsung in record time. She would be pleased.

Fastjack, the legendary decker, has just finished a task using his Electronics (B/R) Skill, which has a Rating of 7. The gamemaster had assigned a basic time of 10 hours for the job, based on his assessment of the modifications Fastjack wanted to include and an overall Target Number of 3. The decker rolled successes with all seven of his dice. He used three successes to get a Noteworthy Success, possibly improving the ratings of his modifications. The other four successes went to reducing the time (10 ÷ 4 = 2.5, which rounds to 3). He has finished in three hours.

THE SKILL WEB

Each skill connects to one or more others by a network of relationships called the Skill Web. Using the web allows a character with one skill to perform functions properly belonging to another skill. He will, of course, not be as likely to succeed as someone who has the proper skill.

There are two ways to use the Skill Web: by using a related skill or defaulting to an attribute.

When using a related skill, trace a path from the desired skill to one in which the character has a rating. You need not trace the shortest path. Count the number of circles you pass, with each circle raising the Target Number by 2.

When defaulting to an Attribute, trace the path to where the Attribute you want to use enters the Skill Web.

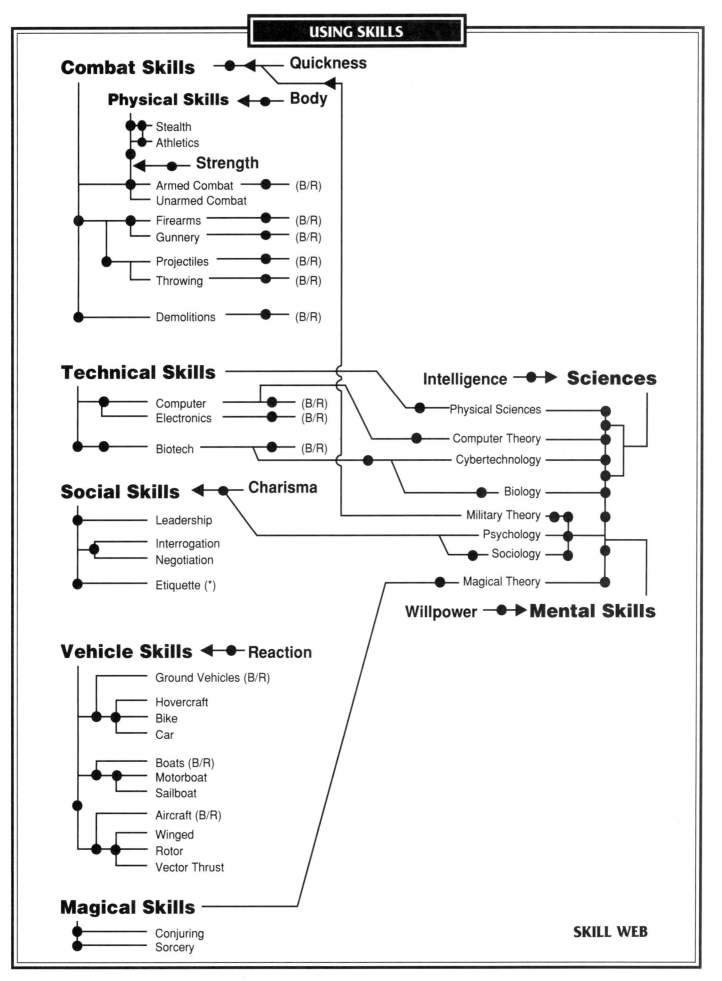

Combat Skills ← Quickness

  Physical Skills ← Body

- Stealth
- Athletics

← Strength

- Armed Combat — (B/R)
- Unarmed Combat
- Firearms — (B/R)
- Gunnery — (B/R)
- Projectiles — (B/R)
- Throwing — (B/R)

- Demolitions — (B/R)

Technical Skills

- Computer — (B/R)
- Electronics — (B/R)
- Biotech — (B/R)

Intelligence → **Sciences**

- Physical Sciences
- Computer Theory
- Cybertechnology
- Biology
- Military Theory
- Psychology
- Sociology
- Magical Theory

Social Skills ← Charisma

- Leadership
- Interrogation
- Negotiation
- Etiquette (*)

Willpower → **Mental Skills**

Vehicle Skills ← Reaction

- Ground Vehicles (B/R)
- Hovercraft
- Bike
- Car
- Boats (B/R)
- Motorboat
- Sailboat
- Aircraft (B/R)
- Winged
- Rotor
- Vector Thrust

Magical Skills

- Conjuring
- Sorcery

SKILL WEB

CONCENTRATIONS AND SPECIALIZATIONS

Players have the option of giving their character a concentration in a particular form of a skill, i.e., the character has spent most of his study and practice time on mastering that form of the skill. By narrowing his focus this way, the character obviously cannot give as much attention to related forms. For example, two characters who have the same ratings in Stealth will have different *effective* ratings if one of them concentrates in Stealth (Urban). The urban fellow will be better than the other guy on the city streets but worse in the wilderness.

Use of the chosen concentration applies +1 to the rating, while other uses of the general skill apply –1 to the rating. Thus, a character decides to concentrate on Pistols within his Firearms Skill. He has a Skill Rating of 4. He will use pistols at a Rating of 5 and all other types of firearms at a Rating of 3.

Specialization takes the process a step further, limiting the character to a particular item or activity. Thus, a character already concentrating on pistols may choose to specialize in a particular weapon. Skill use in the specialization applies a +2 to the general rating. A character has his normal rating with skill uses within the area of concentration, but any other uses of the skill applies a –2 to the general rating. Thus, the pistol specialist from above has a rating of 6 with his chosen weapon, a Beretta Model 101T, a rating of 4 with other pistols, and a rating of 2 with rifles, SMGs, and other firearms.

Starting characters are allowed only one concentration and one specialization per skill. When referring to the Skill Web, use the lowest of the values, that is, the Modified Rating for the general skill.

When a beginning character elects to concentrate or specialize, the maximum Skill Rating applies to the general skill, not the narrowed skill. Thus, a Street Samurai with Firearms 6 can specialize in Beretta Model 101T, giving him a rating of 8 with that particular pistol, 6 with other pistols, and 4 with other firearms.

If concentration or specialization would reduce the general Skill Rating below 1, it stays at 1 instead.

SKILL CATEGORIES

Shadowrun groups skills into five broad categories: Active, Build and Repair, Knowledge, Languages, and Special Skills. All have ratings that improve as the character becomes more experienced. In the description of a skill, you will find a list of suggested concentrations. You can create others if your gamemaster approves them. Possible specializations appear in parentheses after the concentration name. You can create other specializations with the approval of your gamemaster.

ACTIVE SKILLS

Active Skills usually apply toward achieving a specific, short-term result, such as hitting a target with a weapon, performing a difficult maneuver in a vehicle, climbing a wall, casting a spell, and so forth. An Active Skill includes maintenance of equipment commonly needed to use the skill and includes the user's understanding of the skill's application. An Active Skill does not include the ability to design new equipment. Active Skills are arranged into groups to simplify the func-

tion of the Skill Web, making it easier to represent which skills are related.

Combat Skills

Most combat skills have the designation "SW" in parentheses, where you would normally expect to find a list of the specializations. This means that you should choose any specific weapon (SW) from the concentration group if you wish to specialize.

Melee Combat

These are the skills for using all sorts of melee weapons, martial arts techniques, and implant weapons.

Armed Combat governs the use of hand-held melee weapons.

Concentrations: Edged Weapons (SW), Pole Arms/Staff (SW), Whips/Flails (SW), Clubs (SW)

Unarmed Combat governs the use of martial arts techniques and implant weapons.

Concentrations: Grapple, Cyber Implant Weaponry (SW)

Ranged Combat

These are skills that affect combat with a distant target.

Firearms governs the use of all types of firearms, from pistols to grenade launchers.

Concentrations: Pistols (SW), Rifles (SW), Submachine Guns (SW), Grenade Launchers (SW), Tasers (SW)

Gunnery governs the use of heavy weapons, whether on tripods, vehicle mounts, pintles, or in fixed emplacements.

Concentrations: Machine Guns (SW), Missile Launchers (SW), Assault Cannon (SW), Vehicle-Mounted Cannon (SW), Artillery (SW)

Projectile Weapons governs the use of muscle-powered projectile weapons.

Concentrations: Bows (SW), Crossbows (SW)

Throwing Weapons governs the use of weapons thrown by the user.

Concentrations: Non-Aerodynamic (Grenades, Knives), Aerodynamic (Shuriken, Airfoil Grenades)

Demolitions governs the preparation, measuring, and setting of chemical explosives.

Concentrations: Commercial Explosives, Plastic Explosives.

Physical Skills

Physical Skills require agility and general body control, strength, and stamina. A character's load has a large effect on his Physical Skills. See the **Behind the Scenes** chapter for more details.

Stealth governs sneaking around, moving quietly, tracking (and covering one's tracks), and trailing another character without his awareness (and giving a tail the shake). Each particular aspect of the skill may become a specialization for any environmental concentration.

Concentrations: Urban (by Aspect), Wilderness (by Aspect), Farmland (by Aspect)

Athletics governs exceptional training in a particular aspect of physical endeavor. Specialization involves increasing one's concentration, rather than working in a specific form. Thus, a character specializing in Climbing applies +2 to his Athletics Rating when climbing and −2 when using a different Athletics concentration.

Concentrations: Running, Climbing, Lifting, Jumping, Swimming.

Technical Skills

Technical Skills deal with all types of machines, including electronics and those implanted into the body.

Computer governs use and understanding of computer technology and programming. This skill is absolutely essential to anyone who wishes to jack into cyberspace and run the Matrix.

Concentrations: Hardware (Main Frames, Micros, Interface Tech, Implant Tech), Software (Decking, Matrix Programming, Non-Matrix Programming, Interface Programming, Implant Programming)

Electronics governs the use and understanding of electronic devices, which in 2050 is most everything in common use in a city. Specialization involves increasing the depth of concentration, as in Athletics. Thus, specializing in Maglocks applies a +2 to that concentration but a −2 to all other Electronics concentrations.

Concentrations: Control Systems, Electronic Warfare, Maglocks, Linking Between Devices, Diagnostics.

Biotech governs basic medicine, first aid, and implant operations. A character with this skill understands basic medicine in a hands-on sense, as a paramedic rather than a physician. Though familiar with the techniques and materials of Cyberware, he would still need a computer expert to collaborate on the interface systems.

Concentrations: Transimplant Surgery (Headware, Bodyware, Organic Replacements), Organ Culture (by Organ or Limb), Replacement Construction (by Organ or Limb), Extended Care, First Aid

Magical Skills

Anyone may study Magical Skills for the inherent knowledge, but only a magician can use these skills to manipulate magical energy. The **Magic** chapter explains this use.

Conjuring governs the calling and banishing of spirit powers. Only Mages can call Elementals, and only Shamans can call Nature Spirits.

Concentrations: Elemental Type, Nature Spirit Type

Sorcery governs the control of magical energy in the form of spells.

Concentrations: Spellcasting (by Spell Purpose Category), Ritual Sorcery (by Spell Purpose Category)

Social Skills

Social Skills concern the interaction of the player characters and non-player characters. For interaction among player characters, the players should rely on their real social skills.

Leadership governs a character's ability to get others to do what he wants through example and authority. It includes an aspect of problem-solving, but is not intended to substitute for clear thinking and good planning on the part of the players. Successful use of the Leadership Skill depends on the subject's Intelligence Attribute Rating.

Concentrations: Political, Military, Commercial. Specializations for each concentration include Strategy (general plans), Tactics (topical plans), and Morale

Interrogation governs the extraction of information from an unwilling subject. Its success depends on the subject's Willpower Attribute Rating. It is usually ineffective when applied against more than a single subject at a time.

Concentrations: Verbal, Machine-Aided (Lie Detectors, Voice Stress Analysis)

Negotiation governs any interactions in which each side seeks to come out ahead, either through careful and deliberate bartering or through fast talk. Its success depends on the adversary's Willpower Attribute Rating.

Concentrations: Bargain, Bribe

Etiquette is a special kind of skill that requires a concentration. Each concentration represents a particular subculture. Etiquette Skill allows a character to function within the subculture without appearing out of place. It also allows him to recognize prominent figures within the subculture and to have a general idea of their strengths, weaknesses, likes, and dislikes. Attempting to manipulate someone within a subculture by using Etiquette depends on the subject's Charisma Attribute Rating.

Specializations of Etiquette differ with the subcultures. A concentration of Etiquette (Street) would have specializations in each gang, criminal elements, and so on. Particular tribes, specific tribal interests, or intertribal politics would be appropriate for Etiquette (Tribal). Particular corporations, corporate hirelings, and intercorporate relations apply to Etiquette (Corporate).

Concentrations: Corporate, Media, Street, Tribal

Vehicle Skills

The type of vehicle in use and the driver's familiarity with it affect the chance of success when a character attempts a difficult maneuver or takes the vehicle through difficult terrain and conditions. Ordinary operation of the vehicle requires no die roll. In fact, many 21st-century vehicles can operate almost on their own.

Most Vehicle Skills have a concentration of Remote Operation. This refers to vehicles whose operator is not present in the vehicle. The vehicle responds to transmitted orders. Specialization in a Remote-Operation Concentration does not specify a particular vehicle, but a category instead. If the category is the concentration, then a specific vehicle (SV) is the specialization.
Ground Vehicles

Hovercraft are all hover vehicles, regardless of their purpose.

Concentration: Passenger Craft (SV), Transport Craft (SV), Racing (SV), Remote Operation (Category)

Bike refers to all motorcycles, motortrikes, and bikes with sidecars.

Concentration: Two-wheeler (SV), Three-wheeler (SV), Racing (SV), Remote Operation (Category)

Car refers to a motor vehicle with four or more wheels.

Concentrations: Passenger Vehicle (SV), Truck (SV), Racing (SV), Remote Operation (Category)
Boats

Motorboat refers to any motorized watercraft.

Concentrations: Pleasure Craft (SV), Transport (SV), Racing (SV), Remote Operation (Category)

Sailboat governs the control of sail-powered watercraft.

Concentrations: Pleasure Craft (SV), Transport (SV), Racing (SV), Remote Operation (Category)
Aircraft

Winged Planes governs the control of fixed or swing-wing aircraft (jet, prop, or turbo prop) and unpowered aircraft.

Concentrations: Gliders (SV), Jets (SV), Propellers (SV), Racing (SV), Remote Operation (Category)

Rotor Craft refers to fixed and tilt rotor aircraft.

Concentrations: Tilt-Rotor (SV), Fixed-Rotor (SV), Remote Operation (Category)

Vectored Thrust encompasses aircraft relying on vectored thrust for lift and propulsion. This includes Low-Altitude Vehicles (known colloquially as panzers), military craft that use this motive power but do not normally operate at altitude because of their heavy loads or armor and armament.

Concentrations: Vertical Take Off and Landing (SV), LAV Craft (SV), Remote Operation (Category)

BUILD AND REPAIR SKILLS

There is a corresponding Build/Repair (B/R) Skill for many of the Active Skills and they are noted on the Skill Web. The B/R counterpart implies the character's access to the tools and/or equipment commonly used in that skill area. Thus, Armed Combat (B/R) allows a character to make or repair swords and other melee weapons. Ground Vehicles (B/R) allows him to fix a car, a bike, or a hovercraft equally well.

The character still needs time, tools, and materials to build something from scratch. Even a character with superb levels of skill can do little without the proper tools and materials. If he is trying to make something new, he also needs theoretical knowledge to design it unless someone presents him with detailed blueprints for its construction. See **Behind the Scenes** for details on how to use Build and Repair Skills.

Concentrations for Build/Repair Skills are for types of equipment when they relate to named skills and by the category of equipment when they apply to groupings. Thus, a concentration in Armed Combat (B/R) works for Edged Weapons but not

for other melee weapons, and a concentration for Ground Vehicles (B/R) could be Bikes, excluding Car and Hovercraft.

KNOWLEDGE SKILLS

Knowledge Skills give a character access to specific information. This is especially useful when the character is an expert in a field in which the player is ignorant.

Many Knowledge Skills also provide the character with the theoretical basis of actions related to the field of study and the basis for new designs in an area.

Physical Sciences include engineering as well as physical sciences. Specializations are the various branches of each discipline, which are too numerous to list here.

Concentrations: Engineering, Physics, Chemistry, Geology

Computer Theory covers computer design and architecture.

Concentrations: Hardware (Main Frames, Micros, Interface Tech, Implant Tech), Software (Decking, Matrix Programming, Non-Matrix Programming, Interface Programming, Implant Programming), Matrix Theory

Cybertechnology covers the design of implant and cybernetic control technology. Specializations are for Specific Devices (SD).

Concentrations: Headware (SD), Bodyware (SD)

Biology covers general life sciences. Specializations include all the specific branches of each discipline, which are too numerous to list here.

Concentrations: Zoology, Botany, Medicine, Parazoology, Parabotany

Psychology includes covers behavioral science in analytical and predictive forms. Specializations are all specific types of behavior and personality types.

Concentrations: Individual Behavior, Group Behavior, Deviant Behavior

Military Theory covers theoretical studies of men in combat and military organizations.

Concentrations: Military History (by Continent or Period), Tactics (Air, Land, Sea)

Sociology covers historical and observational sciences concerning Humans and Human interactions. Specializations are by continent or culture.

Concentrations: History, Anthropology, Archaeology

Magical Theory includes a general understanding of the functions and functioning of magic. It is vital in the design of new spells.

Concentrations: Design (Shamanic, Hermetic), History (by Continent)

LANGUAGE SKILLS

Language Skills are an exception to the basic rule that each language is a specialization of its family of languages. Thus, a character will have some facility with related languages, but he will not be well-versed unless he adds a specialization in that language as well. Different language families are not considered to be related. Each family is listed in bold type, followed by the specific names.

Players should note that there are no formal Troll, Dwarf, or Ork languages. These characters use the languages of their mothers and fathers, most of whom are Human.

Algonkian: Algonkin, Arapaho, Blackfoot, Cheyenne, Cree, Micmac, Mohican, Ojibwa, Shawnee, Wiyot, Yurok

Armenian

Athabascan: Apache, Chipewwyan, Navaho

Baltic: Estonian, Latvian (Lettish), Lithuanian

Basque

Caddoan: Caddo, Pawnee, Wichita

Celtic: Breton, Irish Gaelic, Scottish Gaelic, Welsh

Chukchi

Common Tongues and Hybrids: City Speak (see **Special Languages,** below), Esperanto, Interlingua

Dravidian: Gondi, Kannada, Kurukh, Malayadem, Tamil, Telugu, Tulu

Elvish: See **Special Languages,** below

Eskimo

Finnic: Cheremis, Finnish, Karelian, Lapp, Livonian, Mordvin, Veps, Votyak, Zyrian

Germanic: Afrikaans, Danish, Dutch, English, Flemish, German, Icelandic, Norwegian, Swedish, Yiddish

Greek

Hamitic: Beja, Berber, Galla, Hausa (Chadic), Somali, Tuareg

Indic: Assamese, Bengali, Bhili, Gujarti, Hindi, Konkani, Marathi, Oriya, Punjabi, Rajasthani, Sindhi, Sinhalese, Urdu

Indo-Iranian: Baluchi, Kurdish, Persian (Farsi), Pushtu

Iroquoian: Cayuga, Cherokee, Erie, Huron, Iroquois, Mohawk, Onandago, Oneida, Seneca, Tuscarora

Japanese and Korean: Japanese, Korean

Khoisan: Bushman, Hadza, Hottentot, Nama, Sandawe

Malayo-Polynesian: Bahasa, Cebuano, Ilocano, Javanese, Kiriwina, Madurese, Malayan, Maori, Melanesian, Micronesian, Misima, Panay-Hiligaynon, Polynesian, Samar-Leyte, Samoan, Sundanese, Tagalog, Taluga

Mayan: Guatemala, Kekchi, Mam, Quiche-Tzutujil-Cakchique, Yucatan

Mon-Khmer (Annamite): Cambodian (Khmer), Mon, Vietnamese (Annamese)

Mongolic: Khalkha (Mongolian)

Muskogean: Chickasaw, Choctaw, Creek, Seminole

Niger-Kordofanian (Bantu): Anyi, Ashanti, Azande, Bassa, Baule, Bemba, Birom, Bulu, Efik, Ewe, Fang, Fante, Fula, Ganda, Ibo, Igbo, Kikuyu, Kituba, Kongo, Kpele, Kru, Luba, Lunda, Makua, Mande, Mbundu, Mende, More, Mossi, Ngala, Ngbaudi, Nyamwezi-Sukuma, Nyanja, Rundi, Rwanda, Shona, Sotho, Sukuma, Swahili, Temne, Tiv, Tswana, Twi, Wolof, Xhosa, Yao, Yoruba, Zande, Zulu

Nilotic: Bagirmi, Dinka, Fur, Kanembu, Kanuri, Koman, Luo, Maban, Masai, Nuer, Sango, Shilluk, Songhai, Wadai

Oto-Manguan: Mixtec, Otomi, Zapotec

Papuan Family: Dayak, Negrito, Papu

Romance: Catalan, French, Galician, Italian, Portuguese, Provencal, Rumanian, Spanish

Salish: Chehalis, Okanagon, Salish

Semitic: Amharic, Arabic, Harari, Hebrew, Neo-Aramaic, Tigre, Tigrinya

Sino-Tibetan: Burmese, Cantonese, Hakka, Kashmiri, Lao, Mandarin, Min, Nepali, Shan, Thai, Tibetan, Wu, Yueh

Siouan: Catawba, Crow, Dakota, Hidatsa, Omaha, Osage

Slavic: Bulgarian, Byelorussian, Czech, Georgian, Macedonian, Polish, Russian, Serbo-Croatian, Slovak, Slovene, Ukrainian

South American Indian: Arowakan, Cariban, Quechua, Tupi-Guarani, many others

Tlinglit

Tsimshian

Tungus

Turkic: Azerbaijani, Chuvash, Kazakh, Kirghiz, Tatar, Turki, Turkish, Uzbek, Yakut

Ugrian: Magyar (Hungarian), Ostyak, Vogul

Uto-Aztecan: Aztec, Comanche, Hopi, Paiute, Papago, Pima, Shoshoni, Ute

Zuni

SPECIAL LANGUAGES

City Speak is one of several languages that are not part of any formal language group.

Many beings know about Elvish, but it has few speakers because few of its fluent speakers have been willing to cooperate with linguists in recording its vocabulary and grammar. These few Elvish speakers, who are rumored to be from the distant past, guard the dissemination of this language carefully, almost as carefully as they guard their own identities. Most Elves cannot speak Elvish, and it is rare for any other race to have more than passing knowledge of it.

SPECIAL SKILLS

Special Skills is a catch-all category of skills intended to round out a character as an individual. Such skills cover hobbies, interests, artistic endeavors, and other unusual skills. Be creative.

COMBAT

"Sure I believe in peace—peace through superior firepower."
—Scuz the Ork merc, mid-21st Century

hen it's time to get down to the action, the game proceeds in turns. Each character acts in order, the fastest first, in a turn roughly approximating 3 seconds of game time. During a combat turn, each player describes his character's action. The gamemaster, in turn, describes the actions of the non-player characters and the results of all actions.

COMBAT TURN SEQUENCE

The sequence of a combat turn is as follows:
1. All characters determine initiative result.
2. The character with the highest result selects an action or decides to do nothing.
3. Resolve that action. If the action is conditional on the actions of other characters, wait until the condition occurs. If it does not happen during the turn, the character wastes his action.
4. The character with the next highest initiative result selects an action.
5. Resolve the action, as in step 3.
6. Repeat these steps until all characters have taken their actions.
7. Start another combat turn.

INITIATIVE RESULTS

To determine a character's initiative result, roll 1D6 and add the result to his Reaction Attribute. Thus, when Fastjack, who has a Reaction Attribute of 5, rolls a 3, he has a result of 8. Some characters have advantages due to Cyberware or spells that increase their Reaction or give them extra dice to roll.

The character with the highest result acts first. Characters act in order, from highest result to lowest. In case of a tie at any point in the sequence, the character with the highest Reaction Attribute acts first. If there is still a tie, roll 1D6. The player with the higher result goes first. Actions are not considered to be simultaneous. The effect of actions, damage, for instance, applies immediately.

EXTRA ACTIONS

When a player rolls a high initiative result, he gets extra actions in that turn. Depending on the result, your character might get up to four actions. Here's how it works.

An initiative result over 10 gives you one extra action. Subtract 7 from the initiative result to determine where that action will occur in the turn sequence. If a tie occurs, the player rolling for an extra action will follow a player rolling for his normal first action.

If the initiative result exceeds 16, the player gets three actions in the turn. Subtract 7 from the initiative result for the timing of the second action, and subtract 14 from the initiative result to get the timing of the third action. In case of a tie, third actions lose out to other players' second and first actions.

If the initiative result exceeds 22, the character gets four actions in the turn. Subtract 7 from the initiative result for the timing of the second action, 14 for the third, and 21 for the fourth. Fourth actions lose out to other players' third, second, and first actions in case of a tie.

EXTRA ACTION TABLE	
Initiative Result	**# of Extra Actions**
1–10	One action per turn
11–16	Two actions per turn
17–22	Three actions per turn
23+	Four actions per turn

The Ork slammed through the door, leaving Grinder the Troll no doubt that it was time to play. The ponderous Troll was slow, even compared to someone without hardwired reflexes. The Ork pumped a burst from his silvergun at Grinder and cut back out of the room. The door slammed shut, but Grinder didn't care. He slammed his fist right through the door. As he felt his fist connect with the Ork's belly, his grin exposed his yellowed teeth.

The Ork's initiative result of 15 gave him two actions. The first at 15, and the second at 15 – 7, or 8. Grinder got a 7 result, one action. For his first, the Ork fires at Grinder and moves out of the room. His lack of effectiveness might have been due to his movement or to the Troll's thick hide. In either case, he must have figured he had run into too much trouble. For his second action, the Ork tries to shut and lock the door, hoping to keep the troll from following him. When Grinder's action comes around, he steps up and unloads a punch through the door.

ACTIONS

When taking an action, a character gets to do something, or move, or combine movement with other activity. The following list is just a sampling of typical Actions.

TYPICAL ACTIONS

Call on a spirit.

Cast a spell.

Drink a potion, take a pill, slap a patch, and so forth.

Fire a gun.

Make a physical attack, armed or unarmed.

Move a number of meters equal to the character's Quickness Attribute. (This can be combined with another action.)

Pick up, put down, or otherwise manipulate an object.

Reload a weapon. (Some weapons need additional actions to finish.)

Run. Running cannot be combined with other actions, and so may be selected only for one action in a turn.

Scrutinize an opponent or area.

Shift to or from Astral Space.

Throw a knife, shuriken, or grenade.

Use a bow or crossbow.

Use any simple device.

Use magic.

Draw or holster a weapon

On any action, a character gets to move a number of meters equal to his quickness. If a character combines movement with another action, there is a penalty. If that action already requires a Success Test, apply +1 to the Target Number. If the movement is over rough ground or obstacles, apply +2 to the Target Number.

If the action is normally automatic, it now requires a Success Test. Use the character's Quickness Attribute, with a Target Number of 4. If a character has been subject to melee attack in the same turn, apply +1 for each opponent to the Target Number for his actions.

Instead of a normal move, a character can run. A character with multiple actions can run only once in a turn, but he can squeeze out some more meters with regular movement. A character *cannot combine running with other actions*. When running, multiply movement by the run modifier for the character's race, per the following table.

RUNNING TABLE

Race	Modifiers
Human	x4
Dwarf	x3
Elf	x4
Ork	x4
Troll	x3

INTERCEPTION

If movement takes your character within one meter past an opponent, the opponent can make a melee attack out of normal sequence. This melee attack does not count as an action. If the opponent has a weapon ready, he uses his normal Skill Rating for Armed Combat; otherwise, he uses Unarmed Combat. The

Target Number is 5, or 6 if the attacking character has already moved this turn. The only modifiers are those applied because of the attacker's condition.

PURSUIT

Occasionally, a character chases another. This is best handled outside a regular combat turn. Both characters are, of course, running. In addition to the usual distance covered, each runner covers a number of meters equal to the result of (Quickness)D6. If the pursuer gets close enough for combat, start a combat turn. The pursuer gets an extra die for his initiative result roll.

DICE POOLS

A Dice Pool is a number of additional dice that you may roll when determining your success at something or resistance to something. Each player starts combat with all Dice Pools at their full allowance. These dice can be used as needed, but each is used only once during the turn. Each of the character's Dice Pools is renewed to full value at the beginning of any of his actions, at which time all remaining dice from the previous action are lost. The Pools are not renewed at the beginning of the following combat turns, but only at the beginning of the character's action.

Dice Pools may not be used during a combat turn in which a character has been surprised.

Three people are shooting at Grinder, starting combat. Grinder gets two actions this turn on 11 and 4. The first shooter fires on 17. The Troll needs to draw on his Dodge Pool. Not knowing that the other guys want him for a target, he uses all of his starting Dodge Pool dice to avoid getting creamed by the first shot. A second shot comes in on 12. Grinder has yet to refresh his Dodge Pool and so the Troll cannot dodge.

Grinder gets plugged again on 10, but he had replenished his Dodge Pool at the start of 11, so he is at full strength again. To avoid this shot he again uses all of his dice. When the third shot comes in at 3, Grinder will get access to his full Dodge Pool again, as it was refreshed on 4. However, if the combat goes on for a second turn, Grinder will not be able to refresh the dodge Pool until the start of his next action.

FIRE COMBAT

Resolve Fire Combat according to the following steps. Each step is explained in turn. Together, these steps constitute a Resisted Success Test.

1. Find the Base Target Number.
2. Apply Target Modifiers.
3. Make the Success Test Roll.
4. Count Successes.
5. Calculate Damage.
6. Reduce Damage.
7. Apply Damage.

TARGET NUMBER

Check the distance to the target, then consult the Weapon Range Table below to find out the range category for your weapon.

WEAPON RANGE TABLE

Weapon	Range in Meters			
	Short	Medium	Long	Extreme
Light Pistol	0–5	6–15	16–30	31–50
Taser	0–5	6–10	11–12	13–15
Shotgun	0–10	11–20	21–50	51–100
Assault Rifle	0–15	16–40	41–100	101–250
Heavy MG	0–40	41–150	151–400	401–800
Bow	0–5	6–50	51–150	151–300
Thrown Knife	0–3	4–6	7–12	13–20
Shuriken	0–5	6–10	11–20	21–25

Once you have determined the range category, consult the Target Number Table to determine the Base Target Number.

TARGET NUMBER TABLE

Range	Target
Short Range	4
Medium Range	5
Long Range	7
Extreme Range	9

Image modification systems reduce a weapon's range category. Each system has a rating that indicates the number of categories reduced. Short range is the minimum. A Magnification 2 Scope reduces a shot at the weapon's long range by two categories to short range. A shot at medium range would also end up at short range because that is the minimum.

TARGET MODIFIERS

Weapon accessories, intervening terrain, atmospheric conditions, and the movement of the attacker and the target can change the Target Number. Of course, as with any skill or attribute use, your character's condition affects the Target Number as well. Effectively, the Target Number will never go below 2, because a 1 on a die roll is always a miss. Find the applicable modifiers on the following table.

WEAPON MODIFIERS TABLE

Situation	Modifier
Recoil	Number of Bursts
Blind Fire	+8
Cover, Partial	+2
Cover, Full	+4
Target Running	+1
Attacker in Melee Combat	+1 Per Opponent
Attacker Running	Cannot Shoot
Attacker Moving	+1
Attacker Moving (difficult ground)	+2
Visibility Impaired	See Visibility Table
Smartgun	–2
Smart Goggles	–1
Image Magnification	Special
Target Standing Still	–1
Recoil Compensator	Up to Rating
Gyro Stabilizer	Up to Rating

Recoil can spoil your aim when you are using automatic weapons. The modifier is usually the number of bursts. See the rules for **Autofire Weapons** later in this chapter.

Blind Fire means the attacker cannot see the target but knows his general vicinity. The target may be behind cover or may be invisible.

Cover means that the attacker cannot see all of the target. **Partial Cover** means more than half the target is in view. **Full Cover** means that less than half is in sight.

Target Running refers to any character who has already run during the turn or declares his intention to do so later in the turn.

Attacker in Melee Combat means an opponent has already assaulted him this turn. For each opponent engaging him in Melee Combat, the attacker adds 1 to his Target Number for Fire Combat. In addition, if the attacker is firing at the character engaging him in Melee, or attempting to grapple, there is a further modifier based on the type of firearm. If he is firing a hand weapon with a silencer, the modifier is +1. It is +2 for an SMG and +4 for a rifle or heavy weapon. If being grappled, the attacker's modifier is +1 for a handgun, +2 with silencer, or +4 with an SMG. Rifle and heavy weapon attacks are prohibited for characters being grappled.

Attacker Moving or Running refers to movement in the same action as the Fire Combat. Remember that a character who is running cannot combine it with any other activity.

Difficult Ground includes rubble, slippery surfaces, mud, water-covered ground, stairways, ladders, and so forth. A gyro-stabilizer can offset movement modifiers.

Visibility Impaired refers to reduced light level, mist, glare, heavy fog, and smoke. Find the attacker's type of vision and the visibility conditions on the Visibility Table below to determine the modifier.

Smartgun is a link between a weapon and its user's brain. It includes a targeting system.

Smart Goggles refers to a weapon-sighting system. Its effect is not cumulative with a smartgun.

Image Magnification refers to systems that have the effect of reducing a weapon's range category. This was discussed under **Target Number** and is included on the Modifiers Table only as a reminder.

Target Standing Still refers to a character who is unaware he is about to be fired on (as in an ambush situation) or who is literally standing stock still (perhaps sighting a target or operating a machine).

Recoil Compensators counter the effects of recoil. Each has a rating that indicates the amount of recoil penalties it can offset. These devices can never apply a negative modifier to the Target Number. They can only negate the plus modifiers of recoil.

Gyro-Stabilizers counter the effects of the attacker's movement. The device's rating is the maximum movement penalty it can offset. Any excess penalty still affects the attacker, and Gyro-Stabilizers can never reduce a modifier below 0.

Condition	Normal Vision	Low-Light Vision	Thermographic Vision
Full Darkness	+4	+2	0
Glare	+2	+4	+4
Mist	+2	+2	0
Reduced Light	+2	0	0
Smoke or Heavy Fog	+4	+4	+2

SUCCESS TEST ROLL

To determine the outcome of your weapon fire, make a Success Test using the number of dice equal to the character's skill in the appropriate weapon. Remember that each die result of 1 is automatic failure and each result of 6 entitles the player to an additional roll, to be added to the result.

Each die result that equals or exceeds the Modified Target Number counts as a success. If you get none, you missed, chummer. If you get some, remember the number of successes and proceed to **Calculating Damage.**

CALCULATING DAMAGE

First, find the weapon's Damage Code in the table on page 135. The Damage Code is a number, a letter, and another number. In this code, the first number is the Power Level, the letter represents the severity of the wound, or Wound Category, and the last numeral is the Staging Number, or Staging.

The Staging Number shows how many **extra** Successes it takes to shift the Wound Category. For each number of Successes equal to the Staging Number, increase the Wound Category by one step. A Light Wound becomes a Moderate Wound, which becomes a Serious Wound, and so on. Extra successes that do not reach the Staging Number are dropped. If the weapon's Staging Number is 2, for instance, and the attacker rolled five **extra** successes, he would shift the Wound Category two steps. Each step past a Deadly Wound eliminates one point of armor from the target.

The Power Level comes into play when determining the target's ability to withstand damage.

Note that sometimes the Wound Category follows an Attribute, such as Strength. In this case, use the character's Attribute Rating as the weapon's Power Level. If you must divide the Attribute Rating to obtain the Power Level (indicated by Attribute÷x), drop all fractions.

SAMPLE WEAPON DAMAGE CODES

Weapon	Damage Code
Light Pistol	3M1
Assault Rifle	4M3
Bow	(Strength)M2
Thrown Knife	(Strength÷2)L1
Katana	(Strength)M3

REDUCING DAMAGE

Now is the time for the target to save his skin, by means of a Resistance Test. The target uses his Body Attribute plus any dermal armor. Archetypes with dermal armor already incorporate its effect into their Body Attribute Rating. In addition, the target may use dice from his Dodge Pool.

The Target Number for the Resistance Test is the Power Level of the weapon. The exterior armor rating gives the target that number of automatic successes. Each type of exterior armor has two ratings, ballistic and impact. The Ballistic Rating applies to damage from firearms and explosives. The Impact Rating applies to projectile weapons, throwing weapons, melee weapons, and guns that fire flechette munitions. If the character wears more than one piece of armor, use the highest applicable rating. The effects of several pieces of armor are not cumulative.

The target's successes reduce the Wound Category step-by-step, again using the Staging Number and dropping fractions of steps. If the dice from the Dodge Pool (and only these dice, so use a different color die or something) push the total of successes on the Resistance Test higher than the attacker's original number, it's a clean miss.

If the target reduces the Wound Category below Light, he takes no damage. He has still been hit, however, and faces the effects of any attack that requires only touch to do damage.

> Sally yelped as something struck her painfully on the back. Her fringed duster whirled open as she spun to face a chagrined MCT corpcop readying for another shot.
>
> Sally is wearing an armor jacket (5/3) under her Lined coat (4/2). Ballistic protection, the first rating, is what's needed against the corpcop's assault rifle shot. Only the best applies, which is the jacket's 5. Because Sally didn't know the cop was there, she doesn't get to use her Dodge pool, so she really needs her armor. The weapon's Damage Code is 4M3. It has not changed because the corpcop got only 2 successes on his Weapon Success Test, and that was not enough to increase the wound category. Sally rolls her Body dice, with results of 3, 4, 4, and 6. Rolling the 6 again is unnecessary because her successes are good enough as is. She has rolled 3 successes and with the 5 for her armor, this gives her a total of 8. Three of those cut the wound category to L, or light. Another three cut it to nothing.

APPLYING DAMAGE

If the Wound Category has not been reduced to nothing, it takes immediate effect on the victim, filling blocks on the Condition Monitor in his Character Record Sheet per the Wound Damage Table below.

WOUND DAMAGE TABLE	
Category	Blocks Filled
Light	1
Moderate	3
Serious	6
Deadly	All

CONDITION MONITORS

The Condition Monitor in the Character Record Sheet charts your character's physical and mental status. Damage reduces a character's effectiveness. Modifiers for each status are cumulative, so that if you get a +1 from a Light wound and you become lightly fatigued (also +1), you will be at +2.

DAMAGE MODIFIERS TABLE		
Physical/Mental Damage	Target Numbers	Initiative Rolls
None	—	—
Light	+1	−1
Moderate	+2	−2
Serious	+3	−3

Each time a character sustains damage, start with the empty block closest to the bottom of the Condition Monitor, filling in the number of blocks corresponding to the wound category. When either column is full, the player is unconscious. If a character takes more Mental Damage after that monitor is full, the excess goes over to his Physical Damage status.

If a player is unconscious with his physical monitor full, he will die without prompt attention. Emergency medical attention from a character with Biotech Skill or following the instructions of a medkit give the character a chance to cheat death. Tending to such a character takes one minute of uninterrupted work. The Target Number for either Medical Success Test is the number of minutes the character has been lying there wounded.

That same number of minutes of bleeding and dying is the character's Target Number for a Body Attribute Test. If he gets at least one success, he is alive. In rough shape, but still alive.

COVER AND BARRIERS

When firing at a target behind cover, the attacker normally aims at exposed portions of his target. If the attacker wants to fire through the cover, his Target Number rises by 8 because of the Blind Fire penalty. The kind of cover may also affect damage. There are three categories of cover: soft, hard, and impenetrable.

Soft cover only affects vision, making a target harder to hit, but offering no physical protection. Bushes, paper walls, and tinted glass are examples of soft cover.

Hard cover conceals the target and offers protection besides. Wood, thin metal, armor glass, and plastic are examples of hard cover. Each has a rating of its protection. This Barrier rating gives an equal number of automatic successes on the Resistance Test, just as with worn armor. Hard Cover Ratings are given on the table below.

Impenetrable cover will not let the attack through. Examples include vehicle armor, concrete support pylons, brick walls, steel beams, and so on.

HARD COVER PROTECTION

	Barrier Rating			
Material	Thin	Normal	Thick	Reinforced
Wood	0	1	2	4
Armor Glass	1	2	4	8
Plywood	1	3	6	12
Construction Plastic	2	4	8	16
Impact Plastic	2	5	10	20
Steel Sheet	3	6	12	24
Ballistic Composite	3	7	14	28
Concrete	4	8	16	32

AUTOFIRE WEAPONS

Some weapons can fire in full automatic mode, continuing to fire as long as the trigger is depressed until the ammunition runs out.

When a character elects to fire a weapon on full automatic, he can fire a number of shots equal to his Firearms Skill Rating (or appropriate concentration or specialization) +1. A gun cannot fire more than seven shots, nor more than the number of shots remaining in its magazine or clip. Treat each shot as a separate attack, making a Firearms Skill Test with the recoil modifier (the number of shots) added to the Target Number. Thus, seven shots would add a +7 modifier to the Target Number.

When using automatic fire, use the weapon's normal Damage Code, with the Power Level increased by 1 point.

A character using autofire may sweep from one target to another, thereby performing an action called "walking the fire." Each meter of distance between the targets requires one burst of sweeping fire. A smartgun can walk autofire past a friendly character without hitting him.

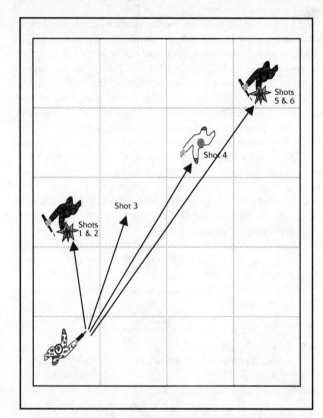

Ghost spun as the two badges barreled through the door, Mitsuhama logos blazing on their jackets and guns blazing in their hands. The goons, a Troll and an Elf, cut wide around Sally as she stood locked in a trance. Wondering if MCT had some kind of affirmative action program for metahumans, Ghost decided to create a couple of openings in the corporate ladder, effective immediately. He swung his Ingram in an arc, sending a hail of automatic fire at the badges.

There were two meters between the goons, with Sally standing there. Ghost raked his fire across the room. Ghost's player decided to fire only six shots, even though Ghost has a Firearm Skill of 7. Ghost put the first two into the Elf, walked the fire with two through the distance to the Troll (missing Sally because of his smartgun link-up), and put the last two into the Troll. Besides whatever modifiers apply to each target, each shot gets +6 to the Target Number because of recoil.

MULTIPLE TARGETS

Whether using an automatic weapon or a semi-automatic weapon, a character can split fire. He simply divides up the number of dice needed for his Firearms Skill Test among the possible targets. The division need not be equal.

Resolve each attack separately. When splitting autofire among multiple targets, the total number of bursts fired is the recoil modifier for all attacks.

> In circumstances that Ghost faced in the last example, he could have split his shots between the Elf and the Troll. He could have used three of his Firearms dice to shoot the Elf and four to shoot at the Troll. With normal shots, there is no recoil penalty.
>
> He also could have split the shots and used autofire. Using six bursts, he could have applied three to each target. He would roll three dice for each burst against the Elf, applying the recoil penalty of +6 to each Target Number. Each of the three bursts against the Troll would use four dice, also applying the +6 to the Target Number.

GRENADES

Grenades are area-effect weapons that work differently from direct-fire weapons. Extra successes do not increase the wound category for these weapons, but increase the accuracy of the throw instead.

When throwing a grenade, designate a target point and make a Success Test based on the appropriate skill, concentration, or specialization. The gamemaster checks the potential amount of error of the throw or shot. His first roll indicates the direction of error, as shown on the following diagram.

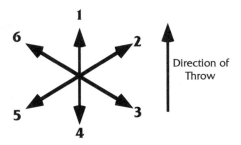

The gamemaster's second roll indicates the maximum number of meters the grenade can fall from its target. For this roll, the gamemaster should use 3D6 for aerodynamic grenades, 2D6 for non-aerodynamic grenades, or 4D6 for grenade launchers.

The attacker reduces the error distance by 3 meters per success for non-aerodynamic grenades or by 5 meters per success for aerodynamic grenades and grenade launchers. The Target Number depends on the attacker's range to the target, per the table below.

GRENADE RANGES TABLE

Types	Target Number				
	4	5	7	9	
	Short	Medium	Long	Extended	Scatter
Aerodynamic Grenade	0–10	11–20	21–60	61–100	3D6
Launcher	5–50	51–100	101–150	151–300	4D6
Non-aerodynamic	0–10	11–15	16–40	41–60	2D6

With its impact point determined, the grenade affects anyone within its area. The damage done by a grenade is determined by its Damage Code, reducing the Power Level for a character's distance from the point of impact, as shown on the following table.

GRENADE DAMAGE TABLE

Type	Code	Power Level Reduction
Offensive	6M3	−1 per 2 meters
Defensive	6M3	−1 per 1 meter
Concussion	4M3 (Stun)	−1 per 1 meter

A character hit by a grenade blast then makes a Resistance Test using his Body Attribute.

MELEE COMBAT

Melee Combat, whether armed or unarmed, works somewhat differently from Fire Combat. When a character announces his intention to make a melee attack, the defender may choose whether to counterattack or to avoid combat. If the defender is trying to avoid combat, the attacker makes an Armed or Unarmed Success Test, as appropriate. The Base Target Number is 4. If the attack succeeds, the defender makes a Resistance Roll, reducing damage exactly as in **Fire Combat**, using the Impact rating of any armor.

If the defender decides to counterattack, he makes an Opposed Success Test. If these are the only two characters involved, they use their Armed or Unarmed Skill Ratings against one another. In the good possibility that a third character becomes involved, the gamemaster should use the following procedure in all cases. The original attacker uses his Armed or Unarmed Skill Rating. The defender uses his Defense Pool, which is based on the character's Armed Combat Rating if a melee weapon is ready or on his Unarmed Combat Rating if not. The distinction is that the dice from the Defense Pool may be used only once. If another character attacks the defender before he replenishes his Defense Pool, the defender can use only those dice he chose not to use the first time. The attacker and defender both use a base Target Number of 4.

Whoever gets more successes may cause damage to the opponent. The loser of the melee can then reduce damage with a Body Attribute Resistance Test, except that he cannot use his Dodge Pool.

The Damage Code for an Unarmed Attack is (Str)M1 stun.

Visibility and movement modifiers are the same for Melee Combat as they were for Fire Combat. The only special modifiers for Melee Combat are for longer reach and superior position. Either of these advantages gives a –1 modifier to the player's Target Number.

Longer reach can refer to weapons (See **Equipment**) or to longer arms (See table in **Critters**). Superior position can mean any tactical advantage. Fighting from horseback against a footman, fighting from elevated ground, or fighting against an opponent who is clinging to a ladder are all examples of superior position. A combination of tactical advantages or an extreme case can merit larger modifiers.

Ghost slipped the punch from the guy on his left and traded shots with the other one. Nothing changed, but as soon as he got an opening, he slashed his razors at the first guy. The goon went down, leaving a grinning Ghost facing only one opponent. The badge ran.

Ghost is in his second action. He waits for one goon to attack, relying on his Dodge Pool to add to his resistance if the guy connects. He counterattacks the other. The street samurai has no weapon in hand, so his Defense Pool springs from his Unarmed Combat Skill.

The first goon hits, but Ghost's Resistance Test reduces the damage to nothing. The second goon attacks, and Ghost delivers a counterattack. Both players roll an Opposed Success Test, but they get the same number of successes. Neither does damage. On Ghost's next action, he attacks the goon on his left. The street samurai uses his skill for the attack, and the goon counterattacks with dice from his own Defense Pool. Ghost gets four extra successes, pushing the wound category of his hand razors from Light to Serious. The Badge flubs his Resistance Test. As he already had four blocks filled on his Condition Monitor, he falls unconscious.

You can split up skill dice to attack several targets at once. Resolve each attack separately, in the order you want them to occur, allowing you to abort later attacks if you get clobbered in the first.

CRITTER COMBAT

Critters do combat in much the same way as characters. Aside from special powers, a critter uses its Reaction Rating as its Unarmed Combat Skill. A critter has an Attack Code that works exactly as a weapon's Damage Code. Intelligent critters (those whose attacks are designated as humanoid) use normal combat rules. They use weapons and have skills.

A critter's Reaction Rating also forms its Dodge Pool. Critters dodge hand weapons, but they rarely dodge missile attacks. A critter gets no Defense Pool. A critter makes a normal Resistance Test to offset damage, using its Body Attribute.

SUBDUING

In **Shadowrun**, there are two kinds of attacks designed to subdue rather than kill. The first is standard combat using stun weapons or attacks. The second is grappling.

Combat with stun weapons proceeds as normal until the damage step. Some weapons carry the denotation of Stun. Others have stun ammunition available or may be used in a particular way to stun, like hitting with the flat side of a sword. Apply damage from stun weapons and attacks on the character's Mental Condition Monitor to represent the bruising and battering he receives. This represents the fact that such attacks have a greater effect on the victim's will to fight than on his long-term physical condition.

Trying to use lethal weapons for stun attacks is tricky. Add +2 to the Target Number when you try it.

If you attempt to subdue somebody who is unaware of your presence, you automatically hit. The victim must make a Willpower Resistance Test with a Target Number equal to the weapon's Power Level and the Damage equal to Deadly. Unless his successes reduce the Wound Category to nothing, the victim falls unconscious.

The second type of subduing is an attempt to restrain another character. This is called grappling, and involves a modified Opposed Success Test. The grappler makes a Success Test using either his Strength Attribute or Unarmed Combat Skill, with a Target Number equal to his opponent's Unarmed Combat Skill or Strength Attribute, whichever is higher. The opponent makes a similar Success Test, but his Target Number is equal to the grappler's Strength Rating plus the number of the grappler's successes.

If the grappler wins, he holds his opponent helpless. If the opponent wins, the would-be grappler may take damage, treating the situation as though the opponent had successfully completed an Unarmed Combat counterattack.

VEHICLES AND COMBAT

Shadowrun is not a vehicle combat game, but characters will sometimes engage in combat involving vehicles. If it involves only one vehicle, use the basic Combat rules. The driver of the vehicle may adjust its movement or use its capabilities during his actions. If the combat involves more than one vehicle, use the special Vehicle Combat Turns.

VEHICLE RATINGS

Vehicles have Attribute Ratings much like those of characters. Remember that Vehicle Ratings are not directly comparable to Character Ratings.

Handling refers to the maneuverability of the vehicle. The higher the rating, the more difficult it is to control the vehicle.

Speed is a split rating giving the standard cruising and the top speeds in meters per combat turn. Some vehicles, like fixed-wing aircraft, have a minimum speed as well. Speed is given in meters per combat turn. For movement in a Vehicle Turn, multiply the Speed Rating by 20.

Body is a measure of the ruggedness of the vehicle. It also counts as personal armor for anyone shot at while within the protection of a vehicle.

Armor rates the vehicle's protection. Vehicle armor will stop anything but heavy weapons.

Signature represents the electronic and heat signatures of the vehicle. This rating is the Target Number for any sensors attempting to get a fix on the vehicle. The larger the number, the harder the vehicle is to spot.

Pilot represents the autopilot's ability to control the vehicle and perceive threats to its progress. Separate ratings may be used for internal systems, especially gunnery and sensors. If the vehicle has no autopilot or if a passenger tries to take control, replace the Pilot Rating with the Skill Rating (or Ratings) of those using the vehicle. The driver's applies to maneuvers, the gunner's for weapons.

CHARACTERS ONBOARD

Characters may perform one of four functions on a vehicle: driver, gunner, technician, or passenger.

The driver controls the vehicle's movement. The driver may perform one minor function for each point of Quickness Attribute he has. Minor functions include altering speed, making a turn, avoiding an obstacle, firing a fixed weapon, and engaging or disengaging an automatic system. A rigger who is jacked into the vehicle is not limited in the number of functions he may perform. He may use all of the vehicle's functions in a single action, with the proviso that he may only apply his own skill to a single weapon system. Any other weapons use the vehicle's Pilot Attribute.

The gunner controls the vehicle's weapons, firing under the normal Combat rules. If a gunner is not attending a weapon in a turret, it cannot be fired.

A technician operates various subsystems, most commonly communications and electronic warfare equipment. If a technician is not attending to a system, it operates with the vehicle's Pilot Attribute.

Passengers are usually along just for the ride. If windows, firing ports, or other openings are available, passengers may fire personal weapons. This does make them vulnerable to return fire. They are also subject to the modifiers for the vehicle's movement.

The vehicle provides some protection for characters inside. An armored vehicle protects characters from light firearms and projectile weapons. If it has no armor, it still provides a barrier and cover against attacks. Heavy weapons that hit a character double the listed Power Level and Staging Number. They also increase the Wound Category by one step.

MOVEMENT

Vehicle combat and pursuit use a special turn sequence. A Vehicle Turn is one minute long, representing the fast-paced dodge and weave as drivers push their vehicles to the utmost. Fast turns, tricky maneuvers, and violent changes of speed are all part of the turn as the drivers seek tactical advantages. First, determine initiative. To obtain initiative results, the drivers use their appropriate skills or the vehicle's Pilot Attribute.

[NOTE: This rule applies to vehicles operating at comparable speeds. If one vehicle has a significant speed advantage over the other, the player controlling that vehicle can decide where to position his vehicle in combat.]

The driver with the highest result acts. He may choose to increase, decrease, or maintain the same distance between vehicles. If the opposing drivers agree with the choice, it happens. The distance between the vehicles changes by the difference in their current speeds. If they disagree, the drivers make an Opposed Success Test based on their Skill Ratings. Each uses the Handling Attribute of his own vehicle as the Target Number. The winning driver chooses what occurs.

Play then shifts to combat turns. The Vehicle Movement Table shows the number of combat turns before the next movement change. The driver who won the Opposed Success Test may use any extra successes to raise or lower the number of combat turns. His vehicle also gets the superior position modifier for any combat. If players agreed on adjusting distance, they should now make an Opposed Success Test to see who can adjust the number of combat turns.

VEHICLE MOVEMENT TABLE		
Terrain	Combat Turns	Safe Speed
Open	8	Maximum
Normal	6	Maximum x 2 ÷ Handling
Restricted	4	Cruising ÷ Handling
Tight	2	Cruising ÷ Handling ÷ 2

Open terrain means flat areas without buildings, trees, or other significant features. For aircraft, this means cloudless skies, and for boats, it means smooth water.

Normal terrain means typical countryside and winding roads, mostly open but with some obstacles. For aircraft, it means partly cloudy skies, and for boats it is light seas.

Restricted terrain can be suburban streets, light woods, hilly areas, and so on. Fog, rain, or darkness change Normal terrain to Restricted. Overcast skies and rain constitute Restricted conditions for aircraft, and high seas are Restricted for boats.

Tight Terrain include urban mazes, badlands, and dense woods. Mist, glare, or low light changes Restricted terrain to Tight. Smoke, heavy fog, or total darkness change Normal terrain to Tight. High winds constitute Tight conditions for aircraft, and gales create Tight conditions for boats.

VEHICLE COMBAT TURNS

Each Vehicle Combat Turn follows the pattern of a standard combat turn except that the driver must attend to the vehicle or risk a crash. Use all normal combat modifiers, except for the movement modifiers from the table below.

COMBAT AND HANDLING MODIFIERS	
Speed	Modifier
1 – 20	+1
21 – 60	+2
61 – 200	+3
201 – 600	+4
601 – 2000	+5

Restricted terrain doubles the modifier; Tight terrain triples it. Boats double the modifier; aircraft halve it, with a minimum modifier of +1. Wheeled vehicles rated as Off-road reduce the Terrain category by one step.

Weapons mounted on any vehicles include automatic Level 1 Gyro-Stabilization. Additional Gyro-Stabilization may be installed.

Ramming

Two vehicles that have closed to zero distance may ram one another during a combat turn. An attempt to ram counts as the driver's action. To conduct a ram, make an Opposed Success Test based on each vehicle's Body Attribute. The Target Number is the Body Attribute plus the Armor Attribute of the other vehicle. The faster vehicle applies −1 to the Target Number. The loser of this Opposed Test must make a crash check.

Crash Checks

A crash check is required at the beginning of any vehicle turn when the vehicle is moving faster than the maximum safe speed for the terrain and conditions. A crash check is also required during a combat turn when the vehicle takes Serious damage, is ignored by the driver during his action, loses a ram contest, or hits an obstacle.

To make a crash check, the driver makes a Resistance Test using his skill against a Target Number equal to the vehicle's Handling plus applying modifiers for conditions, speed, and terrain. Use this Target Number for determining the results of the crash as well.

If the driver fails the test, the vehicle crashes. A crash has a damage category of Deadly and a Staging equal to one-half the crash Target Number. When a vehicle crashes, anyone onboard must make a Resistance Test as if he had been hit by a weapon with a Damage Code = (crash Target Number ÷ 2)D2.

A character may not use his Dodge Pool, but the vehicle's Body Attribute counts as automatic successes in resisting the damage.

VEHICLE DAMAGE

Each vehicle has a Condition Monitor to record damage and display the effects of damage.

If a vehicle is destroyed, all characters in it take damage as if it had crashed.

MAGIC

"Magic is not tuxedos, white rabbits and fake flowers anymore. It is Power."
—*Arthur Garrett, Chairman, Department of Occult Studies, UCLA*

 here are two magical traditions in **Shadowrun**, and you must choose one or the other. This choice is for life. No changes later on!

If you choose the Shamanic Tradition, you will be a shaman. Shamans get their magic from the world of nature and the power of their emotions. They form a link with nature through an animal figure called a totem.

If you choose the Hermetic Tradition, you become a mage. A mage sees the universe as a pattern of abstract energies, which he can control with complex symbols and formulae of power. Hermetic magic is more intellectual in its approach, and mages need elaborate library facilities and equipment to use magic effectively.

The tradition you choose will affect how easily you learn and use some kinds of spells and the kinds of spirits you can summon. It may also impose requirements on how you act. The choice also colors your character's whole outlook on life, his relationships with other characters, and his motives in studying magic.

THE SHAMANIC TRADITION

A shaman's magic comes from stones, herbs, shells, and the animals known to his people. In the past, some "civilized" scholars seemed to disparage shamanism, calling it "primitive" nature worship. When the Awakening came, these "backward" primitives knew how to use their new power to pay back the governments and corporations that had oppressed their people for so long. Indeed, shamanism had developed even among some city-dwellers during the boom in occultism at the close of the 20th century. When the magic came back, these "urban shamans" found that the old ways worked well in cities, too.

To a shaman, the universe is alive. Animals, plants, stones, Mother Earth herself, are all potential allies who can be contacted magically. Before the Awakening, a shaman could only do this by use of hallucinogens, hours of chanting and dancing to the hypnotic beat of drums, or even self-inflicted torture. Now he still uses chant and dance, but a few words or motions are all it takes to make the magic happen.

CHOOSING A TOTEM

When you create a shaman or choose a shaman Archetype, you must also select a totem. A totem will help you with some kinds of magic, but there are rules and possible disadvantages to following a particular totem.

A shaman adds extra dice to his Magic Pool when casting spells that his totem is able to assist. Some totems will *cost* the magician dice from his Magic Pool when he is casting other spells. These dice bonuses or penalties are called Totem Modifiers.

Shamans also get totem modifiers for using Conjuring Skill to summon or banish some kinds of Nature Spirits.

When you create a shaman, you must choose a totem from among the wilderness or urban totems. Wilderness totems are animals that live in the wild: Eagle, Wolf, Bear, and so on. Urban totems are animals that have found niches in urban ecology: Rat, Raccoon, Dog, and others.

There are hundreds of possible totem animals, but space here to describe only a few. If you want to play a shaman who belongs to a different totem, you and the gamemaster can work out its characteristics, advantages, and disadvantages.

You will notice that insects do not appear in the list because insect totems are rare in the shamanic tradition. When they do show up, it's often as a dangerous or evil influence. They are better left alone.

TOTEMS

Wilderness	Urban
Bear	Coyote
Coyote	Dog
Eagle	Raccoon
Raccoon	Rat
Raven	Snake
Snake	
Wolf	

Choose a totem whose characteristics you'll be able to roleplay. A Bear shaman should be deliberate, ponderous, and with a clumsy shamble that looks slow until he has to move fast. A Rat shaman might be unwashed and fond of dark corners, always keeping an eye out for an emergency exit. When he has to, Rat will fight like a cornered...well, you know.

Players should note that a totem is not just "a bear" or even "*the* bear". The totem is Bear, the archetype of all bears in the world. A totem is not just an animal, but the essence, or spirit, of that animal.

Bear

Characteristics: Bear is powerful in body and slow-moving unless he has to move fast. He seems clumsy and unaware of his surroundings, but he is in harmony with the world and what goes on around him. He is slow in speech but powerful in battle. Bear is a powerful healing totem found in shamanic cultures wherever bears are known, be it North America, central and northern Europe, or Asia.

Bear is a healer. Unless a Bear shaman has a good reason, he cannot turn down someone who needs healing.

Environment: Forest

Advantages: +2 dice for all Health Spells; +2 dice for conjuring Forest Spirits

Disadvantages: A Bear shaman can go berserk when wounded. Whenever this shaman is wounded, he must make a Willpower Success Test with a Target Number of 4. He will go berserk for 3 turns, minus 1 turn for every success. If he scores 3 or more successes, he won't go berserk. A berserk shaman will attack the closest living thing, using his most powerful weapons (either magical or physical). If the shaman kills or incapacitates an enemy, or when the time is up, he snaps out of it.

Coyote

Characteristics: Coyote is the Great Trickster, unpredictably bold one moment, cowardly the next. He can be a friend or a dark joker who leads you into danger. Coyote is also the great magician. A Coyote shaman is too independent to be bound by anything except his word. Like Grandfather Coyote in the legends, he is intensely curious. He is often greedy and fond of taking risks just for fun.

Environment: Anywhere on land

Advantages/Disadvantages: None. A Coyote shaman wouldn't let himself be tied down by such concepts. He is beyond rules and lives by his own wits.

Dog

Characteristics: Dog is loyal to friends and family. He fights furiously to defend his home and holdings, but is not generally aggressive outside his own territory. Dog loves people and defends them pitilessly from dangerous spirits or evil magic. Once a Dog shaman gives his loyalty or love, he sticks to it even if the person he loves is unworthy. A Dog shaman will try to protect humanity from evil magicians at any cost.

Environment: Urban

Advantages: +2 dice for Detection Spells; +2 dice for conjuring Field and Hearth Spirits

Disadvantages: Dog is single-minded, to the point of stubbornness. A Dog shaman must make a Willpower Success Test with a Target Number of 4 to change his plans or tactics. The test itself requires one action as Dog struggles to change his mind.

Eagle

Characteristics: Eagle is the highest-flying bird in the sky, and so comes closest to heaven. He faces the rising sun at dawn and is lord of the highest peaks. Eagle is proud, solitary, and sees everything that happens on the Earth over which he flies.

Environment: Mountains

Advantages: +2 dice for Detection Spells; +2 dice for conjuring Wind Spirits

Disadvantages: An Eagle shaman will not tolerate evil or ignoble actions. He is a fierce defender of the land and the purity of nature, with a strong distrust of technology and its tools. Polluters and others who would damage the land for profit are Eagle's enemies, and he will brave any danger to defeat them.

Double all Power Losses caused by adding cyberware, because of the psychological impact this has on the Eagle shaman.

Raccoon

Characteristics: Raccoon is a clever bandit who can break open any trap to remove the bait. He can also escape any danger, for his paws are like cunning hands. Raccoon fights when he must, but prefers strategy and trickery.

Environment: Anywhere but the desert

Advantages: +2 dice for Manipulation Spells; +2 dice for conjuring City Spirits

Disadvantages: A Raccoon shaman is a loner. Like Coyote, his intense curiosity makes him ignore danger in a quest for information. Raccoon can be greedy (this is a thief totem) and Raccoon shamans like to steal the very best, finding petty thefts and violent robberies beneath their dignity. Raccoon shamans suffer a –1 die modifier for Combat Spells.

Rat

Characteristics: Rat is a stealthy thief who is too selfish to share anything, even with his companions. He is a reluctant warrior who would rather run than fight. Where mankind goes, Rat goes, too, for who else's bounty can sustain him?

Environment: Urban

Advantages: +2 dice for Detection and Illusion Spells; +2 dice for conjuring all Spirits of Man

Disadvantages: Rat shamans are usually dirty and unkempt. Rat is also a coward, but when he must fight, he fights to kill. Rat dislikes working out in the open, for a muttered spell from the shadows (or a silenced pistol from a doorway) is more his style. Subtract 1 die for Combat Spells.

Raven

Characteristics: Like Coyote, Raven is a trickster, clever and devious. Raven is also the transformer, responsible for changes. He is a living contradiction, greedy and generous by turns.

Environment: Anywhere under the open sky

Advantages: +2 dice for Manipulation Spells; +2 dice for conjuring Wind Spirits

Disadvantages: Raven shamans are either overweight or else rail-thin. In either case, they are gluttonous and always hungry, finding it next to impossible to refuse an offer of food. Raven dislikes fighting, preferring to see others handle that part of life. Subtract 1 die for Combat Spells. If not under the open sky, Raven shamans suffer a +1 to all Target Numbers.

Snake

Characteristics: Snake is a wise healer who dwells in many places and knows many secrets. Snake is a good councilor, but exacts a price for her advice. Snake is adaptable, and can confuse the senses of enemies.

Environment: Anywhere except Mountains

Advantages: +2 dice for Healing, Illusion, and Detection Spells. As a wilderness totem, +2 dice for conjuring any one Spirit of the Land (shaman's choice). As an urban totem, +2 dice for conjuring any one Spirit of Man (shaman's choice).

Disadvantages: Snake doesn't fight unless she must defend herself or hunt to eat. Snake shamans have a –1 die modifier for *any* spells cast during combat. Snake shamans are obsessed with learning secrets and will take enormous risks to do so.

Wolf

Characteristics: Wolf is the hunter and warrior. He is brother to all his pack, and fiercely loyal to his mate and cubs. As the ancient saying goes, Wolf wins every fight but one, and in that one, he dies.

Environment: Forest, Prairie, or Mountain

Advantages: +2 dice for Detection and Combat Spells; +2 dice for conjuring Forest or Prairie Spirits (shaman's choice).

Disadvantages: A Wolf shaman is loyal to his friends and family until death. Nothing can make him betray those bonds. He will not show cowardice. When a Wolf shaman extends his protection to another or otherwise accepts a responsibility, nothing will make him betray that bond. However, Wolf can go berserk as Bear does.

ROLEPLAYING THE SHAMAN

If you're playing a shaman, he's got to act in character for his totem. Otherwise, the shaman can lose his link to the totem and maybe lose all his magic. If you are not sure you want to stick your character with a lot of requirements, try playing a Coyote shaman, who has more freedom of action.

Shamans are human and a totem is not a religion, though it gets close. There are no commandments the shaman has to follow. The totem is important because it is what makes him a magician. Gamemasters should be lenient about occasional minor goofs.

If a shaman consistently behaves out of character for his totem, the gamemaster should punish him. At first, the punishment will be the loss of any advantages due to his totem. For really persistent behavior, the gamemaster can reduce the shaman's Magic Attribute by a point.

A Shaman can retrieve his lost powers once he starts to behave properly again. A special shadowrun that is particularly appropriate to the totem might be required as a final purification.

THE SHAMANIC MASK

Before the Awakening, most shamans wore masks, usually modeled on their totem animal, when doing magic. With the Awakening, it became apparent that the wearing of masks was a practice based on ancient memories of how shamanic magic worked. When a shaman performs magic, he assumes the physical characteristics of his totem. The more powerful the magic, the more noticeable the animal traits become. A complete shape change does not occur, but the effect can be striking.

For example, an Eagle Shaman performs a minor spell, one not particularly relevant to the Eagle totem. His features might take on a sharper cast, or his chant might resemble the shrill cry of the mighty bird. When casting a more demanding spell, the shaman's crooked fingers become the talons of an eagle or his eyes become the piercing eyes of a hunting bird. Calling on a powerful spell, his features would be obscured by the image a mighty eagle's head.

THE MEDICINE LODGE

A Medicine Lodge is a place that a shaman fills with his magical gear. It creates a little world where he can do serious magic or get in touch with the spirits that give him power.

A Medicine Lodge must be in an environment suitable to your totem. A Bear Lodge should be in the woods, for example, and a Rat Lodge would be anywhere in a city. The Lodge can be indoors, in a cave, or even in an open campsite, as long as you mark off a boundary. You need at least a three-meter by three-meter area; bigger if you plan to have a group of shamans working in it.

Medicine Lodges have a rating. When you need a Lodge, the Lodge's rating is determined by the shaman, depending on his abilities, money, and time. A shaman has to have a Medicine Lodge to learn a new spell. The Lodge must have a rating at least equal to the Force of the spell he is learning.

Most tribes have permanent Lodges: a big hogan, teepee, kiva, cave, or pueblo fixed up as a Lodge. Because many shamans stay on the move, they often lug their Lodge around with them. The actual material would be animal pelts, bones, drums, painted hides, sand for sand painting, minerals and crystals, and so on. All this is reusable, and need not be replaced after purchase unless the Lodge is destroyed. Any talismonger can sell you the magical gear that goes into a Medicine Lodge.

It is best to set up a permanent Lodge. If that is not possible, haul the materials to the right kind of site and set one up. It takes one day per Lodge Rating Point to do this, though, because you have to charge the new Lodge with magical energy to link it to the Earth. That's why permanent Lodges are more convenient.

THE HERMETIC TRADITION

Though some mages may like the country life, most are urban types. Their magic is based on a complicated set of theories that describe the way Astral Space contacts our own world.

Hermetic magic attracted much interest before the Awakening. Even engineers and scientists studied the disciplines of the mage, many of whom discovered the magic to be working when the Awakening occurred. As many of these people were corporate employees, the corps picked up on hermetic magic very early on. To this day, you'll find numerous wagemages working for the big companies, but very few shamans punching a corp clock.

Mages see the magical universe as a complex of abstract forces. By opening yourself up to these forces, you can cast spells, summon spirits, and so on. Before the Awakening, the process required lengthy, complex ceremonies, but now you can make magic with a few gestures and key syllables of invocation. The elaborate rituals and equipment are only needed for special situations.

The desire of the mage is to know firsthand the inner reality of the universe. He may practice magic for its own sake, or for the nuyen it earns, or for power, but a mage is a scholar whose art keeps him studying much of the time.

HERMETIC LIBRARIES

Mages spend a lot of time doing research. They need extensive reference libraries for many activities: learning new spells, designing magical rites, summoning spirits, and so on.

Each hermetic library is specific to a given skill. That is, a mage will need separate libraries in Sorcery, Conjuration, and Magical Theory. Libraries don't have concentrations or specializations.

In 2050, print is almost dead, but many mages are old-fashioned enough to enjoy the feel of a physical book. Libraries can consist of printed books and papers (hardcopy). Though bulky, they are usable anywhere, and not subject to power failures. Alternatively, a library can be stored on CDs or optical chips, like any other information, but you'll need a data reader or computer to access them. Datasoft libraries are available, but they are expensive and cannot be shared with other mages. A library can mix all three types of storage.

Mages can share libraries. Access to the Thaumaturgical section of any big university library or corporate reference department lets any number of mages pursue projects at the same time. These large research facilities will have whatever rating you need. Of course, if you don't have legitimate access, you may find that the owners take exception to your using their data.

A mage needs a Sorcery Library to learn a new spell. The mage determines the rating of his library, which must be at least equal to the Force of the spell he is learning.

Library Ratings aren't cumulative. If you combine a 2-point library with a 3-point library, you end up with 3 points, not 5. When two mages share or copy materials, the lower-rated library is raised to match the higher-rated one. This also applies to stealing materials from a library.

THE HERMETIC CIRCLE

Sometimes, mages need to set up an Hermetic Circle. It can be in any convenient, private place, indoors or out, but should be secluded, so that operations won't attract gawkers.

Hermetic Circles are prepared for a specific spell, conjuring, or enchantment. For example, if you want to use Ritual Sorcery to cast a Stink Curse on someone, you must prepare a Circle for that spell. You cannot use the same Circle to cast a Mask Spell the next day, but must draw a new one. The same goes for spirits. A Circle used to conjure a Fire Elemental is useless for summoning Water Elementals.

Once a Circle is prepared, you *can* re-use it for the same operation. You could draw a Circle for summoning a Fire Elemental, leave it in place, and use it later to summon another Fire Elemental.

Hermetic Circles have ratings, and you can make one with any rating you want if you have time and enough room. Drawing the Circle takes a number of hours equal to its rating. A Circle is 3 meters in diameter, plus a number of meters equal to its rating. This rating must be at least equal to the required score for a specific operation. For example, conjuring an Elemental with a Force of 6 takes a Circle with a rating of at least 6.

MAGICAL ABILITIES

A magician can do things that mundanes cannot. First, of course, he can use the magical Skills of Sorcery and Conjuring to make magic happen. Second, he is strongly tuned in to the parallel universe of Astral Space, and so he can use Astral Perception and Astral Projection.

MAGIC RATING

Magicians have a special Attribute, that of Magic. Like Essence, Magic has a starting rating of 6. Whenever the Essence Rating is reduced, the Magic Rating is rounded down to the nearest whole number. A magician who replaces his eyes with 20/20 Cyber Eyes has an Essence Rating of 5.8, but a Magic Rating of 5. Major wounds, illness, and other factors can also reduce the Magic Rating. A magician whose Magic Rating is too low faces death every time he uses spells. It stinks. You can see it in the burned-out magician who goes the refit route, using danger and Cyberware like drugs to satisfy his craving for spells. You see it with the old gray mage who has to fumble with amulets, powders, and potions to cast a spell he once invoked with a flick of his fingers. It's a pathetic picture, any way you look at it.

If a magician's Magic Attribute ever drops below 1, he cannot use spells at all. He has lost the necessary connection with Astral Space and is now a mundane.

DRAIN

A magician chooses the Force of the spell he will cast, and he gets a number of dice equal to the Force Rating to make a Success Test. Spells bring energy into the world from Astral Space through the magician's nervous system. This causes damage. After casting any spell, the magician must make a Willpower Resistance Test to avoid fatigue. The Target Number is normally equal to the Force of the spell. The Magic Pool can be used to resist Drain. A spell's Drain Code shows the amount of Mental Damage (Fatigue) it causes the magician in the same way a weapon's Damage Code shows its effect. The letter in the Drain Code indicates the starting Fatigue Category, followed by the Staging Number, which shows the number of successes the magician needs to reduce the category.

If the magician's Resistance Test fails to offset the Drain, it shows up as Fatigue (same as Stun Damage) on the Mental Damage track of the Condition Monitor. When the magician casts a spell with a Force Rating higher than his Magic Attribute, Drain goes on the Physical Damage track, wounding the magician with burns, bursting blood vessels, and muscle spasms, all caused by the energy overloading his system.

> Sally the mage casts a spell with a Force of 5. The Drain Code for this spell is M2. Regardless of the outcome of the spell, Sally must make a Willpower Resistance Test with a Target Number of 5. Every two successes reduce the Fatigue Category one level. Against a Drain Code of M2, Sally must roll 4 successes to avoid Drain completely.

MAGICAL ITEMS

Many kinds of items are useful to a magician. Some have no inherent magical nature. Others are enchanted. Enchanted objects are called focuses, which are useless to mundanes because they need magical power as a trigger. A magician must have a Magic Attribute Rating of at least 1 to use a focus. There are five classes of enchanted items:

Spell focuses to help in Sorcery.
Spirit focuses to help in Conjuring.
Power focuses to store Magic Ratings.
Spell Locks to sustain spells.
Magical weapons are power focuses in the form of weapons.

Magical items have variable ratings with virtually no limit. They are commonly available from a Talismonger at all ratings, limited only by cost. A magician may not be able to use an item with a high rating, however. Before he can use any magical item, a magician must bond that item to his magical energy by expending Karma. This is discussed in greater detail in the **After the Shadowrun** chapter. Only one magician may bond a single item at a time, and only that magician can use it.

A magician must activate an item to use it, using one action to activate and another to use. He may keep active a number of items equal to his Intelligence Attribute. Once activated, an item works as long as it is on his person, be it worn, carried, hand-held, on his head, or in a pocket or pouch. If an item is snatched away or dropped, it is immediately deactivated.

Spell Focuses

Spell focuses give a magician extra dice for use with a specific spell or class of spells. Spell focuses do not help a magician to learn spells.

The Spell Purpose Focus applies to all spells within its a purpose category: combat, detection, health, illusion, or manipulation. The rating of a Purpose Focus is the number of dice available in any one action. Any or all of these dice can be added to rolls for or against spells in the purpose category. This includes resisting such spells cast by another magician. By permanently sacrificing the focus's rating points, the magician can receive an automatic success instead of a die. One Rating Point buys one success. Once the rating is reduced to 0, the item is no longer enchanted.

A Specific Spell Focus provides extra dice for one spell, and only for casting the spell, not resisting its use by another magician. Specific focuses have ratings like purpose focuses, and rating points may be permanently sacrificed to buy extra successes in the same way.

Spirit Focuses

Spirit focuses provide extra dice for Conjuring a specific type of spirit (desert spirit, water elemental, and so on). Spirit focus dice may be used with any roll connected to summoning, banishing, or controlling a spirit.

Power Focuses

Power focuses increase a magician's Magic Attribute, allowing him to cast more potent spells safely. They also provide extra dice that go straight into his Magic Pool. These dice can augment any magical test. Rating points may be sacrificed to buy extra successes for any magical test in the usual manner.

Spell Locks

Spell Locks are power focuses with a Rating of 1 made for a single purpose: to lock a spell onto a target permanently. A magician must attach the focus physically to the target after the spell has succeeded. It can be stuck into a pocket, worn, hung, nailed on, or whatever. The magician who cast the spell need not be the one who attaches the lock, but only a magician can do it. Once in place, the lock maintains the spell automatically, drawing power from Astral Space.

There are drawbacks to using spell locks. If a magician removes the lock from the target, the spell is broken. A mundane cannot remove a spell lock; he cannot even touch it. It is in another dimension as far as he is concerned. As long as the focus is working, a thread of astral energy connects it to the spell's caster. This can be traced through Astral Space, becoming a material link that makes the caster vulnerable to Ritual Sorcery. Magicians do not leave these things lying around!

Magic Weapons

Any weapon can be enchanted, giving it a rating as a power focus and other magical properties. A mundane can touch and use the weapon, but gets none of the special benefits.

A magic weapon can perform all the functions of a standard power focus. It also can damage spirits or other magical creatures that are immune to normal weapons. A magician can take a magic weapon into Astral Space and use it against any beings there. If the weapon incorporates the magical metal orichalcum, the weapon's rating adds to the magician's skill in Armed Combat. Orichalcum is a magical alloy of copper, gold, silver, and mercury, a metallurgical nightmare that cannot even exist without magic. It is a rich yellow-orange color, and legend has it that it was discovered in Atlantis.

SORCERY

Sorcery draws heavily on a magician's Magic Attribute, and it can take two forms. The Skill can be used to cast quick spells with limited range (Spellcasting concentration). It can also use elaborate, lengthy rituals to cast long-term spells over greater distances (Ritual Sorcery concentration).

A magician must learn a spell before he can cast it. Once he has learned it, he can cast a spell anytime, each time making a Resistance Test against Drain.

SPELL TYPES

Spells differ in Drain Code, area classification (physical or mental), purpose category, duration, and special effects. Combat Spells also have a Staging Number like firearms.

All spells affect living things. Only a physical spell can affect inanimate objects. Only mental, or mana, spells can affect a purely magical or mental target, such as a spirit, emotions, other spells, and so forth.

There are five purpose categories for spells:

Combat Spells generate violent, destructive energy.

Detection Spells enhance the senses or analyze the environment.

Health Spells heal damage, illness, madness, and other afflictions.

Illusion Spells fool the senses.

Manipulation Spells can transform, transmute, control or animate matter or energy.

Spells have three possible durations:

Instant spells take effect and vanish in the same action. Their effects are usually lasting. Combat spells fall into this category.

Sustained spells can be maintained over time. As long as the magician sustains the spell, it remains in effect. When he drops it, the spell's effects disappear.

Permanent spells must be sustained for some specified period of time before their effects become permanent. Health spells are one example. If the magician drops such a spell before it becomes permanent, its effects disappear.

SPELL FORCE

Magicians choose the maximum rating of a spell when they first learn it. A magician can cast a spell with lower Force if he wants, but to increase the maximum Force of the spell, the magician must learn it all over again. [See the **Learning Spells** section in the **After the Shadowrun** chapter for details.] The Force is the number of dice that the magician gets for his Success Test when he casts a spell. The Force also becomes the Target Number for his Resistance Test against Drain. If the chosen Force exceeds the magician's Magic Attribute, any damage from Drain shifts from Mental (Fatigue) to Physical Damage (Wounds). Force modifiers, derived from magical equipment or from the process of learning the skill, can affect this procedure.

SPELLCASTING

Spellcasting is the branch of Sorcery concerned with the here and now, quick spells of limited range and relatively small effect. The Spellcasting concentration applies to all tests in this section.

Spellcasting should use the following steps:

    Refresh Magic Pool

    Spell Declaration

    Success Test

    Resistance Test

    Determine Results

Refresh Magic Pool

Use the character's Sorcery Skill Rating as the Magic Pool for the action. If the character used any dice before this action to defend against a spell, those dice are not available.

Spell Declaration

At this point, name the spell or spells the character is casting, whether the character is maintaining or dropping other spells, the target or targets, the Force, the timing (immediate, delayed, or conditional), and the radius for area-effect spells.

If the magician is casting a single spell and has been maintaining no other spells from previous actions, the first part of this stage is easy. Some spells carry an Exclusive designation. This means they cannot be combined with another spell, either being sustained from an earlier action or thrown as part of this action. If the magician is sustaining a spell, it adds +2 to all his Target Numbers, magical or not, because of distraction. If the magician wants to cast a spell at more than one target, he simply divides up the Force dice any way he wants. It is important that he declare the order, however, and make a Resistance Test to avoid Fatigue after casting each spell. The magician can cancel spells he had intended to cast at any time in the sequence.

In choosing a target or targets, the magician can cast a spell at anyone he can see. Binoculars, glasses, and other devices can enhance his vision, as can magic or technology that penetrates darkness. A magician cannot, however, cast spells at invisible beings or characters in Astral Space by using enhanced vision or Astral Perception. Remote vision, such as through a telecomm screen, is also useless for casting spells.

Next, the magician chooses the Force of the spell. He will often choose the maximum Force of the spell he has learned, but there are several reasons why he might choose a lower Force. He might want to reduce the possibility of Fatigue. Oftentimes, he will want to save dice from his Magic Pool for spell defense. These dice can be used for Resistance Rolls for the magician or his buddies when an enemy starts flinging fireballs.

Most spells take effect immediately. Some spells can have delayed effect, and a character can also make a spell conditional ("I will throw a Power Bolt if the enemy tries to come through that door."). If the condition does not occur, the character does not cast the spell. It aborts harmlessly (no Drain, no pain).

If casting an area spell, you may want to change the spell's radius of effect. The basic radius is a number of meters equal to the magician's Magic Attribute. The magician can attempt to increase or decrease this distance, removing dice from his basic Success Test to control the area of effect. He can increase the radius by one meter for each die he withholds; he can narrow the radius by one meter for each two dice he withholds. Controlling this kind of power is much more difficult than letting it loose.

Success Test

Casting the spell is a Resisted Success Test based on the Force Rating. The Target Number is usually equal to the rating of the attribute that will be used for the Resistance Test. Any extra dice the target may receive for its Resistance Test do not increase this Target Number.

Any wounds, distractions, and visibility conditions affecting the magician and any cover protecting the target do apply modifiers. Use the list given in Fire Combat, except that the modifier for target movement does not apply. Cover protects targets from either physical spells or mana spells. A magical barrier (Hermetic Circle or Medicine Lodge) adds a modifier to the Target Number equal to the barrier's rating.

The Target Number for Healing Spells is 10 minus the target's Essence Attribute Rating. For other spells that are not followed by a Resistance Test, use a Target Number of 3.

The magician may get extra dice from magical devices and totem modifiers. He may also add dice from his Magic Pool. A magician must declare the total number of dice he is rolling before making the test. When casting an area-effect spell, the magician rolls his dice for his Success Test only once, but Target Numbers may vary for each character within the effect radius. Count the successes separately for each target within the radius.

Neddy tosses a fireball with a Force of 7. There are three targets in range of the spell. Neddy uses 7 dice for his success test and rolls 1, 3, 4, 5, 5, 6, 6. He rerolls the two sixes, scoring 1 and 6. He rerolls the 6 again, scoring 4. His final scores are 1, 3, 4, 5, 5, 7, 16. Neddy has no Target Numbers as yet.

The first target is in the open. He has a Body Attribute of 4, and so Neddy's Target Number is 4. Neddy scores 5 successes against him.

Target 2 is behind a low wall, which the gamemaster rules as partial cover, worth +2 to the Target Number. Target 2 also has a Body Attribute of 4, and so Neddy's Target Number against him is 6, giving Neddy 2 successes.

Target 3 just dove through a doorway near the edge of the blast radius. The gamemaster rules that he has almost full cover, adding +4 to Neddy's Target Number. Target 3 also has Body Attribute 4, so Neddy's Target Number is 8, for only one success.

Resistance Test

Some spells, such as healing, help the target. For these, there is no Resistance Test. Other spells require a Resistance Test, even if the target is an inanimate object. This represents the environment's natural resistance to magic. The Target Number is the casting magician's Sorcery Skill Rating, with no modifiers.

Physical Spells attack the body, and Mana Spells attack the mind. Living beings use their Body Attribute Rating to resist Physical Spells or their Willpower Attribute Rating against Mana Spells. Armor does not count as an automatic success against physical spells in this Resistance Test, and dermal armor increases the Body Rating. A shaman adds totem dice when resisting a spell, if appropriate. A magician may also get extra dice because of a magical device.

Inanimate objects have a resistance based on how close to nature they are. This rating is the magician's Target Number in his Success Test.

OBJECT RESISTANCE RATINGS	
Category	**Rating**
Natural Objects	3
(Trees, Soil, Unprocessed Water)	
Manufactured Low-Tech Objects and Materials	5
(Brick, Leather, Simple Plastics)	
Manufactured High-Tech Objects and Materials	7
(Advanced Plastics, Alloys, Electronic Equipment)	
Highly Processed Objects	9 or more
(Computers, Complex Toxic Wastes)	

Spell Defense

Magicians can help themselves or other characters by adding dice to Resistance Tests. If the magician designated some of his Magic Pool for spell defense, those dice can add to a Resistance Test for anyone the magician can see. He can do this repeatedly, with all dice so allocated, up to a number of times equal to his Sorcery Skill. The addition of spell defense dice must be declared when the spell is cast, before the opposing magician makes his Success Test.

There was a mage in the doorway, and he was open for business! Neddy yelled something just as a jet of hissing green stuff came flying at us. It burned paint off the walls and ate a desk that was in the way, then washed over us like a wave of death. I figured I was gone right then, but somehow the stuff just slid right off me and Iris. Grinder was swearing a lot, even for a Troll, but at least he was still standing. We geeked the mage and kept on traveling. Neddy claimed he saved our butts, but Neddy would claim he keeps the sun shining if he thought anyone would believe him.

Neddy allocated four dice to spell defense on his last action. These dice added to the Body Ratings of the other characters when they made their Resistance Tests to the toxic wave spell. The added dice did, indeed, save their ungrateful, mundane behinds. Note that each person added four dice; the defense dice were not divided up among the three of them.

Determine Result

If the Force Success Test yielded more successes than the target's Resistance Test, the spell takes effect. The net Successes are like all successes in **Shadowrun**, the more you get, the better the result. This works a little differently for each spell purpose category.

If the target's successes equal or exceed the caster's successes, a combat spell still goes off but does no damage. If the caster gets extra successes, you determine damage for combat spells in much the same way as for regular combat. All Combat Spells have an initial combat code of "L" plus a Staging Number. The lower the Staging, the more lethal the spell. Each block of extra successes equaling the Staging Number increases the Wound or Fatigue Category. Then, as in normal combat, the victim makes a Resistance Test to lower the damage, again using the spell's Staging Number. Armor counts as automatic successes against physical spells but not against mana spells.

Most Detection Spells involve an Unresisted Success Test and require only a single success. Extra successes increase the amount and detail of information the player receives.

Extra successes reduce the time that it takes to cast a Health Spell, with the number of extra successes becoming the divisor for the base healing time of the spell.

Extra successes make illusion spells stronger, increasing the extent of distraction or making the illusion more difficult to penetrate (as for invisibility). See each spell for special effects.

Manipulation Spells can transform or control matter and energy. Most Manipulation Spells have a threshold of successes needed to work. If the caster gets insufficient successes to meet this Threshold Number, the spell fails.

Regardless of the spell's effect on its target, the caster must make a Resistance Test against Drain after using a spell. Remember, he uses his Willpower Attribute with the Force of the spell providing the Target Number. The spell's Drain Code provides the maximum damage and Staging Number.

With the effect of the spell and the magician's fatigue determined, the spell duration becomes a factor. Instant spells are easy; they happen and that is it. Their effects may last, but the spell itself is instantaneous.

Sustained spells alter reality only as long as the magician concentrates on channeling magical energy to them. When the energy stops, the spell ends. A magician can sustain a number of spells equal to his Sorcery Skill. Each sustained spell adds +2 to all of the magician's Target Numbers, magical or nonmagical, because of distraction.

Permanent spells work as sustained spells until the magician sustains them for the minimum maintenance time, after which the spell becomes permanent. Once the spell becomes permanent, the magician no longer needs to concentrate on it. If his concentration lapses before then, the spell disappears.

Neddy yelled something magical and waved his hands like he was swattin' bugs. The charging Ork froze solid and turned all white, his hand still clenching the grenade.

"Hey, Neddy, I thought you said magic couldn't turn people to stone?"

"It's not stone, chip-brain! I calcified his tissues and...WILL YOU GET RID OF THE FRAGGIN' GRENADE?"

"Sheesh, wizards!" I slammed the statue's wrist with the butt of my rifle and cracked loose the hand holding the grenade, then tossed it out a window. As I turned back into the room, the slottin' thing blew up and the Ork started howling and spouting blood from the stump of his wrist. I wish Neddy wouldn't drop those spells so quick.

RITUAL SORCERY

Ritual Sorcery builds up spells gradually, taking hours. This lets magicians cooperate, pooling their skills. It also allows magicians to cast spells on targets that are not within visual range. Use the Ritual Sorcery Concentration Rating for all tests in this section.

A shaman must be in a Medicine Lodge with a rating at least equal to the Force of the spell. A mage must be in a Hermetic Circle for the spell he is casting, with a rating at least equal to the spell's Force.

Ritual Sorcery requires special materials. These materials are generalized, and the magician must only pay the cost and keep track of which materials he has on hand. Materials to perform Detection Ritual Sorcery cost 100¥ times the Force of the spell. Health materials cost 500¥ times the Force, Illusion materials cost 100¥ times the force, and Manipulation materials cost 1,000¥ times the Force of the spell. Magicians cannot cast Combat Spells using Ritual Sorcery. Casting the spell expends the materials regardless of the outcome of the spell.

MATERIAL LINK

If the magician cannot see the target, he needs a material link to perform Ritual Sorcery. If the target is a living being, the material link is a tissue sample that contains his DNA pattern. If the target is not a living being, the magician needs an integral piece of its structure. He could target a building using a brick pried from one of its walls, but not a picture that used to hang inside.

RITUAL TEAMS

Ritual Sorcery lets magicians cooperate in casting a spell, but all members of a ritual team must know the spell. The magicians must belong to the same tradition, but shamans of different totems may cooperate in a ritual team. The maximum size of a ritual team is the lowest rating in Sorcery Skill among the members. A chain is only as strong as its weakest link. If a magician has a Sorcery Skill Rating of 4, only three other magicians can be on his team.

Once the ritual begins, the magicians are all linked together magically. The entire ritual counts as one spellcasting action. This affects how magical items are used. A focus with a Rating of 4, for example, adds four dice over the course of the ritual, not at each stage of the ritual. The player should designate one magician as the leader. All tests use his modifiers for totems and equipment, not those for the totem of the Medicine Lodge.

At the beginning of the ritual, all the magicians combine their Magic Pools into one. Because the entire ritual is a single action, this pool is not refreshed and team members cannot use their individual Magic Pools without withdrawing from the team. When a member does this, reduce the remaining dice in the pool by his Sorcery Skill Rating. If this ever exhausts the pool, the spell aborts and all team members must make a Resistance Test against Drain, whether they have pulled out or not.

A team member can "spot" the target from Astral Space, making a material link unnecessary. This team member does not contribute to the Magic Pool for the rite, but he is subject to Drain along with everybody else. If this forward observer is killed or driven away from the target, the spell aborts and all team members make Resistance Tests against Drain. The observer must stay in Astral Space until the Sending of the spell is complete.

Modifiers affecting one member of the team (wounds, for example) affect only that individual. They do not change the overall effectiveness of the team unless it is the leader who is affected.

SORCERY PROCEDURE

The stages in casting a spell by Ritual Sorcery are:
Preparation
Form Magical Link
Sending
Determine Effect
Resist Drain

The last step must occur even if the Ritual Sorcery aborts at any stage along the way.

Preparation

After preparing the place of working (the Medicine Lodge or Hermetic Circle), the team members combine their Magic Pools. The leader declares the Force of the spell to be cast. Team members cannot maintain other spells when working in Ritual Sorcery, and so they must drop any such spells as part of the preparation step.

Form Magical Link

If the target is in sight or being observed in Astral Space, skip this stage. Otherwise, the team must lock onto the target using the material link. This takes a number of hours equal to the Force of the spell. At the end of that time, the leader allocates dice from the combined Magic Pool for an Unresisted Success Test. The Target Number depends on how closely the team can pinpoint the target's location, per the table below.

MAGIC LINK TABLE	
Target Location	Target Number
City or County Known	5
State, Province, or Country Known	7
Continent Known	9
Unknown	11

A single Success is sufficient. If the team achieves no Successes, the spell aborts and team members make Resistance Tests against Drain.

Sending

This stage builds up the power of the spell and directs it at the target. The leader allocates dice from the common Magic Pool for an Unresisted Success Test. Get the Target Number from the following table.

SENDING TARGET NUMBERS	
Target Type	Target Number
Specific Place	6
Human or Metahuman	6
Specific Object	8

There are two possible modifiers to this Target Number. If the target is moving, apply +2. This modifier refers to movement faster than running, as by a plane, car, or train. If the team is casting an area spell, apply a −1 modifier to the Target Number.

The time required for the Sending is a number of hours equal to the spell's Force, divided by the number of successes rolled. The minimum time is one hour. If the player rolls no successes, the spell aborts and all members of the team make Resistance Tests against Drain.

During this time, any magician who sees the target will know what is happening. If the target is a magician, he will recognize at once that he is the subject of a Sending. The use of certain Detection Spells or Astral Projection will let a magician trace the Sending back to the ritual team. Defensive magic can increase the target's resistance to the spell. For example, several magicians could maintain spell defense to assist the target in resisting.

The ritual team can be located and attacked in Astral Space (see **Astral Combat**). During the Sending, the ritual team is considered to be present in Astral Space and therefore vulnerable to Astral Combat.

If time and distance allow, defenders can mount a physical assault on the ritual team. If the team has no physical defenders, this works very well. Either the magicians do not pull their dice out of the pool, which makes them sitting ducks, or they do, which aborts the ritual.

Determine Effect

If this is an area spell, the base radius in meters is equal to the leader's Magic Attribute, and he can alter it by subtracting dice from the pool.

Make a normal Resisted Force Success Test. The leader's Sorcery Skill Rating is the Target Number for the victim's Resistance Test. Modifiers for cover, visibility, terrain, and so on do not apply to the Target Number, but the leader's own wounds and distractions would still apply. If the leader is a shaman, his totem modifiers apply.

If the spell-caster's successes exceed the successes of the target's Resistance Test, the leader may allocate any remaining dice from the Magic Pool to maintain the spell. A ritual spell may be maintained for a number of days equal to these dice. Mages can use an Elemental to maintain the spell (see the **Elemental** rules later in this chapter). It is possible to combine dice from the Magic Pool with the Force Rating of the Elemental for this purpose.

The magicians on the ritual team may also maintain the spell themselves. They can simply stay locked into a team, concentrating on the spell. This still leaves an astral path leading back to the team, though, and also counts as maintaining a spell, adding +2 to the Drain Resistance Roll for all team members.

Resist Drain

The ritual team now resists Drain. Each member of the team acts as if he had cast the spell himself, making a Willpower Resistance Test. Each magician also receives extra dice equal to any dice left in the Magic Pool. If team members have extra dice for the spell because of magical devices or spirit aid they have not previously used in casting this spell, then they may add those dice as well.

CONJURING

Conjuring can summon, control, and banish different kinds of spirits. Magicians and occultists are still arguing about whether spirits have any separate existence or spring from the formless energies of Astral Space when they are conjured. Most folks figure it does not much matter.

There are many kinds of spirits. Each can appear with any Force Rating, chosen by the magician who is conjuring. Two that can be summoned with relative ease are nature spirits and Elementals. Nature spirits personify the forces of the environment. Only a shaman can summon or control a nature spirit. Elementals arise from the four hermetic elements: Fire, Water, Air, or Earth. Only a mage can summon or control an Elemental. The abilities of nature spirits and Elementals appear in the **Critters** chapter.

There are other kinds of spirits in the Sixth World. Most of them can be contacted only by very experienced magicians with Karma to spend, and will be described in future **Shadowrun** products.

SUMMONING NATURE SPIRITS

A shaman can summon a spirit only in its home environment. The shaman first declares the Force of the spirit he wants to call. This is his Target Number for an Unresisted Conjuring Success Test.

After adding dice for totem modifiers, the shaman makes his test. Each success represents one service the spirit will do for him. If the shaman rolls no successes, no spirit comes. The sha-

man makes a Resistance Test against Drain whether a spirit comes or not. If fatigue knocks the shaman out, the spirit is uncontrolled. The spirit's attributes equal the force of the spell.

Nature spirits vanish at sunrise and sunset, no matter what. All services end at that time. Any services left unused or unspecified by that deadline are lost.

> Man-Who-Sees-Many-Things heard the buzzing engines of sandbikes. The corp guards had caught up with him. The uncaring sun beat down, robbing his body of precious moisture.
>
> Raising his hands, he rasped out the song of power through cracked lips. The tones of the song rose to the beaten copper sky in the hissing tones of Snake, and the shaman's skin grew scaly with the bright, diamond-shaped markings of his totem.
>
> Many-Things is summoning a desert spirit with a Force Rating of 6. His Conjuring Skill is 7. He gets two extra dice because he is a Snake shaman with an advantage for conjuring Desert Spirits. He rolls 9 dice, scoring 3 successes.
>
> A burning wind sprang up. It grew from a sibilant whisper to a roaring gale, as a whirling funnel of sand rose before the chanting shaman. Its core shimmered and glowed with the heat of the desert sun.
>
> Many-Things pointed toward his pursuers, their speeding machines visible in the distance, and his voice rose to a wail. The wind roared higher, and the approaching foes vanished in a cloud of dust as the sandstorm struck.
>
> The magician's song sank to a crooning note, and cool shade wrapped him from the burning sun. Many-Things turned and began to glide over the desert. He moved with the speed of a running man, though his steps were no faster than they had been before.
>
> The shaman rolled three successes, earning him three services of the spirit. In this case, he had the Desert Spirit use its Attack power on his enemies, and then he invoked its powers of Guard and Transport.

SUMMONING ELEMENTALS

Only a mage can summon an Elemental. He may summon an Elemental of any desired Force Rating, given the necessary equipment and time, but he needs a Conjuring Library and an Hermetic Circle with ratings at least equal to the Force of the spirit. The rite requires special materials, available from the local talismonger and generalized by simply paying their cost, 1,000¥ per Force Rating of the Elemental.

Each Elemental also needs a source. Fire Elementals arise from a great bonfire (indoor mages, beware of sprinkler systems), a fireplace, or large brazier. Water Elementals come from a large pool or tub of water. This requirement is satisfied if the Hermetic Circle is near any open body of water. Air Elementals need great quantities of burning incense (watch out for smoke detectors, too). An Earth Elemental needs a large heap (man-size) of earth, clay, or rock. This requirement is satisfied if the place of working is on open ground.

The ritual takes hours equal to the spirit's Force Rating. At the end of this time, the mage makes an Unresisted Conjuring Success Test. His Target Number is equal to the Force Rating of the Elemental. He can get extra dice if he has a spirit focus.

The number of successes is the number of services the Elemental will do for the mage. If the player rolls no Successes, no spirit comes, but all the materials gathered for the rite are used up. The magician must make a Resistance Test against Drain whether the Elemental comes or not. If a spirit comes but fatigue knocks the mage out, the Elemental is uncontrolled.

An Elemental that owes services to a mage is bound. The magician need not use services all at one time. To use the services of a bound Elemental, the mage must spend an action calling upon the spirit. It will appear before him immediately, in Astral Space, visible as a slight shimmering in the air. The more powerful the spirit, the more noticeable this is.

Until a bound Elemental is summoned, its powers are not available to the mage. A mage can simultaneously bind a number of Elementals equal to his Charisma. If he is at his limit and wishes to conjure an additional Elemental, he simply releases one of the spirits he controls from its bond.

An Elemental stays in Astral Space by preference. The Elemental manifests physically only if it must do a specific job for its boss.

With the exception of a remote service, the Elemental must remain within sight of the mage. The use of astral senses, clairvoyance spells, or other magical senses fulfill this requirement, but electronic viewing does not. You cannot "remote control" an Elemental using a trideo camera. If the magician controlling an Elemental is knocked out or killed, the spirit immediately becomes uncontrolled.

The magician who summons an Elemental can order the spirit to obey another character, magician, or mundane. Mundanes cannot use Elementals to cast spells, but otherwise they receive the same services as a mage: aid sorcery (the spell defense potion), physical services, and so forth. Elemental bodyguards are rare, but they do protect politicians, corporate execs, oyabun, and other big noises.

There are five types of services that an Elemental can perform: aid sorcery, aid study, sustain spells, physical service, and remote service.

Aid Sorcery

An Elemental can give the magician extra dice for casting spells. The Elemental acts like an auxiliary Magic Pool of dice the magician can use at any time until the spirit is used up and disappears. These dice can augment rolls at any stage in Sorcery, including spell defense.

Each type of Elemental can only help with one spell purpose category.

> Fire Elementals aid Combat Spells.
> Water Elementals aid Illusion Spells.
> Air Elementals aid Detection Spells.
> Earth Elementals aid Manipulation Spells.
> No Elemental can aid Health Spells.

The number of dice is equal to the Elemental's Force Rating. Each die you use reduces the spirit's Force by 1. When the Force reaches 0, the spirit vanishes. It can be called again if it is still bound. When the spirit comes back, its Force is at full value again.

You can also use these dice to buy automatic successes by permanently reducing the spirit's Force by 1. If this reduces the Elemental's permanent Force to 0, the spirit is destroyed. Otherwise, when called again, the spirit has only its remaining Force.

> "Oh bloody-fraggin—AAAAAAAAIIIIIGH!" I whirled around in time to see Neddy go up in a blast of blue fire from the wagemage's spell. We lost our wizard, and on this little run in the shadows, that made us dead meat.
>
> A shimmering haze appeared around the flames. Neddy told me once that meant he had an Elemental taggin' along. It just flickered, then flickered again, getting smaller and weaker, like a match burning low. Then it went out. The whole thing only took a split-second. If I hadn't been chipped so high, I would not have seen anything special.
>
> Suddenly, there was Neddy. He should have been fried, but he was looking O.K. "Sorry, old fella," he muttered, "but I needed all of it. And YOU, you sorry bleeder…chew on THIS!"
>
> Wow! I had never seen Neddy do one of those before. The wagemage looked surprised, too, while he still looked like anything at all.
>
> Neddy failed to resist the effects of a Combat Spell. He needed three more successes to do so. As it happened, he was attended by a Fire Elemental with a Force of 3. By sacrificing all 3 of the spirit's dice, Neddy canceled the remaining effects of the spell, thus avoiding damage.

Aid Study

An Elemental can provide extra dice to help its master learn new spells. It can help only for a spell with the appropriate purpose category: fire for combat, water for illusion, air for detection, or earth for manipulation.

Sustain Spells

A magician can call upon an Elemental to use its Force to sustain one spell of its purpose category. The Elemental can maintain the spell for three seconds for each point in its Force Rating. Then it vanishes. The magician can take over the spell maintenance before the spirit vanishes, so that the spell will not disappear with the Elemental.

The magician can also bind an Elemental to a spell to maintain it for longer periods. The Elemental maintains the spell for a number of days equal to its Force Rating, but this service exhausts the spirit's Force. When this task is finished, the Elemental disappears even though it would have been bound to the magician for more services. If the spirit is banished before this period expires, the spell ends. Once an Elemental has been assigned to this duty, it cannot perform any other service. The magician can release it before it runs out of Force in order to end the spell ahead of schedule, but the spirit is still freed of its bond and will disappear.

Whereas each spell had its own Drain Code in Sorcery, a magician using Conjuring draws the Drain Code from the difference between his Charisma Attribute and the spirit's Force Rating.

If the Charisma equals or exceeds the spirit's Force, the Drain Code is M1, and any damage is applied as Fatigue on the Mental Damage track.

If the spirit's Force exceeds the magician's Charisma, the Drain Code is S1, and any damage is applied as Wounds on the Physical Damage track.

If the spirit's Force is more than double the magician's Charisma, the Drain Code is D1, meaning the magician will die if he does not offset Drain with his Resistance Test. Remember that if the character has powerful friends in a position to help, death is not always the end of the line in **Shadowrun**.

If the magician falls unconscious from Drain, the spirit is uncontrolled. When conjuring a spirit, most magicians have assistants present to try to banish the spirit if the conjurer loses control.

"By the Powers of the Deep, I summon thee!" The closing words of the invocation echoed and died away. Harlequin was bending the full force of his magic to open the gates to the power of the astral planes. The space within the complex binding pattern shimmered with blue-green light as the Water Elemental began to materialize. "Gotcha, babe," the mage murmured.

His smug grin vanished as a bolt of pain jagged through him. The sickening realization that he had overextended his powers was cut off with his consciousness. The last sight Harlequin saw was the amorphous bulk of the Elemental as it began to flow from the now-useless binding pattern into the circle.

Harlequin has a Charisma Rating of 3 and a Magic Rating of 5. He was conjuring an Elemental with a Force Rating of 8. Calculate Drain:

Target Number = Force of spirit = 8.

Charisma is less than half the Force = D1.

Harlequin had to resist a Drain of 8D1 with his Charisma. Rolling only three dice, he gambled that he could make at least one success. Harlequin rolled 3, 3, 5. He was pushing the rite, so when he blew the Drain, it killed him. Of course, had it simply knocked him out, the Elemental would have had him for lunch, so maybe Harlequin got an easy out.

Physical Service

The mage can call upon the Elemental to manifest itself and use its powers to do some job. You could call a Fire Elemental to burn through a door, for example, or an Earth Elemental to move a great weight, or any spirit to fight some enemy. See the **Critters** chapter for the physical powers of Elementals.

Remote Service

A magician can demand remote service of an Elemental only when it first appears. If a magician wants the use the Elemental for a remote service, he cannot make it bound to him. A remote service, therefore, forfeits extra successes and other services.

The mage sends the spirit off to perform a particular job, like a physical service. Once it has orders, the Elemental will pursue them single-mindedly until it either carries them out or is banished. Even the summoner cannot halt an Elemental once it is set loose. The spirit will do as ordered unless it is destroyed.

DRAIN

A magician using his Conjuring Skill must resist Drain in a way very similar to the procedure for Sorcery. There are important differences, however. In Sorcery, the magician uses his Willpower Attribute in the Resistance Test, but in Conjuring, he uses his Charisma Attribute. The magician can use extra dice from items or totems.

UNCONTROLLED SPIRITS

If an Elemental or Nature Spirit is uncontrolled, it is freed of any remaining service and may become violent. Roll 2D6. If the result is greater than the spirit's Force Rating, it simply vanishes. If not, it manifests physically and attacks its former master and anyone or anything else that gets in its way.

If its master is dead, the Elemental will vanish. It will also flee if it is taking too much damage, losing Force due to a banishing, or generally having too tough a time.

CONTROL CONTESTS

Two magicians can contest control of a spirit. Only a shaman can try to take over a nature spirit; only a mage can try to take over an Elemental.

The magician trying to take control declares the attempt as his action. The magician controlling the spirit may resist, whether he has actions available or not. The challenger is attacking the strength of the bond already created with the spirit, so this out-of-sequence action is a special case and does not reduce the dice available to the defending magician in future actions.

The contest is an Opposed Conjuring Success Test between the two magicians. Both have the same Target Number, the Force Rating of the spirit. Both magicians can use additional dice from spirit focuses or totem modifiers.

If the controlling magician wins, he retains control of the spirit and only the challenging magician makes a Resistance Test against Drain. If the challenger gets control of the spirit, each magician must make a Resistance Test against Drain. If neither rolls any successes, then both check for Drain and the spirit is uncontrolled. Drain is the same as when summoning the spirit. If the magician who won the contest is knocked out by Drain, the spirit immediately becomes uncontrolled.

BANISHING

Banishing requires great concentration, using the Conjuring Skill as if the magician were casting an exclusive spell. The magician can sustain no other spells, nor take any other actions while trying to banish a spirit.

A magician of either tradition may banish a spirit of either type. He first makes an Opposed Success Test using his Conjuring Skill against the spirit's Force Rating. Spirit focus and totem modifiers apply. If he is the magician who originally summoned the spirit, he adds dice equal to his Charisma Rating. The magician's Target Number is the spirit's Force Rating. The spirit's Target Number is the magician's Magic Rating.

The winner's net successes temporarily reduce the loser's rating by 1 point each. For example, if the magician rolls 4 successes and the spirit rolls 2, reduce the spirit's Force Rating by 2.

The winner of the test decides whether there will be another round. If he decides to continue the contest, neither character may do anything else until the winner's next action; they are locked in magical combat.

Repeat the process until one participant is overcome or the winner of a round decides to break off the contest. If a spirit's Force reaches 0, it is utterly destroyed. If the magician's Magic Rating drops to 0, he passes out, totally fatigued, and the spirit is free to go about its business. Generally, when a spirit decides to break off a contest, it will flee. Otherwise, the magician (or another magician) could try to banish it again.

Lost ratings return at a rate of 1 point per hour.

ASTRAL SPACE

Astral Space, or the astral plane, is a parallel dimension that touches the physical world. It is the source of magical energy and the medium through which it travels. Though vastly different from physical space, Astral Space shares the common dimension of time. Everything that exists on physical Earth has an astral counterpart. However, the laws of physics known to scientists do not apply to Astral Space.

Magical things (spirits, focuses, spells, some magical creatures, ritual teams, magicians using astral projection or perception, and so on) are living entities in astral space. They are visible, corporeal, and capable of action in Astral Space. Beings in Astral Space can see physical objects and assense magical energy given off by the astral forms of all living things. Assensing is the sixth sense that perceives magical energy and astral forms.

Nonmagical living things have dormant astral forms that are visible and corporeal in Astral Space but do not act on other astral forms. The Earth is a living thing in magical terms, and thus corporeal in Astral Space. Vegetation also blocks movement in the same way it does in the physical world. Water, air, and fire are also tangible in Astral Space, but astral beings can pass through them because of their low density. Water and fire do no harm to the astral traveler, but they do reduce his range of assensing.

Inanimate objects are visible because of reflected light, and they block the passage of magical energy and emotions, two primary elements of the astral form or aura. Because such objects block the flow of aura, astral beings cannot assense through them. These objects have no aura or astral form themselves, however, and so astral beings can freely pass through the astral position corresponding to the object's physical space. In Astral Space, you cannot see or assense through a wall, but you can easily walk through it.

Astral Space pulses with the primal energies of life. Artificial symbols, objects of the intellect, are not directly perceptible in Astral Space. If you examined the astral counterpart of this or any book, you would not be able to read the words, but you would sense the emotions of each passage. Books of poetry, for example, are rewarding when assensed astrally. Technical manuals are virtually blank. Scanning a computer screen in Astral Space would not let you read its contents, but you would detect the emotional context of the file—whether it was public data or secret, legal or illegal, personal or technical or business-oriented.

No, you cannot read the street signs either, so you had better know where you are going before you leave, right?

When viewed in Astral Space, all things reveal their true forms and natures. Auras do not lie. Disguises, whether physical or magical, simply do not work.

ASTRAL PERCEPTION

Any magician can perceive Astral Space, but he must spend an action to switch from normal senses to astral senses or back again. When he looks into Astral Space, he can:

Assense anything that is actually there;
Assense the magical energy surrounding an item;
Assense a Ritual Sorcery Sending;
Assense a being's aura to determine its true nature.

The magician can assense all spirits, magical creatures, and so on, whether they are visible in the physical world or not. If he has a spell that affects Astral Space, he may cast it (any Mana Spell will work). The magician is also vulnerable to Astral Combat.

The magician can assense magical energy surrounding anything that is itself magical or that is being affected by magic:

enchanted items, characters under the effects of spells, magicians casting or maintaining spells, and so forth. He can assense spells, focuses, and other magical items as living beings.

The magician can detect the Sending of Ritual Sorcery. An assensable web of energies leads back toward the source of the spell, allowing the magician to trace it using Astral Projection. Spells being sustained through Ritual Sorcery and spell locks also display such a web, leading to the spell's caster.

Astral Perception allows the magician to view the aura of any living or magical thing. Viewing the aura reveals information about the true form or nature of the being. A shapeshifter always shows its animal form in Astral Space, for example. A character under a disguising spell would also show his true form. The spell's aura identifies it as a thing of Sorcery. Focuses are visible as such. The auras of living beings reveal their general state of health, wounds, diseases, active drugs in the system, and so on. The magician also can assense their Essence and Magic Attributes. The gamemaster may choose not to reveal actual numbers, instead informing the magician if the score is higher, lower, or about the same as his own Magic Attribute. The aura of a magician shows both Magic and Essence, thus revealing the magician's nature.

The magician can gain further information about magical things by making an Unresisted Skill Test. Sorcery would be used to divine the nature of a spell. Conjuring or Sorcery, respectively, would be used to bind the Force and Magic Ratings of spirits or enchanted items. Use a Target Number of 4. The number of successes controls the amount of information revealed. One or two successes mean the magician learns the general class of the thing (a Fire Elemental, a Manipulation Spell, a Combat Spell Focus). Three successes tell him the Force or Magic Rating, and four or more reveal everything there is to know about the thing. The magician can make additional rolls to try to get more information, up to a maximum equal to his skill. Each additional try adds +2 to the Target Number.

ASTRAL PROJECTION

Any magician can use Astral Projection by sinking into a trance. While in this trance, he is dead to the world; his pulse and respiration are almost nil, and his senses are turned off. In magical terms, the magician "leaves his body" to travel in Astral Space. Until he returns, the physical body is comatose.

The magician's astral form has attributes based on his attributes in the physical world, as follows:

His Charisma becomes his Astral Strength.
His Intelligence becomes his Astral Quickness.
His Willpower becomes his Astral Body.

The magician's Special Attributes do not change when he enters Astral Space.

The magician's astral form appears as his idealized self-image. Of course, the idealized self-image of an Ork shaman or a coldly murderous corporate hitmage can be a pretty scary assensement.

Astral copies of the magician's fetishes and magical items accompany him on his journey. Non-magical gear stays with the comatose body in the physical world. The astral magician may form any garments or ornaments he wants, simply by willing it, but such things have no magical or armor value. It is just razzle-dazzle.

Tweezil glanced with the obnoxious pity of youth at the frail figure of his master before he entered his own trance. As Astral Space enveloped him, a voice from behind boomed, "What kept you boy?" Tweezil whirled and stared at a vibrant figure, powerfully muscled, robed in garments of light. He bore a familiar broadsword and his hands lightly held a staff Tweezil had assensed before. "B-b-boss?"

"You young snots never figure it out, do you?" the mage said with a laugh. "Over on this side, you are what you will, not what you think! Now follow me. We've got work to do."

ASTRAL MOVEMENT

Movement through the landscape of Astral Space proceeds at normal rate or fast rate. Normal movement is Astral Quickness multiplied by 3 for Dwarfs and Trolls, or by 4 for Humans, Elves, and Orks. This is the number of meters traveled per three-second turn. There is no danger of fatigue. Characters use this rate when they need to pay attention to the surroundings.

Fast movement is fast indeed! The magician can move at his Magic Attribute times 1,000 kilometers per hour. At this speed, the magician's surroundings will be a blur. He knows where he is and can dodge astral obstacles, but he cannot assense or see the scene in detail without slowing to normal movement. Combat can occur between two characters who are both using fast movement.

At either speed, the magician can fly, that is, he can move freely to any altitude up to the limits of atmosphere. Do not leave the atmosphere (50 miles). Magicians who have tried to break this barrier have usually died or gone mad, and the survivors' memories of the journey have been badly scrambled by some kind of profound mental trauma.

WHILE YOU WERE OUT

The longer a magician is in Astral Space, the weaker his physical form becomes. He has taken his Essence with him into Astral Space, and so his body begins to die.

The physical body loses 1 point of Essence every hour the magician is astrally gallivanting. If the Essence is reduced below 0, the magician dies. The magician's astral form has its full Essense and Magic Attribute Ratings even though the physical body is withering. Once the magician returns to his body, the Essence returns at a rate of 1 point per minute, up to the original rating.

While in Astral Space, the magician is unaware of the environment of his physical body unless he can still see it. If someone, or some thing, moves his body while he is in aura-land, he will not know it until he returns. When he gets back to where he left his physical shell, he will find it gone and must search for it. The search is a Success Test using his Body or Willpower Attribute, whichever is higher. The Target Number is 4, and the time for the search is equal to 6 hours divided by the number of successes. At the end of that period, presuming the magician has not run out of Essence, he will be in the presence of his body. Of course, if his enemies removed it, the magician may find astral opponents blocking his way back home.

A magician's enemies could simply kill the physical body. Almost any wound to the comatose form will drive it into fatal shock. A magician in Astral Space knows at once if his body dies. His astral form survives until he would have used up his Essence, at which point it evaporates. Such a wretch may decide to spend his remaining hours seeking vengeance, and the gamemaster can use such no-bodies as ghosts.

ASTRAL COMBAT

Any magical thing or being with a presence in Astral Space can engage in Astral Combat. Things that do not have an active astral presence cannot fight or be hurt in any way in Astral Space.

Astral combat works like Melee Combat, with an option for a counterattack resulting in an Opposed Success Test. The nature of Astral Space prevents ranged attacks. Movement, cover, and so forth have the same effect in Astral Space as they do in physical space, with the differences noted herein. A magician can attack other astral forms during his actions, receiving no penalties for "movement."

But wait, you say! What about spells? Glad you asked. In Astral Space, a spell is a living thing. From the astral plane, if you watch a magician cast a spell, you assense the spell form a living shape around the caster, then charge toward the target at high speed. Reaching the target, it vanishes, exiting into real space, where it releases its power.

A magician in Astral Space can intercept a spell within his line of assensement and fight it, preventing it from reaching the target for as long as he fights it. If he destroys it, it never gets to its target. When the magician fights the spell, however, it can damage or kill him.

The procedure for Astral Combat varies slightly with each type of astral form.

Other Magicians

Magicians in Astral Space function with their normal Mental and Special Attributes, but have their Astral Physical Attributes. For all actions in Astral Space (dodging, fighting, reducing damage), magicians have only one dice pool, the Astral Pool, drawn from the magician's Sorcery Skill, Magic Attribute, and Astral Quickness Attribute Ratings. It combines the functions of the Dodge and Defense Pools in regular combat and the usual functions of the Magic Pool. Allocate your dice carefully!

Actual attacks are like Melee Combat, using Sorcery Skill rather than any combat skill for the Success Test. The Target Number is 4. The magician who wins the round of astral combat can cause impressive damage.

The magician being attacked has the option of counterattacking using his Astral Pool as his Defense Pool. The number of net Successes determines the Wound Category. One does a Light wound, two inflict a Moderate wound, three a Serious wound, and 4 net successes count as a Deadly wound.

Resistance Tests are made per the normal procedures, using the Astral Body Attribute Rating with the opponent's Sorcery Skill Rating as a Target Number. The Staging is 1 if the opposing magician attacked barehanded. If the magician used a magic weapon, the Staging Number equals the weapon's rating. Remember that if you counterattacked, you cannot use your Astral Pool to dodge.

Because of the occult phenomenon of "repercussion," the physical body manifests the damage. That means that if you are lightly wounded in astral space, your physical body is lightly wounded at the same moment. If you are killed, your astral and physical bodies die at the same moment. Healing techniques used on one body also heal the other, whether they are magical or mundane.

Magical Barriers

Hermetic Circles and Medicine Lodges act as barriers in Astral Space. To pass through a barrier, a magician must destroy a barrier's resistance. The barrier remains intact against all other intruders. Spells cast at targets inside such barriers must penetrate the barrier before passing through to attack their targets. The spell still carries any wounds it got fighting the barrier. The creator of the barrier will know whenever someone is attacking it.

The barrier will resist an intrusion attempt, but it will not persist in fighting the intruder who drops his attempt. If you let an action go by without attacking the barrier, it repairs all damage and you have to start again. The attempt to penetrate a barrier is an Opposed Success Test, with a single net success sufficient to allow passage through. If the barrier prevails, it causes the same damage as would an opposing magician, increasing the Wound Category with each net success. The barrier's rating is used for the Success Test and its Resistance Test if it loses the Success Test.

Magical Items

Like barriers, magical items fight only if they are attacked. Also like barriers, they repair damage as soon as the assailant pauses in his assault. When "destroyed," a magical item loses its enchantment, but its physical form rarely changes. The item's rating serves as its attack value in the original Success Test and as its Body in the following Resistance Test.

Magical Creatures

The two types of magical creatures are dual beings and astral beings.

Dual beings exist on both planes all the time. They have the same characteristic ratings on both planes. Astral beings live in Astral Space, with most having the ability, but not the inclination, to manifest themselves in the physical world.

Dual beings must move on both planes together, as must astral beings when they manifest themselves in the physical world. They cannot be in one place in the physical world and another in Astral Space. Thus, they are limited to their physical-plane rate of speed.

Combat with magical creatures follows the general rules for the environment, physical or astral, where the battle is taking place. In the physical world, use the creature's attributes for appropriate tests and so forth as if it were a Human or metahuman. For example, you would use Body for Resistance Tests. For Astral Combat, use the creature's Essence Attribute Rating for all purposes.

Ritual Teams

Magicians engaged in a Ritual Sorcery Team are present in Astral Space during the Sending or if they are sustaining a ritual spell. The Hermetic Circle or Medicine Lodge acts as a barrier in Astral Space, but any team members except the leader may sortie outside the barrier to engage astral attackers. They cannot cast spells from inside the barrier, but they can do so freely outside the barrier. If a team member dies or loses consciousness, reduce the Magic Pool for the ritual by his Sorcery Skill. If this reduces the pool to 0 or if the leader loses consciousness, then the ritual aborts and all remaining members of the team make Resistance Tests against Drain. Those outside the Circle or Lodge take the Drain as Physical Damage.

Spells

A spell uses its Force Rating for all rolls in any contest with a magician in Astral Space. The caster of the spell, though in the physical world, knows he is being attacked and can allocate dice from his Magic Pool, and any focuses or totem modifiers he has for that spell, using these as a Dodge Pool to help his creation survive.

A spell is mindless. If unopposed, it will ignore any other astral forms and proceed to its target, reaching it in the action of its creation. If blocked, the spell will fight. This again works much like Melee Combat, with the winner of each round (the intercepting magician or casting magician) deciding whether to continue. If the attacker gets out of its way (or it kills the blocker) after one or more actions of combat, the spell proceeds on to hit its original target. Any damage inflicted in Astral Space does not reduce the spell's Force when it hits the target.

If a magician in Astral Space intercepts a spell, its caster can assist, as described above. He can keep doing this as long as he wants, until the spell wins the fight, or it is destroyed, which cancels it out. He can, on any action, decide to stop casting the spell, which promptly vanishes. He can cast other spells (subject to the magic rules) while trying to support the one in combat. His support counts as a distraction as if he were maintaining the spell. The casting magician makes a Resistance Test against Drain in the action he worked to cast the spell, no matter what. If Drain or anything else knocks out the caster, the spell vanishes.

Unless neither magician breaks off such a contest, it continues until the spell is destroyed or the intercepting magician dies trying. Each round is an Opposed Success Test with a Target Number of 4, pitting the spell's Force against the magician's Sorcery Skill. The net successes determine the Wound Category, as with other forms of Astral Combat. The loser makes a Resistance Test to reduce the Wound Category, the magician using his Astral Body Attribute with a Target Number equal to the spell's Force, and the spell using its Force with a Target Number equal to the magician's Sorcery Skill. The spell prevails in such a contest when it knocks out the magician. The magician destroys the spell if he inflicts a Wound Category equal to the spell's Force Rating.

A magician in Astral Space cannot cast a spell at another spell, but he can cast one at any other astral being. Such a spell cannot be intercepted. Only spells that would affect the thing or being physically will work. You cannot use a Sleep Spell to damage a magical item, but it would work against a magician in Astral Space.

When a magician casts spells in Astral Space, Drain always causes Physical Damage (Wounds), regardless of the Force of the spell.

GRIMOIRE

All spells are from *The Manual of Practical Thaumaturgy*, 14th edition, 2050, reprinted by permission of Ambrosius Publications, New York

COMBAT SPELLS

Damage from combat spells works in the same manner as damage from weapons, with the Staging Number of a combat spell used just as a weapon's Staging. All combat spells have an initial Wound Category of Light. Any Successes from the Force Success Test increase the Wound Category each time they equal the Staging. The lower the Staging, the more lethal the spell. With a Staging of 3, every 3 Successes increase the spell's Wound Category by one. Staging 2 needs two Successes to increase the Wound Category, and Staging 1 is nasty, with each Success raising the Wound Category.

Then the victim makes a Resistance Test to reduce the Wound Category in the same manner, based on the Staging of the spell. Remember that the target uses his Body Attribute against physical spells and his Willpower Attribute against mana spells. Armor does not count as Automatic Successes against physical spells or against mana spells. If the victim's successes reduce the Wound Category beyond Light, the spell does no damage, though it still goes off.

Power Dart
Drain: L2   **Type:** Physical   **Duration:** Instant
Mana Dart
Drain: L1   **Type:** Mana   **Duration:** Instant
Special Effect: A bolt of magical power that causes Physical Damage. Staging is 3.

Power Missile
Drain: M2   **Type:** Physical   **Duration:** Instant
Mana Missile
Drain: M1   **Type:** Mana   **Duration:** Instant
Special Effect: A bolt of magical power that causes Physical Damage. Staging is 2.

Power Bolt
Drain: S2   **Type:** Physical   **Duration:** Instant
Mana Bolt
Drain: S1   **Type:** Mana   **Duration:** Instant
Special Effect: A bolt of magical energy that causes Physical Damage. Staging is 1.

Powerball
Drain: S2   **Type:** Physical   **Duration:** Instant
Manaball
Drain: S1   **Type:** Mana   **Duration:** Instant
Special Effect: An area spell that causes Physical Damage. Staging is 2. The mana version affects only living targets, and physical cover offers no protection.

Fireball
Drain: D3   **Type:** Physical   **Duration:** Instant
Special Effect: An area spell that causes Physical Damage. Staging is 2. The spell can ignite combustible materials in its blast area.

Hellblast
Drain: D4   **Type:** Physical   **Duration:** Instant
Special Effect: An area spell that causes Physical Damage. Staging is 1. The spell can ignite combustible materials in its blast area.

Sleep
Drain: S1   **Type:** Mana   **Duration:** Instant
Special Effect: An area spell that causes Mental Damage to living targets only. Staging is 1.

Ram
Drain: S2   **Type:** Physical   **Duration:** Instant
Special Effect: The spell damages inanimate targets, creating a one-meter-wide hole when it reduces the Barrier Rating to 0. Staging is 1. Make a Resistance Test using the Barrier Rating, with the spell's Force as the Target Number. If the spell gets enough successes to penetrate, each extra success increases the width of the hole by one meter.

DETECTION SPELLS

Some detection spells, those called hypersenses, give a magician new senses as long as they are maintained. To determine the range at which the hypersense operates, make an Unresisted Force Success Test against a Target Number of 4. Multiply the Successes by the magician's Magic Attribute for the distance in meters at which the new sense will work.

Certain detection spells, those called general, are not aimed at a specific target or targets, so you need not make a Resistance Test for each of the umpteen-hundred people in range of a Detect Life spell, for instance. First, the magician declares the nature of the information he is seeking. This sets the Target Number, which is 4 if the magician is exploring all targets within sight, 6 for all subjects out of sight, or 10 for beings in Astral Space. For subjects who are out of sight behind a magical barrier, add that barrier's rating to the Target Number. The magician then makes an Unresisted Force Success Test.

A single success gives him a reading, but the number of successes determines how good the reading is. A single success yields only general knowledge, no details. Two successes give the magician detailed information, but some minor parts are inaccurate. Three successes means all details are accurate, but minor parts are obscure or missing. Four successes give the magician accurate and detailed information. If a magician sustains a general detection spell, he picks up new subjects as they enter the area covered by the spell. The results from his original Success Test still apply.

Analyze Device
Drain: S2   **Type:** Physical   **Duration:** Sustained
Special Effect: The magician can analyze the purpose and basic operation of a device or piece of equipment. The magician's previous familiarity with the device or similar objects counts as a base success level (automatic successes) for analysis.

Analyze Truth
Drain: M1   **Type:** Mana   **Duration:** Sustained
Special Effect: Hypersenses spell. The magician can tell whether a target is telling the truth. The target makes a Resistance Test using his Willpower Attribute. The spell does not work on written materials. The magician must hear a statement to know if it is true or not.

Clairvoyance
Drain: M1   **Type:** Mana   **Duration:** Sustained
Special Effect: Hypersenses spell. The magician can see distant scenes as if he were present, to the range of the new sense, regardless of walls or other obstructions. He must concentrate to use this sense, and while using it, he does not use his physical vision. A magician cannot cast spells at a target he sees using Clairvoyance.

Combat Sense
Drain: S2   **Type:** Physical   **Duration:** Sustained
Personal Combat Sense
Drain: M2   **Type:** Physical   **Duration:** Sustained
Special Effect: Hypersenses spell requiring a voluntary subject. The subject becomes able to subconsciously analyze combat or other dangerous situations. Theory suggests that the spell allows precognition, with the subject sensing events a split second before they happen. Add the magician's successes to the subject's Reaction Rating. The Personal form of the spell affects only the magician himself.

Detect Enemies
Drain: S1   **Type:** Mana   **Duration:** Sustained
Special Effect: Area-effect, general detection spell. The magician detects living beings in range who have hostile intentions toward him personally. This would not detect a trap (it is not alive), nor a terrorist about to shoot into the crowd at random (the intention is not personal).

Detect Individual
Drain: L1   **Type:** Mana   **Duration:** Sustained
Special Effect: Area-effect, general detection spell. The magician detects the presence of a particular individual. The magician names the individual when he casts the spell. If the individual does not want the magician to find him, he makes a Resistance Test using his Willpower Attribute.

Detect Life
Drain: M1   **Type:** Mana   **Duration:** Sustained
Special Effect: Area-effect, general detection spell. The magician detects all living beings within range and knows their number and position. In a crowded area, the spell is effectively useless, picking up a blurred mass of traces.

Detect (Life Form)
Drain: L1   **Type:** Mana   **Duration:** Sustained
Detect (Object)
Drain: M2   **Type:** Physical   **Duration:** Sustained
Special Effect: Area-effect, general detection spell. The magician detects a specified type of target: Detect Ork, Detect Dragon, Detect Guns, Detect Computers, Detect Cameras, and so forth. Each variation is a separate spell.

Mind Probe
Drain: M1   **Type:** Mana   **Duration:** Sustained
Special Effect: The magician can telepathically probe a subject's mind. The target makes a Resistance Test using his Willpower Attribute. If the target fails to offset all the successes, the number remaining determines the extent to which the magician can probe the target's mind. One success indicates the magician can read surface thoughts. The magician knows what the target is thinking about at that instant, but he cannot influence the thoughts or draw other information from the target. Two successes allow the magician to probe for thoughts. The magician can find out anything the subject knows consciously. Essentially, he can ask any question, and the target must answer with the truth as he knows it. Three or more successes allow the magician to enter the target's subconscious. The magician can tell the difference between fact and opinions. He can see scenes witnessed by the subject as if he had been there himself. He can also get an insight into the character's psychology.

HEALTH SPELLS

Health spells can cure diseases or inflict them, detoxify poisons or drugs, or mimic their effects, and some can temporarily modify attributes. Unless otherwise specified, the magician must touch his target to use a health spell.

Many health spells are curative, healing physical damage and diseases. No techniques known to magic can erase fatigue or cure mental conditions. Each curative spell has a maximum Wound Category that it can affect. Heal Moderate Wound is useless for someone who is seriously wounded. If a magician uses a more powerful spell than is needed (Heal Serious Wound to heal moderate damage), he still resists the normal Drain for the spell. This goes for spells that cure disease, too. The maximum category the spell can affect is what determines Drain.

The Target Number for a curative spell does not come from the subject's Willpower Attribute because the magician is pumping mana into the subject's own healing mechanism. The Target Number for the Force Success Test is equal to 10 – the subject's Essence Rating, rounded to the nearest whole number. Curative spells are all permanent duration spells. Remember that passing time applies modifiers to this Target Number.

Unlike Drain, the base time required for the spell depends on the Wound Category it is trying to heal, or the drug it is neutralizing, or the disease it is curing, not on the maximum Wound Category of the spell. The Healing Table gives the base times for all healing spells. Divide the base healing time by any extra successes from the Force Success Test. If the magician drops the spell or if the patient is wounded during this time, the spell fails and no damage is healed. Any poisons or drugs are free to continue on their course. Each retry at healing the same subject increases the Target Number for the Force Success Test by +2, whether the spell was interrupted or the Force Success Test simply scored no successes.

HEALING TABLE

Category	Time
Deadly	20 Turns
Serious	15 Turns
Moderate	10 Turns
Light	5 Turns

Antidote (Wound Category) Toxin
Drain: (Wound Category)2
  Type: Physical   **Duration:** Permanent
Cure (Wound Category) Disease
Drain: (Wound Category)2
  Type: Mana   **Duration:** Permanent
Special Effect: These curative spells act on the toxin (poison or drug) or the disease, not the person it is affecting. The Force Success Test is unresisted and has a Target Number equal to the Virulence Level of the infection or toxin. The spell must score a number of successes at least equal to the Staging to take effect. Additional successes may reduce the time for the spell to take effect. The Wound Category of the spell must equal or exceed the Wound Category of the disease or toxin. For example, if curing someone infected with a 6S2 disease, the Force Success Test has a Target Number of 6 and needs 2 successes to cure the

patient. The magician must use Cure Serious Disease or Cure Deadly Disease spell. The Antidote spell must be used before the toxin damages the victim. Cure can be used at any point after infection, killing the germs in the patient's system and eliminating any symptoms at once, but it does not heal damage already done by the disease. That takes a separate Healing spell. There are separate Antidote and Cure spells for each Wound Category.

Decrease (Attribute)
Drain: Special **Type:** Physical   **Duration:** Sustained
Special Effect: The spell can be cast at a distance and uses a normal, resisted Force Success Test. There are three separate spells for each Attribute to Decrease, with Staging 1, Staging 2, and Staging 3. The Staging of the spell thrown determines the Drain Code, L2 for Staging 3, M2 for Staging 2, and S2 for Staging 1. The target resists using the attribute that is attacked, not necessarily his Body Attribute. If an attribute is reduced to 0, the target is helpless. If this is a Physical Attribute, the victim is unconscious or paralyzed. When a Mental Attribute is reduced to 0, the victim is standing about mindlessly. A version of the spell exists for Reaction, but the other Special Attributes may not be affected. This is a physical spell and will affect targets with Cyberware modifiers to their attributes.

Detox (Wound Category) Toxin
Drain: (Wound Category –1)2
  Type: Physical   **Duration:** Permanent
Special Effect: Detox relieves the effects of a drug or poison. It must overcome the toxin as Antidote does, but because relief is symptomatic, the Drain Code is reduced (minimum is Light).

Detox does not heal damage done by toxins, but it eliminates any other effects they may have on the victim (dizziness, hallucinations, nausea, pain, whatever). Detox is the hangover cure of choice among those who can afford it. Each Wound Category is a separate curative spell.

Increase Attribute +1
Drain: L2   **Type:** Mana   **Duration:** Sustained
Increase Attribute +2
Drain: M2   **Type:** Mana   **Duration:** Sustained
Increase Attribute +3
Drain: S2   **Type:** Mana   **Duration:** Sustained
Increase Attribute +4
Drain: D2   **Type:** Mana   **Duration:** Sustained
Special Effect: The spell increases a Physical or Mental Attribute or Reaction. That version will act like wired reflexes, increasing initiative dice as well as the attribute. The spell does not work on other Special Attributes. The Force Success Test is unresisted, with a Target Number equal to double the rating of the attribute to be increased. A single success is sufficient. This spell does not affect cybernetic features. That would take a Physical spell, with higher Staging in the Drain Code. This means that anyone with Muscle Replacement will get no benefit from an Increase Strength spell. Each attribute has four specific spells, and so you might have a magician who knows Increase Strength +2, Increase Quickness +1, and so on.

Treat Light Wounds
Drain: L1   **Type:** Mana   **Duration:** Permanent
Treat Moderate Wounds
Drain: M1   **Type:** Mana   **Duration:** Permanent
Treat Severe Wounds
Drain: S1   **Type:** Mana   **Duration:** Permanent
Treat Deadly Wounds
Drain: D1   **Type:** Mana   **Duration:** Permanent
Heal Light Wounds
Drain: L2   **Type:** Mana   **Duration:** Permanent
Heal Moderate Wounds
Drain: M2   **Type:** Mana   **Duration:** Permanent
Heal Severe Wounds
Drain: S2   **Type:** Mana   **Duration:** Permanent
Heal Deadly Wounds
Drain: D2   **Type:** Mana   **Duration:** Permanent
Special Effect: Treat spells must be applied within one hour after a subject was last wounded. Heal spells may be applied at any time. Both are curative spells.

ILLUSION SPELLS

No matter how realistic they are, illusions cannot permanently harm a character, mentally or physically. They can cause distractions, loss of balance or orientation, and even symptoms like nausea or pain. Such symptoms vanish as soon as the magician drops the illusion.

Many illusions are meant to deceive or distract. For these, the target makes a Resistance Roll using his Willpower Attribute with the Force of the spell as the Target Number, as usual. Some illusions are meant for voluntary subjects, in which case the spell's Force Success Test is unresisted, with a Target Number of 3.

Illusions can be designed as area spells, so that all in the area sense the illusion, or designed for a single subject so that only he senses the illusion. A magician can also cast the spell on a subject, so that all who see him perceive an illusion.

Obvious illusions are usually used for entertainment, though powerful spells can at least distract enemies, even though they know they are illusions. Single-sense illusions seem real to only one physical sense. Full sensory illusions seem completely real to the targets.

Chaos
Drain: S2   **Type:** Mana   **Duration:** Sustained
Special Effect: A target who fails to resist is subject to massive distractions. The spell consumes his senses in a cloud of blinding sights, fierce odors, and tickling sensation. He suffers a major distraction (+2 to all his Target Numbers) for every extra success the spell has. This spell affects electrical sensing devices in addition to a character's own senses.

Chaotic World
Drain: D2   **Type:** Mana   **Duration:** Sustained
Special Effect: This is an area-effect version of Chaos.

Confusion
Drain: S1   **Type:** Mana   **Duration:** Sustained
Special Effect: An area spell. Visual illusions fill the area, making it a place of shifting forms, dazzling lights, and pools of shadow. Those who fail to resist suffer a distraction equal to the number of extra successes. Add each victim's number to all his Target Numbers. This spell does not affect electronic sensing devices.

Entertainment
Drain: L1   **Type:** Mana   **Duration:** Sustained
Special Effect: This area-effect spell requires voluntary subjects. It creates obvious, but entertaining illusions for all who wish to watch. The number of successes measures how entertaining the audience finds the illusion.

Invisibility
Drain: L2   **Type:** Mana   **Duration:** Sustained
Special Effect: The caster must touch the subject, who becomes invisible to normal light. Thermographic vision can still detect body heat, and the subject is completely tangible and detectable by the senses of hearing, smell, and so forth. Double the number of successes to get the Target Number for an observer's perception Success Test. If he succeeds, he notices the invisible person or thing. The spell does not affect observers with thermographic vision, those using audio detectors, chemoreceptors, or similar devices. It does affect cameras that use visible light and cybereyes without thermographic vision.

Mask
Drain: L1   **Type:** Mana   **Duration:** Sustained
Special Effect: This spell requires that the magician touch a voluntary subject. The subject assumes some physical appearance (same basic size and shape), chosen by the caster. The number of Successes becomes the Target Number for perception rolls by observers.

Stimulation
Drain: M1 **Type:** Mana **Duration:** Sustained
Special Effect: The voluntary subject experiences a full sensory illusion of whatever the caster wishes. This is usually a luxury spell bought by the jaded and rich, seeking sensations they cannot find in the real world. Successes measure the pleasure of the subject.

Stink
Drain: S2 **Type:** Mana **Duration:** Sustained
Special Effect: This area spell stimulates the sense of smell. Subjects within the area of effect make normal Resistance Tests using their Willpower Attributes. Each extra success increases all of the victims' Target Numbers by 1 due to the sickening effect of the stench.

MANIPULATION SPELLS

There are thousands of possible manipulation spells, and these are potentially the most powerful class of spells in **Shadowrun**. Manipulation spells can transform or control matter and energy. Control spells affect the actions and the thoughts of living beings. Transformation spells change the material structure of a target. Telekinetic spells are various forms of mind-over-matter, from wild poltergeist phenomena to subtle work controlling machinery.

Many manipulation spells have a Threshold. If the spell does not get enough successes, after the target's Resistance Test, to equal this Threshold, the spell has no effect. For example, most control spells have a Threshold equal to the target's Willpower Attribute. The magician must score this many successes or the spell has no effect.

Control Manipulations

Control Actions
Drain: M2 **Type:** Mana **Duration:** Sustained
Special Effect: The magician controls the physical actions of a target, like a puppet. The victim's consciousness is untouched, but he is a passenger in his own body. The victim uses any skills he possesses at the magician's orders, but with +4 to all his Target Numbers. The Threshold is the target's Willpower Attribute.

Control Emotion
Drain: L1 **Type:** Mana **Duration:** Sustained
Special Effect: The subject feels some overwhelming emotion. This can be anything the magician chooses when he casts the spell. He can make the victim love somebody, hate somebody, whatever single emotion he wants. The Threshold is the target's Willpower Attribute. The effects of this spell require roleplaying more than they do scores or numbers. The spell's victims believe the emotion wholeheartedly but not mindlessly. As a rule of thumb, if a character is doing something that is in keeping with the emotion (fighting while filled with anger or hate), no penalties apply. If he is doing something that is not relevant to the emotion (trying to drive while laughing wildly), he is surely distracted (+2 or more to Target Numbers). If he tries to go directly against the emotion (trying to shoot a magician he "loves"), he must pass an Unresisted Willpower Success Test with the spell's Force as his Target Number. He will have a distraction penalty even if he succeeds.

Control Thoughts
Drain: L2 **Type:** Mana **Duration:** Sustained
Special Effect: The magician controls the thoughts of the subject. The victim will carry out orders wholeheartedly as long as the magician sustains the spell. This is the magical equivalent of deep hypnotic suggestion. The Threshold is the target's Willpower Attribute. Actions that are terribly destructive to the victim or his loved ones allow him to fight the spell. He must pass an Unresisted Willpower Success Test with a Target Number of the spell's Force. If the magician is not present, a single Success will do. If the magician is present, make an Opposed Willpower Test to determine if the target can break control.

Hibernate
Drain: L2 **Type:** Physical **Duration:** Sustained
Special Effect: The magician must touch a voluntary subject. The spell puts the subject in a form of suspended animation. Double the Successes from the Force Success Test to get the factor by which bodily processes are slowed. If you scored 4 Successes with Hibernate, you would slow the subject's metabolism by a factor of 8. If your subject has suffered a Deadly Wound, the Target Number for his saving throw against death would increase by 1 for every eight minutes before treatment was given, instead of every minute. If he were suffering from a disease that weakened him every hour, it would now take eight hours. If he were sealed into a chamber with enough air to keep him alive for a day, it would last eight days.

Telekinetic Manipulations

Levitate Item
Drain: L2 **Type:** Physical **Duration:** Sustained

Levitate Person
Drain: M2 **Type:** Physical **Duration:** Sustained
Special Effect: Levitation allows a magician to lift an item or person from the ground and move it around. The maximum height in meters is the magician's Magic Attribute times the number of extra successes. The magician's Target Number for the Force roll is increased by +1 for every 100 kilograms of mass he is trying to move. A magician can move a levitated object anywhere as long as he maintains the spell and keeps the object in sight. Objects move with a Quickness equal to the magician's Magic Attribute.

Magic Fingers
Drain: M2 **Type:** Physical **Duration:** Sustained
Special Effect: Magic Fingers is classic telekinesis. The magician creates "invisible hands" and can hold or manipulate items by mental power. The Force Success Test is unresisted, with a Target Number of 6. The number of successes becomes the spell's Ratings for the Strength and Quickness. The magician can use his own skills with Magic Fingers, but all Target Numbers receive a +2 due to the problems of remote control. Even simple actions may require a Quickness Success Test (like picking up a drink and spilling it into a corp's pants, right Sally?). The magician can fight, pick a lock, whatever, using Magic Fingers. The Fingers can reach any point the magician can see, but he can use Clairvoyance or even remote viewing technology to get a close-up of the scene. The spell comes in handy for disarming bombs.

Poltergeist
Drain: S2 **Type:** Physical **Duration:** Sustained
Special Effect: Within the area of this spell, all small objects and debris, up to a kilo in mass, whirl around in random patterns. This reduces the visibility factor of the area (+2 to all Target Numbers to a maximum visibility modifier of +4). The spell does Stun Damage as well, whacking targets with flying debris. Targets within the area use their Quickness Attribute, not Body, for their Resistance Tests against such damage with a Target Number of the Force of the spell. The Wound Category is Light, and the Staging is 3. Armor provides no protection against this damage.

Transformation Manipulations

Armor
Drain: L3 **Type:** Physical **Duration:** Sustained
Special Effect: A voluntary subject is required. The magician gives the subject built-in armor, knitting his tissues into tougher compounds. Treat the successes rolled in the Force Test as the rating of dermal armor for as long as the spell is maintained.

Barrier
Drain: D2 **Type:** Physical **Duration:** Sustained

Mana Barrier
Drain: D1 **Type:** Mana **Duration:** Sustained
Special Effect: Area spell. The magician forms a force field of crackling energy. The Force Success Test is unresisted, with a Target Number of 6. The magician may form the barrier as a normal area spell, which would create a dome of energy, or he may create a wall. The wall's height is the spell's Force in meters. Its length or radius is equal to the magician's Magic Attribute. This length may be adjusted in the same way as the radius of an area effect, by withholding dice from the Success Test. The magician may make the wall any shape. Anything the size of a molecule (or less) can pass the barrier, including air or other gases. Anything bigger treats a physical barrier as a hard cover with a rating equal to the spell's Force. Attacks directed through the barrier face reduced visibility. Mana barriers do not stop physical weapons, but they do block movement by living beings. Unliving things (like bullets) pass right through. Passengers inside closed vehicles are not affected by a mana barrier, but it would knock the rider off a motorcycle. Mana barriers also act as a defense against spells. Add the barrier rating to the Target Numbers of all magicians casting spells across the barrier. The barrier's rating counts as automatic successes for Resistance Tests of those protected by it. It is also an astral barrier.

Ignite
Drain: S4 **Type:** Physical **Duration:** Permanent
Special Effect: The magician accelerates molecular speed in a target, causing it to catch fire. Anything that can burn is subject to this spell. The base time to ignite the target is 10 turns, divided by the magician's extra successes. Once the target ignites, it is burning until it burns up or is extinguished by smothering, water, or fire extinguisher. The Threshold for Ignite is the Body of living targets or the base barrier value of inanimate objects. The Ignite spell wraps a being in flames, causing 6M2 damage on the first turn. The Staging increases by +1 per additional turn. Apply damage at the end of each turn. Ammo or explosives carried by the victim may go off. If flames are not extinguished, they burn out in 1D6 turns.

Petrify
Drain: M3 **Type:** Physical **Duration:** Sustained
Special Effect: Any living target turns to a stone-like substance, flesh altering into a calcium carbonate of marble-like consistency. Clothing, equipment, and Cyberware are unaffected. The victim is not conscious while calcified. The Threshold is the victim's Body Attribute.

Toxic Wave
Drain: D4 **Type:** Physical **Duration:** Instant
Special Effect: A wave of toxic acid fills the area, attacking physical objects, people, you name it. The Resisted Force Success Test has a Staging Number of 1. Worn armor does help resist the spell, but armor values are halved. In addition, visual conditions apply a +4 visibility modifier to all Target Numbers in the area for the rest of the turn due to corrosive fumes.

Turn To Goo
Drain: S4 **Type:** Physical **Duration:** Sustained
Special Effect: This spell transforms the target into thick sludge, its molecular cohesion broken down. The Threshold is the Body Attribute of living targets or the basic barrier rating of inanimate objects.

THE MATRIX

"Live and learn. Die and forget...unless you are an Expert System."
—Zapper Weisman, Legendary Decker

he Matrix, or the Grid, is the network of all computer systems interconnected by the world telecommunications system. If a computer is connected to any part of the Grid, then you can get to it from any other part of the grid.

ACCESSING THE MATRIX

There's only one ticket into the Matrix and that's a "Matrix Imaging Cybernetic Interface Device," or cyberdeck. There are other interface devices around, but they are old tech. The cyberdeck is the only choice for someone who wants the edge. Leave the big, ugly, slow stuff for the corporate wageslaves.

To connect into the Grid, all decks have a fiber-optic cable with a standard data plug like those found on home telecom systems. With the right tools, you can drop a neat little tap into any existing comm line to accommodate the plug. Then power up, hit the GO button, and you're going places in the Matrix.

After a second of disorientation, you (that is, the construct that is your persona) appear in the Matrix at the point where you tapped into the Grid. If you enter from an illegal tap in the back room at Matchstick's Bar & Grill, you'll appear in the telecom line that serves the joint.

You'll be standing next to your deck's construct. This is usually a small, white pyramid, the same as a legal cyberterminal. You can make it assume any shape you want, but most deckers like to keep a low profile and leave the appearance of their entry point alone. It's true, though, that some of the really hot deckers don't care drek whether they get spotted or not. The late, great St. Louis Blue used to image his deck construct like a carnival tent, with a neon sign that said "This deck belongs to the meanest dude in the Matrix." Damn shame about old Blue.

Usually, you've plugged into the Local Telecommunications Grid, or LTG. In an antique telephone system, the LTG would be an area code. Getting into the LTG is easy. It's when you want to travel to another part of the Grid, or to any computer system that's linked to the LTG, that things get interesting.

TIME AND MOVEMENT IN THE MATRIX

For some reason, the data world in 2050 is rather paranoid. The corporate sector seems to feel threatened by the deckers running loose through the Matrix, and with good reason. Information is the largest industry in the world, and the market is always hungry for that little piece of data that will incriminate an exec or give the R & D boys an edge on the competition. Financial records make specially tempting targets for the data sharks of cyberspace. Billions of nuyen exist solely as data, and like any data, can be erased, modified, or transferred.

To get anywhere legally in cyberspace, you need passcodes. Even entering the LTG requires a passcode so that the phone company knows whom to bill. Fortunately, LTGs are wide open if you have the right hardware. Even a deck that's last year's piece of techno-junk lets you in for free.

The point where two systems or grids connect is called a System Access Node, or SAN. This is just one of many kinds of nodes that form the Matrix. Entering a SAN usually requires a passcode, because the system owners want to know who's accessing their equipment. They install protective software (Intrusion Countermeasures, or IC) to keep out unauthorized people.

IC will deny access to any user who cannot provide a legitimate passcode. Users with the right passcodes can go right through, but their passcode is logged. They are now on file. The system owners know who they are, and the bill is in the mail.

Deckers can get around IC in various ways. They might have someone else's passcode or software that can trick the IC. But with a hot deck and the right programs, you don't need them. You're the Ghost in the Machine.

PASSCODES

Apparent movement in the Matrix is instantaneous as long as you're not crossing a node. When you reach a node and start playing pattycake with its IC, that's when you slow down.

If you have a legitimate passcode, you breeze through. Flash the code and pass the node. If you ain't got the code, you must deal with the IC somehow—kill it or trick it—to get past the node it guards. Whatever you try, you go through Cybercombat turns to do it. If it takes you two turns (six seconds) to defeat the IC and get through the node, it takes two turns in the world outside the Matrix as well.

HELLO, OPERATOR

OK. Here we are in that LTG. Each Local Telecommunications Grid is part of a Regional Telecommunications Grid, or RTG. If an LTG is a local area code, then an RTG is the long-distance system. The map shows the North American RTGs and their associated Security Classifications. The corps know that deckers are out there, trying to bust into their systems and using telecom networks without paying for it. That's why every System Access Node has a Security Classification, or Code. See **Security Codes**, below.

When you are in an LTG, you have several choices. You can:

•Try to deck into any computer system hooked into the same LTG, if you know its address. The Security Code depends on the individual computer system. See **Mapping Systems.**

•Try to enter another LTG within the same Regional Grid. This requires that you cross one SAN to make the connection. The SAN has the same Security Code as the RTG.

•Try to enter the RTG. The SAN always has the Security Code for the RTG you are trying to enter.

To enter systems outside your immediate area, you have to get into the RTG. Once there, you can enter any other RTG in the world, building a connection across landlines, trans-oceanic cables, and/or satellite links. Entering a new RTG means you must go through a SAN with that RTG's Security Code.

For example, Fastjack taps into LTG 2206 in Seattle. He's headed for a Renraku mainframe on LTG 4206. Changing LTGs within the Seattle RTG (Security Code Green-4) means he has to cross one System Access Node. The SAN has a Code Green-4.

If he were going after a computer in Tir Tairngire, he'd have to move from the Seattle RTG (NA/UCAS-SEA) to Tir Tairngire's RTG (NA/TT). The destination RTG has a Code Orange-5, and he'd have to pass a SAN with that Security Code. Darn touchy about their privacy, those elves.

SECURITY CODES

All computer systems in the Matrix consist of a group of nodes, which are connected to the LTG through a SAN. All the nodes in the Matrix have a general Security Code. This Security Code reflects the relative ease or difficulty with which a decker can manipulate that node. In addition, each node can have an additional protection program known as Intrusion Counter-measures (IC) assigned to it.

The general Security Code of a node is denoted by a Color and a numeric Security Rating. The Security Code is very important, because whenever you attempt to do *anything* to any part of the node, you must first overcome the node's general Security Code, so that it will start to *execute* your orders, which are given via a program.

By the way, most IC programs will be trying to get *your* deck to execute *their* programs in order to dump you out of the Matrix or something equally nasty. Though this attempt might manifest itself as an actual attack against your Persona in the artificial environment of the Matrix, in the real world, the nasty Corp IC is really trying to muck up the insides of your deck, just like you are mucking with the insides of their mainframe. Symmetry is a grand thing, is it not?

The color-coded Security Level indicates the difficulty of getting that node to execute unauthorized programs or instruction, and let's face it, anything *you* do in the Matrix is unauthorized. The higher the Security Level, the more successes you need to get a node to even listen to you. For example, getting a Blue database to execute your order to download a file requires one success on a Computer Skill Test. Getting a Red database to execute the same instruction takes three successes.

Blue nodes are open and have no appreciable security. Small personal computers, free advertising databases, public service networks, and so on are Blue nodes. Getting a Blue database to download its information requires one success on a Computer Skill Test.

Green nodes have minor levels of security. These are usually systems with limited membership or that charge fees for access. Public library databases, subscription services, and most telecom grids are Green systems. Breaking a Green Code requires one success on a Computer Skill Test.

Orange nodes are considered quite secure. This is the typical Security Level for any government or corporate system not containing highly classified data. Computer systems belonging to criminals are often Orange as well. To crack an Orange security code requires two successes on a Computer Skill Test.

Red nodes are "top secret." Classified government systems, corporate financial and R&D systems, and the systems belonging to organized crime syndicates are typical examples. To break this top-secret code requires three successes on a Computer Skill Test.

BREAKING A CODE	
Security Level Code	Successes Required
Blue or Green	1
Orange	2
Red	3

Note that the numeric Security *Rating* is usually the Target Number you have to beat when attempting to do something to the node. For example, when attacking an IC program on a Code Red-4 node, your Target Number to hit the program is 4.

DIRECTORY ASSISTANCE

The Interlocking Local Telecommunication Grids are too complex to map in detail. Such a map would be a jumble even if the system addresses didn't move around constantly in the paranoid data world of 2050. So how the heck does a decker trying to steal a dishonest nuyen find a system to rob?

System addresses are the LTG codes by which computers can be accessed. They are "unlisted phone numbers" and valuable information. In an adventure, the gamemaster may leave a clue for the characters that tells them where to find the address of the bad guys' mainframe. Fixers and other contacts may offer addresses at a price.

And if you can't get it from somebody else, you have to jack into an RTG and hunt it down. You must know what you are looking for. That is, you have to tell the gamemaster something like "I'm searching for Aztechnology's private LTG," or "I want the mainframe for that Yakuza clan on Fifth Street." Then make an Unresisted Computer Skill Test, with a target number equal to the RTG's Security Rating. The color of the Security Level tells you how many successes you need. What you are actually doing is scanning all the databases that store access codes for that RTG and its dependent LTGs, which is equivalent to looking in a phone book a few million pages long.

If at first you don't succeed, try again, applying +2 to your Target Number for each new test. Each time you make the Computer Skill Test, you risk triggering an alert on the system you are attempting to access. The gamemaster will be secretly rolling 1D6. If the result is less than or equal to the number of tests it took you to find the place or less than or equal to the

MAP KEY:
UCAS: All RTGs are Code Green-4
  Northeast (NA/UCAS-NE)
  North Central (NA/UCAS-NC)
  South (NA/UCAS-SO)
  Midwest (NA/UCAS-MW)
  West (NA/UCAS-WE)
  Seattle (NA/UCAS-SEA)
QUEBEC: (NA/QU) Code Green-2
CAS: All RTGs are Code Green-3
  Seaboard (NA/CAS-SB)
  Gulf (NA/CAS-GU)
  Central (NA/CAS-CE)
  Texas (NA/CAS-TX)
NA/NC States:
  Sioux (NA/SIO) Code Orange-3
  Algonkian-Manitoo (NA/ALM) Code Green-4
  Athabascan (NA/ATH) Code Green-3
  Ute (NA/UTE) Code Orange-3
  Pueblo (NA/PUE) Code Orange-4
  Salish-Shidhe (NA/SLS) Code Green-3

California Free State: (NA/CAL) Code Green-4
Tir Tairngire: (NA/TT) Code Orange-5
Trans-Polar Aleut: (NA/TPA) Code Green-2
Tsimshian: (NA/TS) Code Orange-5
AZTLAN: All RTGs are Code Orange-3
  Norte (NA/AZ-NO)
  Centrale (NA/AZ-CE)
  Sud (NA/AZ-SU)
  Baja California (NA/AZ-BA)
  Yucatan (NA/YU)
CARIBBEAN LEAGUE
  South Florida (NA/CL-FLA) Code Green-2
  Cuba (NA/CL-CU) Code Orange-3
  Jamaica (NA/CL-JA) Code Green-3
  Grenada (NA/CL-GR) Code Orange-4
  Bermuda (NA/CL-BER) Code Green-2
  Virgin Islands (NA/CL-VI) Code Green-2

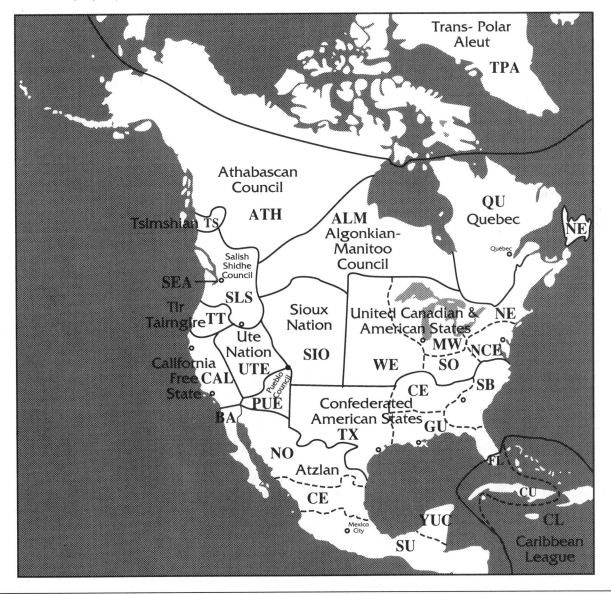

number of tests made before you gave up, the system you were seeking to access will be on an Internal Alert when you come to call. See **Alerts** for details. If you leave the system alone for a couple of weeks, they will cancel the alert. They'll probably also change their address.

LEAVING THE MATRIX

A decker can leave cyberspace anytime by jacking out, or pulling the plug that connects his datajack to the deck. Keep in mind that a Persona is only a program running on the computers of the Grid. It does not really go anywhere and has no independent consciousness. Despite decker legends, you cannot get "trapped" in Cyberspace.

If you get kicked out of the Matrix involuntarily, you have been dumped. The rapid cut-off of the deck's simsense signal can cause mild disorientation called dump shock. This lasts up to 30 seconds, during which time you are disoriented. This adds +2 to all Target Numbers except when making an Unresisted Willpower Test to reduce the time of disorientation. For that test, your Target Number is 4. Divide 30 seconds by the number of successes scored for the time of disorientation.

MATRIX GEOGRAPHY

The Matrix is mapped by locating the nodes and their connections. Each piece of a computer system is some kind of node. Each node has a Security Code and may contain IC.

The gamemaster should be ready with maps for systems that are part of an adventure. When designing a system, he may assign any Security Code he wishes to each node, and any rating to IC.

NODES AND THEIR FUNCTIONS

The Matrix is composed of billions of nodes. A group of nodes that work together is called a system. A system is a single computer, usually a mainframe (a big, non-portable computer).

To perform a system operation inside a node, the decker makes an Unresisted Computer Skill Test, with the system's Security Rating as his Target Number. To accomplish anything, he must score enough successes to overcome the system's color code. The decker may try more than once, with +2 applied to the Target Number for each new attempt.

After a Persona performs a system operation, or gives up after several tries, the gamemaster should roll 1D6. If the result is less than or equal to the number of attempts, the system goes into an Internal Alert. See **Alerts**.

Nodes are connected by datalines, which have no Security Code. There is no IC on a dataline, nor can Cybercombat occur there. If an opponent chases you into one, combat continues in the node to which the line connects. Datalines look like narrow bridges or pathways of energy, pulsing as data flows through them.

Following are descriptions of the six basic types of node: what they are, how they appear from inside (the construct), what you can do when inside (system operations), and to which kinds of nodes they connect.

CENTRAL PROCESSING UNIT

Every system has one and only one Central Processing Unit, or CPU. It is the heart and brain of the system. Most systems have powerful IC guarding the CPU.

Construct: A huge octagonal room, built of massive circuit boards pulsing with dazzling energy. Screens display the data flowing through the computer and the status of the other nodes in the system.

System Operation

Display Map: The gamemaster must show you a map of the system. It shows its nodes and their security codes, but no IC, files, or anything else. [NOTE: Gamemasters should make a separate map for their own use when drawing a system.]

Shutdown: This crashes the system and dumps the decker.

Cancel Alert: Cancels an Internal Alert. If there is an External Alert in progress, that is beyond your control. If you trigger one, it won't prevent any further alerts you may trigger.

Change Node: This is a "Teleport" straight into any node in the system. Once there, you cannot "teleport" back to the CPU.

Connectivity: The CPU can connect to any other type of node in the system. Because of the node's extreme importance, however, it is usually protected from the other nodes by a "layer" of SPUs, so that no access port can get directly to the CPU.

DATASTORE

Datastores hold information, or files. From the decker's point of view, this is where the loot is. Datastores also tend to be heavily loaded with IC.

Construct: A maze of rectangular blocks of energy, files filled with swirling letters and numbers in different colors. Each file is 2D6 x 10 Mp in size.

System Operation

Transfer: Copy data to a cyberdeck's storage (downloading) or from storage to the datastore (uploading). This is governed by the deck's I/O speed. The decker must stay in the node until the transfer is complete, or else it aborts.

Erase: Wipe out one file (e.g., erase a police record).

Edit: Change contents of a file (e.g., award someone straight A's on a college transcript).

Read: Reading a file works like downloading it. You don't actually copy it, so you don't need storage to hold it. You are skimming its contents. If you want to find the private comm number for a corporate officer, read the personnel files. The gamemaster is the judge of what a decker can get from a file by reading. Simple facts like names, dates, phone numbers, addresses, and so on are easy to remember. Highly technical data cannot be memorized. For example, if you want to sell a complex formula, you must download it.

Connectivity: Datastores can connect to other Datastores, SPUs, or the CPU.

I/O PORTS

An I/OP is a limited-access node that opens the system to various data input/output devices: terminals, cyberdecks, printers, graphics displays, data readers for optical chips, and so on. You can jack into the system through these devices using a cyberdeck or a program carrier. Dodger invaded the Mitsuhama mainframe via a security terminal, an I/O port. In big systems, a single I/OP node could be the access point for hundreds of devices.

Construct: A pyramid-shaped, white chamber. If the I/OP controls a number of terminals, you are in a cluster of pyramids connected by dataline, usually radiating out from a large, central pyramid.

System Operation

Display Message: Display a message on the terminal the I/OP controls.

Lockout: Lock the I/OP out of the system. Nothing it controls can contact the computer now. If the I/OP represents a cyberterminal that someone is using, the decker must crash the terminal through cybercombat first.

Connectivity: I/OPs can connect to SPUs or the CPU (rare).

SUB-PROCESSING UNITS

An SPU is a small computer that is "slaved" to a more powerful one. The CPU gives it orders, and the SPU does various jobs for the boss node. Some SPUs are just "traffic cops," connecting datalines to other nodes. Others might lead to datastores or other goodies.

Construct: A large chamber filled with pulsing banks of circuits and sizzling lines of energy.

System Operations: None.

Connectivity: SPUs can connect to any other type of node in the system.

Standardized Cybersystem architecture mapping symbols. All symbols are to be drawn in the color of their security level. Place a numeral in the circle to indicate the node's security rating.

CENTRAL PROCESSING UNIT (CPU)

SYSTEM ACCESS NODE (SAN)

SUB-PROCESSING UNIT (SPU)

INPUT/OUTPUT PORT (I/OP)

SLAVE MODULE (SM)

DATASTORE

SYSTEM ACCESS NODE (SAN)

A SAN connects to other systems or to the Grid. They are the doorways into systems.

Construct: Complex doorways or airlocks through the walls of the system architecture.

System Operation

Lockout: The decker can lock the SAN, preventing any other persona from using it.

Connectivity: SANs can connect to an SPU. They can also connect to the CPU, but this is rare.

SLAVE

A Slave Node controls some physical process or device, anything from an electric coffeemaker to an assembly line to the elevators for a corp HQ building. You can jack into the system through a Slave Node, but only by using a program carrier and going naked.

Construct: A small, cubical room, its walls covered with flashing patterns of light. The more complex the slaved system, the larger the room and the more complex the pattern of lights.

System Operations

Control: You can control whatever the Slave Node controls, whether it be making all the coffee boil over or shutting down the assembly line.

Sensor Readout: You can read any sensors or cameras run by the Slave Node. For example, the Slave controlling building security would let you use the security cameras.

Connectivity: SNs can connect to SPUs and to the CPU.

NODE CONNECTIVITY TABLE

Node Data Type	CPU	Store	I/OP	SN	SPU	SAN
Central Processing Unit (CPU)	No	Yes	Yes	Yes	Yes	Yes
Datastore	Yes	Yes	No	No	Yes	No
I/O Port (I/OP)	Yes	No	No	No	Yes	No
Slave Node (SN)	Yes	No	No	No	Yes	No
Sub-Processing Unit (SPU)	Yes	Yes	Yes	Yes	Yes	Yes
System Access Node (SAN)	Yes	No	No	No	Yes	No

MAPPING SYSTEMS

The gamemaster is responsible for mapping systems for deckers to invade. The **Behind the Scenes** chapter suggests a method to generate systems randomly when you haven't either the time or the inspiration to design one. To create one of your own, read on.

To map a system, start by drawing a rectangle to represent the SAN on a sheet of paper. Choose a color—let's say orange—and outline the box with that color, or write "Orange" next to it. Next, choose a number randomly or roll 1D6 + 2 for the rating. You roll a 4. If you want to put IC in the node (and who doesn't?), choose one. Let's select Access for this example. Now pick another number or roll 2D6. You get a 9. Write Access-9 in the Orange-4 SAN. That's all there is to designing a node.

Keep adding nodes and connecting them with datalines until the look of the system suits you. We advise gamemasters to go easy on the deckers until you've got a feel for running adventures in the Matrix, however. Killing all the characters in the SAN is bad for their confidence.

The loot usually goes in a datastore. Files are 2D6 x 10 Mp in size. Assign a monetary value to the file. If the decker is looking for some specific file or clue, you'll have to note which datastore contains that item.

You can also hide "loot" in places like I/OPs (forcing the decker to access someone's personal computer to get that incriminating evidence), Slave Nodes (letting them spy on the bad guy using the building security cameras), or even the CPU (stashing a program in the CPU that unlocks the villain's bank account in the Swiss L5). Credit balances are loot, too. Money is data, like everything else, and can be lifted from a datastore. You still have to fence nuyen that you steal from a computer, because if it isn't laundered, it's easily traced back to you. See page 147 for fencing your loot.

Read over the IC descriptions in the section on **Intrusion Countermeasures** and try to be fair about what IC you install. No corp can afford the programming expense of putting Black IC on every node.

Typical Matrix architecture will have several areas of datastores, I/OPs, and SPUs, with varying degrees of security. High-security areas are generally guarded by Orange or Red SPUs, with nasty IC installed. The CPU usually is Orange or Red as well, and runs Killer or even (gulp) Black IC.

SECURITY CODE TABLE

Security Level	Number of Successes	Initiative	Security Rating	IC Rating
Blue	1	NA	1D6	None
Green	1	5+rating	1D6+1	1D6+1
Orange	2	7+rating	1D6+2	2D6
Red	3	9+rating	2D6	2D6+1

MAPPING THE TELECOMMUNICATION GRIDS

It is impossible to map the telecom grids in detail. They contain billions of possible connections and are constantly changing, with each RTG containing many LTGs. The simplest way to keep track of LTGs is to assign them a numeric code and keep a log of important systems that connect to those LTGs, kind of like a private phone book. For example, an LTG 2206 in Seattle would be designated as NAUCAS-SEA-2206. Any number of LTGs may be in an RTG. Keep notes showing what systems hook into each LTG. For example:

NAUCAS-SEA-2206: Lone Star Public Security Records
NAUCAS-SEA-2708: Intercontinental Bank of Japan
NAUCAS-SEA-4938: Matilda's (A betting parlor and house of ill-fame, also a front for the Yakuza)
NAUCAS-SEA-4206: Hemdall Group Regional HQ
NAUCAS-SEA-9431: EBMM District Sales Office

Players should not know what is in the gamemaster's phone book because system owners guard their LTG locations jealously. Player characters will have to hunt down an access code or acquire it during an adventure to know where an LTG system connects. Let them keep their own phone books.

Private LTGs

The highest levels of security are found among the megacorps, the government, and private citizens who can pay for it (like the local Yakuza *oyabun*). This is a private LTG. The trend toward these had already started by the 1990s, when large corporate skyscrapers in New York City were assigned their own area codes within the normal 212 area code that served Manhattan.

Private LTGs are designated by an ID code appended to the LTG code.

NAUCAS-NE-3617-EBMMHQ
Private LTG for EBMM UCAS headquarters in Boston.
Accounting
R&D
Public Relations
Security
Each system would belong to an EBMM operation in the Boston area.

A regular LTG has the same Security Code as its RTG. It will come as no surprise that private LTGs are not bound by this rule. They have whatever Security Code their owner can afford, and usually are Orange or even Red.

CYBERDECKS

Cyberdecks are stunningly complex devices, even by the standards of 2050. Not only do they contain a simsense interface that lets you experience the Matrix in full-sensory splendor, but they have more processing power than a warehouse full of 20th-century computers. Let's take a look at the most important components of a deck.

MASTER PERSONA CONTROL PROGRAM

The MPCP is an optical chip that is the heart of the deck. It contains the master operating system that integrates your programs. It lets you control the appearance of your Persona and translates Grid signals into sensory input that you can see, hear, and smell. It also turns your neural signals into computer instructions when you do something in cyberspace. If the MPCP crashes, you're immediately dumped.

The MPCP has a Program Condition Monitor for your Persona. It also has a rating that represents its ability to cope with damage before it crashes. The number of dice rolled to resist damage is equal to this rating.

The appearance of your Persona is pretty much up to you, within certain limits. First, your Persona will always have a "technological" look to it, whether it be a silver-skinned siren, a high-tech knight in electro-armor, a cyber-samurai armed with laser katana, or a cartoon clone with a squirt gun. Whatever it is, if you want to play tech, then you've got to look tech!

Your size remains "Human" in scale to the Matrix. That towering database you are about to hack into will stay towering, whether you look like Little Bo Peep or a Tyrannosaurus Roborex.

A Utility program can appear in any form, but it must be proportional to its rating. An Attack-1 program cannot appear as a megaton nuclear field howitzer. Nor will an Attack-7 program look like a derringer.

Hardening

This is "armor" in the Matrix. If an attacker wins a damage test against your Persona, reduce its extra successes by your Hardening Rating.

Onboard Memory

This is the RAM (Random-Access Memory) of the deck. The total size of the programs running at any given time cannot exceed this rating. If you have 10 Megapulses (Mp) of onboard memory, then you can't run an 11 Mp Utility. When you load a Utility, it takes up RAM. The standard size of a program is equal to its rating. A loaded program stays in memory until erased.

Onboard RAM uses standard optical memory chips, and you can load as much of it onto a deck as you can afford, at the regular prices for non-cyber memory: 20¥ per Mp.

Storage

This is the built-in program storage in your deck. It works just like the disk drives in an old personal computer, but consists of banks of optical data chips, with nanosecond access times. You carry Utilities in storage, ready for loading. Storage is also where you stash downloaded data, fresh off the Matrix and ready to sell to the highest bidder.

Like onboard memory, storage can be expanded at 20¥ per Mp.

Load Speed

This controls the speed at which Utilities load from storage to onboard memory. It takes an action to activate the load process. Loads are then measured in turns. If the program size is less than or equal to half the Load Speed, it loads in the same action. For example, on a deck with a 50 Mp/turn Load speed:

A 25 Mp program would load in the same action during which the decker invoked it.

A 50 Mp program would be loaded by the end of the turn.

A 100 Mp program would be loaded by the end of the next turn, and so on.

While a load is taking place, the Persona suffers a +2 to all Target Numbers. You can only load one program at a time. Programs stay loaded until erased.

I/O (Input/Output) Speed

This is the amount of data that your deck can download or upload in a turn. A 10 Mp I/O speed would let a deck download 10 Mp per turn. The rules are the same as for Load Speed. While transferring data, the Persona suffers a +2 to all Target Numbers and cannot move into a different node. Movement will abort the transfer.

CYBERDECK SPECIFICATIONS

Standard Hardware for all cyberdecks includes:

A fiber-optic connector cable terminating in an STJ-400 standard telecommunications jack.

A keyboard with standard keys, numeric spreads, and a wide variety of function keys.

Prepared slots on the MPCP motherboard for the Persona program chips.

CYBERDECK OPTIONS

Following are some optional features available to cyberdecks.

Response Increase

This is analogous to wired reflexes, increasing the decker's Reaction Attribute in cyberspace. Co-processors are installed with the MPCP to support this feature. If the deck is destroyed by a Trace & Burn or similar IC, so are the co-processor chips. Each level of Response adds +2 to the Reaction Attribute and a 1D6 to the initiative roll, but only within the Matrix.

Cost: Level 1 – 25,000¥
Level 2 – 100,000¥
Level 3 – 250,000¥

Hitcher Jacks

These are simsense electrodes that let other characters tag along with the decker on his run through the Matrix. Hitcher jacks allow these companions to perceive everything the decker does and to communicate with him. They offer absolutely no control over the run.

Cost: 1,000¥ per jack

Vidscreen Display

This is a floppy screen attachment displaying the decker's point of view in cyberspace. The decker can also display text messages to viewers on this screen. However, viewers cannot communicate with the decker via this readout.

Cost: 500¥

USING CYBERDECKS

Only one decker can jack into any one deck at any one time. If more than one decker is going on a run, they jack in separately. Each uses his own deck. Personas can communicate in the Matrix, if within Contact Range. Characters observing a run using hitcher jacks don't count. They can see the Matrix and talk to the decker, but they can't do anything on the run.

CYBERDECK TYPES								
Model	MPCP	Hardening	Memory	Storage	Load	I/O	Design Pts.	Cost
Radio Shack								
PCD-100	2	0	10	50	5	None	5	6,200¥
Allegiance								
Alpha	3	1	10	50	5	None	11	13 200¥
Sony CTY-360	6	3	50	100	20	10	108	111,000¥
Fuchi Cyber-4	6	3	100	500	20	20	138	150,000¥
Fuchi Cyber-6	8	4	100	500	50	30	352	364,000¥
Fuchi Cyber-7	10	4	200	1,000	50	40	490	514,000¥
Fairlight								
Excalibur	12	5	500	1,000	100	50	960	990,000¥

Two decks cannot share programs directly, but deckers can give other deckers data or Utility programs. This takes time. The material must be uploaded to the Matrix by the owner, then downloaded from the Matrix by the recipient. If the recipient is getting a Utility, he must then load it from storage to onboard memory. This is fine when two deck-dancers are swapping programs in a "hacker heaven," but not exactly the way to go with combat IC locking in for a kill.

You can't mess with the deck hardware during a run in the Matrix. If anyone does, the decker dumps. This means no transferring programs or data to or from storage, and no replacing burned out chips. No nothing.

The decker must be physically connected to his deck through a fiber-optic to his datajack. The deck must be physically connected to the Grid through a communications line or system access point of some kind. If anyone has developed wireless deck connections yet, they aren't telling.

CYBERPROGRAMS

You need a cyberdeck to get into the Matrix and you need programs to do things while you're there. Without the right programs to razzle-dazzle the IC, you'll always have to give legitimate passcodes and settle for whatever those passcodes let you do. Programs are freedom! They get you into the places where the corps don't want you to be and they show you things you might be better off not seeing. But those are the only things *worth* seeing, right, technomancer?

The programs that run on your deck come in two breeds: Persona programs and Utility programs. All your programs are integrated by the central processor in your deck, the Master Persona Control Program, or MPCP.

Persona programs (P-programs) are firmware, encoded chips installed directly into the main circuit board of the deck. Each program runs on its own little computer, plugged into the cyberdeck hardware. These programs are your Persona's attributes.

Utility programs (Utilities or U-programs) are software. Utilities are your skills and gear in the Matrix. When you need one, you pick it up. When you're done with it, put it away.

PERSONA PROGRAMS

The MPCP maintains your persona. If the MPCP crashes, you're dumped out of the Matrix. Without a running MPCP, you cannot perceive Cyberspace and must return to what passes for reality outside it. You'll be keeping a program condition monitor for your MPCP to track any reduction in capacity due to attacks. When setting yourself up as a hotshot decker, you must buy or build your own cyberdeck, and then install the P-program chips. See **Cyberprogramming** at the end of this chapter.

Because Persona programs are installed in chips, they do not use up any of your cyberdeck's onboard Random Access Memory (RAM). However, it's important to know the size of a P-program when you are writing your own. The size in Mega-pulses (Mp) of a Persona program is its rating times a multiplier given for each program. (See the **Equipment** chapter for ratings.)

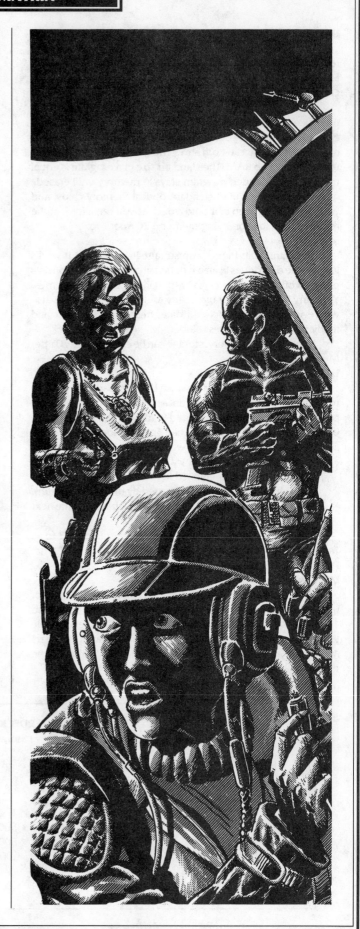

There are four Persona programs. Their ratings are usually used as target numbers by anything that attacks or opposes you in cyberspace.

Bod

This is your persona's "Body" attribute. It is normally used as a Target Number by IC that has successfully *executed* an attack program against your deck and is attempting to crash it. See **Cybercombat** for details.

Size: 10 x Rating

Evasion

This attribute allows your persona to evade unauthorized programs and commands by IC. It is directly analogous to a node's Security Rating.

Size: 5 x Rating

Masking

This is your persona's ability to "blend in" with Matrix nodes. The attribute helps to defeat various tracer and identification programs.

Size: 5 x Rating

Sensors

This attribute lets your Persona detect things in the Matrix.

Size: 3 x Rating

UTILITY PROGRAMS

All other programs are Utilities, your skills and gear in cyberspace. Utility programs must be loaded into your deck's memory to run. Each Utility has a rating that measures how well it works. It also has a size multiplier that measures its complexity. The rating times the multiplier is the program's size in Megapulses.

Utilities tie up onboard memory, even after they have crashed. If you want to load a new Utility and you don't have enough free memory to hold it, you must erase one or more of the programs currently loaded. Erasing one program from memory requires an action.

To load a Utility from storage to memory takes an action, but large programs may require several turns to complete. See **Cyberdeck Specifications** for details.

You can load only one copy of a given Utility in onboard memory at any one time.

DEGRADABLE UTILITIES

Some Utilities become less effective each time they are used. There are many reasons for this, ranging from the Grid's own error-correction capability to the way the program works. Some Utilities become "degraded" every time they run. Degradable programs lose one point of rating each time they are used on a given run. After you jack out, this reduction is canceled.

RUNNING UTILITIES

Your Computer Skill Rating (or your rating in Software Concentration or Decking Specialization) is the only one that really matters once you are jacked into the Matrix.

Whenever you want to give orders to a node or use any of the Utilities listed below, you must determine whether you can get the node to *execute* the programs. Your programs and instructions can only affect the node where you are located (see **Nodes And Their Functions**).

To get a node to *execute* your utility program, make a Resisted Success Test using your program's rating for the number of dice. The Target Number is the node's numeric Security Rating. Use the node's Security Rating for its Resistance Test. The Target Number will be your Persona's Bod, Sensor, or Masking Rating, as appropriate. To execute your program, you need enough successes to beat the node's Security Level. Failure means that the security system protecting the node rejected your Utilities program. If rejected, you can try to *execute* the program again, but apply +2 to the Target Number for each new test.

Combat Utilities are a special case and their use and effect are detailed in the **Cybercombat** section.

The number of dice in the Hacking Pool is equal to your Computer Skill (or your Concentration in Software or Specialization in Decking, if applicable) plus your Reaction Attribute. Wired reflexes and vehicle control rigs do add bonuses to Reaction, but you do not get the extra dice for the initiative roll. Again, remember that the numbers given in parentheses for Reaction in the section on **Archetypes** already include the effects of wired reflexes. You also add any Response Increase built into your deck to your Hacking Pool.

When using a Utility program or when making any other Computer Skill Test, you can use Hacking dice in the same manner described in Combat to augment these tests.

PROGRAMMING ON THE FLY

If you need a Utility program that isn't loaded (or that you don't even own), you can write a one-shot version using your Hacking Pool. Every *two dice* you take from your Hacking Pool gives this program 1 point of rating. Degradable programs can only be improvised once during a single run in the Matrix. As always, dice allocated from a pool are expended until your next action.

COMBAT UTILITIES

Combat Utility programs are weapons used in Cybercombat either to crash IC or another Persona that is protecting a node. You must be in Contact Range of the IC or Persona to use a Combat Utility.

Combat Utilities are complex programs designed to crash rather than simply manipulate a construct. By 2050, constructs are designed to resist such gross modifications through the means of unique coding processes. To have any chance at doing damage, the decker will have to make last-second adjustments to tailor the attack program to the specific construct he is up against. Borrowing from a real-world analogy, he must carefully "aim" his "attack" to even hope to "hit" his target.

To reflect this, a decker uses his Hacking Pool to make a Success Test against the node's Security Code. If the program hits, then make a Resisted Success Test to determine the level of damage. Full details on target numbers and effects are given in the **Cybercombat** section.

Attack Program

The Attack program is your main weapon in Cybercombat and does damage to its target after you successfully *execute* it. Once the Resisted Success Test is made, each extra success is a single "wound" on the target's condition monitor. Ten wounds crash any Matrix construct. See **Cybercombat** for details.

Size: 10 Mp x Rating

Slow Program

A Slow program will slow down IC, but it has no effect on another Persona. After the Resisted Success Test is made, extra successes are subtracted from the target's Reaction. If the Reaction is reduced to 0 or less, the IC program is frozen and stops working. Frozen IC cannot initiate any alarms or trigger traps.

Size: 10 Mp x Rating

DEFENSE UTILITIES

Defense utilities improve the Persona's ability to avoid or resist damage. Because they are run on your deck, they *do not* require a Success Test to execute them, but you will make one to find out how much damage is repaired. Use the Program Rating for the number of dice. Programs that repair damage to your persona also fall into this category.

Medic Program

A Medic program repairs damage to the Persona. The Target Number depends on the Persona's current wound level, per the table below. You cannot augment this die roll from the Hacking Pool.

PROGRAM REPAIR TABLE	
Wound Level	Target Number
Light	4
Moderate	5
Serious	6

Every success rolled heals one "wound," clearing one box on the program condition monitor. Whether or not a medic program succeeds, it degrades each time you use it in the Matrix.

Size: 10 Mp x Rating

Mirrors Program

By adding its rating to a Persona's Evasion Attribute, a Mirrors program makes it harder for unauthorized programs to be executed against your Persona in Cybercombat. No test is required to *execute* this program. A Mirrors program is degradable, with the bonus reduced by 1 point per turn after it is triggered.

Size: 10 Mp x Rating

Shield Program

A Shield program acts as auxiliary armor for the Persona and its programs. The program automatically stops a number of wounds equal to its rating. A Shield program degrades, losing 1 rating point every time it stops damage.

Size: 10 Mp x Rating

Smoke Program

A Smoke program simulates a burst of high-volume system activity, confusing perception around your Persona. Executing a Smoke program requires an action. No Success Tests are required. While you are in the node, the Smoke program's rating is added to every Target Number needed by anything in that node, including your own tests. A Smoke program is degradable, with its effects reduced by 1 point every turn. The effect "follows" the persona if it changes nodes.

Size: 3 Mp x Rating

SENSOR UTILITIES

Sensor Utilities analyze data or other elements of the Matrix. You must be in Sensor Range to use a Sensor program. (See **Perception in the Matrix**). This usually means the Persona is not close enough to the IC to "trigger" it, and that gives you a chance to scope it out before having to deal with it. Exceptions to this may occur when the IC system is in an Alert.

To execute a Sensor program requires a Resisted Success Test. To make the Test, use the program's rating for the number of dice and the node's Security Rating for the Target Number.

Like most Utility programs, Sensor programs are complex. This allows the node a chance to abort the program before it can do any significant "damage," even if successfully executed. To abort a Sensor program, the defending node or program makes a Resistance Test, using its rating for the number of dice and the Persona's Sensor Attribute as the Target Number. To execute, the Sensor program must have extra successes equal to or greater than the color Security Level of the node.

Gamemasters are advised to use secrecy in resolving this test to avoid giving away information. If the player knows the Target Number, he knows the node's Security Rating. If he then notices that he rolled two extra successes and did not get an execution of his program, he will know that the node has a Red Security Level. Unless otherwise specified, the decker can try again if a Sensor program fails. Each new attempt to execute increases the program's Target Number by +2.

> Fastjack has a Sensor Rating of 5. He uses Analyze-6 to scan a node with a Security Code of Red-4. He rolls 6 dice (his Program Rating), with a Target Number of 4 (the Security Rating), to see if his program is executed. Fastjack must beat the node by at least three extra successes, because the node has a Red Security Level. Fastjack gets 3 successes. The node makes its Resistance Test by rolling 4 dice (its Security Rating), with a Target Number of 5 (Fastjack's Sensor Rating). It gets 1 success, aborting Fastjack's Analyze program before it could give him any useful information. Fastjack can try to execute again, but his new Target Number is 6.

Analyze Program

An Analyze program analyzes constructs or nodes. If used against an IC program, the IC makes a Resistance Test using its own rating for the number of dice and the Persona's Sensor Rating for the target. The decker's Resisted Success Test still uses the node's Security Rating as a Target Number. An Analyze program will not reveal any information about another Persona.

If the decker's test succeeds, he learns the name of the construct or gets a brief description of its function. For example: "You are facing a Barrier IC program," or, "This is a slave node controlling the employee coffee station on the 37th floor." You can also use this program to analyze the Security Level for the node you are in. ("You are in a Red-8 node. Please observe all safety precautions.")

Size: 8 Mp x Rating

Browse Program

A Browse program analyzes the contents of datastores. You must specify the subject matter of your search. For example: "I am looking for data on the corporate security division's covert activities." If the decker is successful in running the program, he knows what files in the datastore contain references to that subject, and their sizes. He doesn't learn any details. See **Nodes And Their Functions** for details on datastores and files.

Size: 3 Mp x Rating

Decrypt Program

A Decrypt program defeats Scramble IC. Scramble turns data into garbage if someone tries to access it without knowing the right passcode. Use the rating of the Scramble IC for its Resistance Test in aborting the Decrypt. Failure to beat Scramble can trigger instructions to wipe out the data it is guarding. See **Intrusion Countermeasures (IC).**

Size: 3 Mp x Rating

Evaluate Program

An Evaluate program is a complex expert system that scans datastores looking for any information of value on the open market. The program rapidly becomes obsolete as the market changes.

If the node fails to abort the Evaluate program, the program finds any "paydata" files in the datastore. Evaluate tells the decker how many valuable files are present and the size and market value of each one.

If you are on a mission to find information on a specific subject or subjects, Evaluate will also tell you if the datastore contains that information, just as Browse does.

Evaluate is degradable, whether you use it or not. After every run you make into the Matrix, reduce its rating by 1 point. This reflects the way changing data markets render Evaluate obsolete. If you write your own Evaluate, you can upgrade it from time to time to offset this loss.

Size: 5 Mp x Rating

MASKING UTILITIES

Masking utilities attempt to fool IC into leaving the Persona alone. You must be in Contact Range to use a Masking utility. To execute the program, the decker uses his program's rating for the number of dice, as usual. His Target Number is the Security Rating of the node. The IC makes a Resistance Test, with its rating for the number of dice and the Masking attribute of the Persona as the Target Number. The program must have a net success equal to or greater than the color Security Level of the node to execute.

If the IC wins the test, it may trigger Attack IC or a System Alert or take other programmed action. If the decker's test succeeds, but he does not have enough extra successes to overcome the Security Level, the IC does not react and the decker can try again. Each new Test increases the decker's Target Number by +2.

Deception Program

A Deception program generates fake passcodes to deceive IC. These passcodes are logged by the IC, so Deception does leave a trail of sorts. Deception can defeat Access and Gray IC. It does not affect Barrier or Black IC.

Size: 5 Mp x Rating

Relocate Program

A Relocate program defeats Trace IC, security software that tracks a decker back to his entry point into the Matrix. If the decker makes a successful test to execute a Relocate program, it sends the IC on an endless wild goose chase through the Matrix. The IC will think it is doing its job and will not trigger any alarms.

Size: 5 Mp x Rating

Sleaze Program

A Sleaze program bypasses Access, Barrier, Gray, or Black IC without leaving tracks. If the decker succeeds at Masking, his persona is "invisible" to the IC. Sleaze does not work if the IC is already attacking or otherwise activated.

Size: 8 Mp x Rating

DECKING

Let's go down the checklist, cowboy. Got your cyberdeck?
Check!
Installed your Persona chips?
Check!
Got Utilities in storage?
Check!
Loaded your first-choice programs into memory?
Check!
Decided where you're gonna go?
Check!
Tapped into the grid?
Check!
Got your life insurance paid up?
Che…what?
Then hit the GO button, boy, and welcome to reality!

MOVEMENT IN THE MATRIX

Movement in the Matrix is virtually instantaneous unless you are engaged in Cybercombat, attempting to deal with IC, issuing system instructions, transferring data, or loading programs. The Grid transmits data at megabaud rates (that's fast, folks), and system response is measured in microseconds. Only when dealing with something that requires your attention does the action slow down to where you can notice time passing.

When moving in the Matrix, you are moving from one local or regional grid to another; within a system, from one node to another. The distance is entirely relative in cyberspace. It is a matter of commline connections, available memory in subsystems, and switching systems and transmission rates, not actual meters and kilometers. Distance is what you perceive it to be. Which brings us to…

PERCEPTION IN THE MATRIX

Inside the Grid, distances appear vast and scale is enormous. Inside a system, the area looks like a glowing neon maze of connections, circuits, and dataflows. But keep in mind that there is no "real" distance involved. In technical terms, the question is whether your Persona (remember, it's only a program) is able to access the data space of other programs or the controllers for hardware elements in a system.

There are three effective "ranges" in cyberspace.

Observation Range

You are in Observation Range of every node adjacent to the node of your current location. In a Grid, you can, theoretically, see the System Access Nodes connecting your node to other LTGs, RTGs, and computer systems. If there are many of them, it might obscure your vision. If you are in a computer node, you can see all the adjacent nodes in the system, but you can't tell what they are, only that they're there.

Sensor Range

You are within range to use any Sensor programs loaded when you enter a node but before you overcome any IC guarding it. This allows deckers to cruise up to a node and scope it out before they actually try to enter it.

In Sensor Range, you can tell what kind of node you are in and identify the general nature of constructs that you see: IC, files, and Persona are recognizable. For more information, you'll need to use Analyze.

When an Alert exists on a system, Gray and Black IC may react to Persona that are within Sensor Range.

Contact Range

You can be in Contact Range of anything that is located in the same node as you. All you have to do is decide to move into Contact Range. Most things in the Matrix will sit still, allowing you to decide when to move. Unfortunately, the things that don't sit still are the dangerous ones: other Persona and Gray or Black IC.

Any Utility can be used in Contact Range.

TORTOISES IN THE MATRIX

Not everyone in the Matrix uses a full-blown cyberdeck to do his job. For one thing, decks are expensive. For another, the corps don't hand out Fuchi-7s to every keypuncher and file clerk in the office.

The **Shadowrun** equivalent of an old-fashioned terminal is a keyboard with either a viewing screen or simple sensory electrodes and maybe some antiquated paraphernalia like a mouse or joystick. They have the same basic stats as cyberdecks.

On the positive side, Black IC can't hurt a terminal user. It can only kick him off-line. What's more, terminals cost only one-tenth as much as an equivalent cyberdeck.

Tortoises are penalized in their Hacking Pool and for determining Initiative. Subtract 1D6 from their Reaction (minimum value = 1).

Tortoises reduce all their Program Ratings by 1, to reflect their lack of fine control.

Tortoises have terminals that are locked-in with a rating of 3 in all Persona programs.

NAKED IN THE MATRIX

By now, some of you must be wondering how Dodger got onto Mitsuhama's system without a cyberdeck. The Elf was pulling one of the flashiest and most dangerous stunts in the decker's bag of tricks: going naked into the Matrix. Boys and girls, don't try this at home!

This feat requires a Program Carrier to let you slot Persona chips loaded for Sensor, Masking, and Evasion into a suitable port. You have to jack into a dataport at the same point. To get in, you need an Input/Output Port or Slave Module (see **Nodes And Their Functions**).

"Wait a minute," you say, "what about the Bod program? Where's the MPCP?" Well, chummers, your Willpower is the MPCP when you do this electron dance. Any damage the MPCP would take, you take personally. It's marked off on your Mental Condition Monitor. If you get knocked out, you're dumped. Black IC still kills you, just like always.

You can use headware memory space for downloading data, and you have an I/O rating equal to your Intelligence. Utilities? No, you can't carry those. You have to write all your programs on the fly, using your Hacking Pool.

On the upside, if you have wired reflexes or a vehicle control rig, you do get the dice bonus to your Initiative Roll, but if you run into anything nasty, that may only mean you get to die faster.

CYBERCOMBAT

Cybercombat proceeds in turns and actions, just like combat in the real world, and a turn in cyberspace is the same as a turn in the real world: approximately three seconds. Constructs must be in Contact Range to fight in cybercombat.

INITIATIVE

Multiple actions are determined exactly as in Physical Combat.

Deckers roll 1D6 and add it to their Reaction Attribute. Remember that wired reflexes or a vehicle control rig do not add dice to the Initiative Roll while you are in cyberspace unless you are going naked into the Matrix.

Deckers with Increased Response on their decks add +2 per level of Response to their Reaction Attribute, and roll an extra 1D6 per level for Initiative.

Tortoises on a terminal reduce their Reaction Attribute by 1D6 to a minimum of 1. They still roll 1D6 to get their Initiative result.

IC Reaction Time is based on the node Security Code. The Security Code color gives a basic speed. Add the Security Rating to this for the Reaction. Then make the usual 1D6 roll. Thus, an IC on an Orange-3 node would have a Reaction of 7 (Orange Level) plus 3 (the rating), for a total of 10.

PROGRAM REACTION TIME	
Security Level	**Reaction**
Blue	Not Applicable (no IC)
Green	5 + Rating
Orange	7 + Rating
Red	9 + Rating

ACTIONS IN CYBERSPACE

Following are typical action possibilities in cyberspace.

Execute A Utility. If this is a Combat utility, you attack your target(s). Otherwise, the Utility does whatever it is programmed to do.

Change Range. You may move closer to a construct, or try to get farther away. See **Decker Dogfights** for details.

Jack out! The only time jacking out might not succeed is when you are fighting Black IC.

Load. Load a program from storage to onboard memory. It proceeds at the load speed of your deck. A load in progress applies +2 your Target Numbers.

Download Or Upload A Program. Download or upload from deck storage into the Matrix. This proceeds at the I/O speed of your deck. I/O in progress applies +2 to your Target Numbers.

Erase A Utility From Onboard Memory.

Execute A System Operation. This action occurs only if no IC is operative on the node. (See **Nodes and their Functions.**)

Executing A Combat Utility

A Persona can attack if it has a Combat utility loaded. IC with combat ability always attacks.

Before a Combat utility can be executed, the decker must modify it so that it can "hit" its intended target. This is because Attack utilities work at a level where each Construct or Persona is unique. Therefore, the off-the-shelf Attack-7 program that just wiped out the Black Killer IC protecting the Yakuza's database is not going to work against the Black Killer IC protecting the SAN that you are trying to leave. But it's just that kind of special programming that being a decker is all about. It may drain your Hacking Pool, but making the small changes in the program is not going to take any appreciable time.

Hitting a target requires an Unresisted Success Test. A decker rolls as many dice as he wishes from his Hacking Pool.

(He may *not* use the rating of the Combat utility, as in other cases.) If attacking another Persona, he uses the the other Persona's Evasion Rating as his Target Number. If attacking IC, the Security Rating is the Target Number, and the decker must score enough successes to overcome the Security Code.

Extra successes are added to the Combat program's rating for the Damage Success Test.

The decker can attack multiple targets by allocating Hacking Dice among them. He can use the same program to attack multiple targets.

If IC is attacking, use dice equal to its rating, with the Persona's Evasion Rating as the Target Number. Simple success is all the IC needs. Any extra successes improve its ability to do damage.

"Wounded" Personas suffer penalties according to their status on the MPCP's Program Condition Monitor. If the decker is also wounded, those penalties apply as well. "Wounded" IC also suffer penalties.

Smoke and Mirrors can affect Target Numbers, as described in **Defense Utilities**.

Hitting The Target

If you are successful in hitting the target, the results depend on who or what was hit and what hit them. One way or the other, all damage is determined by a Resisted Success test.

A Hit On A Persona

The attacking program rolls dice equal to its rating, with a Target Number equal to the Bod of the Persona. Any extra successes on this "To-Hit" Roll increase the *rating* of the attacking program. The Persona makes a Resistance Test using the deck's MPCP Rating, with a Target Number equal to the Computer Skill of the attacker, if hit by another persona, or the node Security Rating, if hit by IC.

A decker can augment his results in this test by adding dice from the Hacking Pool, either as attacker or defender. If the defender wins the test, he takes no damage. Otherwise, each of the attacker's extra successes is potential damage.

If the Persona has a Shield program running, it reduces the damage by the Shield Rating. Remember that a Shield program degrades every time it reduces damage.

The Hardening Rating is also subtracted from the potential damage.

Each point of remaining damage fills in one box on the MPCP's Program Condition Monitor. Ten "wounds" crashes the MPCP and dumps the decker.

A Hit On IC

The attacker will always be a Persona because IC does not attack IC. Roll a number of dice equal to the Combat utility's rating. Remember to add one die for every extra success scored in the "To-Hit" Test. The Target Number is the node's Security Rating. The IC makes a Resistance Test based on its rating, with a Target Number equal to the Computer Skill of the attacking decker.

If the IC wins, it is "unwounded." If it loses, the IC suffers a "wound" for every extra success won by its attacker. Fill in one box per wound on the IC Program Condition Monitor. Ten wounds crash it.

Fastjack cursed and spooked left as the IC roared out of the shimmering data maze. Dammit, that was close! He wasn't going to take the time for an Analyze, but the whole place smelled Red and deadly.

Fastjack has triggered Killer-5 IC in a Red-6 node. Jack himself has MPCP 6, Bod 5, Evasion 7, and Hardening 2. His Reaction Attribute is 7, because he is running a Response +1 deck. He has Decking Skill 8.

Jack whipped out Old Betsy. The glowing construct of the humongous Attack-6 blunderbuss flickered into life in his hands. He threw the stock to his shoulder then yelped in dismay as the IC closed in. The son-of-a-glitch was faster than he was!

Fastjack rolled 2D6 for Initiative, scoring 6. His Initiative result is 7 + 6, or 13. On a Red-6 node, the IC has a Reaction Time of 15 + 1D6. Scoring a 3, the IC has an Initiative result of 18. Look out, FJ!

The IC attacks. It rolls 5 dice (its own rating) with a Target Number of 7 (Fastjack's Evasion Attribute). It scores 3 successes on the hit. The IC rolls 8 dice in the damage test: 5 for its rating, and 3 for the successes. Its Target Number is 5 (Jack's Bod Rating).

Jack resists this with 6 dice (his MPCP Rating) and has a Target Number of 6 (Security Rating of the node). He also decides to add 4 dice from his Hacker Pool, for a total of 10 dice.

The IC scores five successes. Jack scores two successes, allowing the IC a potential damage of three "wounds." His Hardening stops two of them, but he takes the third as damage to his MCPC's Program Condition Monitor.

"Drek!" snarled Jack, as sparks blew out of his ears. He took careful aim with Old Betsy. Somewhere, in another world, a wiry figure sat in half-lotus on a dirty cot, cradling a complex keyboard in his lap. In electron reality, Betsy spat a charge of spreading code-shot at the hovering Ice.

Jack's action comes up. His Hacking Pool is usually 15 (Decking Skill plus Reaction), but he's already used 4 dice, so he has only 11. He allocates 5 for an attempt to hit the IC. His Target Number is 6 (the Security Rating of the node) + 1 (Light Wound), and he has to make at least 3 successes to hit (Red Security Level). He rolls 4 successes. The one extra success augments Old Betsy's Attack Rating.

In the Damage Success test, Jack rolls 7 dice (6 for his Attack program Rating +1 for the extra success). His Target Number is 7 (6 for the node rating +1 because his Persona is lightly wounded). The IC rolls 5 dice (its rating) with a Target Number of 8 (Jack's Decker Skill). The IC blows it and gets no successes. Jack scores 4 successes, which Moderately Wounds the IC. It's hurt, but is still going to be a dangerous opponent.

Decker Dogfights

By taking an action, a mobile construct such as a Persona or IC program can try to change range relative to an opponent in Cybercombat. If the opponent wants to prevent that, there is an Opposed Success Test. Personas use their Evasion Attribute, and IC will use its rating for the number of dice rolled. The Target Number for each is the rating used by the other. If Fastjack (Evasion 7) tries to run from the IC (Rating 5), he rolls 7 dice, with a Target Number of 5. The IC rolls 5 dice, with a Target Number of 7. A decker can add dice from his Hacking Pool to this roll.

The winner can move closer by one step, farther away by one step, or leave things as they are. To move out of Sensor Range, a Persona must leave the node. To move out of Observation Range, the Persona must not be in any node adjacent to its opponent.

Gray and Black IC will try to remain in Contact Range with a Persona. If a Persona manages to get out of Observation Range, the IC will return to where it was first encountered. IC always tries to close once it starts fighting. It never runs away.

A decker may pursue a fleeing opponent. Every time the running decker slows down (i.e., gets back into Cybercombat time), roll 2D6. If the die result is greater than or equal to the fleeing Persona's Masking Rating, the pursuing decker has located his prey and will show up in one turn. Of course, this assumes that the pursuer has free run of the system. If not, he can be slowed up by having to make his way through nodes, too. If he is slowed down, the pursuit is cut off.

INTRUSION COUNTERMEASURES (IC)

Intrusion Countermeasures (IC) may be installed in any node with a Security Code of Green or higher. Ice, as it is also known, makes life difficult for deckers. Some Ice tries to make life impossible for deckers. Every IC program has a rating, which is usually its "skill."

There are three classes of IC: White Ice, Gray Ice, and Black Ice. White Ice offers passive resistance. Gray Ice actively attacks intruders or traces their entry point into the Matrix. Black Ice will try to kill deckers. Each is more fully described in the following sections.

WHITE IC

White IC reports or logs system access, blocks illegal access, and encrypts data. White IC is passive. When a Persona comes into Contact Range, the IC detects it. The Persona must use a legitimate passcode to identify himself, or else activate a Utility that can defeat the IC. Things shift into Cybercombat only if the utility fails or the IC is attacked. On its actions, the IC tries to trigger the alert. A decker can try to jam the IC by using dice from his Hacking Pool. He makes an Opposed Success Test with these dice, using the IC's Security Rating as the Target Number. The IC uses its rating for the number of dice rolled and the Persona's Masking rating for its target number. If the IC wins, it triggers the alert. White IC does not fight back against an attacking Persona.

Access, Barrier, and Scramble programs are examples of White Ice.

Access

Access looks like a barrier of shimmering light, made up of billions of tiny alphanumeric characters swirling at ultra-high speed. A decker can defeat Access with Deception or Sleaze or crash it using a Combat Utility. If attacked by Slow, Access cannot issue an alert unless the decker fails to damage it. On its next action, it tries to set off an alarm.

Barrier

Barrier is a solid security lock on a node. It resembles a wall of jagged, pulsing lightning bolts. Barrier can be defeated with Sleaze or killed with a Combat utility. It reacts to Slow in the same way that Access does.

Scramble

Scramble is found in datastores or even on individual files. It resembles a softly glowing light across the entrance to the datastore or wrapped protectively around the file. If a Persona tries to touch the data, the light glows brighter and gives off a humming sound. If it is still present when you read or download a file, the file is garbled junk. Scramble can be defeated by Deception or Decrypt or crashed with Combat utilities. Instead of trying to sound an alert, Scramble will try to destroy the data it is guarding. The Persona can try to jam this program the same way it jams alarms. If attacked by Slow, Scramble reacts like Access.

A Persona can try to download a file protected by Scramble, transferring both the data and the IC into storage. This adds the IC's rating to his target number for operation of that system. Though the downloading file is still protected, the decker can work on it in a more leisurely fashion once he jacks out.

GRAY IC

Gray IC is capable of attacking a Persona. It looks like White Ice and has the same functions but also contains particularly nasty traps. You won't know whether it's White or Gray without successfully scanning it.

All Gray IC requires a trigger of some kind. In other words, once the program sets off an alert the way White IC would, the Gray IC emerges and attacks the Persona. The Gray IC is activated even if the Persona jams the alarm. If the Persona defeats the White IC without using a Combat utility, the Gray IC is also fooled and stays quiet.

Gray IC usually waits for the Persona to reach Contact Range. If the system is in an Alert, the IC closes to Contact Range and demands the passcode as soon as the Persona is in the same node (Sensor Range).

Blaster

Blaster is attack IC, and engages the Persona in Cybercombat, doing normal damage. See **Cybercombat**. If it crashes the Persona, however, the IC tries to damage the deck! The IC makes an Unresisted Success Test, with a Target Number equal to the MPCP Rating of the deck. If the test succeeds, the IC fries the deck, turning it into junk.

Killer

Killer IC attacks the Persona in Cybercombat. See **Hitting the Target** in **Cybercombat** for details. Killer tries to destroy the Persona.

Tar Baby

Tar Baby is a nasty form of trap IC. It resembles White IC, but if attacked or if an attempt to fool it fails, it crashes and takes the Persona's Utility program with it! The crashed utility must be reloaded.

Tar Pit

Tar Pit is similar to Tar Baby, but when it does its trick, it poisons all copies of that Utility in storage. The program cannot be reloaded! The "pits," indeed!

Trace

Trace locks onto the decker's access path and locates his entry point into the Matrix. When it finds the entry point, the trace is completed.

When Trace IC is activated, make a Success Test using its rating for the number of dice and the Persona's Masking Rating for the Target Number. The time IC needs to complete the trace is 10 actions, divided by its successes. If it rolls no successes, it cannot get a lock-on to the decker's access path and must try again on its next action. Note that the clock keeps running even while the decker is fighting Trace or if he runs away from it. It will not pursue him because it doesn't need to.

The Persona can try to kill the Trace before it completes. Like White IC, Trace IC only fights defensively. A decker can also use Relocate, instead of a Combat utility, to try to head it off.

There are three types of Trace, each one nastier than the previous.

Trace and Report: When this Trace completes, it reports to an operator, automatically triggering an external Alert. The trace reports the real-world address or location of the decker's entry point to the system owners. Do you hear someone at the door?

Trace and Dump: This program resembles Trace and Report, but the decker is also automatically dumped if the Trace works.

Trace and Burn: This program resembles Trace and Dump, but the IC also tries to fry the cyberdeck. If the Trace works, the MPCP and the IC make an Opposed Success Test. Each uses its own rating for the number of dice and the other's rating for the Target Number. If the MPCP wins, the decker is dumped, but neither he nor his deck is harmed. If Trace wins, the decker is dumped and the cyberdeck is scrap, its delicate circuits destroyed. Hardening gives the deck its rating in automatic successes for this test.

BLACK IC

Black IC fights just like Killer, but it damages the decker, not his Persona! Black IC is usually programmed to do physical damage, but can be set to do mental damage if the system owner does not want to kill intruders. Dead men tell no tales, but prisoners can be made downright talkative. See **Cybercombat** for details.

Black IC requires a trigger, just like Gray IC. Once triggered, it attacks.

Once Black IC scores a hit on a Persona, the decker has only two options. He may either Hang Tough or Cut and Run. In either case, he may not augment his roll with dice from the Hacking Pool.

Hang Tough

The decker resists damage so he can keep fighting. Brave move, chummer! The IC makes a Resisted Success Test using its rating for the number of dice and the decker's Body Rating for the Target Number. The Decker rolls dice equal to his Body and uses the IC's rating for the Target Number. If the IC wins, it does one Light Wound for each extra success. Hardening on the cyberdeck acts as armor against this damage, and a Shield utility still has no effect.

Cut and Run

The decker tries to jack out. Wise move, chummer! Make an Unresisted Willpower Test, with the IC's rating as the Target Number. The number of successes needed depends on the system security code. If the decker succeeded, he's out of the Matrix and safe. If not, then the IC makes an Unresisted Success Test, using its rating for the number of dice and the decker's Body Rating for the Target Number, *not* the Bod Rating of the Persona! Each success the IC rolls is a Light Wound. The Hardening of the cyberdeck defends as usual against this damage, but a Shield utility has no effect.

ALERTS

IC can set off two kinds of alerts, Internal and External.

Internal Alert

This means that the computer is not sure that it has been invaded, but is going to be careful. All IC increase their ratings by 50 percent (drop fractions). Internal Alerts last for an hour or so at most, because they slow down other processing. If a second Internal Alert is triggered when the system is already on alert, then it triggers an External Alert.

External Alert

This means the computer decides it has been invaded. It notifies its human operators, who will take whatever action the gamemaster thinks appropriate. This usually means sending one or more deckers into the system after the invader.

The controlling operator's only other response to an External Alert is to shut down the computer. He will take this action if it looks like the invader has beaten any defenders sent in after him, or if the alert was triggered from a highly sensitive node like the CPU or a Red datastore. It takes 2D6 turns to shut down without damaging the system. This triggers various alarms in the Matrix as programs wind down and files close safely. The Persona sees flashing red lights and hears klaxons going off. If the Persona is still in the system when it shuts down, he is dumped.

THE OPPOSITION

Hostile deckers come in several grades, none of whom need Deception programs because they have passcodes for all the nodes. (No, chummer, you can't mug one of them in the Matrix and steal the codes.) Use the rules for pursuit in **Decker Dogfights** to see if one of the hostiles finds the invader.

Following are several examples that may help you design your own defending deckers as the rules become more familiar. Keep the odds balanced so the player decker has to sweat, but try to avoid throwing an army (or Godzilla) at him.

Bush League

A Decker Archetype working on a cyberterminal starts hunting around the system, beginning in the node where the alert was triggered. Use the Decker and put him on a cyberterminal version of a Fuchi-4 carrying Attack 4.

Minor League

A Decker Archetype is sent into the system using a Fuchi-4 with Attack 4 and Shield 2. Persona programs are all rated 3.

Major League

Use the Decker Archetype for the hostile, but give him a Fuchi-5 with Level 1 Response Increase. He's carrying Attack 6, Shield 2, and Mirrors 2. His Persona programs are all rated 5.

Heavy Hitter

This is the same as a Major Leaguer, but his Persona programs are all rated 6 and he's got Response Increase 2.

CYBERPROGRAMMING

Writing your own cyberprograms uses Computer Skill. (Software concentration or Matrix Programming specialization are appropriate substitutions). The maximum rating a character can program is equal to his Computer Skill. Programmers need:

A Microtronic tool kit with a rating at least equal to the rating of the program you want to create. See **Equipment**.

A computer. Though a mainframe is ideal, most deckers must make do with personal computers. A personal computer must have enough memory to hold the program. Mainframes always have enough memory.

Chips with enough memory to hold the code for a Persona program. The usual price for these is 20¥ per Megapulse.

Time! The base time to write a cyberprogram is the program size in days. When the character decides to write the program, he makes an Unresisted Success Test using a Character's Computer Skill, with a Target Number equal to the program's rating. Divide the base time by the successes rolled. If there are no successes, it takes twice the base time to write the code. Only one roll is allowed. If the programmer does not like the result, tough luck. The only way he can reroll is by improving his programming skill. He can, of course, use Karma to improve the results of a roll.

When working on a personal computer, apply +2 to the Target Number. For Computer Theory Skill greater than or equal to the program rating, apply a –2.

Programming can be done in stages. A decker can work on a program for ten days, go on an adventure, come back a few weeks later, put in five more days on the program, go spend a week getting some cyberware, come back and work on the program again, and so on. It is the player's job to keep track of the status of all projects his decker is juggling.

You can upgrade programs you have written yourself. Upgrading a program from a 4 rating to a 6 rating is like writing a program with a rating of 2.

Programs you write are not copy-protected, but they're cheap. Commercial software costs big nuyen, but is copy-protected. You cannot make backups of copy-protected codes or give anyone else a copy, either. To defeat copy protection, make an Unresisted Success Test using a character's Computer Skill, with a Target Number equal to the program rating. If you fail, the master copy is wiped out. Go buy another.

With an unprotected program, you can make as many backups as you wish, and can give or sell copies of the program to others.

BUILDING CYBERDECKS

Deckers can build or modify cyberdecks, if they have lots of time. It also takes Computer, Computer Theory, and Computer (B/R) Skills.

First, program the MPCP chip with Computer Skill. This is just like writing a Persona program with a size of 10 x the rating. Maximum rating is still the programmer's skill.

Second, design the rest of the deck. Pick your Hardening (maximum = 5) and the Load and I/O speeds (maximum = 100 Mp/turn). Calculate the Design Points.

If you are adding options such as Response Increase, see the **Cyberdeck** Design Table below and add those Design Points now.

Third, determine the costs. This requires an Unresisted Success Test using Computer Theory, with a Target Number equal to the Design Points divided by 100. The minimum Target Number is 2. The cost of components to build this deck is (1,000¥ x Design Points) divided by the successes. No successes mean you pay full price. To get a reroll, you must either rewrite the MPCP to correct the bugs you obviously programmed into it or else improve your Computer Theory Skill. If you're upgrading an existing deck, use only the Design Points you're adding to the previous total for calculating cost.

Fourth, use Computer (B/R) Skill to build the deck (or substitute Interface Tech of Computer Skill). Once you've purchased the components, that is. You also need access to a microtronic workshop. To find out if you have the ability to assemble the components, make an Unresisted Success Test using Computer Theory, with a Target Number = Design Points÷ 1,000 (Minimum 2). Divide the base time by the successes, and that is how long it will take to build the deck. If upgrading an existing deck, the total Design Points are still the base time, because you are tearing the deck down and rebuilding it.

PROGRAM SIZES

Persona Programs:
- Bod: Size = 10 Mp x Rating
- Evasion: Size = 5 Mp x Rating
- Masking: Size = 5 Mp x Rating
- Sensors: Size = 3 Mp x Rating

Utility Programs:
- Size = Rating x Multiplier
- Multiplier 10 Programs: Attack, Medic, Mirrors, Shield, Slow
- Multiplier 8 Programs: Analyze, Sleaze
- Multiplier 5 Programs: Deception, Evaluate, Relocate
- Multiplier 3 Programs: Browse, Decrypt, Smoke

PROGRAM COSTS

Program Rating	Persona Program	Utility Program
1 – 3	100¥ x Size	50¥ x Size
4 – 6	500¥ x Size	100¥ x Size
7 – 9	1,000¥ x Size	500¥ x Size
10 or more	5,000¥ x Size	1,000¥ x Size

CYBERDECK DESIGN TABLE

Design Formulae

Design Points = MPCP x [Hardening + ((Load Speed + I/O Speed)÷2)]

Cost = (1,000¥ x Design Points) + (Memory x 20¥) + (Storage x 20¥)

Design and Construction Time
- Hardware: (Design Points÷10) x rating in days
- MPCP Programming: 15 x rating in days
- Other Programming: Programming size in days

Options

Response Increase:

Level 1:	+ 25 Design Points
Level 2:	+ 100 Design Points
Level 3:	+ 250 Design Points
Hitcher Jack:	+ 1 design point
Vidscreen Display:	+.5 design point

Standard Hardware is factored into the cost. It includes:

Fiber-optic connector cable terminating in an STJ-400 standard telecommunications jack.

Keyboard.

MPCP motherboard for the Persona program chips.

EQUIPMENT

"When you cut someone nowadays, you don't know if they'll bleed or leak hydraulic fluid."
—Evil Eye, Tiger Gang Member

fine selection of items from the Grid-catalogues, fixer shops, and talismonger haunts of 2050.

PERSONAL WEAPONRY

Katana: The two-handed "samurai" sword is favored by Yakuza with a taste for the romantic and old-fashioned. 1,000¥

Knife: Your basic all-purpose street cutter. 30¥

Monofilament Whip: A monomolecular cord, it is swung with a weight at the end for control. It is extremely sharp and will cut through just about anything. If the user misses an attack, he must pass an immediate Skill Test with a Target Number of 8 or be attacked by his own weapon. 3,000¥

Polearm: You are not likely to encounter such a weapon. It is included to give you an idea of weapon types. 500¥

Staff: This is popular with magicians, for that traditionalist look. 50¥

Stun Baton: The standard riot-control weapon, this weapon delivers an electrical charge. The baton needs only to touch a victim to cause five turns of disorientation (+2 for all Target Numbers). The victim makes a Body Resistance Test, reducing the duration by one turn for each success. 750¥

Sword: This refers to any of a variety of ceremonial styles and also covers some of the longer and more vicious knives. 500¥

IMPACT PROJECTILE WEAPONS

Bow: This can be either a traditional longbow of fiberglass or wood or a modern compound and pulley bow. 300¥ (plus 100¥ per 10 arrows)

Crossbow: These come in three grades. Lights are cocked by hand, while the heavier models use a built-in, side-wheel gear to assist recocking. 300¥ for Light, 400¥ for Medium, 500¥ for Heavy (plus 100¥ per 20 bolts)

Throwing Knife: Any of a variety of slim knives or spikes. 20¥

Shuriken: A multi-edged or spiked airfoil throwing blade. 20¥

FIREARMS

Firearms are primarily slug throwers. The principles have not changed much over the years. Many weapons offer two versions, for standard loads or for caseless ammunition, though the latter is far more common in 2050. In either case, a digital ammunition counter is standard. The readout usually appears on the rear sight, where the user can see it when he is firing.

Most guns use an ammunition clip, which holds many bullets. Changing clips takes only one action. Other guns offer a variety of reload methods, including break action, in which the user inserts bullets into the barrel by hand; cylinders, like in revolvers, where part of the weapon opens to accept bullets into a rotating carrier; and internal magazines, where the gun has a port to accept individual bullets. All of these types have slower reload speeds. A character may insert a number of rounds equal to his Quickness in one action. Weapons capable of firing on full automatic often have belts of ammunition, eliminating the need for reloading in a short firefight.

Shotguns are area-effect weapons, with a Power Level reduction rate of –2 per meter. Only targets directly to the left and right of the target are affected.

Pistols

Unless otherwise noted, pistols may not use autofire.

Streetline Special: This is a common hold-out pistol found among the lowest level of society. Made of composite materials, it is small, lightweight, and extremely concealable. 100¥

Walther Palm Pistol: This European hold-out design packs one large caliber round in each of its over-under barrels. A select switch allows the user to fire both barrels simultaneously. 200¥

Colt America L36: This light American design is very popular among the style-conscious because of its sleek profile, which also makes it easy to hide. 350¥

Beretta Model 101T: This slim-line light personal weapon is favored by corporate personnel worldwide. 350¥

Fichetti Security 500: Designed for light security work, the Fichetti 500 accepts a full range of pistol accessories. Mint models come with the standard 10-round clip, as well as an extended 22-round optional and a detachable shoulder stock. 400¥

Ares Predator: Considered by many the premier heavy pistol, the Predator is a menacing weapon very popular among mercenaries and security services. 450¥

Browning Max-Power: This is the primary contender against the Ares Predator as the toughest heavy pistol. 450¥

Ruger Super Warhawk: This heavy revolver accepts all standard accessories except, of course, a silencer. 300¥

Remington Roomsweeper: The Roomsweeper heavy shotgun is popular with the urban fighter for its high take-down capability and significant intimidation factor. 500¥

Ares Viper: This pistol fires flechette ammunition (already factored into its Damage Code). The silvergun has the range of a heavy pistol even though it is really a light pistol. The Viper features a built-in silencer. 600¥

Rifles

All assault rifles are capable of autofire. Other rifles are semi-automatic.

FN HAR: This assault rifle is common in Europe and increasingly popular with corporate response teams and private security forces specializing in high-threat areas. It comes with integral folding stock, laser sight, and gas-vent recoil compensator (Rating 2). 1,200¥

AK-97: Originally a Soviet weapon, this assault rifle is now found worldwide. The SMG Carbine form, with its integral folding stock, is almost as common. Mounting a grenade launcher on either model is extremely difficult, though the AK-98 features an integral mini-grenade launcher. 700¥ for AK-97, 800¥ for Carbine, 2,500¥ for AK-98

Remington 750: Long and sleek, the 750 sport rifle and its heavy-duty sister, the 950, have been the choice of hunters for nearly 50 years. Both use a smooth bolt-operated action of supreme reliability. A top-mount magnifying scope (Rating 1) is standard with either model. No under-barrel mounting is present. 600¥ for 750, 800¥ for 950

Ranger Arms SM-3: The SM-3 is a must for those jobs when the first shot has to count. Silencer, and imaging scope magnification (Rating 3) and thermographic or low-light circuits are standard equipment. Like most of its breed, it disassembles completely for fit in a standard briefcase. Ideal for the assassin on the go. 4,000¥

Enfield AS7: This assault shotgun provides massive firepower. It has integral laser sight and is fitted with a 10-shot clip or 50-shot drum (–3 to concealability, +2 to weight). 1,000¥

Defiance T-250: A popular autoloading shotgun available in full size and short barrel (use heavy pistol ranges) versions. It has no under-barrel mount. 500¥

Sub Machine Guns (SMGs)

All Sub Machine Guns are capable of autofire.

Uzi III: This is a worthy descendent of the famous Israeli Uzi. The Fabrique Nationale model, officially manufactured for the French government, is one of the commoner street weapons. It features an integral folding stock and laser sight. The very similar Ingram Mk. 22 omits the laser sight. 600¥

Heckler & Koch HK227: This is the SMG of choice with many corporate security, military police, and base security units worldwide. The standard model boasts a retractable stock, integral laser sights, and a gas-vent recoil (Rating 2). The S variant, popular with corp strike teams and special forces, substitutes an integral silencer for the recoil system. 1,500¥ (1,200¥ for S variant)

Light Machine Guns

All Light Machine Guns are capable of autofire.

Ingram Valiant: Popular with merc units around the world, this is the commonest model of light machine gun. Models like the Ares Light Machine Gun and Ingram Valiant have a hip-brace recoil pad (Rating 1) and an ammunition bin slung over the back or hip to feed belted ammo to the weapon. Smart goggles and a gas-vent recoil system (Rating 2) are standard equipment on these popular models. 1,500¥

FIREARM ACCESSORIES

Pistols and SMGs accept only accessories that mount on the top or barrel of the weapon.

Concealable Holster: Custom fitted to the wearer, the holster may be made to wear over the hip, in the small of the back, under the arm, on the forearm, or on the ankle. (Concealed weapons require a perception test to spot. The Concealability Rating is the Target Number.) 100¥

Grenade Launcher: Actually a weapon in its own right, though rarely used in modern forces except as an under-barrel addition to an assault rifle, the launcher fires a round from its integral magazine with either a thumb-press button or a separate trigger. These weapons fire mini-grenades. 1,700¥

Laser Sights: This device projects a laser beam to produce a glowing red spot on the target point. The sight activates when the user touches the trigger. Such sights may not be used with smart guns or goggles. 500¥

Imaging Scopes: A variety of imaging scopes are available, including low-light, infrared, and simple magnification. Scopes may not be used with smart guns or goggles. 1,500¥ for low-light or thermographic, 500¥ for Rating 1 magnification, 800¥ for Rating 2 magnification, 1,200¥ for Rating 3 magnification

Recoil Compensators: There are several ways to compensate for the recoil of autofire. The character can mount Shock Pads (Rating 1) on either the shoulder or hip. Gas-Vent Systems (Rating 2 or 3) fit onto the weapon's barrel. A Gyro-Stabilized Mount is a rigid harness, with a 1/1 Armor Rating, that supports a free-swinging, articulated arm projecting from one side of the harness. Standard military gyro-stabilized mounts include smart goggles with a reinforced cable. Smartguns may, of course, feed into standard palm induction links. A gyro-stabilized mount also reduces firing penalties for the user's movement. 200¥ for shock pads, 450¥ for a Rating 2 gas-vent system, 700¥ for Rating 3, 2,500¥ for a gyro-stabilized mount, 6,000¥ for the deluxe model

Silencers: A silencer is a sound and flash suppressor mounted on the front of a weapon's barrel. Its use precludes any other barrel-mount accessories. Of course, no suppressor will truly silence a weapon, merely reducing the distance at which it can be heard. Only automatic and semi-automatic weapons can use sound suppressors (any weapon with a cylinder reload system cannot be silenced). 500¥

Smart Goggles: This is a pair of oversized goggles that connect by fiber-optic cable to a weapon rigged as a smartgun. The chips in the gun feed the receptors in the goggles, producing a red crosshair in the user's field of vision centered on where the gun is pointing. The gun's ammo status appears in the user's field of vision as well. This system may be built into a helmet or, for enough nuyen, rigged as mirror shades. In addition to simple targeting, goggles may be set up for low-light or infrared reception. 3,000¥

Smartgun Adapter: This adapter is a retrofit version of the standard smartgun hardware. The system provides a feedback circuit relating the gun's angle of fire to the shooter's line of sight. Without a receptor (datajack, smart goggles, or smartgun link), the hardware is simply dead weight. Cost: 1.5 x cost of gun. Built-in smartgun hardware makes the gun cost double its normal price.

TASER WEAPONS

Police and security units favor these electroshock weapons in low-threat environments. The standard model fires a dart that trails a 10-meter wire. An electric charge surges down the wire to incapacitate the target as long as the current flows. The Victim makes a Body Resistance Test with a Target Number of 10 to avoid the effect. After the current stops, it takes the victim some time (10 – Body Rating in turns) to recover from the muscular convulsions. A variant on these weapons fires darts that contain high-capacitance batteries. The darts discharge on contact, stunning the target, effectively paralyzing him for 2D6 turns. The victim makes a Body Resistance Test with a Target Number of 6, and each success reduces the number of turns of paralysis.

Defiance Super Shock: The most popular taser weapon in service with UCAS law enforcement agencies, the SS packs side-by-side heavy darts. Standard issue pistols have integral low-light imaging scopes.

AMMUNITION

In **Shadowrun**, each kind of gun can trade ammo with another of its kind. Thus, all light pistols share ammo. Use the categories on the Range Chart. Shotgun weapons, whether pistol or rifle, can share ammo.

Explosive rounds: Very tiny versions of grenades, this type of ammunition comes with standard military weapons. Unpopular with the troops because of the disastrous results of a weapon malfunction or misfire (a fumble roll can blow up all remaining ammo in the weapon), these rounds remain in wide use, both civilian and military. Exposure to intense heat such as flames or fireballs can also cook the touchy things.

Flechette rounds: Tiny, tightly-packed slivers function as the business end of a Flechette round. They are devastating against unprotected targets, and will cut through standard ballistic protection (Ballistic Armor Rating is halved). Impact armor, however, can easily stand up to this ammunition (double Impact Armor Rating against these rounds). Use the highest of the two modified ratings.

Gel rounds: Designed as a non-lethal round for riot control, these rounds use a hard jelly-like substance to achieve their effect. Impact armor is very effective (double Rating), and ballistic armor has normal effect.

Stun rounds: Also designed for riot control, these rounds work only in large-bore weapons such as shotguns. Impact armor is effective, but ballistic armor is useless against the relatively high mass and low speed of these rounds.

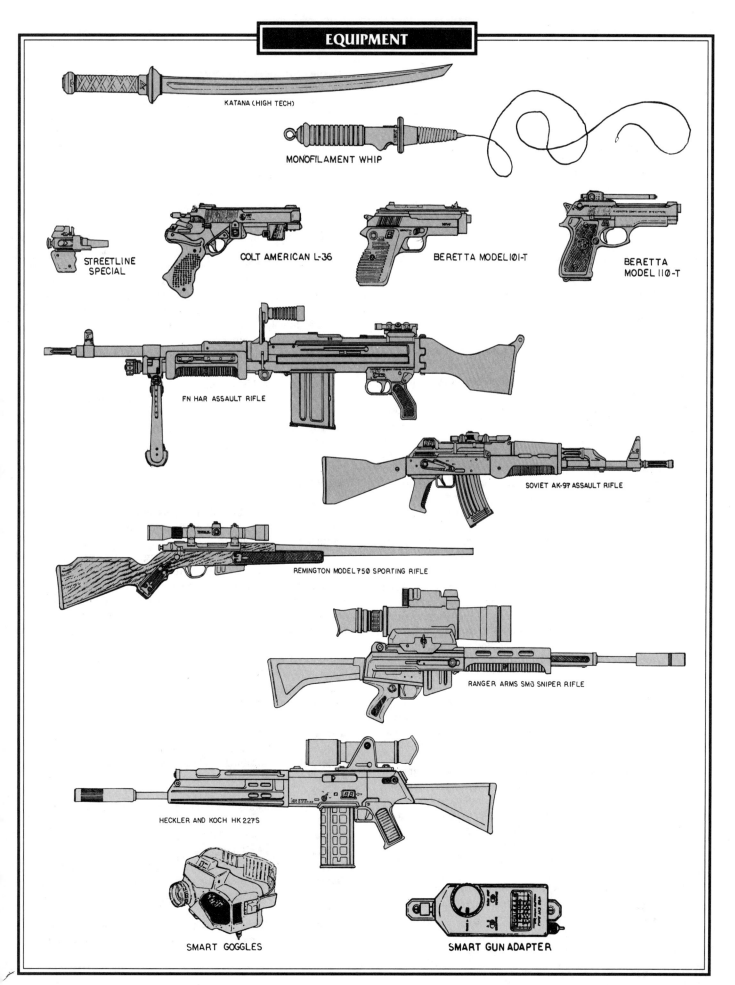

KATANA (HIGH TECH)

MONOFILAMENT WHIP

STREETLINE SPECIAL

COLT AMERICAN L-36

BERETTA MODEL 101-T

BERETTA MODEL 110-T

FN HAR ASSAULT RIFLE

SOVIET AK-97 ASSAULT RIFLE

REMINGTON MODEL 750 SPORTING RIFLE

RANGER ARMS SM3 SNIPER RIFLE

HECKLER AND KOCH HK 227S

SMART GOGGLES

SMART GUN ADAPTER

EXPLOSIVES

Hand Grenades: Grenades are small, self-contained packages of explosive, timer, and detonator. They may be set to explode on impact, or at any time from 2 seconds to 2 minutes. Non-aerodynamic models often offer a "booby-trap" setting that detonates by electric signal or pressure release. These models are shaped as spheres or cylinders. Aerodynamic models are rings or disks with superior range capabilities. Explosive grenades come in three types. Defensive grenades have the highest fragmentation effect. Offensive grenades have a smaller circle of destruction, allowing the character to use the grenade as he presses forward. Concussion grenades are intended to have little fragmentation effect at all, relying on blast to stun or injure targets.

Besides explosive types, grenades may also deliver stun gas, smoke, and other chemical and biochemical agents. Such weapons are almost exclusively found in cylindrical, non-aerodynamic forms.

Mini-grenades: Mini-grenades are bullet-like projectiles designed for grenade launchers. They come only with explosive loads and work like hand grenades. They cannot be armed and thrown.

Plastic Explosives: Highly stable, moldable, and slightly sticky, these substances are ideal for certain demolition jobs, such as blowing a hole in a wall. Compounds are usually color-tinted to indicate the level of current needed to detonate them, from the black of magnetic field induction to the chalky white of 440 volt industrial explosive. Each kilogram of explosive used affects an area one meter in diameter. It takes one minute per kilogram of explosive used to prepare the charge. Once the plastic explosives are detonated, a player should make a Resisted Demolition Skill Success Test, using a Target Number of 4. The Barrier Rating of the object being attacked is used for the Resistance Test, with the explosive's rating used as the Target Number. Each extra success reduces the Barrier Rating in the affected area by 1. If the barrier rating is reduced to 0, then there is a hole with the appropriate diameter. All explosives have a Damage Code of 6D3, and are handled like grenades with a reduction in Power Level of –1 per meter.

HEAVY WEAPONS

Heavy weapon Damage Codes are rated on the vehicle scale. If a character is hit by one, double the Power Level and Staging Number, and increase the Wound Category by 1 step.

Machine Guns: These autofire weapons come in two grades, medium and heavy. They normally use belt ammo feeds. Though usually mounted on tripods or pintles or built into vehicles, medium machine guns are occasionally used on gyro-stabilized mounts as mobile infantry support weapons. These weapons double the normal recoil penalties. 2,500¥ for Medium Machine Gun, 4,000¥ for Heavy Machine Gun.

Assault Cannon: This massive weapon fires shells equivalent to explosive bullets, but without the inherent instability. The shells also have limited armor-piercing capability, making the weapon useful in a wide range of applications. It can use belted ammo. 6,500¥

Missile Launchers: The variety of missile and rocket launchers of the previous century have given way to increased emphasis on flexible delivery systems and elimination of the back-blast problems so common in early systems. The typical launcher is reusable and breaks open to load up to four missiles. Its sighting mechanism, shoulder brace, and exhaust tube are foldable, making it a compact bundle when disassembled.

The missiles themselves have gotten smaller and smarter, each now having its own targeting capabilities. Add the missile's Intelligence Rating to the user's Skill Rating for determining the hit. Heavier missiles and launchers exist, of course, but they are rare in the shadows of the city streets. 8,000¥ (1,000¥ per missile)

Anti-Vehicle Missiles pierce a vehicle's armor, and they do not explode if they miss. The missile must lock on to use its bonus. Make an Unresisted Success Test, using the Missile's Intelligence Rating with the vehicle's Signature Rating as the Target Number.

Anti-Personnel Missiles have high explosive and fragmentation warheads. Their Damage Code is not on the vehicle scale. If it misses, the missile lands 3D6 x 5 meters away from its target. Use the **Grenade Scatter** diagram to find where. The burst radius is 5 meters.

High-Explosive Missiles cause general destruction. Misses scatter the same way as Anti-Personnel Missiles. The burst radius is 10 meters.

ARMOR

Besides the armor built into your hide (dermal armor or plating), you can also wear body armor. The two types are cumulative in their effects.

Dermal armor works against anything, adding to your Body Attribute Rating when you try to resist damage.

External armor works differently. It has two ratings: ballistic and impact. No matter how many pieces of armor you wear, you only get to use the highest Rating, which counts as automatic success on Resistance Tests.

Ballistic armor protects against projectiles delivering large amounts of kinetic energy in short amounts of time, mostly bullets. Impact armor protects against projectiles with lesser kinetic transfer: projectile weapons, hand-held weapons, fists, and stun ammunition.

Armor Clothing: The prime choice for an everyday stroll along the streets of 2050. Fashion designers worldwide offer a variety of styles in fabrics made of descendants of kevlar. 500¥

Armor Jacket: Available in a wide selection of tailoring, from chic street styling to the harsh ribbed and padded esthetic of macho militarism, jackets offer substantial protection. 900¥

Armor Vest: The vest provides slimline protection under normal clothing. Additional rigid plates provide improved protection at the expense of subtlety. 200¥ or 600¥ with plates

Helmet: Most corporations provide distinctive headgear for their security personnel. An exception to the basic rule, a helmet does add its rating to other exterior armor. 200¥

Heavy Armors: These are obvious armors, often styled for intimidation as much as for effective protection and ease of movement. They include helmets. Partial suits use rigid plates on the torso and head and occasionally elsewhere. These plates may be integral to an undersuit or attached separately. Full suits use heavier undersuits and more extensive plating. They often offer environmental sealing with minimal preparation. 20,000¥ for full suit, 10,000¥ for partial

Lined Coat: With a variety of styles, the lined coat is a popular form of armor. Its appearance is reminiscent of the long dusters worn in the days of the wild west. It uses rigid plates concealed between layers of ballistic cloth to cover vital organs. 700¥

SURVEILLANCE AND SECURITY

VISION ENHANCERS

Binoculars: These flat, compact digital imagers produce high resolution up to 50x magnification. Optical glass variants are available for magicians. Enhanced models can operate in low-light or function on thermographic principles. 100¥ for magnification, 300¥ for low-light, 350¥ for thermographic

Goggles: Strap-on models or helmet visors allow low-light or thermographic vision. 1,500¥ for magnification, 2,000¥ for low-light, 2,200¥ for thermographic

COMMUNICATIONS

Kleen-tac™ backing makes these items attachable almost anywhere.

Micro-transceiver: This flat 2cm disk transmits on a preselected radio frequency with a range of 5 kilometers. 2,500¥

Micro-recorder: This small (3x3x1.5cm) case can record up to 6 hours. It may be set to voice-activation to increase effective recording time. 1,000¥

Micro-camcorder: The case (3x5x2cm) comes with a three-hour vid cartridge. It may be set to activate with motion. The recording's image carries time indicators from its internal clock. 2,500¥

SURVEILLANCE MEASURES

Surveillance measures and countermeasures oppose each other. Each uses its rating as its "skill" and the other's rating as its Target Number.

Data Codebreaker: This sophisticated device, the size of a briefcase, unscrambles the encryption on a data pulse. It can receive transmissions from dataline taps or accept standard recordings. 10,000¥ times its rating

Dataline Tap: Spliced into a dataline, the tap will transmit a copy of any data to a distant receiver. To avoid detection, many devices are set to conduct burst data transmissions at irregular intervals. 5,000¥

Laser Microphone: This device bounces a beam against a solid object, reading the vibrational variations of the surface and translating them into the sounds that are occurring on the other side of the surface. 1,500¥ times its rating

Shotgun Microphone: This directional microphone (30x8cm polyfoam-protected cone attached to a pistol grip) allows the user to listen in on distant conversations. Solid objects

block reception, as do loud sounds outside of the line of eavesdropping. 1,000¥ times its rating

Signal Locater: This comes in a hard plastic case with a map screen in its lid. Using a detachable sensor, it triangulates on a set tracking signal, displaying its location on its map. The device can also sweep the transmission bands for other tracking signals. 1,000¥

Tracking Signal: This is a homing signal transmitter (4cm diameter disk) with Kleen-tac™ backing. The typical transmission range is 5 kilometers in cities. Smaller versions have correspondingly smaller ranges. The criminal justice system uses a special ankle band sealed on the leg of a criminal to broadcast his location at all times. 100¥ per point of Concealability Rating.

Voice Identifier: This system is designed to defeat voice mask devices. It analyzes the masked voice, offering a variety of possible voices, one of which should be a recognizable version of the original voice. 2,000¥ times its rating

SURVEILLANCE COUNTERMEASURES

Bug Scanner: This hand-held device scans for the micro-induction field created by micro transceivers and other monitoring devices. The scanner will not detect bugs unless they are transmitting. The case's holographic screen displays a directional arrow pointing to the bug. 500¥ times its rating

Data Encryption System: Placed in-line with any fiber-optic transmission device, this system will encrypt the signal so that it can be unscrambled only by a receiver with the proper decode sequence. The keypad on this device allows selection of random or pre-arranged codings. 1,000¥ times its rating

Dataline Scanner: When in-line with a system, this device emits a pulse, measures its return and analyzes the echo to detect the presence of dataline taps, even those that are inactive. The scanner cannot determine the location of the tap. 100¥ times its rating

Jammer: This transmitter overrides broadcast signals, scrambling them by filling the band with garbage. 1,000¥ times its rating

Voice Mask: This small disk (3cm diameter), when worn or held near the throat, creates a resonating frequency to distort the timber and pitch of the user's voice. 3,000¥

White Noise Generator: This device creates a field of random noise, masking the sounds within its area. It is designed to defeat eavesdroppers and long-range microphones. 1,500¥ times its Rating

SECURITY DEVICES

High-Intensity Veracity Examiner: This state-of-the-art device measures voice stress, pulse rate, and minute contractions and expansions in the subject's corneal blood vessels while the operator leads the subject through a series of questions. The machine cross-references the responses and measures the subject's physical reactions and computes a probability of deception. The subject must wear a special glove and rest his chin against a folding frame that supports the eye scanner. The examiner and its peripherals fit in a high-impact carrying case. 50,000¥

Identification Scanners: A variety of devices contain readers (pads for thumbprints and palmprints; eyecup pads for retinal scans) and library files of recording patterns. Most record the patterns of any attempts to use the scanner. ID scanners are often incorporated into locks, opening only to authorized patterns. 200¥ for thumbprint scanner, 300¥ for palmprint scanner, 1,000¥ for retinal scanner

Maglocks: Household and commercial security rely almost exclusively on maglocks, computer-controlled systems operable only by the proper passcode, keycard, or credstick. Usually, the only visible component of these locks is the slot or slot-keypad mount. In high security areas, a thumbpad or retinal scanner may also be present. Maglocks may be linked to the PANICBUTTON™ system to signal an alarm if the lock is tampered with. 100¥ times its rating

Maglock Passkeys: These sophisticated electronic devices fool a maglock into opening. Use of such systems often leave the lock scrambled or sluggish in response, providing a warning that the lock has been violated. 50,000¥

Restraints: Besides the usual metal models, high-tech plastic strips may be heat-fused to a subject's wrists or ankles, remaining in place until cut free. Such restraints can be painful if the wearer resists their constraints. 50¥ for metal, 20¥ for plastic

Squealer: Formally known as a location forbidder, this small box is strapped to the wrist or ankle by corporate employees or visitors. When the wearer approaches within a specified distance of a restricted area, the box emits a polite warning. At a closer distance, the device transmits a call to security and activates a siren to alert guards in the area. 100¥

SURVIVAL GEAR

Chemsuit: This slick, impermeable garment usually consists of booted coveralls, a hooded poncho, and mittens. The hood is often transparent, at least in the face area, and fitted with an air filter. Designer versions are popular in the UCAS and other industrialized areas for the miserable "hard rain" days. 1,000¥

Respirator: This is a small oxygen cylinder (20x10cm) connected by a plastic hose to a full or partial face mask. It provides enough air for several hours of moderate exertion. A pressure regulator allows the wearer to use the respirator under water. 500¥ for respirator, 250¥ additional for pressure regulator

Survival Kit: This rugged bag contains a useful assortment of stuff: flares, small utility knife, lighter, matches, compass, lightweight thermal blanket, several days worth of ration bars, a water-purification unit, a filter mask, and other items. 100¥

WORKING GEAR

Build/Repair skills need tools to do the job. Tools in **Shadowrun** come in kits, shops, and facilities.

A kit is portable and contains the basic stuff to make repairs. Items with Moderate Damage may be repaired with a kit.

A shop is transportable if you have a truck or two. You need it for repairing anything with Serious Damage or to build something from off-the-shelf parts.

A facility is immobile because of all the bulky, heavy machines involved. You need one to repair Deadly Damage to a device or to build something from scratch.

The prices are variable, depending on the type of tools. The base cost is 500¥ for a kit, 5,000¥ for a shop, and 100,000¥ for a facility.

General construction uses basic tools, which have the base cost. Electronic, computer, and cyberware repairs require microtronics tools, which cost triple the base figures.

Vehicle tools cost double the base figures.

LIFESTYLE

ENTERTAINMENT

Music: Recorded music comes in two basic forms, laser-read compact disks (CD) and optical-chip hardboxes (HB). Both formats record to a fidelity far beyond the average person's discrimination. Playback units are little larger than the storage disk, fitting comfortably in the hand or clipping to a belt. Extra speakers can achieve a "total dimension of sound." Headsets or mastoid-implant speakers are available for private listening. Units with roll-out screens are available for disks with video tracks.

Video: Video recording systems long ago switched to digital information storage and crystal liquid screens. Most recorders function in the pseudo-holographic format popularly known as trideo, or trid. Despite technical advances, high-quality holograms in open air still elude technicians. Even those produced under controlled conditions lack proper texture and animation. Trid screens range from tiny 30mm diagonal ordinary wrist-phone displays to wall-sized arrays. Screens capable of displaying recorded imagery have the usual image speed and quality controls, as well as simple special effects distortion and color alteration capability. Recorders are pistol-sized, with a rotating cylinder of six disks, each with a six-hour capacity. Shoulder stocks and gyro-stabilized units are standard. Transmission units may be built in, increasing the size of the unit, or plugged in and worn on the back or belt. Transmission may either be by cable directly linked into the net or by broadcast or laser link to a receiver, which then transfers the signal into the net.

Simsense: Simulated sensory impressions are the latest fashion in entertainment. Developed from the early ASIST (Artificial Sensory Induction Systems Technology), the system deceives the user by inducing false sensory signals in the brain with a lightweight headset unit. The user, despite the imperfect simulation and the undercurrent of sensory impressions from the real world around him, experiences a programmed set of stimuli while neural overrides prevent him from injuring himself or others during playback. Most users prefer programs that are "hosted" by a specific simstar who actually has the sensations that have been recorded, allowing the user a true vicarious experience. Many simstars have cults of fans devoted to them and emulating their every move. The simsense headset is connected by fiber optics to a player unit. A unit may be set up for direct feed into a datajack. Portable simsense recorders are available to the public, but they lack the clarity and editing capability of professional equipment.

Live Performance: Live performances continue to be popular in 2050. Performers, both actors and singers, often have implanted voice amplifiers, either simple volume enhancers or sophisticated transmitting microphones that broadcast to speakers situated around the hall. Such equipment often features voice modifiers and sound-effects generators. The basic shape and style of musical instruments has changed little, but there has been a proliferation in the types that come in electronic versions. Few, if any, pop performers use anything other than synthesized sound. Highly technical musicians work with a synthlink, a special system that operates through a datajack to allow the user to control his instrument cybernetically for greater complexity and subtlety of sound than is otherwise possible.

Networks: Corporate-owned and viewer-supported networks still make up the bulk of transmitted trideo in 2050. Though the term "broadcasting" remains in use, all transmissions are digitized and travel over fiber-optic cables to individual subscribers.

ELECTRONICS

The personal electronics industry, even separating out the enormous computer and cyber subsectors, is one of the major growth sectors of the world economy in 2050. Samples are ubiquitous, and advertising invasive. Everywhere the citizen is bombarded with catch phrases and taglines—compact, flexible, advanced, stylish, tailored. All are buzzwords used to describe the wonders of 21st century technology.

Credstick: A credstick is a combination passport, keyring, credit card, checkbook, and business card. It is a small plastic cylinder tapering to a point. The blunt end houses a computer. The chip in the credstick contains the owner's System Identification Number, his credit balance, financial records, and resumé, as well as passcodes for the owner's locks. When used to conduct transactions or access the owner's records or property, the credstick transmits identification data from a simple ID number (normal) to a thumbprint (gold chips) to a retinal pattern (platinum chips), to the bank or lock. The transmission must match the data on file, and the user must confirm by typing the ID number, thumbing a pad, or submitting to a retinal scan, as appropriate. Once the user is confirmed as the owner of the credstick, the transaction is approved or the lock opened. Credsticks record transactions not already in the financial computer network, but they must be periodically connected to the network to validate such transactions. Failure to do so results in invalidation of all non-network transactions and cancellation of the credstick's financial function. Limited-use credsticks carry a specified credit limit, much like a certified check. Ownership of a certified credstick may be transferred at any computer station.

Telecom: The telecom is the entertainment and communication center of the modern home. It also provides a work station for a home office or the telecommuting corporate worker. The typical telecom functions as a telephone with audio-video reception and transmission (speaker phone is the normal mode, but handsets and headsets, with or without connecting fibers, are available), a computer with display screen, and keyboard (advanced models have datajacks and interface hardware), and a television (the most advanced models feature simsense ports). The exact services accessible through the telecom depend on what the owner subscribes to. Subscription services include the usual entertainment, sales, news, dating, sports, and literary channels; magazine and news services, with printouts available through the computer printer; public data access; phone services on local or long-distance nets; and secretarial services.

Portable Phones: Portable phones range from the common wrist models, with or without flip-up view screen, to "walkie-talkie" handset units, to audio-only earplug models with lightweight boom microphones. Range is limited, but a booster pack may be worn on the belt or placed on any convenient surface or part of the user's clothes. Portable phones without a fiber link-up are subject to electromagnetic distortions and jamming.

Pocket Secretary: The pocket secretary is an office for the businessman on the go. The compact unit functions as a portable phone, a computer (100 Mp), and filing system. Standard software performs call screening, answering-machine functions, automatic teleconfirmation of credit transactions, word processing with standard letters on file and stenographer functions. Pocket secretaries are never equipped for jacking into the Matrix. Cases are shock- and water-resistant for durability and long service.

Personal Computers: The standard personal computer of 2050 is the size of a keyboard. It has a roll-out monitor. A digital radio signal transmits input and output to peripherals. Program and data cartridges are the size of a standard credstick and slot into the ends of the keyboard. Internal program storage is more than sufficient for common programs such as word and data processors, communications software, and games, and the storage is non-volatile (stored indefinitely). Disposable printers for single-color printing come attached to containers of paper, barely increasing the size. Full-color printers add two centimeters to the height of the paper box. Smaller computers exist, usually designed for a particular function. These accept a limited range of spoken commands, and they output data in a synthesized voice. They may be fiber-linked to a monitor. Internal storage capacity is limited, and they do not accept standard program or data cartridges. Some models have miniature keyboards, usable with a stylus, or accept links to standard keyboards.

Data Display Systems: Typical data units have fold-up monitors and will accept on-line input or standard chip cartridges, allowing them to function as a computer's display screen, a television, a video player, or a simple data reader. For people who work with their hands, there are headset units that project data in "heads-up" display on a surface such as a transparent face shield, the lens of a pair of glasses, or a monocle. A headset unit usually only has one slot to accept standard data cartridges (1,000 Mp). Helmets of government and corporate military forces often have headset display units, allowing soldiers to access maps and other important tactical data without disrupting their regular functions.

CYBERWARE

In 2050, they can rebuild you, make you better. Well, at least more efficient. All Cyberware eats away at the very essence of life, replacing meat with machine. This has its consequences. Magicians are well aware of the price they pay for Cyberware. Those who are not magically active pay as well.

Each item of Cyberware has a Cyber Rating. This is the reduction of the character's Essence Rating that occurs when the Cyberware is implanted. If a character's Essence is ever reduced below zero, his life force ebbs and he will die in short order. Even a zero Essence is tough, promoting despair and melancholy. Low Essence folks walk the edge of sanity.

HEADWARE

This hardware, small and complex, requires the replacement of sections of the cranium with plastic plates of artificial bone. There is no loss of skull strength.

Communications

Chipjack: A specialized form of datajack that allows access to a data skillsoft, or memory chip. 1,000¥

Datajack: The almost universal mark of the cyber-conscious user, standard datajacks allow both input and output. 1,000¥

Radio: This headware allows full-band, limited-range communications. The signal quality is rarely as good as a telephone, but the ability to switch bands makes the system more popular with the military or any user expecting active jamming. When transmitting, the user must speak, though it may be in tones inaudible to those nearby. For the cost- or health-conscious, receiver-only models are available. 4,000¥ for two-way radio, 2,000¥ for receiver.

Synthlink: This specialized datajack linked to control systems is a musician's tool, allowing cybernetic use of music synthesizers. 1,000¥

Telephone: A real head phone allows you to access the telenet from your head. Like all mobile phones, the quality of the link is unsuitable for a decking connection. The user may speak normally or, with the pressure on a sub-dermal switch, speak under his breath. 3,700¥

Ears

Cyber replacement of the ears typically features an obvious prosthesis that has perfect hearing within normal ranges. The Cyberear will also accept a minor additional adjustment (one feature of .2 cyber rating or less) without additional impact on the user's system. 4,000¥ for replacement, 2,000¥ for modification

Cosmetic modification: There is an endless variety of shapes and sizes. By far the most popular is the pointing and or extension for metahuman wannabees. 1,000¥

Damper: This modification protects the user from sudden increases in sound level as well as providing partial protection from damaging frequencies. 3,500¥

High Frequency: The user can hear sounds of higher pitch than the normal human hearing range. 3,000¥

Low Frequency: The user can hear sounds of lower pitch than the normal human hearing range. 3,000¥

Recorder: The user can record anything he hears. He can play back recordings inside his head. If linked to a standard datajack, he can play them back through a speaker. 7,000¥

Eyes

Cyber replacement of normal eyes offers 20/20 vision as standard and almost always involves both eyes, as mismatched pairs send imbalanced signals to the brain. The outward appearance of the implants can be indistinguishable from biological eyes (at least without an eye exam) or outlandish, with gold or neon irised effects (complete with gold-lettered manufacturer's logo) to the high chrome, featureless effect. Cybereyes will accept additional vision enhancements up to .5 Cyber Rating without further Essence loss. 5,000¥

Retinal modification, rather than eye replacement, is also an option for the appearance-conscious, but each feature independently impacts on the user's system. Duplication of another person's retinal pattern, either permanently in a retinal modification or as a stored pattern in a cybereye, is a capital crime. It is also of dubious use, because the duplicate rarely is of high enough fidelity to fool retinal scanners on a regular basis. Continual changes also are a health hazard. 50,000¥

Camera: The memory can store a digital copy of any image viewed through the eye (.5 Mp for each image stored). If the eyes are linked to a standard datajack, images may be downloaded to any data system. Otherwise, the image-storage chip must be removed through a port in the eye. 5,000¥

Cosmetic modification: Alteration of iris color is the most popular type, but pupil-shape alteration and cornea pigmentation are also common. 1,000¥

Flare compensation: This protects the user from blinding flashes of light, as well as simple glare. 2,000¥

Low-Light: The user can see normally in light levels as low as starlight. Total darkness, rare in our cities, still renders the user as blind as an unmodified person. 3,000¥

Thermographic: This Cyberware operates in the infrared portion of the spectrum, allowing the user to see heat patterns. Light level has no effect, but strong sources of heat act much like a bright glare does to normal vision, often blinding the user. 3,000¥

Internal Headware

Cortex Bombs: These are an illegal method of coercion offering the ultimate headache. A small amount of explosive is implanted at the brain stem. The triggering circumstance is determined at the time of implant, either set as a timer or prepared for the receipt of an electromagnetic signal. Most cortex bombs are booby-trapped, rigged to explode if it is tampered with in any way. The explosion of a cortex bomb kills the wearer and endangers those around him (one-meter radius, 5D1 explosion). 500,000¥

Memory: This is the definition of the computing power of the chips in your head. It covers the storage space as well. Unless you want to change data surgically, you need a datajack. Memory is the amount of space available in Megapulses (Mp). Raw data, skill software, and certain programs can be stored, but other equipment gives the user access to them. 100¥ times the number of Megapulses

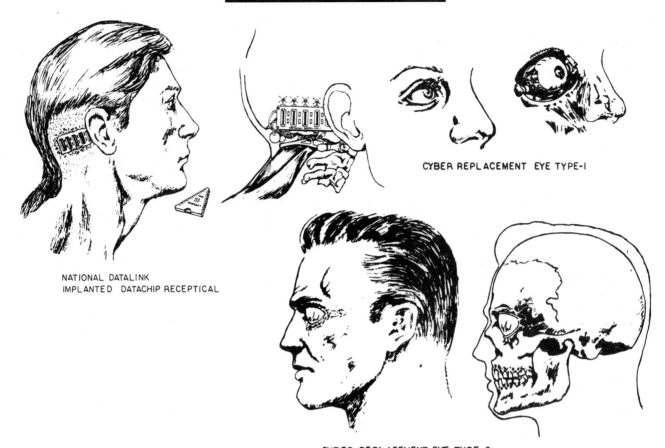

NATIONAL DATALINK
IMPLANTED DATACHIP RECEPTICAL

CYBER REPLACEMENT EYE TYPE-I

CYBER REPLACEMENT EYE TYPE-2

Datasoft Link: This gives the user access to his knowledge skill software. 1,000¥

Display Link: This allows the user to display data on his retina or cybereye, letting him read what is in his head. 1,000¥

Data Lock: This denies the wearer access to his own memory space. Input or output through a datajack requires a special code. This option is very popular for couriers. 1,000¥

Data Filter: This is a special sensory block that prohibits the wearer from absorbing sensory data into his own memory while he is carrying data in his cybernetic memory. Data Filter turns a man into an organic audio-visual recorder, unaware of what he has heard and witnessed while the recording feature is active. This is very popular for confidential couriers and secretaries. 5,000¥

Skillsofts: These chips contain copies of the intricate patterns that occur when a skill is in use. The user can function as if he had the skills or memories himself. The coding systems must override the user's own reflexes or memories, forcing him to rely on the encoded capabilities. Active skillsofts require skillwires to translate the reflexes into reality for the user. Additional chipjacks can accommodate additional skillsofts. Data and language skillsofts may be inserted into a chipjack or a datajack. The user needs no other hardware to utilize the knowledge locked in the skillsoft. With a skillsoft in a datajack, the datajack may not be used for other functions. Skillsofts are usually sold installed in 5-centimeter-long cylinders to protect the chip until it is inserted into a jack. Once the chip is in, the user can leave the cylinder attached for easy removal, or dispose of the holder.

Skill programs may also be directly loaded into headware memory through a datajack. Such programs will fill much of the available space, as shown on the chart below.

SKILL MEMORY CHART

Skill Type	Rating											
	1	2	3	4	5	6	7	8	9	10	11	12
General	10	20	30	200	250	300	700	800	900	2,000	2,200	2,400
Concentration	6	12	18	120	150	180	420	480	540	1,200	1,320	1,440
Specialization	4	8	12	80	100	120	280	320	360	800	880	960
Language	3	6	9	24	30	36	70	80	90	300	330	360

BODYWARE

Bodyware is Cyberware implanted in locations other than the user's head. Some types, such as dermal plating, also involve additions to the skull.

Dermal Plating: This is an invasive protection system that uses hard plastic and metal fiber plates bonded to the user's skin to produce dermal armor. Dermal plating does limit skin flexibility and is obvious. The armor plates may be tailored to any surface texture or color. It comes in three strengths, which affect the level of invasion. 6,000¥ for Level 1, 15,000¥ for Llevel 2, 45,000¥ for Level 3

Filtration Systems: These systems operate to protect the user from specified substances. Toxins and rated gases oppose the system's rating. If the system fails, the toxin takes effect at full value. A replacement trachea fitted with filters protects the user from smoke and most gases. A specialized form, the artificial gill, allows the user to filter oxygen from water. A kidney replacement includes toxin filters to remove foreign agents from the bloodstream. It is effective against most injected drugs and many diseases. There is also a system of implanted filters designed to detoxify a wide range of poisons, including alcohol, taken orally. 15,000¥ times the rating for an air filter, 10,000¥ times the rating for a blood or toxin filter

Fingertip Compartment: This is a small storage space replacing the last joint of a finger. It is ideal for concealing data chips. It is also commonly used for the concealment of a monofilament whip, because the replacement joint can serve as the control weight. 3,000¥

Hand razors: These are 2.5-centimeter chromed steel or carbon fiber blades that replace the user's fingernails. The razors anchor to the user's bones. Retractable versions slide out of sight under synthetic nail replacements. 4,500¥, 9,000¥ for retractable version

Limbs: Substitute limbs come in two basic models, obvious cyberlimbs and fully functional, natural-looking replacements. Replacements offer no special abilities. Other cyberlimbs can offer enhanced strength, but the typical user can rarely apply the limb's full strength. Trying to lift a car single-handed will only bring you grief and pain as the limb rips free from its flesh-and-blood moorings. Cyberlimbs may have spurs and hand razors at no additional loss to the user's system. They also come with a small storage compartment. Small devices, including pistols, may be built into that space. Such devices have no Cyber Rating but cost four times their normal price. Multiple replacements make the user less vulnerable to additional damage. Each pair of limbs replaced counts as one level of dermal armor. 50,000¥ for replacement, 100,000¥ for cyberlimb, plus 150,000¥ for each level of increased strength

Muscle Replacement: Implanted, vat-grown synthetic muscles replace the user's own. Calcium treatments and skeletal reinforcement allow an overall increase in the user's strength. Rating increases apply to Strength and Quickness, but this change does not affect Reaction. The maximum increase is 4. 20,000¥ times the rating

Program Carrier: This is a specialized form of Bodyware for those who work with the Matrix, especially deckers. Three retractable prongs are located in the user's hand to carry any kind of chip. The chips are connected by individual, subdermal fiber optics to the user's datajack. Technicians use program carriers for diagnostic routines, and deckers for persona programs. By inserting the prongs into a suitable station and plugging in a data table, a decker can run the Matrix, as they say, "naked." He will need headware memory storage to stash any data he heists. This is a dangerous way to deck because the user's neural system is extremely vulnerable. 25,000¥

Skillwires: These are an invasive system of neuro-muscular controllers necessary for a user to take advantage of skillsofts containing active type skills. The level of the skillwires limits the rating of the skill-soft, but skillwires are not specific to any one skill. The system includes a chipjack for the insertion of a skillsoft. 10,000¥ times the rating if 1–3, 100,000¥ times the rating if 4–6, 1,000,000¥ times the rating if 7–9

Smartgun Link: This is the feedback loop circuitry necessary to take full advantage of a smartgun. Targeting information appears on the user's retina or cybereye. A flashing crosshair appears at his focal point, remaining solid once the system has directed the user's hand to aim the weapon at that point. Typical systems use a subdermal induction pad in the user's palm to link with the smartgun. 2,500¥

Spur: A narrow blade attached to the user's bone, similar to a razor. Retractable versions must be placed where they can be withdrawn along a long bone. Alternatively, a set of three smaller blades may be anchored to the back of the hand. 7,000¥, 11,500¥ for retractable

Vehicle Control Rig: These are neuro-enhancers and muscular signal transference (MST) interfaces. Each level adds 2 to the user's Reaction. Each level also allows an additional +D6 on the initiative die when the user is controlling a vehicle through his datajack. 12,000¥ for Level 1, 60,000¥ for Level 2, 300,000¥ for Level 3

Voice Modulator: Voice modulators are popular with entertainers. Stage performers commonly make use of the volume feature and singers of the tonal shift. 45,000¥ plus the cost of features. Increased volume makes you into a loudspeaker (10,000¥). Tonal shift alters tones for perfect bird calls, mellifluous singing, and uncanny vocal impressions. Modulations and secondary quavers make detection simple for a vocal pattern recognizer (25,000¥). Secondary pattern, an illegal modification, allows the user to install a second vocal pattern and reproduce it in a form that is almost indistinguishable from an unmodified pattern (50,000¥). Playback allows the user to access an audio record in data storage or fed in through a datajack and reproduce it almost perfectly (40,000¥).

Wired Reflexes: These are implanted neural boosters and adrenalin stimulaters. Each level adds +2 to the user's Reaction. He also gets +D6 on initiative rolls. 55,000¥ for Level 1; 165,000¥ for Level 2; 500,000¥ for Level 3

CYBERDECKS AND PROGRAMS

This gear is described in the Matrix chapter.

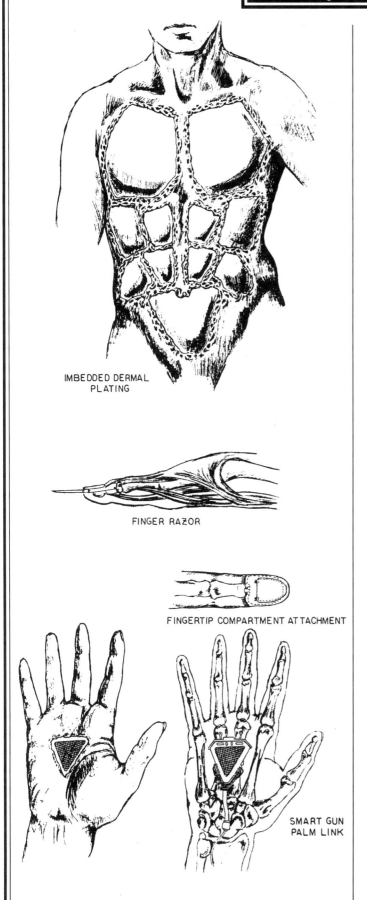

IMBEDDED DERMAL
PLATING

FINGER RAZOR

FINGERTIP COMPARTMENT ATTACHMENT

SMART GUN
PALM LINK

BIOTECH

DocWagon™ Contract: Don't leave home without it! Doc-Wagon™ offers first-class medical care on a 24-hour, house (or street) call basis. Once a call from a platinum card holder is confirmed, most DocWagon™ franchises guarantee arrival of a trauma team in less than ten minutes, or the immediate medical care is free. Resuscitation service carries a high premium, as does High Threat Response (HTR) service. In the latter case, the client (or his heir) is expected to pay medical bills up to and including death compensation for DocWagon™ employees. A DocWagon™ contract requires a filing of tissue samples (held in a secure vault staffed by bonded guards) and comes with a sealed-band, direct-dial wrist phone, which also serves as a homing beacon for the roving DocWagon™ ambulances and choppers. Rupture of the band will, of course, alert the DocWagon™ representative. Gold Service includes one free resuscitation per year, 50 percent reduction on HTR service charges, and a 10 percent discount on extended care. Platinum Service includes four free resuscitations per year. There is no charge for HTR services, but employee death compensation still applies. It carries a 50 percent discount on extended care. 5,000¥ per year for Basic Service, 25,000¥ for Gold Service, 50,000¥ for Platinum Service

Medkit: The 2050 medkit is well equipped to handle most typical medical emergencies. It includes drug supplies, bandages, tools, and even a doctor. Actually, it is an expert system (Biotech 3) to diagnose problems from information given by the user. The system will request more information if the diagnosis is unclear. Having determined a course of action, the kit will advise the user on techniques. The kit may (Unresisted Biotech Skill Test against the toxin's Virulence Level) be able to concoct a specific antidote to a toxin, thereby canceling the toxin's effects. Medkits are, of course, not infallible and a standard waiver of liability must be filed with the manufacturer on purchase of the item. Most models will advise of their inability to supply proper treatment as well as issuing reminders when their stocks of expendable materials are low. Supplies run out if you roll a 1 on 1D6 after a treatment. 200¥, 50¥ for new drugs

Organic Replacements: Vat-grown replacement tissues and organs are readily available. Most common are "Type O" products tailored for minimal rejection reaction, though they require a program of tailored immuno-suppressant treatment to prevent a body's rejection of the transplant. The safest transplant material is grown from samples of the patient's own body. Regrettably, no replacements for brain or nervous tissue are yet available, and full clones of a person remain in the realm of fiction. See **After the Shadowrun** for details.

SLAP PATCHES

Slap patches are adhesive drug dispensers that release measured doses to allow continual, safe administration of necessary chemicals. Patches must go directly against the patient's skin. Dermal armor hinders their effects (reduce the patch rating by the armor rating), and blood filtration implants make all but the trauma patch ineffective.

Antidote Patch: This releases a broad-spectrum toxin antidote to aid the patient in resisting the effects of a toxin. The Patch Rating adds to the subject's body Attribute for Resistance Tests. Multiple patches give no additional effect. 50¥ times its Rating

Stimulant Patch: This releases a non-addictive stimulant to keep you awake at those times when awareness is vital. When used, reduce the number of filled blocks on the Mental Damage track of the subject's Condition Monitor equal to the patch's rating. Magicians should be wary of side effects that may damage their ability to use magic. The magician makes a Magic Resistance Test against a Target Number of the patch's rating. If he fails, he must follow the procedure for possible Essence loss as if he had taken a Deadly Wound. (See **After the Shadowrun** for details.) 25¥ times its rating

Tranq Patch: This is designed to anesthetize patients in preparation for medical attention. Tranq patches are known to be used in some circles to sedate unruly prisoners. The patch and the subject's Body Attribute make an Opposed Test, each having a Target Number of the other's rating. If the patch wins, each success fills a block on the Mental Damage track of the subject's Condition Monitor. 20¥ times its rating

Trauma Patch: This is the last-ditch hope of a victim unable to receive medical care. The trauma patch must be placed over the victim's heart. It allows a second chance against death. The Target Number is the number of minutes since the subject went down, but the patch's rating is added to the victim's Body. Success leaves the character comatose (deadly wounded, but stable). 75¥ times its rating.

Stabilization Unit: An enclosed capsule with carrying handles, this unit is designed to stabilize a critically wounded person until proper medical care can be applied. It is standard equipment on DocWagon™ vehicles and in use with all the better ambulance services. The unit extends the time a character has to escape death. Each minute in the time becomes a number of hours equal to the rating. 10,000¥ for the standard model, (Rating 2), 20,000¥ for the deluxe (Rating 6)

MAGICAL EQUIPMENT

See the **Magic** chapter for item descriptions.

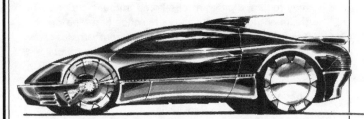

Eurocar Westwind 2000

VEHICLES

GROUND

Vehicles operate on varied forms of power. Economy models and those intended for use with a power grid usually use high-capacity storage batteries that can be recharged at stations, parking garages, or on a grid track. Some have solar cell auxiliaries, but these provide only limited power. Vehicles in use with the tribes or in outlying areas sometimes rely on alcohol fuels easily derived from organic materials. Long-distance vehicles still use some petroleum derivative. Luxury vehicles usually use petrochem. Whatever the form of fuel, the vehicles still handle with similar efficiency, the main differences arising in the cost and availability of the fuel and in the capacity of the vehicle for sustained travel.

Most ground vehicles have limited self-guidance capability. They can follow a programmed map and still react to conditions around them (Car Skill 2). The autopilot is very cautious, often stopping for no reason apparent to the passenger. Unexpected roadblocks confuse the system, prompting it to ask for instructions.

Combat vehicles have hardpoints and firmpoints to contain weapon systems. Some also have weapons incorporated into their structure. Such weapons may not be changed to suit a mission, as can those on a hardpoint. Hardpoints accept any heavy weapon or special weapons designed for vehicles. They provide 1 point of gyro-stabilization. Firmpoints accept any firearm smaller than a heavy weapon. They also provide 1 point of gyro-stabilization. Weapons must be purchased separately. Adaptation of a weapon for a vehicle mount doubles its cost.

Cars

Mitsubishi Runabout: A one-person, three-wheeler that runs on electric power, the Runabout is designed for commuters and short-distance errands. It is affectionately referred to as "the box" due to its blocky shape. 10,000¥

Chrysler-Nissan Jackrabbit: This two-seater's low price and heavy advertising campaign have made it the commonest car on North American highways. The back section may be used as a trunk or space to squeeze in another two passengers. It is available in electric or petrochem models. 15,000¥

Ford Americar: A mid-size sedan. 20,000¥

Eurocar Westwind 2000: A sleek, low-slung speed machine. Side wheel panel covers slide down in parking mode to lock and protect the tires. 100,000¥

Toyota Elite: A full-size luxury car whose interior appointments beggar some penthouse apartments. It has a superior autopilot. 125,000¥

Mitsubishi Nightsky: The limousine of the elite, its interior style and features make the Elite look like a cheap Sri Lankan import. A full suite of anti-theft systems, armor, medkit, rigger controls, telecom with direct satellite link-up, and wet bar are standard features. The autopilot is superior. Concealed defensive weaponry is often retrofitted. 250,000¥

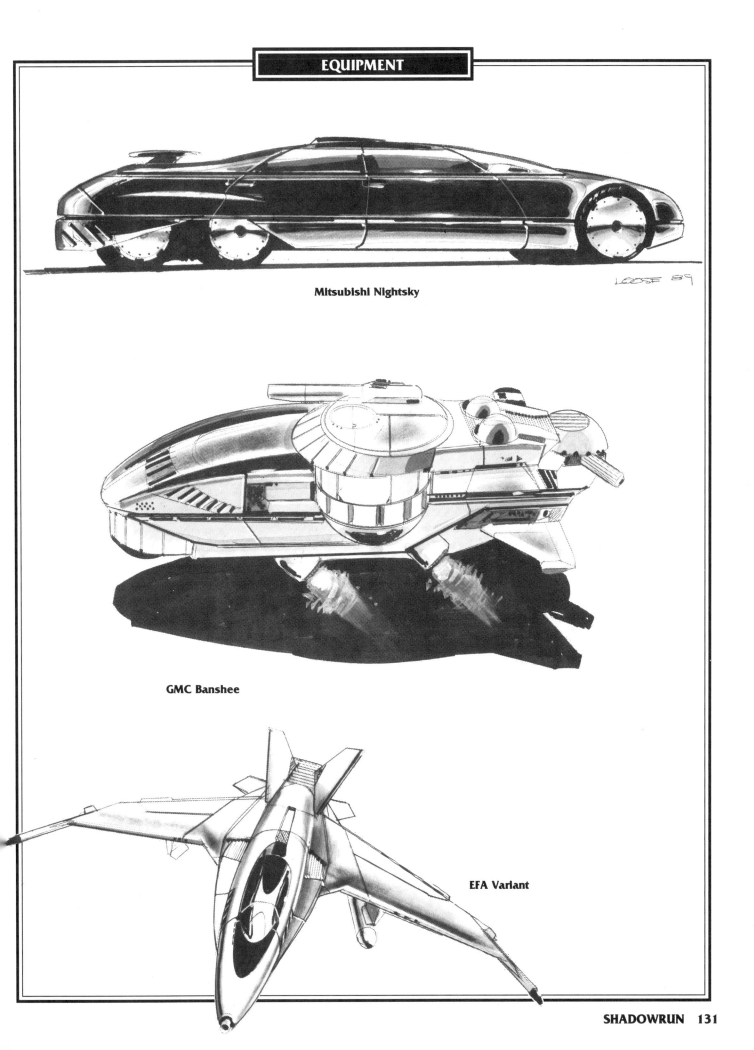

Mitsubishi Nightsky

GMC Banshee

EFA Variant

Bikes

Dodge Scoot: An electric intracity scooter. 2,000¥
Harley Scorpion: A classic heavy-bodied road hog. The Scorpion features folding aerodynamic panels that double as armor. Many consider it a combat bike. It can carry up to three firmpoints. 15,000¥ plus 1,000¥ per firmpoint.
Yamaha Rapier: A fast street machine whose slick styling make it a favorite with go-go-go-gangs. 10,000¥

Hovercraft

Chrysler-Nissan G12a: This is a general-purpose hovercraft that sees duty in passenger and freight versions. The separate driver's compartment seats two, and the six-ton cargo flat may be fitted with a 30-passenger cabin. 50,000¥
GMC Beachcraft Patroller: A swift, lightly-armed patrol craft, the Patroller sees service with coast guards and security corps worldwide. It has two hardpoints. 100,000¥

BOATS

Watercraft feature the same power sources as ground vehicles, with a higher proportion using petrochem fuels. Large freighters are often almost completely robot-controlled. The largest super-freighters and tankers have fusion plants.

Motorboats

Samuvani-Criscraft Otter: A popular mid-size craft fine for pleasure boating, the Otter also does light hauling and utility work. 20,000¥
Aztech Nightrunner: This small, two-seat craft is equipped with auxiliary electric engines for silent running. Its composite hull and non-reflective paint, which reduces its heat signature, make it hard to detect. It has two firmpoints. 30,000¥
GMC Riverine: A popular commercial patrol boat, the Riverine relies on water jets rather than propellers, making it an excellent shallow water craft with superb maneuverability. It has four hardpoints. 75,000¥

Sailboats

Sendanko Marlin: Designed as a pleasure boat, this 15-foot craft has gained notoriety as the favored boat of the infamous smuggler Janos Smoot since the Channel 32 docudrama of the irascible criminal's life. 15,000¥

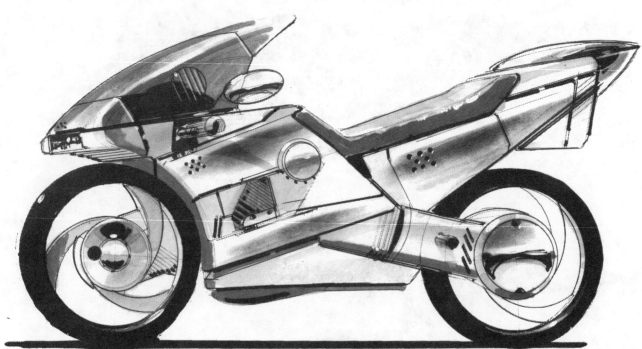

Yamaha Rapier

AIRCRAFT

Save for a few solar-powered pleasure and reconnaissance vehicles, aircraft are petrochem guzzlers. Designs are sophisticated, usually featuring fly-by-wire controls and adjustable airframes. Added to the availability of new composite materials, this has allowed the dreams of 20th century visionary designers to become everyday reality.

Autopilot systems work in a similar fashion to those on ground vehicles, but they are almost always tied into the Navstar position-location system. Aircraft categories are based on the system that provides the major portion of their lift.

Winged Planes

The minimum air speed of these craft is 50.

Cessna C750: A dual prop craft serving as transport, the Cessna C750 can be configured to carry six passengers. The plane also sees service with border patrols and surveillance corporations. 200,000¥

EFA variants: Designed as the European Economic Community's general fighter, this craft has been pirated worldwide, proving to be an extremely durable design primarily because of its ease of maintenance and adaptability to improved electronics and weapon systems. Many corporations maintain a squadron for escorting VIP jets. It carries an assault cannon in its nose and four hardpoints. 500,000¥

Lear Platinum: This sleek flying limousine carries advanced materials and features. It is the flying equivalent of the Mitsubishi Nightsky. 500,000¥

Rotor Craft

Federated Boeing Commuter: A tilt-wing craft, the Commuter is designed for rapid transport to and from sites with limited landing area. It is primarily a passenger carrier. 250,000¥

Hughes WK-2 Stallion: The workhorse helicopter of the mid-21st century, this venerable design has seen a great number of modifications. It features a two-seat tandem cockpit and a cabin that can seat ten people. Armed (two hardpoints, two firmpoints) military variants are common in much of the world. 300,000¥

Ares Dragon: This large, double-rotor helicopter has a variety of military and civilian applications, from passenger transport (it can carry 24 battle-armed troops) through cargo and heavy-lifting duty to serving as a command post. It has two hardpoints. 400,000¥

Hughes Airstar: This luxury helicopter was designed for speed and agility. The standard corporate model carries armor and luxurious appointments. There are many reports of variants with concealed weapons. 600,000¥

Northrup PRC-42 Wasp: This single-man rotorcraft was designed for police and military service. The craft is very stealthy in that the pilot can cut power to the rotors some distance away and descend safely on autorotation effect alone. Combat support variants are beginning to appear. Nicknamed Yellowjackets, they carry one or two hardpoints. 200,000¥ for standard model, 250,000¥ for Yellowjacket

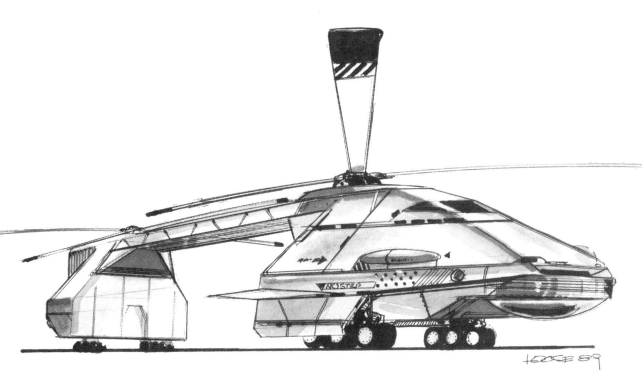

Ares Dragon

Vectored Thrust

These craft are too fuel inefficient except for military and high-threat corporate operations.

Federated Boeing Eagle: A vectored-thrust stealth aircraft designed for air superiority, it has entered limited commercial service. It has two assault cannon in its nose and six hardpoints. Restricted

MILITARY AND RESTRICTED ISSUE

PANZERS

This is slang for a category of Low Altitude Vehicles (LAV) in service with militaries and corporations worldwide. These vehicles are heavily armed and armored and capable of extended operations in hostile environments.

GMC Banshee: This light panzer is designed for reconnaissance and courier duty. It carries two assault cannons, two heavy machine guns, an autocannon in its turret, four hardpoints, and two surveillance/decoy drones.

SECURITY VEHICLES

This classification includes a variety of urban combat vehicles ranging from police squad cars to anti-terrorist assault vehicles. All are well-armored and capable of traversing typical city rubble.

Ares Citymaster: An urban riot-control vehicle, it carries and serves as a command post for 10 riot cops. A roof turret mounts a water cannon and a coaxial light machine gun. The machine gun usually uses gel rounds. 500,000¥

Chrysler-Nissan Patrol-1: A ubiquitous urban patrol car, its armored body features lock-down wheel protection and slide-up window armor with firing ports. In tight situations, the crew may release nausea gas from ports located around the exterior. 100,000¥

REMOTES

Many remotely piloted vehicles are available in surveillance, spotter, and weapons carrier modes. Though operable by any trained user, these vehicles function at their most efficient in the control of a rigger, to whom the feedback is as innate as his sense of balance. Remotes have autopilots and may function independently for short times, but only at risk to the vehicles, as the autopilots can rarely cope with novel occurrences.

Surveillance Drone: This rotor aircraft carries thermographic and low-light video scanners. It can be equipped for direct data transmission, or it can store images for later recovery. 10,000¥

Spotter Drone: This winged, stealth aircraft carries equipment similar to the Surveillance Drone. The spotter is designed for longer missions with increased loiter times. Recovery is more difficult though, because the craft needs a runway or a catch net to avoid a crash on return. 15,000¥

Hunter: This is a designation for armed versions of surveillance or spotter drones. They carry two firmpoints. 20,000¥

Patrol Vehicle: This tracked ground vehicle performs perimeter patrol and defense. These remotes carry one firmpoint, one hardpoint, and armor. The sensor equipment usually consists of only thermographic receptors. 10,000¥

VEHICLE WEAPONS

Autocannon: This is a light cannon with autoloader. 12,000¥

Launcher: This small launcher uses the same missiles as a shoulder-fired launcher. 15,000¥

Water cannon: A high-pressure projector, it always fires on "autofire" and suffers no recoil penalty. The damage code is on human scale, but any hit requires the target to make a Strength Test (Target Number 5) or be knocked over. If the weapon's pump is connected to water source, it does not need to "reload". 20,000¥

RIGGER GEAR

Vehicle Adaptation: Any vehicle can be adapted for rigger control. If not built into the vehicle during construction, a rigger adaptation will increase the base Handling Rating by 1.

Remote Control Device: This is a portable control deck that allows the remote control of a vehicle through a radio link. This control link is subject to disruption by jammers and atmospheric conditions. The deck has a video screen to display the output from a vehicle-mounted camera. It also has a keyboard and a set of switches, dials, and joysticks to manipulate the vehicle's function. Variant decks allow the control of building systems and other devices. Such systems are often hardwired, rather than broadcast.

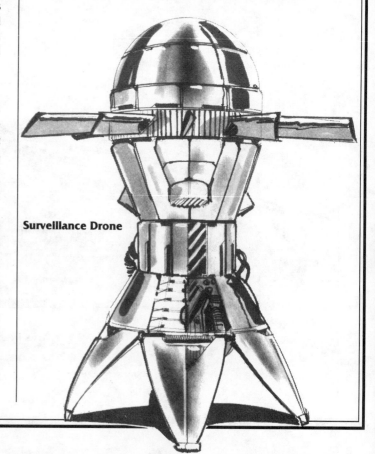

Surveillance Drone

WEAPONRY

MELEE WEAPONS

	Concealability	Reach	Damage	Weight	Cost
Edged Weapons					
Katana	3	+1	(Str)M3	1	1,000
Knife	8	—	(Str÷2)L1	.5	30
Sword	4	+1	(Str)M2	1	500
Pole Arms/Staffs					
Pole Arm	2	+2	(Str)S3	4	500
Staff	2	+2	(Str)M2 Stun	2	50
Clubs					
Club	5	+1	(Str+1)M2 Stun	1	10
Sap	8	—	(Str)M2 Stun	—	10
Stun Baton	4	+1	(5)L2Stun + Special	1	750
Whips/Flails					
Monofilament Whip	10	+2	6S4	—	3,000
Cyber Implant Weapons					
Hand Razors	NA/10*	0	(Str÷2)L2	–	4,500/9,000*
Spurs	NA/9*	0	(str)M2	–	7,000/11,500*

*Non-Retractable/Retractable

PROJECTILE WEAPONS

	Concealability	Reach	Damage	Weight	Cost
Bows					
Bow	3	—	(Str)M2	1	300
Arrows	3	—	—	.1	10
Crossbows					
Light	2	1	4L3	2	300
Medium	2	2	5M2	3	400
Heavy	NA	2	6S2	4	500
Bolts	4	—	—	.05	5

THROWING WEAPONS

	Concealability	Reach	Damage	Weight	Cost
Non-Aerodynamic					
Throwing Knife	9	—	(Str÷2)L1	.25	20
Aerodynamic					
Shuriken	8	—	(Str÷2)L1	.25	30

FIREARMS

Pistols	Type	Concealability	Ammo	Damage	Weight	Cost
Streetline Special	Hold-out	8	6 (Clip)	3L1	.5	100
Walther Palm Pistol	Hold-out	9	2 (Break)	3L1	.25	200
Colt America L36	Light	6	9 (Clip)	3M2	1	350
Beretta Model 101T	Light	5	10 (Clip)	3M2	1	350
Fichetti Security 500	Light	7	10 (Clip)	3M2	1	400
Fichetti Security 500	Light	6	22 (Clip)	3M2	1.25	400
Ares Predator	Heavy	5	10 (Clip)	4M2	2.25	450
Ares Viper	Heavy	6	30 (Clip)	2M3	2	600
Browning Max-Power	Heavy	6	8 (Clip)	4M2	2	450
Remington Roomsweeper	Heavy	8	6 (Magazine)	3M3	2.5	500
Ruger Super Warhawk	Heavy	4	6 (Cylinder)	4M2	2.5	300

Rifles						
FN HAR	Assault	2	20 (Clip)	5M3	4.5	1,200
AK-97	Assault	3	22 (Clip)	5M3	4.5	700
AK-98	Assault	NA	22 (Clip)	5M3	6	2,500
Remington 750	Sporting	3	5 (Magazine)	5S2	3	600
Remington 950	Sporting	2	5 (Magazine)	6S2	4	800
Ranger Arms SM-3	Sniper	NA	6 (Magazine)	6S2	4	4,000
Enfield AS7	Shotgun	3	10 (Clip)	4M3	4	1,000
Defiance T-250	Shotgun	4	5 (Magazine)	3M3	3	500

Submachine Guns						
AK-97 SMG/Carbine	SMG	4	22 (Clip)	4M3	4	800
Uzi III	SMG	5	16 (Clip)	4M3	2	600
Heckler & Koch HK227	SMG	4	20 (Clip)	5M3	4	1,500
Heckler & Koch S variant	SMG	5	16 (Clip)	5M3	3	1,200

EQUIPMENT

FIREARMS (continued)

Light Machine Guns

Ingram Valiant	Light MG	NA	100(Belt)	5S3	9	1,500

Tasers

Defiance Super Shock	Taser	4	4 (Magazine)	Special	2	1,000

Heavy Weapons	Type	Concealability	Ammo	Damage	Weight	Cost
Medium MG	Medium MG	NA	40 (Clip)	8S4/4M2*	12	2,500
Heavy MG	Heavy MG	NA	40 (Clip)	12S4/6M2*	15	4,000
Assault Cannon	Cannon	NA	20 (Clip)	10D4/5S2*	20	6,500
Missile Launcher	—	NA	—	By Type	8	8,000

Missile	Intelligence	Ammo	Damage	Weight	Cost
AVM	4	4 (Break)	12D8/6D4*	3	2,000
APM	3	4 (Break)	5M3	2	1,000
HEM	2	4 (Break)	4M4	2	1,500

*Vehicle Damage

AMMUNITION, PER 10 SHOTS

	Damage	Weight	Cost
Regular Ammo	—	.5	20
Explosive Rounds	+2 Staging	.75	50
Flechette Rounds	−1 Power Level, +1 Staging	.5	100
Gel Rounds	4L1 Stun	.25	30
Stun Rounds	4M4 Stun	1	100
Taser Dart	Special	.5	50
Taser Cartridge	Special	.5	100
Box of 100 Belted Ammo	NA	5	175
Box of 100 Belted Gel Rounds	NA	3	250

FIREARM ACCESSORIES

	Mount	Concealability	Rating	Ammo	Effect	Weight	Cost
Concealable Holster	—	—	—	—	—	—	100
Grenade Launcher	Under	−3	—	6 (Magazine)	—	+2	1,700
Laser Sights	Top	−1	—	—	−1 Target Number	+.25	500

Imaging Scopes

	Mount	Concealability	Rating	Ammo	Effect	Weight	Cost
Low-Light	Top	−2	—	—	Special	+.25	1,500
Thermographic	Top	−2	—	—	Special	+.25	1,500
Magnification 1	Top	−1	1	—	—	+.25	500
Magnification 2	Top	−1	2	—	—	+.25	800
Magnification 3	Top	−1	3	—	—	+.25	1,200

Recoil Compensators and Gyros

	Mount	Concealability	Rating	Weight	Cost
Shock Pads	Stock	—	1	.25	200
Gas-Vent 2	Barrel	−1	2	.5	450
Gas-Vent 3	Barrel	−2	3	.75	700
Gyro Mount	Under	−5	4	6	2,500
Deluxe Gyro Mount	Under	−6	6	8	6,000

Others

	Mount	Concealability	Effect	Weight	Cost
Silencer	Barrel	−1	Special	.2	500
Smart Goggles	Top	—	−1 Target Number	—	3,000
Smartgun Adapter	Top	−2	—	1	x1.5 Gun Cost
Smartgun Variant	—	—	−2 Target Number	.5	x2 Gun Cost

EXPLOSIVES

	Concealability	Damage	Weight	Cost
Grenades				
Offensive	6	6M3	.25	30
Defensive	6	6M3	.25	30
Concussion	6	4M3 Stun	.25	30
Gas (neuro-stun VIII)	5	—	.5	60
Mini	8	—	.1	50
Smoke	5	—	.5	40

Explosives, Per Kilo

	Concealability	Rating	Weight	Cost
Commercial	6	3	1	60
Plastic, Compound 4	6	6	1	80
Plastic, Compound 12	6	12	1	200
Timer	6	—	.5	100
Radio Detonator	8	—	.25	250

WEAPON RANGE

Type	Short	Medium	Long	Extreme
Target Number	**4**	**5**	**7**	**9**
Firearms				
Hold-out Pistol	0–5	6–15	16–30	31–50
Light Pistol	0–5	6–15	16–30	31–50
Heavy Pistol	0–5	6–20	21–40	41–60
Taser	0–5	6–10	11–12	13–15
Shotgun	0–10	11–20	21–50	51–100
Sporting Rifle	0–30	31–60	61–150	151–300
Sniper rifle	0–40	41–80	81–200	201–400
Assault Rifle	0–15	16–40	41–100	101–250
SMG	0–10	11–40	41–80	81–150
Heavy Weapons				
Light MG	0–20	21–40	41–80	81–150
Medium MG	0–40	41–150	151–300	301–500
Heavy MG	0–40	41–150	151–400	401–800
Assault Cannon	0–50	51–150	151–450	451–1300
Grenade Launcher	20–50	51–100	101–150	151–300
Missile Launcher	20–70	71–150	151–450	451–1,500
Impact Projectiles				
Bow	0–5	6–50	51–150	151–300
Light Crossbow	0–10	11–40	41–100	101–200
Medium Crossbow	0–20	21–60	61–150	151–250
Heavy Crossbow	0–30	31–80	81–200	201–300
Thrown Knife	0–3	4–6	7–12	13–20

CLOTHING AND ARMOR

	Ballistic	Impact	Weight	Cost
Armor Clothing	3	0	2	500
Armor Jacket	5	3	2	900
Armor Vest	2	1	1	200
Lined Coat	4	2	1	700
Helmet	1	1	—	200
Vest With Plates	4	3	2	600
HEAVY ARMOR				
Partial Suit	6	4	10+Body	10,000
Full Suit	8	6	15+Body	20,000
LEATHER				
Real	0	2	1	750
Synthetic	0	1	1	250
Ordinary Clothing	0	0	1	50
Fine Clothing	0	0	1	500
Tres Chic	0	0	1	1,000

SURVEILLANCE AND SECURITY

VISION ENHANCERS

	Magnification	Weight	Cost
Binoculars	x50	1	100
Low-Light	—	—	200
Thermographic	—	—	250
Goggles	x20	—	1,500
Low-Light	—	—	500
Thermographic	—	—	700

COMMUNICATIONS

	Rating	Weight	Cost
Micro-Transceiver	1	—	2,500
Micro-Recorder	8	—	1,000
Micro-Camcorder	6	—	2,500

SURVEILLANCE MEASURES

	Rating	Weight	Cost
Data Codebreaker	Maximum 6	5	10,000 x Rating
Dataline Tap	—	—	5,000
Laser Microphone	Maximum 6	1	1,500 x Rating
Shotgun Microphone	—	1	1,000 x Rating
Signal Locator	—	2	1,000
Tracking Signal	Maximum 5	—	100 x Rating
Voice Identifier	Maximum 6	10	2,000 x Rating

SURVEILLANCE COUNTERMEASURES

	Rating	Weight	Cost
Bug Scanner	Maximum 10	1	500 x Rating
Data Encryption Sys.	Maximum 10	6	1,000 x Rating
Dataline Scanner	Maximum 10	6	100 x Rating
Jammer	Maximum 15	3 x Rating	1000 x Rating
Voice Mask	2D6	—	3000
White Noise Generator	Maximum 10	1 x Rating	1500 x Rating

SECURITY DEVICES

	Rating	Weight	Cost
High-Intensity Veracity Examiner	8	5	50,000
Identification Scanners			
Thumbprint	6	—	200
Palmprint	8	—	300
Retinal	12	—	1,000
Maglocks	Maximum 15	—	100 x Rating
Panicbutton Hook-Up	—	—	1,000
Maglock Passkey (illegal)	—	1	50,000
Restraints			
Metal	12	.5	50
Plastic	15	—	20
Squealer	5	—	100

SURVIVAL GEAR

	Weight	Cost
Chemsuit	1	1,000
Respirator	1	500
Pressure Regulator	.5	250
Survival Kit	2	100
Ration Bars (10 Days)	1	30

LIFESTYLE

Entertainment

	Weight	Cost
Music		
Playback unit	—	200
Disk	—	20
Quad Speakers	—	100
Mastoid Implant Speaker (Cyber .1)	—	1,000
Video		
Screen	3	150
Disk	—	20
Recorder Package	2	1,000
Transmission Unit	5	4,000
Simsense		
Player Unit	—	350
Program Chip	—	50
Portable Recorder	5	50,000

ELECTRONICS

	Weight	Cost
Telecom	15	Memory Cost x1.5

PORTABLE PHONES

	Weight	Cost
Wrist Models	—	1,000
With Flip-Up Screen	—	1,500
Handset Unit	1	500
Earplug Unit	—	1,000
Booster Pack	2	500
Pocket Secretary	.5	3,000

PERSONAL COMPUTERS

	Weight	Cost
Table Top	10	Memory Cost
Pocket	1	Memory Cost x5
Wrist	—	Memory Cost x20
Printer	10	1
Computer Memory (Non-Cyber)		20 x Megapulses

DATA DISPLAY SYSTEMS

	Capacity	Weight	Cost
Data Unit	2,000 Mp	2	Memory Cost
Headset	1,000 Mp	1	Memory Cost x2
Heads-Up Display	200 Mp	1	Memory Cost x10

CYBERTECH

HEADWARE

	Essence Loss	Cost
Communications		
Chipjack	.2	1,000
Datajack	.2	1,000
Radio	.75	4,000
Radio Receiver	.4	2,000
Telephone	.5	3,700
Ears		
Cyber Replacement	.3	4,000
Modification	.1	2,000
Cosmetic Modification	—	1,000
Damper	.1	3,500
High Frequency	.2	3,000
Low Frequency	.2	3,000
Recorder	.3	7,000

Eyes		
Cyber Replacement	.2	5,000
Camera	.4	5,000
Cosmetic Modification	—	1,000
Flare Compensation	.1	2,000
Low-Light	.2	3,000
Retinal Duplication (illegal)	.1	50,000+
Thermographic	.2	3,000

INTERNALS

Cortex Bomb (illegal)	—	500,000
Memory	Mp÷100	Mp x 100
Datasoft Link	.1	1,000
Display Link	.1	1,000
Data Lock	.2	1,000
Data Filter	.3	5,000
Program Enabler	.1	1,000

Skill Software and Computer Media Libraries

	Cost
Knowledge	Mp x150
Active skill	Mp x100
Language	Mp x50

BODYWARE

	Essence Loss	Cost
Dermal Plating		
Level 1	.5	6,000
Level 2	1	15,000
Level 3	1.5	45,000
Hand Razors	.1	4,500
Retractable Razors	.2	9,000
Spur	.1	7,000
Retractable Spur	.3	11,500
Filtration Systems		
Air	Rating ÷ 10	15,000 x Rating
Blood	Rating ÷ 5	10,000 x Rating
Ingested Toxin	Rating ÷ 5	10,000 x Rating
Fingertip Compartment	.1	3,000
Limbs		
Simple Replacement	1	50,000
Cyber Limb	1	100,000
Increased Strength	—	+(Level x 150,000)
Built-In Smartgun Link	.25	2,500
Built-In Device	—	x4 Normal Cost
Muscle Replacement (Maximum Level 4)	Level	(Level) x 20,000
Program Carrier	.2	25,000
Skillwires		
Level 1–3	.1 x Level	Cyber Rating x10,000
Level 4–6	.2 x Level	Cyber Rating x100,000
Level 7–9	.3 x Level	Cyber Rating x1,000,000
Smartgun Link	.5	2,500
Vehicle Control Rig		
Level 1	2	12,000
Level 2	3	60,000
Level 3	5	300,000
Wired Reflexes		
Level 1	2	55,000
Level 2	3	165,000
Level 3	5	500,000

CYBERDECKS AND PROGRAMS

CYBERDECKS

	MPCP	Hardening	Memory	Storage	Load	I/O	Cost
Radio Shack CD-100	2	0	10	50	5	None	6,200
Allegiance Alpha	3	1	10	50	5	None	13,200
Sony CTY-360	6	3	50	100	20	10	111,000
Fuchi Cyber-4	6	3	100	500	20	20	150,000
Fuchi Cyber-6	8	4	100	500	50	30	364,000
Fuchi Cyber-7	10	4	200	1,000	50	40	514,000
Fairlight Excalibur	12	5	500	1,000	100	50	990,000

Hitcher Jack	1,000
Off-line Storage	10,000 x Mp
Response Increase	
Level 1	25,000
Level 2	100,000
Level 3	250,000
Vidscreen Display	500

PERSONA PROGRAMS

	Size	Cost
Bod-1	10	1,000
Bod-2	20	2,000
Bod-3	30	3,000
Bod-4	40	20,000
Bod-5	50	25,000
Bod-6	60	30,000
Bod-7	70	70,000
Bod-8	80	80,000
Bod-9	90	90,000
Bod-10	100	500,000

EVASION OR MASKING

Evasion/Masking-1	5	500
Evasion/Masking-2	10	1,000
Evasion/Masking-3	15	1,500
Evasion/Masking-4	20	10,000
Evasion/Masking-5	25	12,500
Evasion/Masking-6	30	15,000
Evasion/Masking-7	35	35,000
Evasion/Masking-8	40	40,000
Evasion/Masking-9	45	45,000
Evasion/Masking-10	50	250,000

SENSORS

Sensors-1	3	300
Sensors-2	6	600
Sensors-3	9	900
Sensors-4	12	6,000
Sensors-5	15	7,500
Sensors-6	18	9,000
Sensors-7	21	21,000
Sensors-8	24	24,000
Sensors-9	27	27,000
Sensors-10	30	150,000

UTILITY PROGRAMS

Attack, Medic, Mirrors, Shield, Slow

Rating 1	10	500
Rating 2	20	1,000
Rating 3	30	1,500
Rating 4	40	4,000
Rating 5	50	5,000
Rating 6	60	6,000
Rating 7	70	35,000
Rating 8	80	40,000
Rating 9	90	45,000
Rating 10	100	100,000

Analyze, Sleaze

Rating 1	8	400
Rating 2	16	800
Rating 3	24	1,200
Rating 4	32	3,200
Rating 5	40	4,000
Rating 6	48	4,800
Rating 7	56	28,000
Rating 8	64	32,000
Rating 9	72	36,000
Rating 10	80	80,000

Deception, Evaluate, Relocate

Rating 1	5	250
Rating 2	10	500
Rating 3	15	750
Rating 4	20	2,000
Rating 5	25	2,500
Rating 6	30	3,000
Rating 7	35	17,500
Rating 8	40	20,000
Rating 9	45	22,500
Rating 10	50	50,000

Brouse, Decrypt, Smoke

Rating 1	3	150
Rating 2	6	300
Rating 3	9	450
Rating 4	12	1,200
Rating 5	15	1,500
Rating 6	18	1,800
Rating 7	21	10,500
Rating 8	24	12,000
Rating 9	27	13,500
Rating 10	30	30,000

BIOTECH	Rating	Weight	Cost
DocWagon™ Contract:			
Basic Service	—	—	5,000 per year
Gold Service	—	—	25,000 per year
Platinum Service	—	—	50,000 per year
Medkit	3	3	200
Medkit Supplies	—	—	50
SLAP PATCHES			
Antidote Patch	Maximum 8	—	50 x Rating
Stimulant Patch	Maximum 6	—	25 x Rating
Tranq Patch	Maximum 10	—	20 x Rating
Trauma Patch	Maximum 6	—	75 x Rating
Stabilization Unit	2	30	10,000
Deluxe Unit	6	35	20,000

MAGICAL EQUIPMENT

	Cost
SPELL FOCUSES	
Specific Spell Focus	Rating x 5,000
Spell Purpose Focus	Rating x 30,000
Spirit Focus	Rating x 30,000
POWER FOCUSES	
Basic	Rating x 10,000
Spell Lock	50,000
WEAPONS	
Knife	Rating x 18,000
Knife With Orichalcum	Rating x 28,000
Sword	Rating x 210,000
Sword With Orichalcum	Rating x 315,000

MAGICAL SUPPLIES	Weight	Cost
Elemental Conjuration Materials	—	Spirit's Force x1,000
Fetishes		
Expendable:	—	—
Combat	—	20
Detection	—	5
Healing	—	50
Illusion	—	10
Manipulation	—	30
Reusable Fetishes	.1	x10 Expendable Cost
Medicine Lodge Materials	2 x Rating	500 x Rating

HERMETIC LIBRARY (ANY MAGICAL SKILL)		
Computer Media	—	Mp x 100
Hardcopy	50 x Rating	2,000 x Rating

RITUAL SORCERY MATERIALS		
Detection Spells	—	100 x Force
Health Spells	—	500 x Force
Illusion Spells	—	100 x Force
Manipulation Spells	—	1,000 x Force

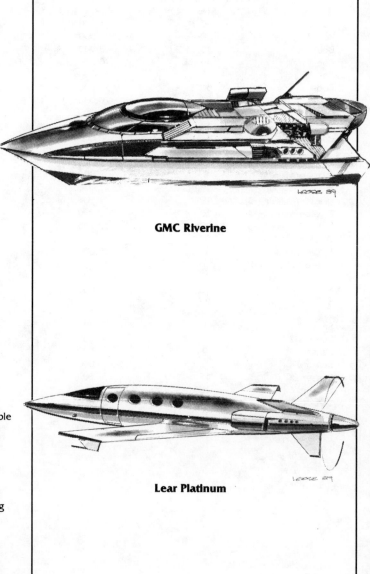

GMC Riverine

Lear Platinum

VEHICLES

G R O U N D
Cars

	Handling	Speed	Body	Armor	Signature	Pilot	Cost
Mitsubishi Runabout	4	25/75	1	0	5	1	10,000
Chrysler-Nissan Jackrabbit	4	40/120	1	0	4	1	15,000
Ford Americar	4	40/120	2	0	2	2	20,000
Eurocar Westwind 2000	3	70/210	2	0	2	3	100,000
Toyota Elite	4	60/160	4	0	3	4	125,000
Mitsubishi Nightsky	4	45/120	5	1	4	4	250,000

Bikes

	Handling	Speed	Body	Armor	Signature	Pilot	Cost
Dodge Scoot	4	22/66	1	0	5	0	2,000
Yamaha Rapier	2	60/175	2	0	4	2	10,000
Harley Scorpion	3	50/160	3	1	3	2	15,000 +1,000 per fimpoint

Hovercraft

	Handling	Speed	Body	Armor	Signature	Pilot	Cost
Chrysler-Nissan G12a	4	40/100	4	0	5	2	50,000
GMC Beachcraft Patroller	3	55/140	4	2	5	2	100,000

BOATS
Motorboats

	Handling	Speed	Body	Armor	Signature	Pilot	Cost
Samuvani Chriscraft Otter	4	15/45	2	0	3	2	20,000
Aztech Nightrunner	3	25/75	2	0	4	3	30,000
Nightrunner using electric motor	3	10/30	2	0	8	3	30,000
GMC Riverine	3	15/50	4	2	3	2	75,000

Sailboats

	Handling	Speed	Body	Armor	Signature	Pilot	Cost
Sendanko Marlin	2	20/30	2	0	5	0	15,000

AIRCRAFT
Winged Planes

	Handling	Speed	Body	Armor	Signature	Pilot	Cost
Cessna C750	5	340/680	3	0	2	2	200,000
EFA Variants	4	950/1,900	4	2	4	3	500,000
Lear Platinum	5	800/1,600	5	1	3	4	500,000

Rotor Craft

	Handling	Speed	Body	Armor	Signature	Pilot	Cost
Federated Boeing Commuter	5	140/420	3	0	3	3	250,000
Hughes WK 2 Stallion	5	170/250	5	1	4	3	300,000
Ares Dragon	5	160/240	6	4	3	3	400,000
Hughes Airstar	4	190/260	4	2	3	4	600,000
Northrup PRC 42 Wasp	4	65/100	1	0	5	0	200,000
Yellowjacket	4	65/100	1	0	5	0	250,000

Vectored Thrust

	Handling	Speed	Body	Armor	Signature	Pilot	Cost
Federated Boeing Eagle	3	900/1,800	5	4	5	3	Restricted

MILITARY AND RESTRICTED ISSUE

Panzers

	Handling	Speed	Body	Armor	Signature	Pilot	Cost
GMC Banshee	3	650/1,000	6	6	5	2	Restricted

Security Vehicles

	Handling	Speed	Body	Armor	Signature	Pilot	Cost
Ares Citymaster	4	40/120	4	4	5	3	500,000
Chrysler Nissan Patrol	4	60/180	3	2	4	3	100,000

Remotes

	Handling	Speed	Body	Armor	Signature	Pilot	Cost
Surveillance Drone	4	70	2	0	3	2	10,000
Spotter Drone	3	35/100	2	0	3	2	15,000
Hunter Drone	*	(-10%)	4	0	3	2	20,000
Patrol Vehicle	3	35/70	3	2	3	2	10,000

* See Vehicle Description

Vehicle Weapons

	Ammunition	Damage	Cost
Autocannon	10 (Clip)	6D2	12,000
Launcher	6 (Break)	By Missile	15,000
Water Cannon	20	4M3	20,000

			Cost
Vehicle Adaptation Rig			+50% of vehicle

	Level	Weight	Cost
Remote Control Device	Slave Ports	2x Level	5,000 x Level

AFTER THE SHADOWRUN

"Never relax. Your run might be over, but someone, somewhere, is just starting his, and the target could be you."
—Kirk Hoff, Street Mage

ou've just been for a run through the shadows. Maybe you got your behinds kicked or maybe the run was sweet and smooth. Either way, you've still got a few things to do.

HEALING UP

Wounds are easy to come by and fragging hard to get rid of. Wounded characters are gonna be laid up, maybe for a day or two, maybe for weeks. The time depends on how bad they're hurting.

Anything but a Deadly wound might heal without medical attention. When the adventure is over, each wounded character makes a Body Success Test with a Target Number determined by his overall wound level. (See Wound Table below.) Dermal armor or plating doesn't help here, chummer.

WOUND TABLE	
Wound Level	Target Number
Light	4
Moderate	6
Serious	8

If the character rolls any successes, he will heal without medical attention, given time. If no successes are rolled, the wounds will not heal without medical treatment. Deadly wounds always require medical treatment.

GETTING BETTER

Healing in Shadowrun occurs in stages. If you are Severely wounded, when you finish healing from that, you are Moderately wounded. Finish healing from that, and you are Lightly wounded.

When you heal one level of wound, your condition monitor drops to the lowest point for the next category. Thus, a character who has a Serious wound level, no matter how many blocks are filled, drops down to having only three blocks filled when he reduces his level to Moderate.

Healing takes time. Fast healing takes time, medical assistance, and money, too, chummer. To speed up the healing process, a doctor has to work on you at least once a day. Each wound level has a base healing time, as shown on the Healing Table. The doc makes an Unresisted Skill Test using Biotech (a Medical concentration of Biological Sciences will do as well). He divides the base time by his successes to determine how fast you actually heal. If the healing process is interrupted, it must start over again.

If you are healing without medical treatment, you need the full base time to recover.

USING THE HEALING TABLE

The Minimum Time column tells you the shortest possible time to heal a wound, with the best doctor and equipment on the case. No matter how many successes the doc rolls, this is the minimum time it takes to heal.

The Doctor's Target Number is the number your doc has to make to speed up your healing. The conditions under which he's treating you can affect his Target Number.

Minimum Lifestyle indicates that the better you take care of yourself, the better you heal. What's your lifestyle? If its lower than this for your wound, then conditions are bad, and your doc's job gets harder. If you are a Squatter or on the Streets, conditions are terrible. See **Lifestyles** for details.

HEALING TABLE

Wound Category	Base Time	Minimum Time	Target Number	Minimum Lifestyle
Deadly	30 days	3 days	10	Hospitalized
Severe	20 days	2 days	8	High
Moderate	10 days	1 day	6	Middle
Light	24 hours	1 hour	4	Middle

DOCTOR'S TARGET NUMBER MODIFIERS

Situation

Intensive Care (only available if hospitalized)	−2
Conditions (only one applies):	
Not in a hospital or clinic	+2
Bad conditions	+3
Terrible conditions	+4
Patient is a magician	+2

Patient's allergy to sunlight is:

Nuisance	+1
Mild	+2
Moderate	+3
Severe	+4

Patient's Body Attribute:

1–3	+0
4–6	−1
7–9	−2
10 or more	−3

Big Grinder staggered into Doc's clinic. The medico could see that the Troll was hurting. The bleeding holes in his massive gut were the first clue.

Grinder is Severely Wounded. His Body is 8. Doc has Medicine 7. Grinder is in a clinic and pays extra for intensive care. Doc rolls 7 dice. His Base Target Number is 8 (Severe damage), −2 for Intensive Care and −2 because of Grinder's Troll-tough Body Attribute, for a final Target Number of 4. Doc rolls 3 successes. The Base Healing Time for Severe damage is 20 days. 20÷3 is about 7, so it takes a week to get Grinder down to Moderately Wounded.

About this time, the bad guys get wind of Grinder's whereabouts, and he has to relocate to an abandoned storm drain. Without the nuyen to add little touches like warmth, food, and water, conditions are terrible. Doc visits Grinder once a day, though.

Doc rolls 7 dice again. This time, his Target Number is 6 (Moderate Wounds), with +4 (Terrible conditions), −2 (Grinder's Body Attribute), for a net target of 8. He only rolls 1 success, so it takes Grinder the full 10 days to get down to Light Wound. At this point, Grinder hits the streets. Since he is not being treated, he will need an additional 24 hours to get rid of his Light Wound condition.

ELECTIVE SURGERY

Surgery does damage. Medical technology won't let you die on the table, but you don't just bop into a clinic, get a full dermal armor implant, and then jog out the next day to kick butt. You have been cut open and glued back together, and recovery takes awhile.

Minor Cosmetic Surgery leaves you Lightly Wounded. This covers anything that does not cost Essence, and consists of minor plastic surgery that does not involve the eyes, muscles, or nervous system. Examples are a nose job or an ear bobbing.

Minor Invasive Surgery leaves you Moderately Wounded. This includes anything costing up to .4 points of Essence, or any cosmetic surgery involving the whole body, or your eyes, muscles, or nervous system. Getting a crest that you can raise or lower (nerve connections required) or a whole-body skin graft would come under this category.

Major Invasive Surgery leaves you Severely Wounded. Any procedure costing .41 to .99 points of Essence is major. This category also includes any organic limb replacements or eye transplants. New eyes are blind until you've fully healed from this surgery.

Drastic Invasive Surgery leaves you with a Deadly Wound, though your condition is stable and you won't die. This is any procedure costing 1 or more points of Essence. This category also includes any organ transplants. Magicians are required to check for Magic loss after healing (see **Magicians and Danage**).

Calculate the Essence costs based on all the cyberware you are having done at the same time. You cannot have additional cyberware done until you finish healing completely anyway, so you may as well get it over with. Surgery costs do not include the cost of recovery!

FIRST AID

All this medical stuff is great if you are in a hospital. What happens when you are face-down and bleeding in some filthy gutter?

Biotech Skill handles first aid in **Shadowrun**. It can reduce wounds that are not Deadly or stabilize Deadly wounds until your buddies can get you to a doctor.

First aid exploits the body's tremendous response to shock trauma within the first hour after a major injury. First aid must be applied during this "golden hour" in order to be effective.

The character using First Aid rolls his Biotech dice, using the wound level of the patient as his Target Number, modified by the conditions.

WOUND TREATMENT TARGET NUMBERS

Wound Level	Target Number	Treatment Time
Light	4	10 minutes
Moderate	6	20 minutes
Serious	8	30 minutes
Deadly	10	Special

Target Number Modifiers

Situation	Modifier
Patient is a magician	+2
Patient has Moderate or Severe allergy to sunlight	+1
Bad Conditions	+1
Terrible Conditions	+3
Patient's Body Attribute:	
1– 3	NA
4 – 6	−1
7 – 9	−2
10 or more	−3

If the wound is not Deadly, successful first aid will reduce the wound level to the next lower one. Divide the basic treatment time by the successes rolled to see how long this takes. If no successes are rolled, the wound cannot be reduced by first aid. If the medic rolls all ones, the wound level is increased. Fill in two boxes on the monitor. Ouch!

In order to be effective, the medic must work on the patient without interruption for the full duration of the required time. To treat multiple patients at the same time, he has to split his dice among them. If he is interrupted, then no healing! If the golden hour has not run out, the medic can begin treatment again after dealing with the interruption.

"Hold still, drek-head," snapped Iris. She slapped another lead from the medkit onto Grinder's torso. "Why ya pointy-eared creep!" snarled the Troll, "Whyn'tcha go back to the woods and chew dandelions…? OW! Watch where you stick those fraggin' needles!"

Grinder, Iris, and company are on a run. The Troll has a Moderate wound level and Iris is trying to patch him up. Iris has Biotech 6, and so rolls 6 dice. The Base Target Number is 6 (Moderate damage) and conditions aren't great, which gives her a +1 modifier. Grinder has Body 8, for a –2 modifier, making Iris's final Target Number a 5. Iris rolls 4 successes. A Moderate wound takes 20 minutes base treatment time. 20÷4 = 5 minutes.

"Aw, c'mon Grinder, I know it hurts, but just a few more min…oh FRAGGIT!" The yakuza soldiers had found the shadowrunners. Nameless and Neddy were offering light refreshments at the door, but the guest list was growing too fast. "Jeez, just as I was startin' to enjoy myself, too," grunted Grinder. He grabbed his shooter and jumped to his feet, ripping loose needles and 'trodes.

Grinder will still be Moderately wounded, because his treatment was interrupted. His wounds can still be treated after the fight, starting from scratch. Of course, if he is Severely wounded during this fight, Iris will have to treat that wound category instead.

If only one success is rolled, a limb or eye has been mangled beyond its ability to heal. A replacement is required, either natural or cyber. This adds to the normal healing costs and may mean waiting to get the replacement before healing can begin. Increase the base healing time by 50 percent.

If two or more successes are rolled, there is no limb or organ damage.

MEDICAL COSTS TABLE

Wound Level	Cost
First Aid	
Deadly	400
Serious	200
Moderate	100
Light	50
Doctor's Services	
Deadly	400 per day
Serious	200 per day
Moderate	100 per day
Light	50 per day
Hospitalization Lifestyle	500 per day
(includes doctor's services)	
Intensive care	1,000 per day
(only if Hospitalization Lifestyle applies)	
Surgery (includes cost of surgeon)	
Minor Cosmetic	1,000
Minor Invasive	5,000
Major Invasive	25,000
Drastic Invasive	250,000
Body Parts (Base Time to Grow)	
Eye (6 weeks)	10,000
Limb (10 weeks)	30,000
Organ (6 weeks)	20,000

Forced Growth (maximum rating 10) Cost x Rating
Divides time to grow by rating
Reduces compatibility by rating

DEADLY WOUNDS AND FIRST AID

Deadly wounds are nasty. First aid just lets the patient check to see if he's already dead! If the medic rolls one or more successes, the patient gets to make a Body Success Test against death, as described on page 67. He rolls dice equal to his Body Attribute, and again, dermal armor doesn't help. His Target Number is the number of minutes before treatment began. If he has even one success, his condition is stabilized. He is still comatose, but can be kept alive until transported to a hospital or other source of major medical treatment.

DEADLY WOUNDS AND ORGAN DAMAGE

Not only can they kill you, Deadly wounds can take the fun out of staying alive, too. Whenever a character suffers a Deadly wound, he may have suffered permanent damage to a vital organ or a limb. Make a Body Success Test (this time dermal armor does help) with a Target Number of 5. If you haven't survived the wound, you need not bother with this roll.

If no successes are rolled, a vital organ has been destroyed. The character must be kept under continuous treatment by someone with Biotech Skill even if the wound is stabilized, and the normal healing process cannot begin until a replacement organ is implanted, costing extra nuyen and extra time. The base healing time for the entire healing process is doubled, not counting the time it takes to come up with the replacement organ!

PIECES AND PARTS

When you lose the odd body part and want an organic replacement, you may not be able to get one off the shelf. If you want a complete DNA match, you'll have to have the part grown. Of course, a DocWagon™ platinum service contract includes a "donor counterpart" that can provide material for immediate transplant starting three months into the contract.

Transplants have varying degrees of compatibility with the recipient. Over time or when subjected to severe stress (like more deadly damage), the transplant may fail, requiring another replacement. The gamemaster decides when to invoke the possibility of failure. If you've got enough troubles, he might be kind and ignore it.

BODY PARTS TABLE			
Grade	Compatibility	Availability	Cost
Clonal	100%	Must grow	Base
Type O	90%	50% chance	Base
Other	3D6 x 5%	Always	Base x.5

Failure Chance of Transplants	
Compatibility	Failure Under Stress
100%	None
90 – 99%	1 in 6
70 – 89%	2 in 6
40 – 69%	3 in 6
01 – 39%	4 in 6

MAGICIANS AND DAMAGE

Magicians have it rough when they get hurt. You've probably noticed that doctors and medics have a harder time treating them. This is because they cannot use a lot of their high-tech gear without risking damage to the patient's Magic Rating. A magician can be treated without the +2 modifier, but then he has to check for Magic loss.

Whenever a magician suffers a Deadly wound, or is treated without the +2 Target Number Modifier, he risks loss of Magic. Roll 2D6. If the result is less than or equal to the magician's Magic Rating, he loses 1 point of the attribute. PERMANENTLY!

If the magician is being treated for a Deadly wound and the treatment does not observe the +2 modifier, check for Magic loss twice.

If a magician requires a replacement limb or organ, it must be cloned from his own tissues. Any other DNA pattern, even that of another magician, will reduce the character's power handling capability and automatically reduce his Magic Rating by 1. This can be temporary. A non-cyber substitute can be replaced later with a limb or organ cloned from the magician's tissues. This restores the lost point of Magic Rating, but organ implants do Deadly surgical damage, and consequently, can risk even greater Magic loss.

Hawkwind the shaman has Magic Attribute 6. The young magician takes a Deadly wound. Hawkwind survives, so check to see if he loses Magic. On a roll of 2D6, the result is 7. Hawkwind's Magic Rating remains at 6. Because the medic used every high-tech trick in his medkit to save Hawkwind and did not use the +2 modifier, check again. This time we get a 4. Hawkwind's Magic Rating is now a 5.

REDUCING MENTAL FATIGUE

Your mental condition monitor fills up from fatigue, strain, non-lethal attacks, Drain, and so on. This "mental damage" heals much faster than physical damage, but there is no real way to treat it. You get rid of fatigue by resting.

Fatigue is reduced in steps, mimicking the process in physical damage.

"Deadly" fatigue is a collapse. The victim is only unconscious, not dying. Magicians who suffer Deadly mental damage do not risk loss of Magic. Any additional mental damage done to an unconscious character counts as physical damage, though.

A character must rest to get over fatigue. He rolls dice equal to his Body or Willpower Rating, whichever is higher. Consult the following table for Target Numbers and Base Recovery Time. Divide the base time by the successes rolled. One or fewer successes means the character needs the full time to recover one wound category. If this resting time is interrupted, the recovery process aborts. Unconscious characters being carried by companions are resting "badly" and suffer a +2 to their Target Numbers.

MENTAL DAMAGE RECOVERY		
Fatigue Level	Basic Time	Recovery Target Number
Deadly	60 minutes	6
Serious	40 minutes	5
Moderate	20 minutes	4
Light	10 minutes	3

Neddy turned white and fell over. He'd been pushin' the spells pretty heavy in this fight, and all that magic finally took it out of him, I guess. I blew away the last yakuza, checked Neddy's pulse, and sat down with my gun locked on the doorway. There was nothin' to do now but wait…

Neddy has a Willpower Rating of 5 and has suffered Deadly fatigue due to Drain. Needing sixes, he rolls 5 dice and scores 2 successes. It will take him 60÷2, or 30 minutes, to regain consciousness. He will now be Severely fatigued. If he continues resting, he may roll 5 dice, with a Target Number of 5, to see how long it will take him to get to Moderate fatigue, and so on. This process continues until Neddy has healed all his Mental Damage or stops resting.

DISEASES AND TOXINS

Toxins (drugs and poisons) and diseases can do damage from which you recover normally. Many also have side-effects that affect your character as long as the nasty is active. Some of these effects only manifest at certain stages.

Countermeasures to toxins and diseases are antidotes. These will increase the victim's dice by their rating for the Body Success Test if no damage has yet been done. If the patient has gone down (Deadly damage level) from the effects of a nasty, the injection of the correct antidote counts as medical attention and permits the patient to make a saving roll against death as usual.

There are also many vaccines, which can be administered before a character is exposed to a disease or drug. These make him immune to the toxin, so that he never needs to resist the damage at all.

Diseases and toxins are rated for the damage they do and the speed with which they take effect.

Speed tells you how soon after exposure the victim will have to resist damage. This is usually immediately for drugs, but can be hours or days for diseases. Some kinds of technological or medical attention must be given during this period if it is to have any effect.

The description of the nasty will specify any side-effects or symptoms. It will also include notes about how it gets into the victim's system and special treatments that might be necessary.

TOXINS

Neuro-stun VIII
Damage: 6S2-Stun   **Speed:** 1 turn
Description: Delivered as a gas in an organic binder, N-S VIII takes effect if inhaled or on contact with the skin. At the end of the turn a character is exposed, he suffers stun damage. Even if he resists this, he suffers disorientation for about an hour, adding +2 to all Target Numbers.

Narcoject
Damage: 4D3-Stun   **Speed:** Instantaneous
Description: Injected. Can be used in drug darts because a touch is sufficient to inject. No side-effects. Narcoject either knocks you out or it doesn't.

Fugu-5
Damage: 3D2   **Speed:** Instantaneous
Description: Injected or eaten. This is a hyped-up version of one of the deadliest neurotoxins in nature. No side effects if you resist damage.

DISEASES

VITAS-3
Damage: 4D3   **Speed:** 12 hours
Description: Aerosol virus transmitted by close contact or sharing confined space with an infected person. After the incubation period, fever, chills, and vomiting occur until damage is reduced to Light.

FENCING THE LOOT

You've got an optical chip full of hot RAM, fresh off some corp's database. On top of that, you nailed some exec's limo, and have the ordnance from half a squad of his bodyguards in the trunk. How do you get rid of it?

If the team had a prearranged deal for disposing of loot, then you don't need these rules. If not, it's time to find a fence. The fence might be one of your regular street contacts like a Fixer or Talismonger, depending on what you've got to sell.

FINDING A FENCE

Finding a fence requires an Unopposed Skill Test using Etiquette (Street). The Base Target Number is 4, subject to the modifiers on the following table.

FINDING A FENCE	
Situation	**Modifier**
Using a regular contact	−1
Disposing of standard gear	−1
Disposing of high-tech or other important loot	+1
Disposing of hot loot	+3
While being sought by police	+1
While being sought by corp or organized crime	+2
Magical loot (focuses, spell formulae, and so on)	+2

THE LOOT

Most fences will buy loot that is easy to dispose of before taking the fancy stuff. Typically, a fence prefers to buy in the following order.

Standard Gear
This includes weapons, clothing, armor, vehicles, jewelry, certified credit sticks (money), and so forth.

High-Tech Loot
This includes ordinary data, equipment, research files, and such.

Hot Loot

This includes unique items, specific datafiles, prototypes, procedurals for new processes, magical items, or anything that belonged to a big, big boy and is irreplaceable.

The team can combine its dice in the Skill Test to find a fence, but all characters who contribute must attend the meeting at which the loot will be sold. If one or more of them doesn't show, the fence will get nervous and won't show either.

The successes from the roll to find a fence can be used in two ways.

Hustle It Along

It takes a base time of 10 days to locate a fence and set up a meet. Successes can be allocated to divide this time (minimum 1 day). Each day spent locating a fence increases the chances that the former owners of the merchandise will learn that you are trying to move it. The gamemaster rolls dice equal to the days spent, with a Target Number of 6. Any success means the bad guys are onto you. If the gamemaster thinks they would come after the team, he can set up an ambush at the meet.

Financing the Fence

Fences don't have unlimited means. They are just ordinary businessmen, trying to turn a dishonest nuyen. Each success allocated from the roll increases the fence's bankroll. The gamemaster secretly rolls two dice and multiplies the result by 100,000¥, to get the base bankroll. He then multiplies the base number by the number of successes the team allocates to get the total amount of money the fence will have available for that meet.

THE MEET

The meet can be anywhere. Once it's going down, make an Opposed Negotiation Test between any one character and the fence. The Target Number for each roll is the Willpower Rating of the other. Naturally, both sides are suspicious of the other (+2). The gamemaster sets the ratings for the fence.

The base price for any loot is 30 percent of its actual value. The price lists in **Equipment** cover the standard loot. For other loot, the gamemaster sets the prices.

Whichever side won the Negotiation test alters the price by 5 percentage points per extra success. If the fence won, the percentage won't go below 10 percent. If the team won, it won't go above 50 percent.

The fence will almost certainly have muscle with him to forestall any unscrupulous business practices by the team. If the original owners of the loot are coming after it, that will happen at the meet as well.

LIFESTYLES OF THE RICH AND SHADOWY

Your character does not, obviously, live in a bar. He has a lifestyle, and so the following information can be used to flesh out events that might occur in his life in between adventures. Even more important, though, is the effect Lifestyle has on healing, which is detailed earlier in this chapter.

Lifestyle measures the quality of your character's daily life and his living expenses, including shelter, food, entertainment, clothing, and so on. It does not cover technical resources, weapons, magical equipment, professional hirelings, or other major impersonal items. You and your gamemaster can decide on any details of the character's lifestyle that interest you.

A character living a Middle lifestyle or higher can support guests at ten percent above his own cost of living per guest. A host can also keep a guest at a lower lifestyle than his own by paying 10 percent of the lower cost of the guest's lifestyle.

LUXURY

This lifestyle offers the best of everything: spacious, ritzy digs, lots of high-tech toys, the best food, drink, and you-name-it. You have a household staff or a maid service or gadgets to do the mundane chores. You have a powerful car, possibly a hot sports model or a chauffeured limo. Whether it's a big house, a snazzy condo, or the penthouse in a top hotel, this is the life for the high-stakes winners in the business: top executives, government big shots, high-level yakuza, and the shadowrunners who pull off the big scores.
Cost: 100,000¥ a month and up-up-up!

HIGH

A high lifestyle offers a roomy house or condo, good food, and the tech that makes life easy. So you don't have the perks that the big boys do, but neither do you have as many people gunning for you. Your home is in a secure zone or protected by some good solid bribes to the local police contractor and gang boss. You have a housekeeping service or enough tech to take care of most chores. You've got a luxury commuter car. This is the life for the well-to-do on either side of the law: mid-level managers, senior yakuza, and the like.
Cost: 10,000¥ a month

MIDDLE

The Middle lifestyle is not the best but far from the worst. It offers a nice house or condo, with lots of comforts. So you eat some nutrisoy as well as natural food, but at least the autocook has a full suite of flavor faucets. You have a commuter car or first-class tube pass. This is the lifestyle for ordinarily successful wage-earners or criminals.
Cost: 5,000¥ a month

LOW

With this lifestyle, you've got an apartment, and nobody is likely to bother you much if you keep the door bolted. Meals are regular. The nutrisoy may not taste great, but it's hot. And you've also got power and water during your area's assigned rationing periods. When you travel, you ride the tube. Factory workers, petty crooks, and other folks stuck in a rut, just starting out, or kind of down on their luck tend to show up here.
Cost: 1,000¥ a month

SQUATTER

Life stinks and most of the time, so do you. You're eating low-grade nutrisoy and yeast, with the flavors added using an eyedropper. You live in a made-over building, converted into barracks, divided into closet-sized rooms, or maybe just renting out coffin-sized sleep tanks by the night. The only thing worse than the Squatter Lifestyle is living out on the streets.
Cost: 100¥ a month

STREETS

You live on the streets! Or in the sewers, steam tunnels, condemned buildings, or whatever flop you find for the night. Food is where you find it, bathing is a thing of the past, and the only security is what you make for yourself. The bottom of the ladder, inhabited by down-and-outers of all stripes.
Cost: Hey chummer. Life ain't all bad. For you, it's free.

HOSPITALIZED

This is a special lifestyle, applicable only when you are sick or injured. You are in a hospital, whether a real one, a clinic equipped as a hospital, or a private location with the necessary equipment installed. You don't own this lifestyle. You are paying for it until you get well or go broke, whichever comes first.
Cost: 500¥ a day for Basic Care. 1,000¥ a day for Intensive Care.

KEEPING UP THE PAYMENTS

A character has to shell out the nuyen each month to keep up a lifestyle. If he misses a payment, he may end up in debt and with a lower lifestyle.

Each month that a character misses a payment, roll 1 die. If the roll is greater than the number of consecutive months he's missed, no sweat. The missed payment is absorbed into his credit, which is part of the cost of his lifestyle. If he makes the next payment, everything is fine again.

If the die roll is less than or equal to the missed months, he's got troubles. The character's lifestyle gets downgraded to the next lower level. This means he gets evicted from his former home, some of his tech gets repossessed, he hocks some clothes, and so on.

He is also in debt, and owes somebody one month's cost of his former lifestyle. If he is mostly legit, this is a credit company. If the character is a criminal or shadow person or now lives a lifestyle lower than Middle, it may mean that he has defaulted on less-formal financial obligations. This can lead to earnest discussions with large persons on the subject of debt management. After the character gets out of the hospital, he can pay back the loan. He'd better. There's always a good market for fresh body parts. "Taking a debt out of your hide" takes on new meaning in 2050.

KARMA

In **Shadowrun**, Karma measures the experience characters get when they go out on an adventure. You don't get Karma for doing the laundry, unless your laundromat is in an urban combat zone. Karma is needed to improve attributes, skills, and special resources.

Karma is awarded at the end of an adventure, not necessarily after a single playing session. The gamemaster decides who gets Karma, and how much they get. Everyone in a group gets it for some things, but some awards go only to individuals.

Each surviving member of a team gets Karma for staying alive, succeeding at a mission, and for the amount of danger in the mission.

Individual characters can get additional Karma for good roleplaying, gutsy fighting, smart planning, sheer luck, and other personal feats.

Once you get it, what do you do with it? You can spend Karma one of two ways: as Instant Karma or Good Karma.

INSTANT KARMA

Characters can spend Instant Karma at any time and can use it on any die roll called for in the game. During an adventure, characters can spend Instant Karma in the following ways.
Reroll Failures
1 point of Karma allows a reroll of any dice in a Test that fails. For example, you roll 4 dice and score two successes. For 1 point of Karma, you can reroll the two dice that failed. This can be repeated as often as you wish until all the dice are successes or you run out of Karma.
Avoid an "Oops"
The Rule of One can only be partially avoided. If all your dice come up 1, you usually have had a disastrous failure. Paying 1 point of Karma will not let you reroll, but turns the disaster into a simple failure. You cannot spend more Karma on this failure.
Buy Success
Two points of Karma will simply buy one success. You can even buy more successes than you have dice. For example, you roll 4 dice and score two successes. You need 5 successes. You can simply blow 6 Karma points, and bingo, you've got 'em.
Improve Your Chances
You can spend your Karma to improve any rolls made by a non-player character who is helping you. If you need to buy a success for the NPC medic trying to stabilize your Deadly Wound, you can do it.
Save Your Butt
You can spend 2 points of Karma to buy off one of the other guy's successes.

GOOD KARMA

Karma is also used between adventures to improve character scores or gain them benefits. Physical and mental attributes can be increased 1 point using Karma. This increase is to natural attributes, not cyberware. The natural attribute can never exceed the character's racial maximum. That is, a Human cannot raise a value above 6 using Karma. Karma can also be used to raise attributes that have been reduced for some reason, but the maximum remains 1 more than the initial rating. Reaction, Essence, and Magic may never be raised directly using Karma, though Reaction may change if you improve Quickness or Intelligence.

The improvement costs Karma equal to the current value of the attribute. This represents time spent exercising, studying, eating health foods, taking various treatments, and so on. For example, raising Strength to 5 costs 4 Karma points.

Skills

Skills are raised using Karma. Once you've paid the Karma, the skill rating goes up 1 point.

Once you've begun the character, improvements in general skills, concentrations, and specializations all happen separately.

KARMA COST FOR SKILLS

General skills	2 x Current Rating
Concentrations	1.5 x Current Rating
Specializations	1 x Current Rating
Languages	1 x Current Rating

Iris has specialized in Firearms Skill, leaving her with general Firearms of 1, Pistols at 3, and Beretta 101T, her chosen weapon, at 5.

Raising her general Firearms Skill from 1 to 2 costs 2 Karma.

Raising her Pistols skill from 3 to 4 costs 4.5, rounded to 5 Karma.

Raising her Beretta 101T skill from 5 to 6 specialization costs 5 Karma.

New concentrations are based on the existing general skill score. If you have Firearms 4 and want to concentrate in pistols, to buy Pistols at 5 would cost 4 x 1.5, or 6 Karma.

New specializations are based on the existing concentration score. If you don't have one, use the general skill. Thus, if you only want to improve with the Remington Roomsweeper, it would cost 4 x 1, or 4 Karma to get 5 in that specialized skill.

Totally new skills cost 1 point of Karma for the first point.

MAGICAL ACTIVITIES

Magicians need Karma to learn spells. Magicians also need Karma to bond an enchanted item to their power so that they may use it.

Learning a Spell

Before you can cast a spell, you have to learn it. You can learn it from a magician who already knows it, or you can do it on your own if you have the spell formula.

Teachers cost numerous nuyen. While he is coaching you one-on-one, for as long as it takes to learn the spell, your teacher cannot do anything else. If he quits before you learn it, all the time you spent is wasted. Teachers charge what the market will bear, but a typical price is 1,000¥ times the Force of the spell, plus living expenses.

Teaching a spell does not take the Magic that casting it does. As long as the magician is still functional (at least 1 point of Magic Attribute left), he can teach spells at any Force the student wants.

A spell formula is the symbolic theory for the spell and is designed using Magical Theory Skill. To learn on your own, you must have a copy of the spell formula that goes with your tradition. A shaman needs a medicine item, like a painting, carving, set of runes, or medicine bag. A mage needs a written text. Once you have the formula, you can learn a spell at any Force you want, with any Force modifiers.

If you happen onto a spell formula for another tradition, you need to translate it before you can use it. Translation is a task like design, but you do not need inspiration, and you get a –2 to your Target Number.

A shaman learning a new spell spends his time chanting, dancing, and carrying on. This whips up the kind of emotional peak shamans need to contact the spell energy. The shaman must study in a Medicine Lodge with a rating at least equal to the Force of the spell. A mage spends his time in meditation, intense study, and formal ritual. He needs peace and quiet and a library of Sorcery with a rating at least equal to the Force of the spell.

Learning a spell is an Unresisted Skill Success Test. You get your dice from Sorcery and Magical Theory Skills. The Target Number is the desired Force. A shaman gets his totem modifier. A mage may get extra dice if he is aided by an Elemental appropriate to the spell's purpose category. All Target Number modifiers for damage to the magician apply, as do distractions for maintaining spells, bad conditions, and so on.

Learning a spell requires a base number of days equal to the desired Force. Divide this by the number of successes. The minimum time is one day. Learning spells costs Karma equal to the desired Force.

If the player rolls no successes, the learning attempt fails. The magician has wasted his time, a number of days equal to Force. Fortunately for him, failed study does not cost Karma, but teachers will still expect to be paid. Never stiff a man who can throw a Fireball, know what I mean?

Force Modifiers

When learning a spell, you can accept limitations on its use. These Force modifiers allow you to cast spells with Force higher than your Magic Attribute without exposing yourself to Physical Damage. Once a Force modifier is chosen for a spell, it applies to that spell permanently. If you want to know the spell with different options, you must learn it all over again. Then you will know both versions of the spell.

Force modifiers are never part of the spell formula. A magician can use the same formula to learn a spell with a variety of modifiers.

Neddy has a Magic Attribute of 6, and he wants to be able to toss a killer Fireball spell. He accepts the Exclusive Spell modifier (–2) and learns the spell at Force 6. Neddy will be able to cast his Fireball spell at Force 8 without exceeding his Magic Rating, but he also must abide by all the restrictions of using an Exclusive Spell.

An Exclusive Spell applies a –2 Force Modifier. When casting an Exclusive Spell, you cannot maintain any other spells or cast any other spells in the same action. When maintaining an exclusive spell you cannot cast any other spells or use another magical skill.

A Fetish-Required Spell applies a –1 Force Modifier for a reusable fetish or a –2 Force Modifier for an expendable fetish. You need some physical object to cast the spell, choosing what it is when you learn the spell. This prop is a fetish. The term comes from anthropology and means a ritual item used in "primitive" magic. Primitive to those mundane chummers, maybe. You must have a fetish in your hand to use it. If you are wearing the fetish, you need only touch it with your hand. The fetish goes with a specific spell. You cannot use the same fetish for different spells.

Fetishes can be bought from a talismonger. His prices depend on the spell s purpose category. You cannot substitute one for another, so don't lie to your fetish supplier. A reusable fetish is a durable object that you can use again and again. An expendable fetish is used up or destroyed when the spell is cast. In other words, the spell needs ammo.

Shamanic Fetishes

Reusable: drums, rattles, knives, tomahawks, spears, carved wooden or bone wands, native jewelry, carvings, masks, and medicine bag, pouches filled with a complex mixture of minerals, herbs, and animal parts.

Expendable: small packets of herbs, curiously shaped twigs, tufts of feathers or animal hair, small stones or crystals, crude miniature weapons, bits of bone, shells, and so on.

Hermetic Fetishes

Reusable: ornate wands, usually jewelled, rings, amulets and other jewelry, complex illustrated scrolls covered with diagrams.

Expendable: small parchment talismans, chemical mixtures or potions, crystals or stones, painted charms, and so on.

MAGICAL ITEM BONDING TABLE	
Item	**Karma Cost**
Specific Spell Focus	Rating
Spell Purpose Focus	3 x Rating
Spirit Focus	2 x Rating
Power Focus	5 x Rating
Spell Lock	1
Magical Knife	6 x Rating
With Orichalcum	7 x Rating
Magical Sword	6 x Rating
With Orichalcum	7 x Rating

All magic items must be bound to their user.

BEHIND THE SCENES

"Why do things happen the way they happen? For all I know the world is just one big game and all of our actions are determined by the roll of a die."
– Dunkelzahn, Great Dragon

ehind the scenes is where you find the person who makes the game happen. In other words, the gamemaster. The gamemaster has many functions, including creating adventures, roleplaying NPCs, and mediating rules and other formalities of play.

To create adventures, the gamemaster can make up the story out of whole cloth, use a **Shadowrun** adventure published by FASA, or adapt a plot from fiction, TV, or the movies. In practice, many gamemasters end up mixing all these elements to create an adventure best suited to their own and their players' interests and personalities.

The gamemaster plays the roles of all the people, computers, critters, or anything else the player characters meet. The **Contacts** section profiles a number of "typical" NPCs from 2050 to get you started. FASA's **Shadowrun** adventures will give you more. Sometimes, it's fun to use a published adventure as a starting point, creating your own NPCs to replace the published ones.

A good gamemaster is always open to discussion about how rules work, but when he makes his decision, it's final. As gamemaster, only you decide how much Karma to award at the end of each adventure.

That sounds like the gamemaster has absolute power, but it really depends on how much power your players are willing to give you. If the players don't like the way you run the game, they won't play it with you. On the other hand, if you don't like the way they play the game, you won't run it for them. The moral of the story is that conducting a roleplaying game requires some cooperation from everybody!

DICEY SITUATIONS

As an adventure unfolds, your players will start to want to use the skills and attributes of their characters to get things done: con their way by a guard, fix a broken detonator before the Trolls find their hiding place, or try to understand what that Japanese corp type is saying to them. You, meanwhile, will want to know whether the player characters saw that all-important clue or whether they kicked it under the trash.

For many of these situations, you will have to rely on your own judgment to decide which skills are needed for the situation, Target Numbers, conditional modifiers, and interpreting what a "success" means. Below are some guidelines and rules to help you to resolve some of the commoner situations.

SOCIAL SKILL USE

To influence a non-player character through Social Skills, use a mental statistic of the NPC as the Base Target Number. If the player character is attempting to influence a group of NPCs who do not have a designated leader, use the average of their ratings. Groups tend to react as a whole, with reluctant members being drawn along by enthusiastic ones. Otherwise, all attempts should be made against the leader of the pack (varooom).

The Base Target Number is modified by circumstances. See the following table.

Situational Modifiers	Target Number
With respect to your character, the NPC is:	
Friendly	−2
Neutral	—
Suspicious	+2
Hostile	+4
An enemy	+6
Player's desired result is:	
Advantageous to NPC	−2
Of no value to NPC	—
Annoying to NPC	+2
Harmful to NPC	+4
Disastrous to NPC	+6

Social Skills are a prime place to use extra successes as a measure of accomplishment. Judge the exact effects according to the specific circumstance.

Dodger wants to do a little snooping at a local Mitsuhama subsidiary. To get in, the Elf tries, with a little fast talk and a somewhat tattered ID card, to Negotiate his way past the gate guard. Dodger has a Negotiation Skill Rating of 4. The Elf uses the other guy's mental attribute as his Target Number, in this case, the guard's Intelligence of 3. The guard is suspicious (+2, it's his job to be suspicious) and will be in trouble if he allows unauthorized personnel into the compound (harmful to him, +4), but the elf's got an ID card (the gamemaster awards a special −1 for supporting evidence). That brings the Target Number to 3 + 2 + 4 −1, or 8.

Because of Dodger's Negotiation Skill Rating of 4, his player rolls 4 dice and gets 6, 6, 6, and 4. The Elf's got a good line tonight. He rerolls the three sixes and gets 2, 3, 5. Adding each result to 6, he gets a final result of 8, 9, and 11, for a total of three successes. One would be enough to get him past the guard, temporarily convincing the poor schmuck that Dodger really is a Mitsuhama employee. That wouldn't last long, though, because the guard's no idiot. Unless distracted, he would begin to notice holes in the Elf's story. Because Dodger has three successes, the guard is convinced enough to wait until the end of his shift before checking his log book to see whether the ID was valid (and because it wasn't, setting off alarms). If the Elf had been skillful enough to get five successes, the guard might never have twigged to the deception and might not even log in Dodger's presence.

BUILD AND REPAIR SKILL USE

Characters performing a Build or Repair task are primarily interested in how long it takes. A very successful character can reduce that time. Divide the time specified for the operation by the number of successes he achieves to determine how long it takes.

As a guideline to the time required to build things, take the price of a comparable item from the price list and divide by a number to get the typical time in hours. Divide by 10 for armed

combat type items, by 20 for vehicles, and by 50 for electronics, cyberware, or other technical gear. Ordinary, everyday equipment would have a Target Number of 4. Fancy or technical stuff gets a 6. The real exotics start at 8.

BUILD/REPAIR SKILL SITUATIONAL MODIFIERS

Situation	Target Number
Working Conditions:	
Bad	+2
Terrible	+4
Superior	–1
Tools are:	
Unavailable	Usually not allowed
Inadequate	+2
References available	—
Working from memory	+(5 – Intelligence)

Dodger's sweating hard, but he can't feel it under the water from the sprinkler system as he fumbles with the soldering iron and probes he scrounged up (inadequate tools +2). He wishes Grinder hadn't blasted the door lock to keep the corpcops from opening it behind them. The runners needed to go through it now, before the whole place blew up in their faces.

Between the sprinkler system and the stress, the gamemaster decides that Dodger is working in Terrible Conditions because the water from the sprinklers splashing on the circuits does not help one bit (+4). To override a door control without a lock would normally be a typical task (Target Number 4). Dodger faces a target of 4 + 2 + 4, or 10. He has Electronic Skill of 4, and so he rolls 4 dice for this Success Test. The results are a 3, 4, 5, and 6. The rerolled 6 gets a 5, for a total of 11, and Dodger breathes a sigh of relief.

The following Skills and Skill groupings have corresponding Build and Repair Skills: Aircraft, Armed Combat, Biotech, Boats, Computer, Demolitions, Electronics, Firearms, Ground Vehicles, Gunnery, Projectile Weapons, Throwing Weapons.

When used as a substitute skill, the Build and Repair Skill enters the Skill Web where it is listed. If it applies to a specifically named skill (such as Armed Combat), the Build and Repair Skill enters as though it were two circles away. That means the character applies a +4 to his Target Number when attempting to use the skill. If the Build and Repair Skill applies to a subgroup (such as Ground Vehicles), enter the web at that point with no additional modifiers.

VEHICLE OPERATION SKILL USE

Normal vehicle operation doesn't require any dice rolls. Unless things are really bad, most people can safely operate a vehicle for which they are trained without any problems. Unfortunately, shadowrunners are not most people. They ask their vehicles to do things that would make the most hardened Driver's Ed teacher drop dead. When those situations come up, the gamemaster can use the Handling rating of the Vehicle as a Target Number and apply the following situational modifiers.

Vehicle Operation Situational Modifiers

Situation	Target Number
Complex controls	+1
Unfamiliar vehicle	
Unstressful situation	+1
Stressful situation	+3
Large vehicle of Type	+2
Very large vehicle of Type	+3
Bad conditions	+2
Terrible conditions	+4
Rigger in Control	–(Rating x 2)

Whizkid's a Rigger. He's also into aircraft, helos to be exact. He's got Rotor Craft at 6. Being a rigger, he has concentrated on Remote Operation and specialized in Fixed-Rotor. He can operate any fixed-rotor aircraft, remotely or jacked in, with a rating of 8.

Whizkid's Ares Dragon has hit a sudden squall and he decides to land before it gets worse. The chopper is big (+2) and the squall makes for bad conditions (+2). With his vehicle Control Rig rating of 1 he gets a -2. Too bad he's never flown a Dragon before (+1), but least he ain't under fire. His Target Number is the Dragon's Handling Rating of 5, plus the modifiers, for a final Target Number of 8. Whizkid gets 1, 2, 3, 3, 5, 6, 6, and 6. Rerolling the three sixes he gets 1,1, and 4, for a final result of 1, 2, 3, 3, 5, 7, 7, and 10. The last one saves his butt since it gives him one success. The Dragon sets down safely.

KNOWLEDGE SKILL USE

Does the player know the capital of Tir Tairngire? What about the metals that make up Orichalcum? What are the normal operating parameters of a Smartgun Link and why does this chipped ork, who the player just offed, have a different type? Players don't know this information, but their characters might. Below is a list of suggested Target Numbers and a Success Table for using the various Knowledge Skills.

KNOWLEDGE SKILL TABLE

Situation	Target Number
Character is seeking:	
General Knowledge	3
Detailed Knowledge	5
Intricate Knowledge	8
Obscure Knowledge	12

 # Number of Successes

1 General Information, no details

2 Detailed Information, with some minor points inaccurate

3 Detailed Information, with some minor points obscure or missing

4 Detailed and Accurate Information

Fastjack has never had much use for magic, but he knows science (Physical Sciences Rating 6). He's got a strange, white rock on his hands and wants to know what it is. Knowing that it's a piece of metamorphosed flesh (see Petrify Spell, in the **Grimoire**), the gamemaster secretly sets the Target Number at 12 because the rock is not natural and magical workings are not common knowledge, especially to Fastjack. Fastjack rolls his dice and manages to get two successes, which is not enough to get the whole story. The gamemaster informs Jack that his analysis shows the rock to be a metamorphic carbonate of unusual structure, possibly a fossil, because of the presence of some apparently biological structures.

LANGUAGE SKILL USE

In using Languages, failure to achieve the required number of success usually means that the attempted communication was only partially successful, possibly misunderstood to your detriment. The gamemaster may want to make any die rolls himself so that the players won't know whether they got across what they intended to say.

LANGUAGE SKILLS TABLE

Situation	Target Number
Speaking Dialect	+2
(variation of a particular language)	
Universal Concept	2
(hunger, fear, bodily functions)	
Basic Conversation	4
(concerns of daily life)	
Complex Subject	6
(special/ limited interest topics)	
Intricate Subject	8
(almost any technical subject)	
Obscure Subject	10
(deeply technical/rare knowledge)	

A beautiful Elven woman comes running up to Dodger, babbling something in Elvish. His knowledge of the language is minimal (Elvish 2). He rolls his two dice and gets two sevens. As it turns out, these are success, and so he understands that she is looking for help because someone is following her (Complex Subject Target Number 6). When she tries to explain just who it is and why they want her (Intricate Subject, Target Number 8), the convolutions become too much for Dodger (he rolls a 2 and a 5) and he loses the sense of what she is saying. Still, she is a maiden in distress, and he must help her!

Alexander

HAULING THE LOAD

Players have a tendency to equip their characters with every conceivable item, from assault cannon to toasters, along with enough ammunition and bread to keep them operating continuously for five years. If your players seem to be getting a bit out of hand, you can impose the following Encumbrance rules.

A character can carry up to his Strength x 10 in kilograms without appreciable effect.

Twice that load will leave him in a state of Light Fatigue (see **Combat**). Three times the load and he's moderately fatigued, cannot run, and his movement is cut in half. Four times and he's seriously fatigued, cannot run, and his movement is cut to one-quarter of its normal value. Any more and the character passes out from exhaustion.

If the character is just trying to lift a load and not go anywhere with it, he gets to add (Strength)D6 kilograms over his maximum load. He can only hold this up for the number of turns equal to his Body, however. Any longer and he increases his fatigue condition one step per turn.

PERCEPTION AND REALITY

The player knows that he is not really in the world of **Shadowrun**, but his character is. Unlike the player, the character can see the world around him in 2050. The player has to rely on his character to notice things.

Normally, the gamemaster will keep the player informed of obvious facts about the character's surroundings. But what about the not-so-obvious facts? Like whether or not that suit

over there who looks like a corp type, is packing heat. Or whether the character can hear that sneaky Elf coming up the alley behind him. Or smell the Chromed Ork hiding under an Invisibility Spell.

To determine such situations, the gamemaster tests the character's perception. Use the character's Intelligence Rating for the number of dice. The Target Number will depend on the circumstances. Some things, such as whether a gun can be concealed, are assigned specific numbers and are listed in the **Equipment** chapter. The gamemaster can decide on the rest.

Either way, the gamemaster asks the player for his character's Intelligence Rating (or the highest rating in the group if there's more than one player character) and make the roll himself. To avoid letting the players know that something is up, every once in a while when you think your players are getting complacent, ask for the rating, roll a couple of dice, and shake your head. Pretty soon the players will start to think Trolls are in every shadow.

QUICK MATRIX SYSTEMS

The following Quick Matrix System lets you whip up a "random" computer system in the Matrix. It will be useful for those times when you have given the players a clue indicating that, say, Crown Imperial Corporation is behind some recent problem of theirs, and the decker pipes up with, "Zero sweat. I'll just hack into their 'puter and see what's on file."

Here's how you prepare a warm welcome for him.

CHOOSE A SECURITY CODE

First, choose a base Security Code or roll randomly on the table below. It is better to choose the code. The hotter the system, the higher its code.

RANDOM SECURITY CODE TABLE	
Die Roll	Security Level
1–2	Green
3–5	Orange
6	Red

DESIGN THE ARCHITECTURE

Next you design the architecture. by making a series of die rolls to position each node in the system. Keep on rolling new nodes until you like what you've got. As you roll up each node, draw its symbol on your map.

The first node you draw is always the SAN that the decker will enter. Draw a second box, which is an SPU (SANs almost always connect to SPUs). Draw a line from the SAN to the SPU.

The SPU is now your current node. Roll 1D6 and consult the SPU Column of the following table to get the next node to draw. Run a line from the SPU to the new node. The new node usually becomes the current node for the next roll. If you don't like the result, you can always reroll or ignore a roll. You may also decide to stay in a node and roll for a second (or third) connecting node.

As you draw each new node, give it a number that you can refer to in your notes during the adventure. So far, we have Node 1 (the SAN) and Node 2 (the SPU).

About the only firm rule is that a system can have only one CPU. If you get the CPU early in the process, you may decide it's too easy to reach and so ignore that roll. If you keep designing after you place the CPU, then you can either ignore a CPU result in another node, or take it to mean that there is a line connecting that node back to the CPU.

Once you have the basic architecture, you may wish to embellish it by adding more nodes, running connecting Datalines, and making it a real maze. By the way, it's a good idea to make one map for yourself and one for your players while doing this. Some decker might get to the CPU and demand to see what the system looks like.

QUICK MATRIX CREATION

Die Roll	Current node: CPU	SPU	DATASTORE
1	SPU	CPU	CPU
2	SPU	SPU	CPU
3	SPU	DATASTORE	SPU
4	DATASTORE	DATASTORE	SPU
5	DATASTORE	*	SPU
6	*	*	DATASTORE

* Add a line to a dead-end node: your choice of an SN, I/OP, or SAN. Stay in the current node for the next roll.

EXAMPLE: Starting from a SAN, connect to an SPU 1D6, with a result of 5. A 5 in an SPU is a dead end. Add an I/OP and stay in the SPU. Make another die roll with a 1 result. A 1 in an SPU is the CPU. Too early. Ignore this roll. Roll again with a result of 3. A 3 in an SPU is another SPU. This SPU becomes current. You roll again, and get a 3. A 3 in an SPU is a Datastore. The Datastore becomes current. Now you roll a 5. A 5 in a Datastore is an SPU. The SPU becomes current node. This time you roll a 6. A 6 in an SPU is a dead end: add an I/OP and the SPU stays current for the next roll. Another die roll, and the result is 1. Finally! A 1 in an SPU is a CPU. The CPU becomes the current node. You roll again, and its another Datastore. You decide to stop here.

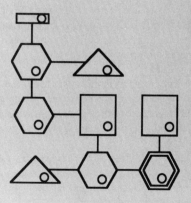

DETERMINE SECURITY CODES

The third step is to set Security Codes. For random systems, you may want to keep the whole system the same Security Level (that's the color) and randomly roll a Security Rating (that's the number) for each node. You can also vary the classifications randomly, assigning different Security Levels, or colors, to different parts of the system.

To vary the Security Level, roll 1D6 for each node. A 1 is one level lower than the Security Code you originally chose. On a Green system, this would mean a Code Blue Level. A roll of 6 is one level higher. On a Green system, this would be an Orange level.

Whether or not you fiddle with the level, choose or roll for (1D6 is good) the Security Rating of each node. Note the numbers on your system map.

INSTALL IC

For each node, roll 1D6 to see if IC is present.
For a Code Green node, IC is present on a roll of 1.
For a Code Orange node, IC is present on a roll of 1 – 2.
For a Code Red node, IC is present on a roll of 1 – 3.
To determine the type of IC present, roll 2D6 and consult the IC Installation Table.

IC INSTALLATION TABLE

Security Code	White IC	Gray IC	Black IC
Green	2 – 8	9 – 11	12
Orange	2 – 7	8 – 10	11 – 12
Red	2 – 6	7 – 10	11 – 12

Now make one more roll on 2D6 and consult the Program Table below to find out exactly what kind of White or Gray Ice is installed. There is no need to make this roll for Black IC. Lethal is Lethal, right? All IC programs have a rating of 2D6–1.

IC PROGRAM TABLE

White IC

Die Roll	Program
2	Trapped IC*
3 – 7	Access
8 – 11	Barrier/Scramble**
12	Trapped IC*

*Trapped IC: There is Gray IC hidden as White IC. Rolling 1D6+4, against the White Table to see what the obvious IC is. Then roll against the Gray Table for the hidden IC.

**Use Scramble only in a datastore. Use Barrier in any node (including a datastore if desired.)

Gray IC

Die Roll	Program
2 – 4	Blaster
5 – 6	Trace
7 – 8	Killer
9 – 11	Tar Baby
12	Tar Pit

INSTALL DATA VALUES

Data is loot. Roll 2D6 and consult the Data Value Table for each datastore. Unless the roll comes up 2 or 12, there will be 1D6 valuable files. The size of each file is 2D6 x 10 Mp. The decker needs the Evaluate program to find the valuable files, though.

Besides stocking this kind of random loot, you should determine the location of any files containing specific information the decker is seeking. This can be scattered around. Let's say the team was attacked by a gang called the Gutter Larks. They suspect that Crown Imperial hired the gang to do them dirty. You might put a file in one datastore that contains a payment from Corporate Account #324A7 to the Gutter Larks. Another file in the other datastore might indicate that Ivan Dragomilov is the officer authorized to release funds from account #324A7. A third file (perhaps back in the first datastore) identifies Dragomilov as a junior executive in corporate security, and gives his address, photo, and so on. This information lets the team find Mr. Dragomilov and ask a few pointed questions in person.

For example, in an Orange Datastore, you roll 2D6 and score 9. The base value is 10,000¥ per 10 Mp of data. Roll 1D6, scoring 3. There are 3 valuable files. For each file, roll 2D6, scoring 7, 9, 4. The files are 70 Mp (worth 70,000¥), 90 Mp (worth 90,000¥), and 40 Mp (worth 40,000¥). If the decker can download them all, the "list price" of the swag will be about 200,000¥ from this datastore. But he has to fence the stuff, which means he will only get 20–100 thou.

| | DATA VALUE TABLE | | |
| Die | Value per 10 Mp of data: | | |
Roll	Green	Orange	Red
2	0	0	0
3 – 4	500¥	1,000¥	2,500¥
5 – 7	1,000¥	2,500¥	5,000¥
8 – 10	5,000¥	10,000¥	50,000¥
11	10,000¥	50,000¥	100,000¥
12	0	0	0

SHADOWRUNNING

The world of 2050 is an exciting, dangerous place with plenty of opportunity for adventure. That's where the player characters come in. Whether they are making a run on some megacorp's mainframe, providing security for a visiting dignitary, or busting a friend out of a detention center, they are the heroes. Your adventures should challenge their wits even more than their guns, with the gamemaster rewarding good roleplaying as much or more than lucky dice-rolling.

TAILOR THE ADVENTURE

When getting a group of players together, is best to learn something about their interests or else your adventures could fall flat. It's important that the mission you have planned is one they'd really like to tackle, but don't expect a lot at first. The players probably know less about the ways of the game universe than you do and may have only vague ideas about wanting to make money, take on a corrupt corp, deal with elves, and so on. Once they get a few runs under their belts and their characters' life stories take some shape, the players' goals and ideas will become more defined. They may want to hunt down a particular enemy, find a lost love, take revenge on a corporation that did them dirty, or find a specific teacher or piece of custom gear. You can and should build these ideas and suggestions into major themes in your adventures.

Encourage the players to write out their character's histories, including background on family, friends, and previous employment. You can then draw on those histories to develop adventures that get everyone involved.

Be Aware!

You have to keep a lot in mind. Listen to what the players say. Keep track of your NPCs' whereabouts, plans, and so on. It's good to have a note pad handy for jotting down memos to yourself as the adventure rolls along.

Be Knowledgeable!

A gamemaster must be familiar with the whole game. That doesn't mean memorizing the complete rule book, but you should be familiar enough with it to find a particular rule or rules quickly. You should also have a good knowledge of the basic game systems.

Keep a written outline of your adventure where you can refer to it. As you gain experience, you'll probably improvise more and more detail, but for starters, it's best if adventures are simple and worked out beforehand.

Be Fair!

Stick to the rules. If you or your players hate something we've written, change it. If you do that, make sure everyone knows what the new rule is.

Remember that you, as gamemaster, know much more about what is happening than the NPCs do. *You* may know the player characters' skills, weapons, spells, and so on, but the NPCs don't. It would be unfair to let the NPCs behave and make plans based on that knowledge.

Be Realistic!

Remember that the NPCs that you play are just people, with all the usual fears, needs, hopes, and desires. By giving them life, the stories that come out of the game will be more memorable for everybody involved.

Play critters like real critters, too. For example, most animals have little or no interest in killing for pleasure. They fight when they need to—to eat, to protect their young, to save their own hides.

Be Flexible!

If a player wants to do something not explicitly covered in the rules, don't just refuse on principle. There is always a skill rating of some kind that you can use for a Success Test. Tell the player what skill or attribute you think applies to the situation and whether his chances are good, indifferent, or terrible. You don't have to tell him precise Target Numbers, just whether or not his goal is possible.

If you come up with a rule to cover a special case during a game, decide later whether it will become a new "house rule" that always applies in future games or a one-shot that may or may not be used again. The middle of a shadowrun is no place to discuss the fine points of game mechanics.

Be Tough!

Challenge the players. If they don't sweat to get that Karma, they haven't earned it. Two goons armed with baseball bats would not be the only security guarding the corporate data center, and the local Yakuza won't keep their main database on a home computer.

Once you and the players are comfortable with the way the rules work, you'll be able to fine-tune the "threat level" of an adventure. For now, keep in mind that on a really rough run, the player characters should, ideally, win it by the skin of their teeth, if they win at all. If you don't get it right at first, nobody's gonna fry you.

Be Kind!

How can you be tough and kind? As gamemaster, you can kill off a character anytime. You can throw enormous risks at the player characters until their luck runs out and they fail a Success Test. But only cheap bullies do that. Gamemasters who measure their success in trashed character sheets soon find themselves without players. Better to be too easy on the characters, rather than too deadly.

When the player characters get in over their heads, remember that bad guys like to take prisoners. Prisoners can be made to talk. Prisoners can be used as hostages. Prisoners can also escape or pay ransoms. Most important, prisoners have a chance to escape and live to fight another day. If fictional villains were smart enough to kill off the heroes at the first opportunity, then all the adventure movies ever made would end after the first ten minutes.

DEATH AND SHADOWRUNNING

In any roleplaying game, death is a touchy subject. Nobody likes it when a favorite character buys the farm. In **Shadowrun**, agricultural property can come very cheap. Characters can get splattered before they know what is happening. Despite all the special rules and high-tech medicine, player characters are going to die.

Sometimes, you may have to cheat to keep them alive. If, in your opinion, the player did everything right and just had bad luck in rolling dice, don't kill him. Knock him out! Stick him in the hospital! Whatever! Don't let a well-developed character die just because the player rolled a 2 when he needed a 3. You can and should decide that he stays alive long enough to get into a hospital.

The same goes for your best NPCs. If the villain you spent hours designing gets hit by a lucky shot and does not resist the damage, you can always bury his body under a collapsing building or some other disaster that "no one could possibly survive." A few months later, he can show up, held together by glue and cyberware, ready for revenge on the player characters.

BEHIND THE SCENES

AWARDING KARMA

As mentioned in **After the Shadowrun**, characters get Karma for surviving an adventure and more Karma if they do well in the process. You make the awards. Give all surviving team members Karma in equal amounts, based on the following criteria.

A typical adventure should be worth maybe 3 or 4 Team Karma points. One for survival, a couple for objectives, and a point for the danger along the way. A real horror show would be worth 6 to 8 points or so, but that needs combat, danger, and powerful opposition, with the objectives wrapped in twisting paths of mystery!

SURVIVAL

Each character should get 1 Karma Point for surviving the adventure.

SUCCESS

For every adventure objective that the team achieves, award them 1 point of Karma. Partial awards are allowed. If they foiled the evil plan and stole the technological gizmo, but the villain escaped, they get 2 out of a possible 3.

THREAT

Award extra Karma for dangerous adventures. A simple mission might not carry any bonus, but a mission against high odds or one where a dangerous enemy is involved is worth 1 or

2 extra Points. A whirling nightmare of combat, confusion, and betrayal is worth 3 Karma Points each to the survivors. Let the level of opposition influence this. Even a simple run against a superior enemy (a powerful corp type or a Yakuza oyabun) is worth extra Karma.

INDIVIDUAL KARMA AWARDS

Team awards are made to everybody who participates in an adventure, even if he didn't get into the spotlight this time around. Individual Karma is awarded to characters who personally advance the story or the overall gaming enjoyment in some way.

If a character has an absolutely amazing run, and the group succeeds at a very nasty mission, he might get up to 10 or 12 Karma Points. A Karma award greater than 12 Points for a single adventure should probably never happen.

Roleplaying

Award 1 Karma Point to players who mostly stayed in character. Really good roleplaying is worth 2 Karma Points. The standards of roleplaying will depend on how you and your group like to play. Be flexible! This is supposed to be fun, not a course in method acting.

Guts

Brave and/or effective fighters should get a Point or two of Karma. Stupidly brave fighters don't earn this award. If they are lucky enough to survive, that's its own reward. This would include gutsy magical battles in Astral Space and desperate Cybercombat in the Matrix as well as shoot-em-ups in the physical world.

Smarts

Players who come up with a clever strategy or solve a puzzling clue or pull off a good scam should get 1 Karma Point for their characters. This includes those smart enough to know when to surrender or run.

Right Place–Right Time

Characters who are in the right place, with the right skill to do some necessary job, should get 1 point of Karma. Don't award Karma just for making good die rolls. The award is for having a skill that is vital and knowing when to use it.

If the players knew they needed a lock picked and so had a character slot Lockpicking Skill beforehand, a Karma award is unsuitable. If the team got trapped in a dead-end alley, with the bad guys closing in, and one of them spotted the old doorway and picked the lock under fire so the team could escape …well, that's different story.

Surprise

Players can surprise you with plans that absolutely kill the story line. A surprising and effective strategy is worth 1 Karma Point to the player who comes up with it. Surprising and silly actions, on the other hand, get zip.

Humor

If a player, acting in character, can paralyze the entire gaming group with laughter, that is worth 1 Karma Point in an adventure. We are in this for fun, after all.

Drama

Similarly, if a player, acting in character, impresses the group with a particular piece of high drama (maybe even if its high melodrama), he too, earns 1 Point of Karma.

GLOSSARY OF SLANG IN 2050

—Courtesy of *WorldWide WordWatch*

KEY

(vul) = vulgar

(jap) = Japanese or "Japlish" loanword

v. = verb

adj. = adjective

n. = noun

Angel n. A benefactor, especially an unknown one.

Arc n. An arcology.

Breeder n. Ork slang for a "normal" Human.

Business n. In slang context, crime. Also "Biz."

Buzz Go away. Buzz off.

Chipped adj. Senses, skills, reflexes, muscles, and so on, enhanced by cyberware.

Chummer n. "Pal" or "buddy".

Comm n. The telephone.

Corp n., adj. Corporation. Corporate.

Dandelion Eater n., adj. Elf or elven. Highly insulting.

Dataslave n. Corporate decker or other data processing employee.

Datasteal n. Theft of data from a computer, usually by decking.

Deck n. A cyberdeck. v. To use a cyberdeck, usually illegally.

Decker n. Pirate cyberdeck user. Derived from 20th-century term "Hacker".

Deckhead n. Simsense abuser; anyone with a datajack or chipjack.

Drek n. (vul) A common curse word. adj: Drekky.

Dumped v. Involuntarily ejected from the Matrix.

Exec v. Corporate executive.

Fetishman n. A talismonger.

Frag v. Common swear word. adj: Fragging.

Geek v. To kill.

Go-go-go n. A bike gang or gang member.

Heatwave n. Police crackdown.

Hoi Hi. Hello. (familiar form)

Hose v. Louse up. Screw up.

Ice n. Security software. "Intrusion Countermeasures," or IC.

Jack v. Jack in, or enter cyberspace. Jack out, or to leave cyberspace.

Jander v. To walk in an arrogant, yet casual manner; to strut.

Kobun n. (jap) Member of a Yakuza clan.

Mr. Johnson n. Refers to any anonymous employer or corporate agent.

Mundane n. adj. (vul) Non-magician or non-magical.

Nutrisoy n. Cheaply processed food product, derived from soybeans.

Nuyen n. World standard of currency.

Oyabun n. (jap) Head of a Yakuza clan.

Panzer n. Any ground-effect combat vehicle.

Paydata n. A datafile worth money on the black market.

Plex n. A metropolitan complex, or "metroplex."

Poli n. A policlub or policlub member.

Razorguy n. Heavily cybered samurai or other muscle.

Samurai n. (jap) Mercenary or muscle for hire. Implies honor code.

Sararlman n. (jap) From "salaryman." A corporate employee.

Screamer n. Credstick or other ID that triggers computer alarms if used.

Seoul Man n. Member of a Seoulpa ring.

Seoulpa ring n. A small criminal gang with connections to others like it.

Shaikujin n. (jap) Lit. "Honest citizen." A corporate employee.

Simsense n. ASIST sensory broadcast or recording.

Slot v. Mild curse word.

Slot and Run v. Hurry up. Get to the point. Move it.

So ka (jap) I understand. I get it.

Soykaf n. Ersatz coffee substitute made from soybeans.

Sprawl n. a metroplex (see Plex); v. fraternize below one's social level.

Suit n. A "straight citizen." See Shaikujin, Sarariman.

System Identification Number (SIN) n. Identification number assigned to each person in the society.

Trid n. Three-dimensional successor to video.

Trog n. (vul) An Ork or Troll. From "troglodyte." Highly insulting.

Vatjob n. A person with extensive cyberware replacement, reference is to a portion of the process during which the patient must be submerged in nutrient fluid.

Wagemage n. A magician (usually mage) employed by a corporation.

Wetwork n. Assassination. Murder.

Wired adj. Equipped with cyberware, especially increased reflexes.

Wizard n. A magician, usually a mage; adj. great, wonderful, excellent.

Wizworm n. slang. A dragon.

Yak n. (jap) Yakuza. Either a clan member or a clan itself.

CONTACTS

"You are who you know."
—Street Proverb

his chapter includes brief descriptions, including Attribute and Skill Ratings, for non-player characters likely to appear in **Shadowrun** adventures. The quotes may help the gamemaster get a "feel" for the character to help him add life and color to his own roleplaying.

BOUNTY HUNTER

"Nobody asked you to like me. I'm just a gal doing a job. You want the guy or not? You want him, I'm the one to get him. I can bring him back alive, but that's extra. It complicates things."

QUOTES

"Dead. Alive. Don't really matter to me. Of course, dead is a lot easier."

"Money. It always comes down to that, doesn't it?"

"Easy or hard. Your choice."

COMMENTARY

The Bounty Hunter is a hard woman. She lives by tracking those people that the corporate cops and hitmen don't have the time or inclination to track down.

ATTRIBUTES	SKILLS
Body: 6	Bike: 5
Quickness: 5	Car: 5
Strength: 5 (6)	Computer: 4
Charisma: 1	Etiquette (Corporate): 3
Intelligence: 4	Etiquette (Street): 5
Willpower: 4	Firearms: 8
Essence: 1.35	Stealth: 4
Reaction: 8	Unarmed Combat: 6
	Special Skills:
	Data Tracing: 3
	Tracking: 3

CYBERWARE

Cyberarm (Strength 1) with holdout pistol and retractable hand razors

Cybereyes with thermographic imaging

Smartgun Link

Wired Reflexes (2)

BARTENDER

"I been tending bar here for a lot of years now. Seen it all in my time. Know all the regulars real good. Their problems mostly, but their happy times, too. We're like family around here. Always looking out for each other. We're peaceable folks, though. Don't like no trouble. Trouble is bad for business."

QUOTES

"Whazappening, man? Ain't seen you for a while. The usual?"

"I caught a little something about that. Not first-hand, mind you. I heard from a man who knows a man. Understand?"

"There was some suits in here asking after you, but I told them you ain't been around."

COMMENTARY

The Bartender is a common source of information on current conditions in the streets and on the club circuit. He is discreet and reliable, for a price. Discounts for old friends and good customers, of course.

ATTRIBUTES	SKILLS
Body: 4	Firearms: 3
Quickness: 3	Etiquette (Street): 4
Strength: 4	Unarmed Combat: 3
Charisma: 3	**Special Skills:**
Intelligence: 2	Rumormill: 5
Willpower: 2	Sympathetic Listening: 5
Essence: 6	
Reaction: 2	

COMPANY MAN

"I'm a company man. I know that doesn't make me very welcome in some places, but that doesn't bother me. I'm not here to make people happy. I'm here to do a job and I'll do whatever it takes to get it done. The company'll take care of the mess afterwards. It always does."

QUOTES

"Nothing personal, friend. It's just business."

"I'm just in it for the money and the benefit package, sweetheart."

"You're being an annoyance to somebody important, chummer. I've been asked to resolve the matter."

COMMENTARY

The Company Man is the special executive agent for the corporation. He does his job, no questions asked. He is loyal, often unto death. After all, the corporation can even fix that.

ATTRIBUTES	SKILLS
Body: 6	Etiquette (Corporate): 3
Quickness: 5	Firearms: 7
Strength: 6	Stealth: 5
Charisma: 2	Unarmed Combat: 6
Intelligence: 4	Vehicle (Gamemaster's discretion
Willpower: 5	for type): 5
Essence: 3	
Reaction: 4	

CYBERWARE

WiredReflexes (1)

Skillwires (5)

CITY OFFICIAL

"We have a fine city here, one of the best-run metroplexes on the continent. All those rumors you may have heard about corruption in the current administration are just smoke from the opposition parties. Smoke and lies from malcontents. We are all hard workers, proud of our city and proud to serve the public as best we can."

QUOTES

"No comment."

"I'm sorry, but I really can't comment on that at this time."

"I assure you that there is no conflict of interest in the present circumstances."

COMMENTARY

The City Official is a typical member of the bureaucracy that runs the metroplex. Though concerned about his public image and the reactions of the voters, he is more concerned about his party bosses and his sponsors. He is most trustworthy during a campaign, but will gladly sell you out for a political or career advantage.

ATTRIBUTES	SKILLS
Body: 2	Etiquette (Corporate): 4
Quickness: 2	Etiquette (Tribal): 3
Strength: 2	Negotiation: 4
Charisma: 5	
Intelligence: 3	
Willpower: 2	
Essence: 6	
Reaction: 2	

CORPORATE SECURITY GUARD

"Sure, I been through hard times, but I've got a good job with the corporation now. I'm a company man all the way. It's got just enough glamor and excitement to keep me happy right now. Someday, though, maybe I'll work my way up, and get myself a slot in the special ops division. Be one of those guys who push all the buttons. Yeah, that would be nice."

QUOTES

"Hold it right there, chummer. Let's see your corp card."

"Are you authorized for this section? Let's see your corp card."

"Your card checks O.K. How about them Sonics? Quite a game the other night."

COMMENTARY

The Corporate Security Guard is a simple man who is really more interested in his own private life and survival than dangerous action and adventure. He greatly values his position with the corporation and will work in its best interests, especially when there is a corporate official nearby watching him.

ATTRIBUTES
Body: 4
Quickness: 3
Strength: 3
Charisma: 2
Intelligence: 2
Willpower: 2
Essence: 6
Reaction: 2

SKILLS
Etiquette (Corporate): 2
Firearms: 3
Interrogation: 2
Unarmed Combat: 3

CORPORATE SECRETARY

"I know what a lot of people think about us here at the company. Believe me, I've heard it all. I also know this is a strange thing for me to say, but...I'm a company woman. All I can say is that the corporation's been very good to me and I intend to do anything I can to keep things that way."

QUOTES

"I'm sorry, but Mr. Johnson is not available at the moment. May I take a message?"

"Could you hold, please?"

"I'm sorry, but Mr. Johnson is still unavailable."

"He'll get back to you as soon as he can."

COMMENTARY

The Corporate Secretary is cool, efficient, loyal, and discreet. You'd want her working for you, if you could have her. She's as much a part of the corporate office as the furniture and telecom.

ATTRIBUTES
Body: 2
Quickness: 2
Strength: 2
Charisma: 4
Intelligence: 4
Willpower: 2
Essence: 4.8
Reaction: 3

SKILLS
Computer: 3
Etiquette (Corporate): 4
Special Skill:
Corporate Rumormill: 4

CYBERWARE
Datajack, 100Mp of Memory

ELVEN HITMAN

"You came looking for the best and now you've found me. I heard of your proposal. Such a sanction is well within my capacity. I can do the work with no noise, no fuss, no trace. Satisfaction guaranteed."

QUOTES

"I do hope you have arranged for quality logistic support. My last employer had a skinflint's tendency to skimp."

"You want the best work, you hire the best."

"What did you say your credit balance was?"

'That will cost extra!'

"I am not mad. You do not want to see me when I am mad."

COMMENTARY

The Elven Hitman is slick and smooth, and he knows it. He is the quintessential gentleman-assassin. He is always impeccably dressed, with accessories of the finest quality. His manners are smooth, with just a hint of dangerous arrogance. Unless, of course, he loses his temper.

ATTRIBUTES	SKILLS
Body: 5	Bike: 4
Quickness: 6	Car: 4
Strength: 5	Demolitions: 4
Charisma: 2	Etiquette (Corporate): 3
Intelligence: 4	Etiquette (Street): 3
Willpower: 4	Firearms: 8
Essence: 3.5	Hover Craft: 4
Reaction: 9	Unarmed Combat: 4

CYBERWARE

Wired Reflexes (2)
Smartgun Link

DWARVEN TECHNICIAN

"I know it's a stereotype, but what do you want? Stereotypes make sense sometimes, you know. I happen to like tech, that's all. It's not like it's in my blood. It's just a knack, an interest. And I am very good at it."

QUOTES

"Nobody appreciates good craftsmanship anymore."

"What do think you're paying for? Some fumble-fingered Ork who doesn't know a circuit board from a bread board?"

"Now ain't that sweet! Them furriners sure like to make their circuits small."

COMMENTARY

The Dwarven Technician may actually be no better than any other, but he does tend to blow his own horn whenever he gets the chance. Maybe he just tries harder, though he would never admit that.

ATTRIBUTES	SKILLS
Body: 4	Computer Theory: 6
Quickness: 2	Computers (B/R): 6
Strength: 3	Electronics (B/R): 9
Charisma: 2	Electronics: 6
Intelligence: 6	Etiquette (Street or Corporate): 3
Willpower: 4	
Essence: 3.8	
Reaction: 4	

CYBERWARE

Datajack, 200Mp of Memory

GANG BOSS

"To live on the streets is to know the streets. Who's on top, who's out, where the turf lines are. You're on my turf now, chummer. Let's here you sing. If I like the tune, maybe I'll let you keep your tongue. But you'd better not bring any trouble my way. I don't like strangers slopping their wars over onto my turf."

QUOTES

"I'm the boss here."

"You want to see action in this part of the plex, you talk to me."

COMMENTARY

The Gang Boss talks tough, and he is tough. He has to be in order to stay on top. But he's not stupid. He's learned a lot of hard lessons growing up on the streets. Just being tough doesn't cut it anymore.

ATTRIBUTES	SKILLS
Body: 3	Armed Combat: 4
Quickness: 3	Etiquette (Street): 6
Strength: 4	Firearms: 4
Charisma: 4	Leadership: 4
Intelligence: 4	Unarmed Combat: 2
Willpower: 4	
Essence: 6	
Reaction: 3	

FIXER

"You say you're looking for a little military hardware? Could be I have just what you need. Money is an amazing thing. Fixes just about anything. Need an expert to run that hardware? I can take care of that, too. You came to the right woman, my friend. I know we can do business."

QUOTES

"Let's see the cred balance, chummer."

"It's hot. Some kind of military program, I think. Its definitely not Israeli, despite the casing."

"Can't give you that kind of price, chummer. A woman's got business expenses to cover."

"Are you sure nobody's tailing you?"

COMMENTARY

The Fixer is a fence and/or arranger, a power broker of the streets who always has the latest in software, equipment, or information. All for a price.

ATTRIBUTES	SKILLS
Body: 2	Computer: 3
Quickness: 3	Electronics: 3
Strength: 2	Etiquette (Street): 5
Charisma: 3	Firearms: 3
Intelligence: 5	Negotiation: 7
Willpower: 5	**Special Skill**
Essence: 2	Evaluate Value of High-Tech Items: 6
Reaction: 4	

CYBERWARE

Cybereyes

Datajack, 300 Mp of Memory

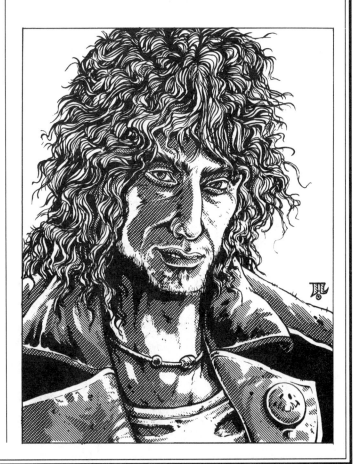

HUMANIS POLICLUB MEMBER

'They're worse than the heathen, these so-called meta-humans. They are perversions, blots upon the sacred honor of true humanity. They and all who side with them must be annihilated if the true way of the world is to be followed."

QUOTES

"Black, white, or yellow is no longer the question at hand. Now it is simply a matter of us and them. Humans and metahumans. Purity and pestilence."

"The hoods are not meant to hide our identities. Rather they protect the pure face of justice staring out at the devil's children."

COMMENTARY

The Humanis Policlub Member belongs to an organization that opposes all legal rights for the Awakened, especially meta-humans. They have been known to twist and bend existing laws whenever possible in order to further their own aims, while at the same time suppressing the rights of the opposition. Even acts of violence are not beyond their scope. In such instances, they usually conceal their faces.

ATTRIBUTES	SKILLS
Body: 4	Bike: 3
Quickness: 4	Car: 3
Strength: 4	Demolitions: 4
Charisma: 2	Etiquette (Street): 3
Intelligence: 2	Firearms: 4
Willpower: 4	
Essence: 6	
Reaction: 3	

NOTES

The individual member will have 1D6 other members he can call to help him.

MECHANIC

"Machines are a lot nicer than people. They never sass you back, never get up on the wrong side of the bed. A woman can understand them. They never complain about grease on your clothes or dirt under your finger-nails. Machines and me, we get along pretty well.

QUOTES

"You broke it good this time."

"How do ya expect me to fix that on yer budget?"

"If ya don't want the weapons registered, it'll cost ya extra. Plenty extra."

COMMENTARY

The Mechanic is the person to see when your transport's down. She also does custom work.

ATTRIBUTES	SKILLS
Body: 2	Aircraft (B/R): 6
Quickness: 3	Computer: 3
Strength: 3	Computer Theory: 6
Charisma: 2	Electronics: 3
Intelligence: 6	Electronics (B/R): 5
Willpower: 4	Ground Vehicles (B/R): 8
Essence: 6	
Reaction: 4	

MEDIA PRODUCER

'The people want to know. That's what I always say. They have enquiring minds, and besides, it's their fundamental right to be informed. At least that's what we'll tell them."

QUOTES

"For us, bad news is always good for the ratings."

"If I can't find any news, I'll just have to make some."

"Look, I been in the business since before you were born. I know what'll play and what won't."

"All the people want is a good show. Just a show. Every day is so full of problems, complaints, and worries that when people come home at night, all they want is their cocktail, their solitude, their entertainment. That's where I come in."

COMMENTARY

The Media Producer is an entertainment entrepreneur, who draws a very fine line between news information and entertainment. She's got an eye for what will make people sit up and take notice, and how to present the stories in a way that won't leave anybody too upset. Broadcasting is a business, after all.

ATTRIBUTES	SKILLS
Body: 2	Computer: 3
Quickness: 3	Etiquette (Corporate): 4
Strength: 2	Etiquette (Media): 4
Charisma: 5	Etiquette (Street): 4
Intelligence: 4	Negotiation: 4
Willpower: 4	Stealth: 2
Essence: 6	Unarmed Combat: 2
Reaction: 3	

METAHUMAN RIGHTS ACTIVIST

"We're all human, you know. It's as simple as that. The disgraceful actions of Lone Star's storm troopers at the O.R.C. rally last week will not be forgotten. They never should have gassed the crowd. There was no real provocation. It was a peaceful demonstration. Disgraceful. I just came from filing a grievance with the city court. We'll see what the governor has to say when her gestapo is slapped with a lawsuit."

QUOTES

"Elves (and Dwarfs and Trolls, sometimes even Orks) are people, too."

"How would you like to be treated like that?"

"You think the March on Fresno was tough. Nothing. I was down in SF on Goblinization Day."

COMMENTARY

The Metahuman Rights Activist may have another job, but her true calling is working to see that all branches of humanity receive equal justice before the law. Then again, any unjust law deserves to be broken. The Activist is a mortal foe of the Humanis cultists.

ATTRIBUTES	SKILLS
Body: 2	Etiquette (Media): 5
Quickness: 2	Interrogation: 3
Strength: 2	Leadership: 3
Charisma: 2	Negotiation: 3
Intelligence: 2	
Willpower: 2	
Essence: 6	
Reaction: 2	

MR. JOHNSON

"Let me assure you that I fully understand your position. I hope you understand mine. We need this work done, and I feel that you are the right people to do it. Let's just say it would be very uncomfortable for all concerned were any news of this to be made public knowledge. I'm quite sure that we can rely on your discretion.

QUOTES

"If you're caught, we never heard of you before."
"This conversation never took place. Understand?"
"It's a small job. Minimal complications."
"Payment will be handled the usual way."

COMMENTARY

Mr. Johnson may not look the same the next time you see him. He may not even be a he. But don't be fooled—he's the man. Mr. Johnson is the generic slang term for a corporate-insider connection. He's got the bucks and he's got the jobs. And he's also got a private army to hunt you down if you cross him.

ATTRIBUTES
Body: 2
Quickness: 2
Strength: 2
Charisma: 4
Intelligence: 6
Willpower: 5
Essence: 3.8
Reaction: 4

SKILLS
Computer Theory: 5
Etiquette (Corporate): 8
Negotiation: 6
Psychology: 8
Special Skill
History: 4

CYBERWARE
Datajack, 200Mp of Memory

SQUATTER

"Watchu staring at, chummer? Ain't ya never seen a poor person? Watchu doing here? This squat's mine! Whoa, calm down. Don't want no trouble. Let's not get violent. I can find another. Always have. Just let me slip past ya. I won't say nothing. Truth. Real truth. Not a word."

QUOTES

"Mind your own biz."
"Ain't seen nothing. Ain't heard nothing."
"I wasn't always like this."
"Dey went dat way."

COMMENTARY

The squatter is a tough victim of the underside of the metroplex, hardened and beaten down by life in the slums. He is a survivor who tries to roll with the punches, and still wants to see another day. In one piece.

ATTRIBUTES
Body: 2
Quickness: 2
Strength: 1
Charisma: 1
Intelligence: 2
Willpower: 2
Essence: 6
Reaction: 2

SKILLS
Etiquette (Street): 3
Special Skills
Know Neighborhood: 6
Scrounge: 6

STREET DOC

"In trouble again? No, don't tell me about it! It's better for both of us if I don't know. Just keep your mouth shut and don't squirm until the local takes effect. I'd wait, but you're the one in a hurry. Your credit better clear this time."

QUOTES

"Stop bleeding on the floor."

"Interested in a good deal on some vat tissue? Source says it's real Chiba stock. I could stitch it down while I've got you opened up. No? Maybe a little cosmetic work since I have the laser scalpels out?"

"This is the third time this year. Haven't you any respect for quality craftsmanship?"

COMMENTARY

The Street Doc may be a quack or he may be a top-flight surgeon, but either way he's an outlaw's best friend. He'll always keep his mouth shut and won't report any suspicious wounds to the corp-sec or register your augmentations with the manufacturer for full-warranty coverage.

ATTRIBUTES
- Body: 2
- Quickness: 3
- Strength: 2
- Charisma: 2
- Intelligence: 4
- Willpower: 2
- Essence: 5.8
- Reaction: 3

CYBERWARE
- Datajack

SKILLS
- Biological Sciences: 6
- Biotech: 8
- Etiquette (Street): 3
- Negotiation: 4

STREET COP

"When I signed on with Lone Star, I believed all their recruitment hype. I was young. I know better now, but I'm still working for them. Guess I like the job. I'd feel better about the job if they were real police, but them days are long gone. We're businessmen now. Still, the streets should be safe. I believe that. Guess that's why I'm still doing the job."

QUOTES

"Look, I'm just doing my job."

"Let's not have any trouble here."

"Dead or alive, you're coming with me."

"Don't try it, chummer. Don't even think it."

COMMENTARY

The Street Cop is a slightly disillusioned, frustrated, but still determined servant of the law. Now, though, he works for an independent corporation rather than the government. It means better benefits, but lesser prestige among the rest of the population. He has learned to live with this, too. A few cops have, as always, succumbed to the temptations of their positions and become "bad cops," but most remain true to their honor.

ATTRIBUTES
- Body: 4
- Quickness: 4
- Strength: 4
- Charisma: 2
- Intelligence: 3
- Willpower: 3
- Essence: 6
- Reaction: 3

SKILLS
- Armed Combat: 2
- Etiquette (Corporate): 2
- Etiquette (Street): 4
- Firearms: 3
- Unarmed Combat: 3

Special Skill
- Police Procedures: 4

TALISMONGER

"If you're looking for the magical goods, I got 'em. Powders, bones, potions. Only the best ingredients and materials. What did you have in mind? If I don't have it, I can make arrangements to get it. I've got a lot of friends all over the 'plex and not a few outside of it."

QUOTES

"First, let's see the cred balance, chummer."

"On my uncle's spirit! It really is Elven (or Dwarven or Orkan or Troll) workmanship."

"Of course, I can't guarantee that it'll work under all conditions."

COMMENTARY

The Talismonger is a broker of magical goods and services, sort of an occult middle-woman. Sometimes she will moonlight as a fence for stolen magical materials as well as information.

ATTRIBUTES	SKILLS
Body: 2	Enchantment: 4
Quickness: 3	Etiquette (Street): 4
Strength: 3	Magic Theory: 8
Charisma: 2	Negotiation: 6
Intelligence: 3	Sorcery: 4
Willpower: 4	**Special Skills**
Essence: 6	Evaluate Magic Goods: 6
Magic: 3	Woodworking: 4
Reaction: 3	Metalworking: 4

TRIBAL CHIEF

"You are sitting in the council lodge of my people, stranger. You do not give orders here. You may make a request, and the council may consider your words, but no demand will be made here. If we find it in the interests of the tribe, we may agree to do as you ask."

QUOTES

"I am the chief. They do the singing."

"Do you play chess?"

"I have a fine horse, so who needs a car? A horse is a renewable resource. Have you had any success breeding your car lately?"

"Before I present you to the tribe, I will have to check your file on the council database."

COMMENTARY

The Tribal Chief is a man wise in the ways of the modern world, not just the ancient traditions. He must be well-aware of technology and the corporations if he is to guide his tribe well. He therefore makes it a point to know what is going on around him at all times.

ATTRIBUTES	SKILLS
Body: 3	Etiquette (Corporate): 4
Quickness: 3	Etiquette (Tribal): 8
Strength: 4	Leadership: 5
Charisma: 4	Negotiation: 4
Intelligence: 4	Projectile Weapons: 4
Willpower: 4	Psychology: 5
Essence: 6	Stealth: 5
Reaction: 3	

YAKUZA BOSS

"The times now are not what they once were. This is life. A man who wishes to be successful must adapt as society changes. We in the yakuza have done so, preserving as much of the old, honorable ways as possible while at the same time learning the new. Society will always need us."

QUOTES

"The new men are nothing more than gangsters and ruffians. They have no real sense of honor. And the Koreans and the Chinese are mere barbarians."

"An accommodation is necessary."

COMMENTARY

The Yakuza Boss, despite his philosophizing and courteous manners, is still a criminal mastermind. His true designs are ruthless, yet he always seeks to spread a veneer of culture and gentility over his rough edges. The older bosses prefer influence-peddling and embarrassment tactics over the crude intimidation and violence favored by the new blood.

ATTRIBUTES
Body: 3
Quickness: 4
Strength: 3
Charisma: 5
Intelligence: 6
Willpower: 5
Essence: 3.2
Reaction: 5

SKILLS
Etiquette (Corporate): 4
Etiquette (Street): 5
Leadership: 5
Negotiation: 6

CYBERWARE
Datajack
Wired Reflexes (1), 60Mp of Memory

TROLL BOUNCER

"Don't make trouble and you won't get hurt."

QUOTES

"I think dat it's time for youse to leave, shorty."
"Dat supposed to hurt?"
"Youse talkin' to me?"
"Closin' time."

COMMENTARY

Troll Bouncers are popular in many clubs, and not just the tougher ones, either. Any club owner would rather see a troublemaker leave without causing a commotion. A Troll is just the right one to get the job done. Few drunks will argue with a mountain of muscle.

ATTRIBUTES
Body: 9
Quickness: 3
Strength: 9
Charisma: 1
Intelligence: 1
Willpower: 2
Essence: 6
Reaction: 2

SKILLS
Armed Combat: 3
Etiquette (Street): 2
Firearms: 2
Unarmed Combat: 6

CRITTERS

"All your weapons and cyberjunk don't mean drek when you hear the barghest howl..."
—Ad copy for simsense thriller Howl

POWERS OF THE AWAKENED

The powers, or innate magical abilities, of the Awakened are varied. Following are general descriptions of these powers, which individual creatures may or may not possess.

Virtually all beings have some form of attack. If they rely on simple physical capabilities, the details are given with their statistics. Specialized forms of attack are also noted. These may range from the painful, but mostly annoying, smack on the head with a frying pan by a Hearth Spirit, through the deadly paralyzing touch of a cockatrice, to the shattering lightning bolts of the Storm Spirits.

[NOTE: When two directly opposing powers, such as Accident and Guard, are applied to the same character, make an Opposed Success Test. Each power uses the other's rating as its Target Number. The winner applies its effects with a rating equal to its net successes.]

ACCIDENT

Accident gives the being the power to cause an apparently normal accident to occur. The nature of the accident and its results will vary according to the terrain the being controls.

ALIENATION

Alienation gives the being the power to enshroud its victim(s) with an aura that makes the victim invisible to others. Treat this as an Invisibility Spell.

ANIMAL CONTROL

Some beings have heightened empathy with animals, which is usually limited to a particular type, such as predators or scaled animals. This power allows the being to automatically prevent that animal from attacking, giving an alarm, and so on. With concentration, the being can control an individual animal, experiencing the world through its senses and directing its behavior. This behavior would fall within what is normal for the animal's type. That is, a controlled monkey could not drive a car. The number of small animals (cats, rats, and so on) that a creature may control is equal to its (Charisma)D6. A being may control a number of larger animals (wolves, lions, and so on) equal to its Charisma.

BINDING

Binding gives a being the power to make its victim "stick" to a surface or to itself. The binding has a Strength Rating equal to twice the being's Essence.

COMPULSION

A being with Compulsion power can compel its victim to perform a specific action, as with a post-hypnotic suggestion. Often a being may only compel one particular action.

CONCEALMENT

This power refers to a being's ability to hide within its terrain rather than to its own ability to become invisible. This power is generally associated with Nature Spirits. A being can use Concealment to hide its summoner and its companions from danger, or alternatively, can use the power to hide something that people are seeking. Concealment adds the being's Essence Rating to the Target Number of any Perception Rolls.

CONFUSION

Confusion gives a being the power to make its victims lose their sense of direction and wander confusedly through the terrain it controls for a number of hours equal to the being's Essence Rating. The consequences may vary widely. A Hearth Spirit causing Confusion in a house might lead to nothing worse than someone bumping into walls or mistaking a closet door for an exit. Confusion in the realm of a Mountain Spirit could easily lead someone over the nearest cliff.

PARANATURALISM

Earth is the home to an almost limitless variety of animals. Even in the trying times of the late twentieth and early twenty-first centuries, new species continued to be discovered while others slipped into extinction. During the turbulent period of the Awakening, more new species and subspecies were identified than in any period since the development of scientific classification (even after discounting numerous mutations or outright hoaxes).

The explosion of novel and variant lifeforms has led to the development of several new fields of scientific study often combined under the heading of paranaturalism. Paranaturalists specialize in species identified after 2009, and many further specialize in aspects such as parabiology, parasociology (especially among the various metahuman and officially recognized sentient species), and paranatural biotechnology. There are even researchers investigating fossil lifeforms for evidence of paraspecies. Research into the origins of these paraspecies has yielded some fascinating theories.

Most paraspecies seem to be a particular expression of DNA in the presence of high levels of magical energy. In these species, one generation gives birth to paraspecies young but remains unaffected itself. In time, the natural species will vanish, completely replaced by the paraspecies.

In certain cases, all or part of the natural species undergoes goblinization as some threshold is crossed in the rising tide of magic. Unless the whole species changes en masse, the natural species continues (as in the Human species), but will produce individuals of the paraspecies at later birthings. Occasionally, an apparently normal individual of such a species will express paranormal traits or capabilities at puberty.

A few species consistently produce young resembling the original natural species but who undergo goblinization at puberty. Most such individuals are hostile and vicious.

The most perplexing problem facing paranaturalists is the existence of several paraspecies of vertebrates that have three pairs of limbs, with one pair typically forming a set of wings. Most familiar of these are Western Dragons and Griffins. The presence of six limbs violates long-standing theories of vertebrate evolution, and no satisfactory explanation yet exists. Even the normally garrulous and opinionated great dragon Dunkelzahn refuses to address the issue.

Even so, careful examination of Dunkelzahn's early interviews with representatives of the world media reveals several references to an "awakening." These very comments were what prompted Holly Brighton to label the new global condition as the Awakened World. The same comments led some researchers to conclude that the great dragons came into being when a mana level was reached, manifesting from some kind of collective unconscious template. Little credence is given this theory in most circles, even though it accounts for their six-limbed form.

A counter-theory posits that the great dragons are visitors from another world where a six-legged form is the vertebrate pattern, but the scientific community gives this little credence. The popular belief that the great dragons awakened from a millennia-long sleep seems equally incredible.

In all cases save the alien-lifeform approach, the theories cannot account for dragons and other six-limbed forms. According to the alien-origin theory, these arrived on Earth, along with other paraspecies, via a "space ark". This is unlikely, as the paraspecies in question appeared at distinctly different times.

—Excerpt from the introduction to *Changeling Terra: A New View of Life*, by Gamiel Shaath and Miguel Martinez

ELECTRICAL PROJECTION

Electrical Projection gives a being the power to strike a target with a discharge of electricity. Depending on the being, results may range from a mild shock to a lightning bolt. A victim can neither dodge nor defend against Electrical Projection attacks. Typically, such attacks do (Essence)M3 damage and disorient the target for a number of turns equal to the being's Essence.

ENGULF

Engulf gives a being the power to draw its victim into itself or the terrain or element appropriate to its nature. The victim is subject to all effects of being submerged in the substance, the least of which is usually suffocation.

ENHANCE PHYSICAL ATTRIBUTES

With this power, a being adds its current Essence Rating to its physical attributes. This power to enhance may be limited to specific attribute(s).

ENHANCED SENSES

This power includes low-light and thermographic vision, improved hearing and smell, heat-sensing organs, sonar, motion detection (ability to detect electrical field disturbances), and so on.

ESSENCE DRAIN

This power allows a being to drain the Essence from another, adding the points to its own rating. The being may increase its Essence Rating to a maximum of twice the maximum for its type. Humanoid beings have a maximum of 12.

Essence is transferred only in the presence of strong emotion. This can be a lover's passion, the terror of an unwilling victim, or the rage of a defeated enemy, but it must be strong and it must be directed personally at the being. This usually requires some transfer of physical material, such as blood for a vampire or flesh for a wendigo, though often only a token amount.

The process of Draining Essence requires some minutes undisturbed. The being may drain as many points of Essence as it currently possesses. The minimum Drain is 1 point.

A being cannot Drain Essence from a fiercely resisting victim. Either the victim participates willingly or he must be physically or magically subdued. The psychic stimulus of the being's touch (such as a vampire's bite) opens an empathic link between the being and his victim, who will feel the same ecstasy at being drained. The release of endorphins and other changes in body chemistry triggered by this experience can be addictive. A victim must make a Willpower Success Test with a Target Number of 4 each time he is drained. Failure indicates addiction, and the subject will actively cooperate in hopes of receiving another session. This will, of course, lead to a rapid loss of Essence and the death of the addict.

Beings can Drain Essence from other beings with Essence Drain Power without the necessity of strong emotional energy,

but the contact still requires undisturbed time. The action requires an Opposed Essence Test with a Target Number of 4 for both of them. The winner drains the other of Essence equal to the extra successes. For example, two vampires with Essence Ratings of 5 each are locked in a transfer. Each rolls five dice. The first scores three successes, the other scores five. The second vampire will drain 2 points of Essence from the first. A vampire whose Essence is reduced to 0 in this manner dies at once and permanently.

FEAR

This gives a being the power to fill its victims with overwhelming fear of either the terrain or of the being. The victim will race in panic for the nearest point of apparent safety.

FLAME AURA

Flame Aura gives a being the power to make its surface ripple with flame, burning any who touch it. Intense forms of this power may make wooden weapons burst into flame at a touch or even melt metal or plastic weapons. The flames add +2 to the Staging Number of the Damage Code of any successful attack.

FLAME PROJECTION

With this power, a being can project flames, often in the form of fiery breath. This attack has a damage code of (Essence)L1.

A being may sustain the attack, but will suffer Drain the way a magician does: Drain (Essence)S2. When sustained, the being spreads the effects over a number of square meters equal to its Essence.

Highly flammable items may be ignited by a Flame Projection attack.

GUARD

Guard gives a being the power to prevent normal accidents within its terrain.

IMMUNITY TO AGE

With this power, a being does not age. Thus, he will never suffer the debilitating effects of advanced age.

IMMUNITY TO PATHOGENS

The being gets automatic successes equal to double its Essence Rating when resisting infections or diseases.

IMMUNITY TO POISONS

The being gets automatic successes equal to double its Essence Rating whenever resisting the effects of a toxin (poison or drug).

IMMUNITY TO NORMAL WEAPONS

The being gets automatic successes equal to double its Essence Rating when resisting damage from ordinary weapons. This power has no effect against magical weapons. Against elemental damage (such as fire, lack of air, water cannon, and so on), the effect is halved.

CRITTERS

Basilisk

(*Varanis lapidis*) p. 180

Cockatrice
(Aveterror lapidaris) p.180

Feathered Serpent

(*Alatuserpens quetzalcoatlus*) p.180

Eastern Dragon
(*Draco orientalis*) p.180

Western Dragon

(*Draco occidentalis*) p.180

Eyekiller
(*Bubovermis fulminis*) p.182

Griffin

(*Alatusleo aquila*) p.184

Harpy
(*Harpyia gregaria*) p.184

Kraken
(*Architeuthis megagiganteus*) p.184

Merrow
(*Merhomo marina*) p.184

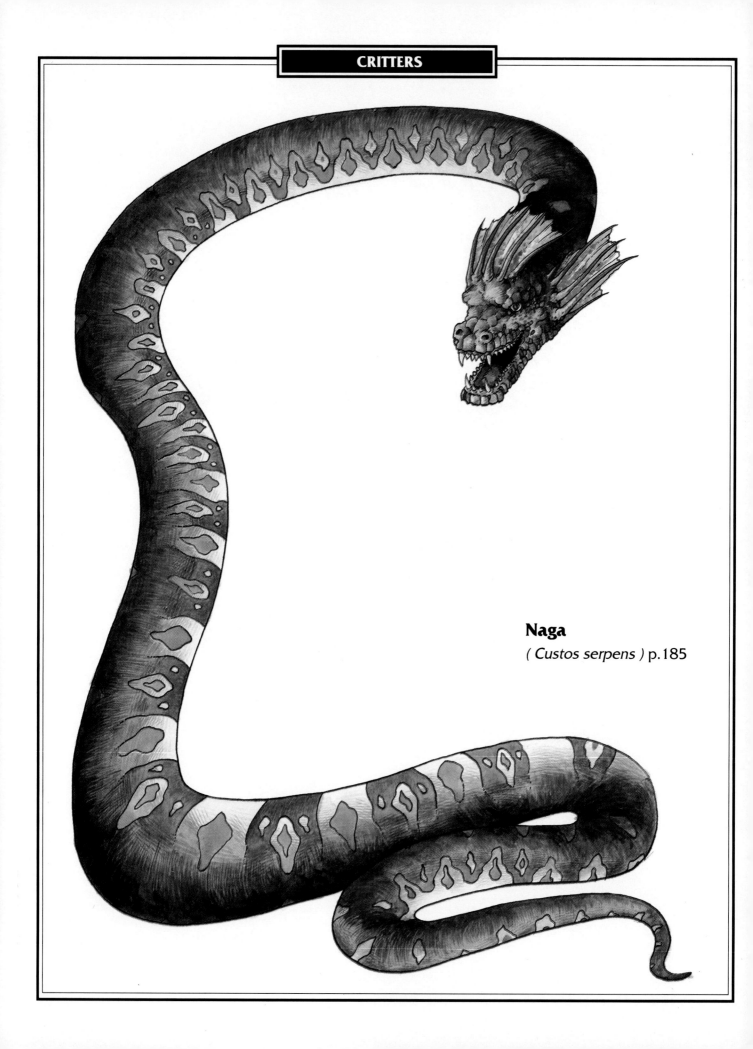

Naga

(*Custos serpens*) p.185

Phoenix
(Phoenix aureus) p.186

Sasquatch
(*Pesvastus pilosis*) p.186

Unicorn
(*Unicornis validus*) p.188

Wendigo
(*Anthrophagus pilosis*) p.189

INFECTION

When a being that Drains Essence (such as a vampire) has reduced a victim's Essence to 0, the victim will sicken and apparently die. Shortly after this "death," the individual will return to life as a being of the type that drained his Essence (Essence still equals 0). Such "newborn" creatures are dangerous. Though they are barely conscious of their new state, instinct will drive them to satisfy their hunger in any way they can.

After their "deaths," Infected characters are no longer under the control of their player, but come under the gamemaster's control.

INFLUENCE

Influence allows a being to insinuate suggestions into the mind of a victim, predisposing that person to some form of action, reaction, or emotion. Match the being's Charisma Attribute in an Opposed against the victim's Willpower.

MAGICAL GUARD

The being's Magical Guard Power is used as Spell Defense by the person it is warding.

MANIFESTATION

An Astral being with Manifestation Power may temporarily manifest in the physical world. When doing so, its Physical Attribute Rating is the same as its Essence Rating, unless some modifier is specified in the description. The minimum Manifested Rating is 1. Moreover, the Essence Rating of these beings functions as Spell Defense.

MIST FORM

The being can transform its body into a mist, apparently by controlling the molecular cohesion of his cells. The Mist can pass through any crack or crevice that is not airtight, even penetrating filtration systems that are proof against gases or pollution. Systems that are proof against bacterial or viral incursions will stop it, however. While in Mist Form, the being has the additional power of Immunity to Normal Weapons, including weapons to which it has a Vulnerability. While in Mist Form, a being can be affected by magic. If the being is exposed to a substance to which it is allergic, it will be forced to return to its corporeal form. (The easiest allergen to apply to this end is sunlight. Other substances require that fine sprays of powder or liquid be directed into the Mist). A being requires a complete action to shift form. If forced out of Mist Form, the change is instantaneous.

MOVEMENT

The being may increase or decrease its victim's movement rate within the terrain it controls, multiplying or dividing the rate by the being's Essence.

NOXIOUS BREATH

The nauseating effects of the being's breath incapacitate the victim. The victim makes a Willpower or Body Resistance Test (whichever is greater) against the spell's Damage Code (being's essence)S2. Damage is applied against the Mental Condition Monitor.

PETRIFYING GAZE

If the victim meets the being's eyes, he must make a Resistance Test using his Intelligence Attribute, with the being's Essence Rating as the Target Number. A being can keep a number of victims petrified equal to its Essence Rating. Failure means that the only actions a victim can perform are attempts to break the spell, which require the same Resistance Test as described above.

PARALYZING TOUCH

Any touch (including an attack that does no damage) reduces the victim's Quickness by the being's Essence Rating for 2D6 minutes.

PESTILENCE

The victim is subject to an infection of a disease similar to VITAS-3.

PSYCHOKINESIS

The being may generate psychokinetic energy with a Strength equal to its Essence Rating.

REGENERATION

The being cannot be killed by wounds except when the damage injures the spine or brain. Check for this whenever the being takes a Deadly Wound or its cumulative wounds take it down. Roll 1D6. A result of 1 indicates that the being is, indeed, dead. Wounds still hurt the being, giving penalties to actions as for normal characters, but if they do not kill it, the wounds vanish at the end of the turn.

Damage from weapons that cause massive tissue damage (fire, explosion, and so on) will also kill on a die result of 1 or 2 on 1D6.

SEARCH

The being may seek any person, place, or object within its terrain. Its rating for perceiving hidden objects or persons is equal to twice its Essence. Use the Opposed Success Test described at the beginning of this chapter.

VENOM

The being's attack is poisonous, with a Damage Code of (Essence)S2. Treat as a Toxin with a speed of 1 turn.

WEAKNESSES

ALLERGY

Many beings have reactions to one or more substances or conditions. Normally, the effects only last as long as the being is in contact with the substance. Common allergy-causing substances include sunlight, ferrous metals, holy objects (such allergies appear to be psychosomatic), plastics, and pollutants.

Nuisance: Annoys the being but has no significant game effects.

Mild: Causes discomfort and distracts the being (+1 to all Target Numbers)

Severe: The touch is painful to the being, often forcing retreat. If contact is prolonged, a reaction will occur. Weapons made of the substance add +1 to their staging.

Extreme: Even the slightest touch results in a reaction and causes physical damage to the being. Weapons made of the substance cause an additional Light wound.

ESSENCE LOSS

The being has no inherent Essence Attribute. It gains Essence only by regularly consuming the Essence of others. The being loses a point of Essence every month.

A being whose Essence is reduced to 0 will die within days, or even hours. During this period, the being is very dangerous because, whatever its normal nature, it now behaves as a starved predator and will hunt fresh Essence with mindless ferocity.

REDUCED SENSES

Any or all of the being's senses may be limited in effectiveness. Typically, Reduced Senses function at half the normal rating.

VULNERABILITY

The metabolism of some beings is disrupted drastically by weapons made of particular substances. Such weapons increase their wound category by one step. For example, a 2L1 wooden club would be a 2M1 weapon against a being vulnerable to wood.

Beings recover (or regenerate) from wounds inflicted by the substance to which they are vulnerable with the same speed as they do from wounds due to other sources.

Simple contact with the substance is treated as a Nuisance Allergy.

CYBERWARE FOR CRITTERS

Critters may be equipped with Cyberware, usually bodyware. Such operations tend to unhinge the animals, making them vicious and barely within control. Cyber-modified animals are as likely to attack their handlers as intended targets. When unleashing such an animal, roll 1D6. If the result equals or exceeds the animal's Essence Rating, it will turn on its handler.

Headware designed to control this tendency makes the animal stupider and less perceptive, as well as lowering its Essence further. Each control implant lowers Essence by 1 while subtracting 2 from the die roll when checking for the animal's behavior. Each implant also lowers the animal's Mental Attribute Ratings by 1.

SELECTED AWAKENED BEINGS

The following descriptions are excerpted from *Field Guide to the Awakened*, Volume 23, in the well-respected Paterson Field Guide Series.

The sizes and weights given in the identifications are typical for an adult member of the species. Larger (often 10–20 percent and occasionally as much as 30 percent) and smaller (typically 60–75 percent in a species displaying gender size differences) individuals are possible. A description of coloration and distinctive physical characteristics follows.

The habitats listed are those preferred by the creature. Obviously, you may encounter creatures away from that environment, especially if the creature is being used in a guardian or watchdog capacity.

Many beings display magic powers without being magicians. Other creatures achieve feats clearly possible only through magic, such as the ability to fly in defiance of aerodynamic laws. This magical capability is described as *innate*. Beings that can function as magicians are termed *active*.

Many paraspecies are known worldwide. The field guide entry lists the area where the species was originally recognized. Usually this was the home range of the natural species from which the paranatural species emerged.

Specific powers and weaknesses observed in the species are listed, as are special characteristics such as Enhanced Senses. The strengths of certain powers (such as various attack forms) are listed with the creature's game statistics.

BANSHEE

Noxplorator letalis

Identification: This creature is indistinguishable from an Elf, save that it may appear very gaunt. All Elven authorities and many paranatural specialists deny that a banshee is an Elf.

Habitat: The banshee prefers desolate places near Human habitations.

Magic Capability: Many innate abilities, including evidence of active magic capability among some specimens

Habits: Nocturnal. The banshee is solitary and reclusive except when hunting. Unlike the vampire, it appears to survive completely on Essence derived from its terrified victims. The creature wails, instilling fear to the point of blind panic in its prey, who flees in mindless terror. The banshee pursues until its victim is physically exhausted, then closes for the kill. The final attack is, apparently, a form of assault, which leaves its target an apparent victim of cardiac arrest. The banshee rarely shows any restraint, almost always draining a victim in the first attack.

Range: Worldwide

Commentary: Paranaturalist Charles Forte has advanced the hypothesis that the banshee is the typical expression of HMHVV (Human-Metahuman Vampiric Virus) in Elves.

Powers: Enhanced senses (low-light vision; hearing; smell), Essence Drain, Fear, Immunity (age, pathogens, poisons), Mist Form, Regeneration

Weaknesses: Allergy (Sunlight; Severe), Essence Loss, Vulnerability (wood, silver)

BARGHEST

Canis inferni

Identification: The barghest's head and body reach 1.5 meters, but its height at the shoulder is only .9 meter. Its tail measures .7 meter, and its typical weight is 80 kilograms. The barghest resembles an oversized mastiff of pure white or pure black. Its fur is very short and lies flat on its body, which sometimes gives the impression of a naked hide. Its ears are sharply pointed and set high on its head. A protruding spine runs along the back. Even in the absence of reflected light, the barghest's eyes glow red and its teeth glow slightly in the dark because of luminescent bacteria in its saliva. Its skull has 42 teeth. The female barghest has 8 mammae.

Habitat: Wilderness forests, tundra, and moors

Magic Capability: Innate

Habits: Nocturnal. The barghest hunts alone or in pairs during breeding season, but may be found in packs of twelve or more during the rest of the year. It feeds on anything available, primarily large mammals that it pursues to exhaustion before closing for the kill. Hunting range is 100 kilometers or more in diameter. Breeding takes place in late winter through early spring.

Range: Northern portions of North America, Europe, and Asia

Commentary: The barghest's howl induces a fear reaction in Humans and many other animals. This is used to herd prey. Once the prey is cornered, the barghest shifts the pitch of the howl, often causing near-catatonia in its victim.

Powers: Fear, Paralyzing Howl (Power opposes Willpower), Enhanced Senses (sonar)

Weakness: Allergy (Sunlight; Severe)

BASILISK
Varanis lapidis

Identification: The basilisk's head and body average 1.5 meters and its height at the shoulder is .2 meter. Its tail is about one meter long and it weighs about 100 kilograms. Its skin is covered with knobby scales in a black and bright yellow pattern, which condenses to a solid black at the muzzle and the end of the tail. The skull has 40 saw-edged teeth that are usually of several sizes and are constantly renewing.

Habitat: The basilisk prefers rainforest or open woodland in warm temperate or tropical zones.

Magic Capability: Innate

Habits: The basilisk is most active during the day, especially in the morning hours. It is normally a solitary animal that is often drawn, possibly by the smell of blood, to the site of a fresh kill. It feeds primarily on small animals, usually mammals, but will devour anything it can catch. Its natural camouflage blends in with the rocky outcrops where it nests. Though fiercely territorial, the basilisk ranges up to ten kilometers from its den to forage for food. Its life expectancy is thirteen years in captivity, eight to ten years in the wild. Its breeding season is in the spring.

Range: Originally confined to the Indonesian archipelago, the species has spread worldwide as specimens trapped or bred for guard functions have escaped and bred in suitable environments.

Commentary: Paranaturalists believe that the basilisk uses a mana spell to calcify the victim. It is believed that in some unknown way the minerals in the victim's body are vital to the creature's metabolism.

Power: Petrifying Gaze

Weaknesses: Allergy (Extreme; reflection of own gaze. Failure to receive two successes on a Body Success Test with a target of 6 results in a crumbling basilisk statue.)

COCKATRICE
Aveterror lapidaris

Identification: The cockatrice's head and body commonly measure 2 meters. Its tail is 1.2 meters long, and it weighs about 40 kilograms. The cockatrice is a long-legged, bird-like, feathered creature whose predominant coloration is yellow. The head has a bright red coxcomb and a sharp, horny beak.

Habitat: The cockatrice prefers open plains and scrubland, but is also known to frequent open woodlands.

Magic Capability: Innate

Habits: Diurnal. Though capable of limited and awkward flight, the cockatrice is better adapted to running. It prefers to chase down its prey, often rising briefly into the air to strike downward with its taloned feet. The cockatrice feeds on animals weighing from 10 to 80 kilograms. Nests are defended by both parents until hatching, when one of them (possibly the female) departs. The other becomes guardian of the chicks for the next several months. Specimens have lived up to 25 years in captivity. Breeding season is in spring.

Range: The cockatrice's range has expanded greatly in recent years. It is now found worldwide.

Commentary: The adult cockatrice has the paranatural ability to paralyze with a touch from its tail. In its leaping attack, it whips its tail around in the attempt to paralyze its target.

Powers: Paralyzing Touch, Invulnerability (own touch)

DRACOFORMS
Within the group of dracoformed Awakened creatures are several related types. Though major physical differences are apparent between the types grouped here, they display a basic similarity even if no true relationship exists. All are of large size and saurian nature, sapient, and matching ancient descriptions of dragons and great serpents from areas where Dragons are now sighted since the Awakening.

Magic Capability: All Great Dragons and some of the lesser dracoforms are magically active. They usually follow the shamanic tradition.

Habits: Dragons are most active at dawn and dusk, but they also operate in full daylight and in the dead of night. They feed on live prey of substantial size, cattle being a favorite food. They prefer to strike from the sky, swooping rapidly on the victim to carry it off before consuming it. Their lairs are caverns in unpopulated areas, which are often accessible only from the air. The dragon's aerial hunting pattern allows it to range more than 200 kilometers from its lair. A dragon's life expectancy is unknown, though it is believed to be very long, indeed. Its breeding habits are also unknown.

Range: Worldwide

Commentary: All dracoforms exhibit a thermal sense unrelated to vision that is as effective as the thermographic vision of other Awakened forms. Dracoforms are also all capable of flight, in defiance of aerodynamic laws, as they appear to utilize some form of un- or subconscious magic in order to lift their mass.

Common Powers: Enhanced Senses (wide-band hearing, low-light vision, thermal sense)

Powers Observed in Individuals: Animal Control (reptiles), Influence, Flame Projection, Noxious Breath, Venom

Feathered Serpents
Alatuserpens Quetzalcoatlus

Identification: Most feathered serpents are 20 meters in length from head to tail, have a wingspan of 15 meters, and weigh 6,000 kilograms. A feathered serpent is a long-bodied dracoform with one pair of wings and one pair of limbs. Its contour feathers and prominent feathered ruff are often a dazzling rainbow of colors. Membranes stretch between the extended finger bones of its large wings. Behind the wings are a pair of limbs that end in paws for ground locomotion. These feet have five digits, one of which is like an opposable thumb, giving it sufficient flexibility to manipulate objects. The skull contains 60 teeth. Some specimens have a tail spine connected to a poison sac, and some have a pair of fangs similarly equipped. The data gathered to date have been insufficient to determine whether such individuals represent a subspecies of *Quetzalcoatlus*, or a completely separate species of *Alatuserpens*.

Habitat: Mountains, open forest, and grasslands

Eastern Dragon
Draco orientalis

Identification: The Eastern Dragon's head and body measure 15 meters. Its height at the shoulder is 2 meters, its tail is 15 meters long, and it weighs 7,500 kilograms. It has a serpentine or lizard-shape, with a broad, low head adorned with a fringe of whiskers on the chin and along the rear portions of the skull. Pairs of horns rise from behind the eyes, and a pair of barbules descend from beneath the pronounced nasal region. Scaly armor covers the body, neck, and tail, which are surmounted by a ridge of membrane-connected spines. The highly dextrous paws are four-fingered, with each digit ending in a large claw; captive specimens have been taught to handle fragile porcelain vases without mishap. The commonest pattern of Eastern Dragon coloration is iridescent green with golden whiskers and belly scutes, but other color patterns are known. The Eastern Dragon's skull has 40 teeth.

Habitat: River valleys, mountains, and coastal cliffs.

Western Dragon
Draco occidentalis

Identification: The Western Dragon's head and body are 20 meters long. It is 3 meters at shoulder height, its tail is 17 meters long, and its wingspan is 30 meters. Its adult weight is about 2,000 kilograms. The Western Dragon has four limbs and a pair of wings. Its horned head is mounted at the end of a long neck. Only its forepaws exhibit the opposable digits and the dexterity of other dracoforms, with the hind paws adapted into feet. Dorsal spines and/or membranes may be present. The Western Dragon is usually a single color, though darker along the spine, with a pale belly. Some specimens have dermal armor formed of bony plates, in addition to the normal heavy scales. Others have small, non-overlapping scales that lend the appearance of smooth skin. The Western Dragon's skull has 40 teeth.

Habitat: Mountains, fens, bogs, and dense forests

Great Dragons
Draco sapiens

Identification: The Great Dragons are extremely large specimens, often up to 50 percent larger than typical lesser dragons. All of the common dracoforms have Great Dragons among them. Size is usually the best indication that an individual is a Great Dragon, but it is not entirely reliable.

These creatures claim that they descend from a common lineage, though have provided no details or proof to back up this assertion. Therefore, despite the differences in their physical appearance, these rare and powerful creatures are grouped in a single entry. All Great Dragons are intelligent, being conversant in at least one Human language and often many. They are also all magicians of great power.

Habitat: Wherever it wants

Known Great Dragons:

Aden, a sirrush, was responsible for demolishing Teheran in 2020, after the ruling Ayatollah declared a jihad against the Awakened. Aden is believed to be lairing on Mount Ararat.

Dunkelzahn, a Western Dragon, is the source of much of the information given here. Shortly after its first appearance, it granted interviews to a panel of media, including Holly Brighton, in return for a substantial portion of the revenue from the interview disks. Since then, Dunkelzahn has retired to the Rocky Mountains, where it lairs in Lake Louise and controls the surrounding area as a private feudal domain.

Hualpa, a feathered serpent, is leader and spokescreature of the Awakened forces responsible for creating Amazonia. It is believed to be lairing in the Yucatan.

Lofwyr, a Western Dragon, bought a controlling interest in Saeder-Krupp Heavy Industries with a massive lump of gold that had been part of its hoard. From that time, Lofwyr has pursued a program of corporate acquisition, so that its diversified holdings are now a major economic force. The full extent of this Dragon's financial empire is unknown, as information on its assets is carefully guarded. It is believed to be currently lairing in Tir Tairngire.

Lung, an Eastern Dragon, was involved in several Tong wars in the decades following the Awakening, sponsoring factions with monetary and magical support. Its current whereabouts are unknown.

Ryumyo, an Eastern Dragon, became the first Dragon sighted by Humans on December 24, 2011, in the vicinity of Mount Fuji. After two further confirmed sightings at Ise and Kyoto, it disappeared.

Sirrurg, a Western Dragon, is believed to be responsible for the loss of EuroAir flight 329 in 2041. It has been identified in several attacks against corporate and government holdings in Europe and may have participated in the coup establishing Amazonia. Its present whereabouts are unknown.

ELEMENTAL SPIRITS
Anima hermetica

Identification: Elemental spirits are embodiments of the classical elements. Each one's appearance is peculiar to its element, with the size of its manifestation almost always indicative of its power.

Habitat: Wherever conjured, which is easiest near a concentration of its element

Commentary: Elemental spirits are the forces of the magical elements (Fire, Water, Air, and Earth) engendered into seemingly self-aware entities. They exist primarily in Astral Space.

Each type of Elemental has special powers and weaknesses. Each is subject to annihilation by contact with an opposing elemental of equal or greater power, during which the stronger Elemental is weakened by the Power of the other as well. Fire opposes Water, and Air opposes Earth. All Elementals can manifest physically.

AIR SPIRIT
Appearance: An air spirit appears as a swirling, smoky shape of vaguely humanoid form.
Powers: Engulf, Movement, Noxious Breath, Psychokinesis
Weaknesses: An air spirit may be confined by airtight seals in containers of remarkably small size; Vulnerability (Earth).

EARTH SPIRIT
Appearance: An Earth Spirit appears as a chunky, humanoid shape of earth and/or rock.
Powers: Engulf, Movement
Weakness: Vulnerability (Air)

FIRE SPIRIT
Appearance: A fire spirit appears as a reddish-orange, lizard-like creature sheathed in an aura of flames.
Powers: Engulf, Flame Aura, Flame Projection (always sustained without causing Drain), Guard
Weakness: Vulnerability (Water)

WATER SPIRIT
Appearance: A water spirit appears as a mass of murky water of indefinite, ever-shifting shape.
Powers: Engulf, Movement
Weakness: Vulnerability (Fire)

EYEKILLERS
Bubovermis fulminis

Identification: The typical eyekiller's overall length is 7 meters, its height at the shoulder is 2.5 meters, and its weight is 200 kilograms. An eyekiller's body tapers from its large head to its thick tail. Its eyes are enormous. The head is covered in contour feathers that form a sound-conducting pattern that aid the creature in hunting, resembling a feature known in owls. The feathers are hairier below the shoulders and became a furry pelt over the limbs and snake-like body. The eyekiller's feathers are commonly gray or brown. The single pair of limbs end in feet with four clawed digits. The skull is beaked.

Habitat: Deserts and chaparral

Magic Capability: Innate

Habits: Nocturnal. The eyekiller feeds on many species. It prefers hunting to scavenging. The female nests in burrows dug into the ground, often near piles of stone that the creature constructs itself. Eyekillers mate for life and hunt in pairs. Its life expectancy is ten years in captivity, seven years in the wild. Its breeding season is in mid-spring.

Range: Western North America

Commentary: The eyekiller generates an electrical impulse strong enough to stun a strong man or cause cardiac arrest in a weak or sickly individual.

Powers: Electrical Projection, Enhanced Senses (low-light vision; Amplified Hearing)

GHOSTS
Larva valida

Identification: The existence of ghosts has been proven beyond any doubt since the second decade of this century. Though hauntings are extremely rare, and debate rages about the survival of consciousness after death, haunting phenomena cannot be denied.

In every case, a ghost is an image of a dead human or metahuman. Individuals who die unexpectedly, yet are aware of their deaths, may become ghosts. Someone who dies under overwhelming psychic pressure, such as an undischarged obligation or unfulfilled need, may also become a ghost.

There are two known classes of ghost: apparitions and specters.

Habitat: Apparitions generally haunt either the place where the individual died or his former earthly home. Specters can appear wherever they wish, but most haunt a specific place or attach themselves to an individual or a family. Specters are often hostile, causing poltergeist phenomena that can injure or even kill, but some act as protective spirits that watch over family members or descendants.

Habits:

Apparitions appear only as illusions. They are almost always visible, usually audible, and may affect other senses with ghostly touches, cold chills, faint odors, and so on. They may frighten the onlooker, but cannot cause physical harm or any other lasting effect on reality. They are usually generated upon the death of someone with an overpowering need to communicate some information to the living world.

Apparitions are frequently associated with violent death. Their behavior tends to be repetition of the actions that led up to the death of the ghost's once-living counterpart.

Specters are more independent in actions than apparitions. They can affect the physical plane, and most display a personality—a strong argument that they are the surviving spirits of deceased persons—but others show little individuality at all. A specter's true form is that of the deceased, but it can usually assume any appearance desired. Hostile specters seem to delight in assuming grotesque, frightening shapes.

Specters may, like apparitions, be motivated by a desire to communicate with the living. On the other hand, they may also have a more concrete motivation, such as seeking revenge for murder or some other injustice, protecting their surviving family, or satisfying the psychological motivations of the deceased.

Range: Worldwide

Commentary: Some schools of thought maintain that a ghost has the actual consciousness, or even the "soul," of the deceased. According to these theories, a ghost refuses to acknowledge its own death, and the spirit cannot rest until exorcised by a magician (using Conjuration), or until some set of conditions is fulfilled.

A less mystical theory maintains that a ghost is an illusion created by the mind of the deceased, but that it does not actually partake of his consciousness. The psychic pressure at the time of death forms the ghost from magical energy and programs it with its motivations. The strength of this mana-manipulation determines the power and behavior of the ghost.

Though ghostly evidence is not admitted in a court of law, a detective-mage tracked down a serial killer in Charleston, South Carolina in 2039 after studying an apparition of one of the killer's victims. The ghost's actions revealed sources of evidence that led to the murderer's arrest and conviction.

Specter Powers: Fear, Manifestation, Psychokinesis. Incidents involving Compulsion (to repeat acts of the deceased), Noxious Breath, and Paralyzing Touch have been reported, but remain unverified.

GHOULS

Manesphagus horridus

Identification: Ghouls commonly stand 1.7 meters tall and weigh 78 kilograms. They are a goblinized form of human or metahuman. The change results in a rough, scabrous hide and loss of all body hair. Skin coloration varies from dead-white to ashen gray, depending on the ghoul's original ethnic group. The fingers of a ghoul's hand elongate and its nails harden into claws. Its skull has slightly enlarged jaws that contain 28 teeth. These are modified to a consistent jagged shape. The females have two mammae.

Habitat: Crypts, abandoned properties near graveyards, and densely populated slums

Magic Capability: Normally innate, but some individuals are magically active

Habits: Nocturnal. A ghoul feeds on dead animals, usually Humans. Its diet and sanitary habits often result in a nauseating odor that emanates from the creature's pores. If no suitable building is available, the ghoul will often dig its own burrow. Though usually found in packs of six to twenty, some ghouls wander alone. Such specimens tend to be extremely aggressive and have greater-than-average physical characteristics. A ghoul's life expectancy is similar to its subspecies of origin. Its breeding season is unrestricted.

Economic Status: Most governments offer a bounty on ghouls. Many jurisdictions also make commerce with, or aid to, a ghoul punishable by fine, imprisonment, re-education, or even death.

Range: Worldwide

Commentary: Many ghouls, though suffering from goblinization trauma, and possibly loss of mental capacity, remain thinking creatures capable of utilizing whatever technology they can acquire. City-dwelling ghouls often mask their odor with perfumes.

Powers: Enhanced Senses (smell, hearing)

Weaknesses: Allergy (moderate, sunlight); Reduced Senses (blind or nearly so)

CRITTERS

GRIFFIN

Alatusleo aquila

Identification: The griffin's head and body are 3 meters long. It stands 1.6 meters tall at the shoulders, its tail is 1.3 meters long, and it has a wingspan of 7 meters. It weighs 150 kilograms. The griffin is a large, winged quadruped. Most griffins have golden-brown feathers on their wings and foreparts, with lightly furred hindparts, though some varieties have white-feathered heads and necks. The sharply hooked beak is bright yellow or occasionally bright red. The forelimbs are scaled and end in four toes, each equipped with a sharp, black talon. The skull is beaked. There are no mammae.

Habitat: Mountains, usually near steppes or open plains

Magic Capability: Innate

Habits: Griffins are active in daylight, mostly near dawn and dusk. Their favorite food is horsemeat, though cattle and other livestock are regularly taken. They nest in mountain clefts or on pinnacles. A griffin's hunting territory is over 100 kilometers in diameter. The longest-surviving specimen in captivity is at least 30 years old. Its life expectancy in the wild is unknown. Its breeding season is early summer.

Range: Northern hemisphere

Commentary: Like most large, flying Awakened creatures, the griffin is believed to use magic to counter its mass.

HARPY

Harpyia gregaria

Identification: The harpy stands only 1.2 meters tall, has a tail 1 meter long, and weighs about 560 kilograms. It is a flying mammal rather than a bird-human mixture, with fur and bat-like wings, unlike its namesake in Greek mythology. Its head is curiously shaped, with an expression resembling a human face distorted with rage. Its color ranges from light brown to almost black. Its skull has 28 teeth. All specimens of harpy encountered to date have been female, with two mammae.

Habitat: The harpy prefers elevated sites for nesting, but is otherwise unrestricted.

Magic Capability: Innate

Habits: Active by day, the harpy feeds on small birds and mammals, but prefers carrion when available. It nests near favorite food sources such as garbage dumps, and ranges up to fifty kilometers from its nest. Harpies aggregate in communities of up to 100 individuals. A harpy may live 20 years in captivity, but only 5 to 10 years in the wild. Breeding season is unrestricted, but details on the harpy's mating habits are lacking.

Range: Worldwide

Commentary: The greatest mystery about harpies is how they breed, as no males of the species have ever been sighted.

Power: Pestilence

KRAKEN

Architeuthis megagiganteus

Identification: The combined head and body length of the kraken averages 25 meters. The length of the ordinary tentacles is 30 meters and the elongated tentacles 40 meters, and its total weight is estimated at over 30 tons. The kraken has a hydrodynamically streamlined body, and ten ordinary and two elongated tentacles, the latter widening at the ends to form oval pads. The creature has some limited color-changing ability, but is basically white with dark blue or brown mottling on its dorsal surfaces. The skull is composed of calcium carbonate and has a horny central beak.

Habitat: Pelagic Ocean

Habits: The kraken is drawn to the lights of ships and ocean platforms, despite an aversion to sunlight that prevents it from appearing on the surface other than at night. It is involved in a predator-prey relationship with beaked whales, in which each seems to be the favorite food of the other. No specimen of kraken has ever been held captive.

Range: Worldwide

LESHY

Incola silvestris

Identification: The average leshy's height is 1.5 meters. Its tail is .1 meter long, and it weighs 60 kilograms. Leshy are humanoid, though their habit of wearing garments of leaves and moss often makes them appear half-vegetable. Their skin is dark and rough, with sparse body hair that is often green-tinged by a harmless algae. The skull has 24 teeth. The female leshy has two mammae.

Habitat: Forests

Magic Capability: A significantly higher proportion of the leshy population are magically active, more than most other metahumanoid species. Leshy magicians are usually shamans. They have additional advantages with forest spirits (+1 die for leshy dealing with forest spirits).

Habits: Capable of activity at all hours, leshy are most active during the early and late portions of the day. They are good climbers and leapers, often taking to the trees to avoid predators or pursuit. Leshy are vegetarians, feeding on fruits and vegetables native to the forest. They nest in hollow trees, in natural or modified windfalls, and in abandoned shelters or buildings. They range up to five kilometers from their nests. The basic social units are small family groups that maintain cordial, if distant, relations with other families whose range abuts theirs. Isolated individuals are quite common. Breeding season is unrestricted.

Range: Worldwide

Commentary: Leshy are exceedingly territorial. Their familiarity with their home range enables them to move through it with almost supernatural speed. They resent intrusions into their range, and set traps to impede anyone passing through. When aroused to anger, they construct deadfalls, spiked pits, and torsion-powered impalement devices, which encourage trespassers to seek alternate routes.

Power: Confusion

MERROW

Merhomo marina

Identification: A merrow is three meters tall and weighs 500 kilograms. Its forelimbs are long and end in two three-fingered hands with opposable thumbs. Rudimentary hind limbs mark the junction of the long, tapering torso and the slender but strong tail. A long mane covers the neck, and a series of extended spinal vertebrae run the length of the torso. The rear half of the body is armored by dermal bone, but the tail remains remarkably flexible. The body coloration is light and usually has a greenish tinge, except for the dermal bone's darker emerald or deep blue-green. The merrow's ears are external and elongated to points. It has red eyeshine and a short-snouted skull containing 36 teeth. The females have two mammae.

Habitat: Coastal waters

Magic Capability: This is normally innate, but evidence of magically active individuals indicates that merrow are a sentient species.

Habits: Merrow congregate in polygamous family groups and associations. They feed on fish and mollusks, with a preference for squid. A merrow swims with an undulating motion, using its limbs for fine directional control, and can achieve remarkably high speeds. They breathe air, but have been observed to stay submerged for prolonged periods, leading to speculation that they possess innate magical ability to extract oxygen from water. Their breeding season is unrestricted.

Range: Worldwide

Commentary: Paranaturalists argue whether the merrow can be considered sapient. The creature has been observed using tools such as nets of seaweed and spears, and using digging and prying tools to collect and open mollusks. There are also unsubstantiated reports of merrow using manufactured items. Indeed, paranaturalist Merdith Perkins, a noted advocate of classifying the species as sapient, maintains that she has observed members of one community consistently gut and clean prey with knives of high-density plastic.

NAGA
Custos serpens

Identification: The naga is ten meters long and weighs 300 kilograms. It has the form of a great serpent, but with an enlarged head containing 28 teeth. Coloration is highly variable, but is almost always a multicolored pattern that fades toward the pale underbelly.

Habitat: Tropical forests

Magical Capability: Innate, with some evidence of spellcasting ability

Habits: The naga becomes inactive in periods of extreme heat or prolonged cold. It eats small mammals and dens in rocky crevices or human-built structures. Though normally solitary, naga may be found in groups of up to two dozen, especially in colder climes during periods of low activity and in all climates during the mating season. The longest-lived naga specimen in captivity is at least 32 years old. Breeding takes place in early spring.

Range: The naga's original range was Sub-Saharan Africa, Southern Asia, and Indonesia. Transport by humans has distributed them in tropical zones worldwide.

Commentary: The naga is clearly more intelligent than other reptiles. The creature can learn verbal and somatic cues to sophisticated behaviors in very short periods of time. Its spellcasting ability strongly argues that the naga should be rated as sentient. The Committee for Recognition of Awakened Intelligence has a petition seeking international recognition of the naga as a sapient lifeform pending before the United Nations. It also calls for sanctions against nations and corporations that employ nagas, on the grounds of involuntary servitude.

Powers: Guard, Magical Guard, Venom

NATURE SPIRITS
Anima naturalis

Identification: Nature spirits rarely appear in any fixed form. When they do manifest, it is often in a form that reflects their home terrain. If conjured by a shaman of great power, they may appear in a shape somewhat similar to that of their summoner, but composed of the matter of their home terrain.

The spirits of man are the major exception to this rule, as they usually assume humanoid form. The ancient legends of "brownies" appear to be memories of these spirits' manifestations.

Magic Capability: Innate

Habitat: Nature spirits can only exist in their home terrain. They cannot be summoned anywhere else, nor will they obey orders that send them from home. Thus, a sea spirit will not move onto land, a prairie spirit will not enter a forest, and so on.

Commentary: Nature spirits are the embodied forces of nature and of place, and the spirits of shamanic tradition. There are four classes of nature spirit: spirits of the land (forest, mountain, desert, prairie), spirits of the waters (sea, lake, river, swamp), spirits of the winds (storm, mist), and spirits of man (city, field, hearth).

City Spirit

Powers: Accident, Alienation, Concealment, Confusion, Fear, Guard, Search

Appearance: Varies widely. City spirits usually appear as small pieces of litter or amorphous masses of garbage. There is, however, a documented case of a spirit in San Francisco that appeared in the form of a cable car, and a shaman in Seattle recently claimed that he conjured a spirit that took the form of a 1947 Hudson automobile.

Desert Spirit

Powers: Concealment, Movement, Search

Appearance: Desert spirits appear initially in the form of small dust devils that, if ordered to attack, grow into raging sandstorms.

Field Spirit

Powers: Accident, Concealment, Guard, Search

Special Power: Field spirits can improve the fertility of crops and livestock. Conversely, they can also damage crop or ranch yield.

Appearance: Field spirits take the form of miniature farmhands dressed in overalls, bandanas, and so on. Reports of field spirits wearing chaps, ten-gallon hats, and elaborate cowboy boots in the Southwest remain unverified at this time.

Forest Spirit

Powers: Accident, Concealment, Confusion, Fear

Appearance: Forest spirits rarely manifest visibly. When they do, they appear as deeper pools of shadow among the trees. If a shaman orders them to take a solider shape, they become vaguely humanoid trees, capable of movement, with great, knobby, branchlike limbs.

Hearth Spirit

Powers: Accident, Alienation, Concealment, Confusion, Guard, Search

Appearance: Hearth spirits often resemble small, bearded humanoids wearing antique clothing.

Lake Spirit

Powers: Accident, Engulf, Fear, Movement, Search

Appearance: Lake spirits usually appear as an area of ripples upon the water. If the shaman conjures them into solider form, they will appear as humanoids dripping with moss and weed, rising from the water.

Mist Spirit

Powers: Accident, Concealment, Confusion, Guard, Movement

Appearance: Mist spirits have no material form, appearing only as swirling clouds of fog.

Mountain Spirit

Powers: Accident, Concealment, Guard, Movement, Search

Appearance: Mountain spirits rarely have physical manifestations. Their arrival is marked by an utter stillness and oppressive, invisible presence. If forced into visibility, the mountain spirit becomes a craggy humanoid of apparently living rock, which despite its small size has an aura of enormous mass.

Prairie Spirit

Powers: Accident, Alienation, Concealment, Guard, Movement, Search

Appearance: Prairie spirits typically appear as erratically moving tumbleweeds or small dust devils. Reports of miniature riders resembling nomadic Human types such as Mongols and Amerindians are under investigation.

River Spirit

Powers: Accident, Concealment, Engulf, Fear, Guard, Movement, Search

Appearance: River spirits usually appear as small whirlpools, but under constraint, they may appear as small, froggy, weed-draped humanoids.

Sea Spirit

Powers: Accident, Alienation, Concealment, Confusion, Engulf, Fear, Guard, Movement, Search

Appearance: Sea spirits usually appear as anomalous surfaces on the water: chop in a calm sea and tranquil patches in a choppy sea. If forced to take on a solider form, they resemble merfolk, mythical creatures with humanoid upper bodies and hind bodies of fish.

Storm Spirit

Powers: Concealment, Confusion, Electrical Projection, Fear

Appearance: Storm spirits initially manifest as cold, damp presences. When conjured with strength, they appear as roiling thunderclouds or whirlwinds. More specific conjuration has been documented of an eagle in the North American west or a red-bearded giant in a goat-drawn chariot in Northern Europe. (Accounts of winged humanoids with bowling balls can be safely discounted.)

Swamp Spirit

Powers: Accident, Binding, Concealment, Confusion, Engulf, Fear, Guard, Movement, Search

Appearance: A swamp spirit typically manifests as a flickering ball of light, which is believed to be the source of the Will O'the Wisp legends. Conjurers have occasionally reported moss-hung trees or rotting masses of vegetation that could only be called humanoid out of charity.

PHOENIX

Phoenix aureus

Identification: With a wingspan of four meters, a height of 1.3 meters, a tail two meters long, and weighing 20 kilograms, the phoenix is a large bird. It has strong, graceful wings and long, flowing tail feathers. Its crested head has golden plumage. Its body feathers are iridescent red and shimmering purple, and its tail is a glittering array of azure shades. The skull has a sharply hooked beak.

Habitat: Open woodlands

Magic Capability: Innate

Habits: The phoenix is a diurnal creature that feeds on small mammals and birds. It nests on the ground in rocky areas, and will defend its nest fiercely. The creature can live up to 20 years in captivity. Its breeding season is in early spring.

Range: Eastern Asia and North Africa

Powers: Flame Aura

SASQUATCH

Pesvastus pilosis

Identification: The sasquatch stands 2.9 meters and weighs 110 kilograms. It is a dark-skinned, upright biped with large feet. Its black or dark brown body hair is double-layered, though the hair may be silver-tipped, especially on the upper back and head of older individuals. The sasquatch can mimic a variety of sounds, including the hunting calls of other creatures. Its ears are small, often disappearing under the head hair, but its nose is prominent and flared. The sasquatch skull has 28 teeth and the female has two mammae.

Habitat: Forested regions

Magic Capability: Sasquatches are presumed to be magically active, most likely as shamans.

Habits: The sasquatch is active at all times. Its way of life is similar to that of the gorilla (now extinct in the wild). It is vegetarian, peaceful, and curious. It fights only when attacked, though it demonstrates elaborate threat behavior. The observer is warned to be cautious, however, for sasquatches have been known to interpret sudden movement by a threatened individual as a trigger to an actual attack. The creatures live in small family groups, though individuals may range far from the group while foraging. Sasquatches nest permanently in groves or caverns, but sometimes prepare temporary nests in thickets when traveling at a distance from the home nest. Life expectancy is believed to be more than 40 years. Their breeding season is unrestricted.

Range: Northern America

Commentary: The sasquatch was recognized by the United Nations in 2042 as a sentient species, despite its lack of a material culture and the inability of scientists to decipher its language. This decision ended years of imprisonment and exhibition of sasquatch individuals. Development of the Perkins-Athapaskan sign language has allowed limited communication with sasquatches. Today, they can be found colonizing forests in Awakened lands worldwide and serving as sound effects technicians in the entertainment industry.

SHAPESHIFTER

Bestiaforma mutabilis

Identification: Variable. In animal form, a shapeshifter manifests as a large, well-formed member of its species, often with dramatic coloration. In human form, a shapeshifter is usually very attractive, but with vestiges of its bestial nature. Viewing the shapeshifter in Astral Space will reveal its identity, as its alternate form is always visible there.

Habitat: The shapeshifter lives in its animal form in the wild. In its human form, it lives as a member of the community.

Magic Capability: Many are active, with potential innate in all others.

Habits: Shapeshifters are capable of activity at all times, but many forms prefer a nocturnal life. Despite many myths to the contrary, shapeshifters are not locked into the cycles of the moon, though many seem to prefer their animal form during the full moon. It is also a myth that they shed their skins in order to become human. Shapeshifters are usually carnivorous, but show no difficulty maintaining an omnivorous diet while in human form. They breed according to the season of their animal form.

Range: Worldwide

Commentary: All shapeshifters display a severe allergic reaction to silver.

Powers: Enhanced Physical Attributes in animal form, Regeneration

Weaknesses: Allergy (Silver; Severe), Vulnerability (silver)

Common Shapeshifters

Bear
> **Origin:** Northern hemisphere
> **Identifying Feature:** Extensive body hair
> **Active Magic:** Rare

Fox
> **Origin:** Japan and China
> **Identifying Feature:** Long tail
> **Active Magic:** Common

Leopard
> **Origin:** Africa
> **Identifying Feature:** Enlarged canines
> **Active Magic:** Common

Seal
> **Origin:** Coastal waters worldwide
> **Identifying Feature:** Webbed toes, possibly fingers
> **Active Magic:** Common

Tiger
> **Origin:** Asia.
> **Identifying Feature:** Reflective eyes
> **Active Magic:** Rare

Wolf
> **Origin:** Northern hemisphere
> **Identifying Feature:** Hairy palms, eyebrows that meet in the middle
> **Active Magic:** Uncommon

THUNDERBIRD

Avesfulmen splendidus

Identification: The thunderbird's head and body measure 3 meters, its tail 1 meter, and its wingspan 10 meters. It weighs 100 kilograms. An eagle-like bird, its head, neck and tail are usually covered with white feathers, but in some specimens these areas are darker. Its torso and the upper wing surfaces range from golden to dark brown. The wing undersurfaces are cream-colored. The skull has a sharply hooked beak.

Habitat: Mountains

Magic Capability: Innate

Habits: The thunderbird is usually active during the day, but reports also indicate nocturnal activity. Thunderbirds hunt terrestrial animals such as antelope and deer, as well as scavenging carrion. They nest in sheltered spots near mountain peaks and may travel hundreds of kilometers from their nest in search of prey. Their breeding season is early summer.

Range: Western hemisphere

Power: Electrical Projection (with area effect)

UNICORN

Unicornis validus

Identification: The unicorn's head and body are three meters long, and its height at the shoulder is 1.4 meters. It weighs 370 kilograms. To all appearances, a unicorn is a horse with a single, spiral horn. It has a long, flowing mane and tail. Coloration is usually white, but all natural horse colors and patterns have been observed. Its skull has 40 teeth, and females have four mammae.

Habitat: Grasslands

Magic Capability: Innate

Habits: Unicorns are active by day, feed on grasses, and keep harems (if male) or stud groups (if female) of horses. The unicorn may range far afield from its herd for extended periods of time. They live less than a year in captivity, but more than 25 years in the wild. The breeding season is unrestricted.

Range: Worldwide

Powers: Magical Guard, Immunity (pathogens)

Weakness: Allergy (Pollutants; Severe)

VAMPIRE

Sanguisuga europa

Identification: Vampires are externally identical to humans or metahumans, though there is enlargement of the upper canines in most individuals. Vampires are detectable biochemically by the Harz-Greenbaum blood series, or virologically by testing for presence of Human-Metahuman Vampiric Virus (HMHVV).

Vampires are not a true species, but rather, individuals of a human subspecies who have been infected with an agent that causes the vampiric condition. The infection only seems to reach its full virulence in a magic-rich environment, but there are indications that both virus and vampires were present before the Awakening.

Habitat: Vampires prey on sentient beings, and so are usually urban dwellers.

Magic Capability: Latent. Active magic is much commoner in humans infected with the virus than among the uninfected. It is unknown whether this is due to side-effects of the virus or preferential selection of magic-capable individuals by its carriers. Vampires absorb the life essence of their victims. With their

prolonged life span, they have the potential to become powerful magicians. It seems likely that legends of vampiric powers are based on the magical prowess of individual vampires.

Habits: The vampire consumes the blood of the living to survive, but also must consume psychic energy along with the blood.

Range: Worldwide

Commentary: Though case histories are often vague, not all vampires fit the stereotype of unrelenting bloodsucker. Many prefer willing partners, and do not drain Essence from a subject more than once. Only when a partner freely accepts the transition to the vampiric life will such a vampire "kill."

Other vampires revel in their role as hunters and killers. Such individuals have a strong sadistic streak and seek out unwilling victims. Initially, the vampire draws sustenance from the victim's terror. Then, if the early attacks have not killed the victim, the vampire will enjoy taking the now-addicted subject's final Essence. Such individuals may have been psychopaths before their transition to vampirism, or it may be the shock of their death and rebirth as a "hunting creature" that pushes them over the edge. These are the monsters of the vampire horror stories made popular over the years.

There have also been cases where a vampire has destroyed the victim's body after draining his Essence, and thereby prevented a new vampire from taking up its new life.

Powers: Enhanced Physical Characteristics, Enhanced Senses (hearing and smell), Essence Drain, Immunity (age, poison, pathogens), Infection, Mist Form, Regeneration, Thermographic Vision

Weaknesses: Allergy (Sunlight; Severe), Induced Dormancy (lack of air), Essence Loss, Vulnerability (wood), and in some, a psychologically based Allergy (Severe; Holy symbols)

Though many of the legendary weaknesses of vampires are not genuine, they do have certain limitations. They do not need food or drink other than blood, but neither can they comfortably ingest anything else. Within a few minutes after eating or drinking, a vampire will evidence obvious distress and will vomit within an hour. Alcohol is particularly distasteful to them, as it causes nausea and vomiting within minutes.

Vampires have less buoyancy than other humanoid beings (+3 to Target Numbers of all Skill or Attribute Success Tests when swimming, trying to stay afloat, and so on). This is presumably the basis for their legendary vulnerability to running water. A vampire can hop across a stream with no difficulty, but if one falls into a lake, he will probably go under, forcing him into dormancy.

WENDIGO
Anthrophagus pilosis

Identification: The wendigo's height is 2.5 meters and its weight is 130 kilograms. This is a white-furred, upright biped. The nails of its hands are elongated and hardened into claw-like weapons. Many paranaturalists believe that this creature is the result of the HMHVV retrovirus in orks, though no specimens have been tested for presence of the virus. Its skull has 28 teeth. The females have two mammae.

Habitat: Forests

Magic Capability: Most are magically active.

Habits: The wendigo is most active at night. It feeds on flesh, and is believed to derive psychic sustenance from its victim. Typically, it induces a victim to partake of a cannibalistic feast. This seems to create a psychological dependence on such meat in the victim, who begins to aid the wendigo in spreading its habits, thus creating a coven or secret society of cannibals. The members of the coven are unaware that they will ultimately be meals for the wendigo itself, which seems to prefer the Essence of such corrupted spirits. The wendigo makes its lair in the abode of a previous victim. Its life expectancy is unknown.

Range: Originally the northern portions of North America and Asia as well as the transpolar regions. Recent reports indicate that it has spread worldwide, leading paranaturalists to suspect that it can maintain an Appearance Spell in addition to its other powers.

Commentary: All known wendigo have been active shamanic magicians. Though most carried fetishes of predatory totems such as the wolf, some had items of unidentified affiliations. All civilized regions outlaw the wendigo, making it subject to an automatic death penalty if convicted of anthropophageous activity. Aiding and abetting a wendigo usually carries a similar sentence. Many jurisdictions offer a bounty on the creature.

Powers: Influence, Enhanced Physical Attributes, Enhanced Senses (sight: low-light and acuity; hearing, smell), Essence Drain, Fear, Immunity (age, pathogens, poisons), Infection, Regeneration

Weaknesses: Allergy (Sunlight; Severe), Essence Loss, Vulnerability (ferrous metals)

CRITTER STATISTICS

All numbers are for a typical specimen. Individuals may vary, especially among sentient species. Physical and mental attributes of an individual may be 50 percent larger than those of an average specimen. A small individual will never have attributes less than half those of the average unless it is sick or injured. Even in the largest and smallest specimens, Essence, reach, attack type, run multiplier, and damage modifiers remain the same.

CRITTER SIZE TABLE
2D6	Size
2	−50%
3 – 4	−20%
5 – 7	—
8 – 9	+10%
10 – 11	+20%
12	+50%

METAHUMAN VARIATION TABLE
2D6	Total Attribute Points
2	−4
3 – 4	−2
5 – 7	—
8 – 9	+2
10 – 11	+4
12	+8

CHART KEY

B: Body. The first number is the rating. Second is any "armor" for the critter.

Q: Quickness. The first number is the Rating. The second is the multiplier for running.

S: Strength.

C: Charisma.

I: Intelligence. The first number is the critter's basic rating, used for puzzles and magic throws. The second number is its perception rating, used to detect prey or enemies when its best sense is working (sonar for bats, nose for dogs, and so forth).

W: Willpower.

E: Essence. If the number appears in parentheses, the critter has a dual nature. If a capital A follows the number, the critter exists primarily in Astral Space. Critters with variable Essence have a range of numbers.

R: Reaction. Some critters' Reaction Rating is a function of their other attributes.

Attacks: This lists the Attack Code for nonintelligent critters or the designation Humanoid for those that can use weapons and follow the normal combat rules for characters. This column also tells which critters have extended reach.

CRITTER STATISTICS

Normal Critters

Name	B	Q	S	C	I	W	E	R	Attacks
Bat	1	5x4	0	–	1/5	1	6	6	2L1
Bear, Large	10/2	4x3	12	–	2/4	2	6	4	9D2, +1 Reach
Bear, Typical	9/1	4x3	9	–	2/4	2	6	5	7S2, +1 Reach
Cat, House	1	4x4	1	–	2/4	2	6	5	2L2, –1 Reach
Cat, Wild	2	4x4	2	–	2/4	2	6	5	4M2, –1 Reach
Deer	4	4x5	4	–	2/3	2	6	3	3M2, +1 Reach
Dog, Large	3	4x4	3	–	2/4	2	6	4	4M2
Dog, Small	1	4x4	1	–	2/4	2	6	4	2L2, –1 Reach
Elephant	15/3	3x4	40	–	3/3	3	6	3	7D3, +1 Reach
Fox	2	4x4	1	–	2/4	2	6	5	3L2, –1 Reach
Goat	2	4x6	2	–	2/3	2	6	3	2L1
Horse	10	4x4	8	–	2/3	2	6	3	5S2, +1 Reach
Leopard	5	5x4	5	–	2/4	2	6	5	5S2
Rat	1	5x3	0	–	2/4	1	6	5	2L1, –1 Reach
Rhinoceros	12/2	4x4	25	–	2/2	2	6	3	8D2
Seal	6	5x4	4	–	3/4	2	6	4	4M2

Note: Running multiplier on land is 2.

Name	B	Q	S	C	I	W	E	R	Attacks
Shark, Large	10/2	5x3	10	–	1/3	2	6	5	9D3
Shark, Typical	5/1	5x4	4	–	1/3	1	6	5	7S3
Tiger	8	6x4	8	–	3/4	2	6	6	8S2, +1 Reach
Wolf	5	5x4	4	–	3/4	2	6	5	5M2

Paraspecies

Name	B	Q	S	C	I	W	E	R	Attacks
Banshee	3	4x5	3	5	3	3	2D6	3	Humanoid

Powers: Enhanced Senses (low-light vision, hearing, smell), Essence Drain, Fear, Immunity (age, pathogens, poisons), Mist Form, Regeneration
Weaknesses: Allergy (sunlight; severe), Essence Loss, Vulnerability (wood, silver)

Barghest	7	6x4	5	–	3/6	3	(6)	6	7S2

Powers: Fear, Paralyzing Howl, Enhanced Senses (sonar)
Weakness: Allergy (sunlight; severe)

Basilisk	4/2	2x3	7	–	1/3	2	(6)	2	4M2, –1 Reach

Power: Petrifying Gaze
Weakness: Allergy (own gaze; extreme)

Cockatrice	3	5x3	4	–	2/3	2	(6)	4	5M2

Powers: Paralyzing Touch, Invulnerability (own touch)

Dracoforms

Powers: Enhanced Senses (wide-band hearing, low-light eyes, thermal sense), [some show: Animal Control (reptiles), Influence, Flame Projection, Noxious Breath, Venom]

Name	B	Q	S	C	I	W	E	R	Attacks
Feathered Serpent	12/4	6x2	30	4	4	8	(2D6)	7	9D2, +2 Reach

Note: Movement multiplier is 4 while flying

Eastern Dragon	14/4	8x3	35	5	4	8	(2D6)	6	10D3, +2 Reach
Western Dragon	15/4	7x3	40	4	4	8	(2D6)	5	10D3, +2 Reach
Great Dragon	+10/6	+3	+10	+5	+5	+5	12	+3	11D4, +3 Reach

Note: Estimates only; individuals vary widely

Elementals

	B	Q	S	C	I	W	E	R	Attacks
Air	F–2	(F+3)x4	F–3	F	F	F	(F)A	F+2	Special

Powers: Engulf, Manifestation, Movement, Noxious Breath, Psychokinesis
Weaknesses: May be confined, Vulnerability (Earth)

Earth	F+4	(F–2)x2	F+4	F	F	F	(F)A	F–2	4S3, +1 Reach

Powers: Engulf, Manifestation, Movement
Weakness: Vulnerability (Air)

Fire	F+1	(F+2)x3	F–2	F	F	F	(F)A	F+1	3M4

Powers: Engulf, Flame Aura, Flame Projection, Guard, Manifestation
Weakness: Vulnerability (water)

Water	F+2	Fx2	F	F	F	F	(F)A	F–1	6D2 Stun

Powers: Engulf, Manifestation, Movement
Weakness: Vulnerability (fire)

CRITTER STATISTICS (Continued)

Name	B	Q	S	C	I	W	E	R	Attacks
Eyekiller	7	4x3	7	–	3/4	3	(6)	4	6S2

Powers: Electrical Projection, Enchanced Senses (low-light vision, amplified hearing)

	B	Q	S	C	I	W	E	R	Attacks
Ghost	—	—	—	2	2	5	6A	5	Special

Powers: Fear, Manifestation, Psychokinesis, [some show: Compulsion, Noxious Breath, Paralyzing Touch]

	B	Q	S	C	I	W	E	R	Attacks
Ghoul	7	5x4	6	1	4	5	(5)	4	Humanoid

Powers: Enhanced Senses (smell, hearing)
Weaknesses: Allergy (sunlight; moderate), Reduced Senses (blind)

	B	Q	S	C	I	W	E	R	Attacks
Griffin	9	7x2	9	–	3/5	4	(7)	6	8S3, +1 Reach

Note: Movement multiplier is 5 while flying

	B	Q	S	C	I	W	E	R	Attacks
Harpy	4	8x2	4	–	2/3	2	(4)	5	4M2

Note: Movement multiplier is 6 while flying
Powers: Pestilence

	B	Q	S	C	I	W	E	R	Attacks
Kraken	12/1	5x3	20	–	3	6	(6)	7	9D3, +2 Reach
Leshy	3	4x4	3	4	3	3	(8)	3	Humanoid

Power: Confusion

	B	Q	S	C	I	W	E	R	Attacks
Merrow	5	7x4	7	3	3	3	(6)	5	Humanoid
Naga	5/1	2x3	6	3	3	4	(8)	4	5M2, −1 Reach

Powers: Guard, Magical Guard, Venom

Nature Spirits	*	*	*	*	*	*	A	*	*
Land	F+4	(F−2)x2	F+4	F	F	F	(F)A	F−2	4S3, +1 Reach
Sky	F−2	(F+3)x4	F−3	F	F	F	(F)A	F+2	Special
Water	F+2	Fx2	F	F	F	F	(F)A	F+1	2D6 Stun
Man	F+1	(F+2)x3	F−2	F	F	F	(F)A	F+1	3M4
Phoenix	3	5x4	4	–	2/4	2	(6)	3	3M2

Power: Flame Aura

	B	Q	S	C	I	W	E	R	Attacks
Sasquatch	8	3x4	7	3	3	2	(6)	4	Humanoid, +1 Reach
Shapeshifter	5	4x5	5	5	3	3	(8)	5	Humanoid

Note: Above statistics are for the Shapeshifter in its own form. As an animal, refer to the animal attributes, designated A, and add the following modifiers.

	B	Q	S	C	I	W	E	R	Attacks
	A+2	(A+1)x(A+1)	A+2	5	3	3	(8)	5	(A+1)(A)(A+1)

Powers: Enhanced Physical Attributes in animal form, Regeneration
Weaknesses: Allergy (silver; severe), Vulnerability (silver)

	B	Q	S	C	I	W	E	R	Attacks
Thunderbird	4	7x2	8	–	2/4	3	(6)	5	5M2

Note: The movement multiplier is 5 for flying
Powers: Electrical Projection (area effect)

	B	Q	S	C	I	W	E	R	Attacks
Unicorn	8	5x6	8	–	3/4	4	(9)	5	6M3, +1 Reach

Powers: Magical Guard, Immunity (pathogens)
Weakness: Allergy (pollutants; severe)

	B	Q	S	C	I	W	E	R	Attacks
Vampire	C	Cx5	C+E	C	C	C	2D6	C	Humanoid

Note: A vampire was originally a character, and it retains most of the character's Attributes, designated C. Its Strength is the character's Strength, plus the Vampire's Essence.
Powers: Enhanced Physical Attributes, Enhanced Senses (hearing, smell), Essence Drain, Immunity (age, pathogens, poison), Infection, Mist Form, Regeneration, Thermographic Vision
Weaknesses: Allergy (sunlight; severe), Induced Dormancy (lack of air), Essence Loss, Vulnerability (wood)

	B	Q	S	C	I	W	E	R	Attacks
Wendigo	6	2x5	5	4	3	3	2D6	4	Humanoid

Powers: Influence, Enhanced Physical Attributes, Enhanced Senses (sight: low-light and acuity, hearing, smell), Essence Drain, Fear, Immunity (age, pathogens, poison) Infection, Regeneration
Weaknesses: Allergy (sunlight; severe), Essence Loss, Vulnerability (ferrous metals)

AVERAGE METAHUMANS

Name	B	Q	S	C	I	W	E	R	Notes
Human	3	3x4	3	3	3	3	6	3	
Dwarf	4	2x3	5	3	3	4	6	2	
Elf	3	4x4	3	5	3	3	6	3	
Ork	6	3x4	5	2	2	3	6	2	
Troll	8/1	2x3	7	1	1	2	6	1	+1 Reach

THE NORTHWEST IN 2050

"When the politicians gave away the damn country to the Indians, I didn't know who to kill first, the politicians or the Indians."
— Humanis Policlub member

The northwestern quarter of North America is bordered by the Pacific Ocean on the west and mountain ranges that divide the coast from the rest of the continent on the east. In between is a diverse assortment of lesser features, including plateaus, river systems, valleys, and smaller mountain ranges. Indeed, the Northwest offers almost every type of environment found elsewhere on the continent. Glaciers and deserts, temperate rainforests and badlands, all exist within the area.

Since the Treaty of Denver (2018), much has changed in the western half of North America. Under the protection of the Native American Nations, much of the land has been returned to its earlier, natural state. The lowered population and the influx of the Awakened has resulted in a landscape vastly different from the shrinking wilderness of the late 20th century. Tall trees stand unmolested by loggers, sheltering strong populations of both natural and paranatural animals. Towns and villages are vanishing under the new growth as the land renews itself.

Politically, the Northwest is no less changed. Several sovereign nations now exist there, with little remaining of the former jurisdictions of the United States and Canadian governments. Today the dominant powers of the region are the various states of the Native American Council and the Elven realm of Tir Tairngire. In and among these large political entities are smaller independent states, most notably, the independent Native American nation of Tsimshan and the various sovereign states of metahumans and Awakened.

TRIBAL LANDS

Most of the Northwest is under the control of assorted members of the Native American Nations, a loosely knit group of independent nations. Though all are officially governed by the Sovereign Tribal Council, few of the members submit without question to the mandates of the STC. As each member seems increasingly intent on following its own path, the STC has become little more than an ineffectual referee in the Council's internal squabbling. The vast, occult power wielded by the shamans of the Great Ghost Dance directed by the STC seems a thing of the past.

The nature of leadership varies within the member-nations. For example, the Salish-Shidhe Council is a loose collection of tribal clusters with no formal governmental structure. Though each chief acts as a sovereign lord on his tribal lands, he is not an all-powerful feudal dictator. The Council Chiefs rule by example and persuasion. Counter-argument is both frequent and expected, on the principle that a chief unable to persuade others to his view should not speak for his tribe. Dissenters are not only tolerated, they are respected for their convictions. In some ways, the Salish-Shidhe represent more of a consensus culture than the Japanese.

Other Council nations have other forms of government, ranging from formal confederations like the Algonkian-Manitou Council to businesslike corporate states like the Pueblo Council.

The Salish-Shidhe Council is one of the largest and wealthiest tribal nations in the Northwest. The Council lands extend over most of former Washington State. With the return of resources to the tribes and land tenants, the Council has become custodian of the region's lucrative mineral and timber resources.

The S-S Council represents Native Americans, metahumans (predominantly Elves), and combined tribes of the two or more subspecies. There are also several tribes of pinkskins, the name often used for non-Amerindians who have adopted the Indian philosophies and objectives. Many of the combined tribes include pinkskin members.

The S-S Council is one of two members of NAN to have a high proportion of metahumans, as reflected by its name. "Salish" refers to the dominant Native American tribes and "Shidhe" (pronounced SHE-hee), the old Irish name for the fairy folk, signifies the metahuman participation. The other nation in this group is the Algonkian-Manitoo Council.

Despite their often primitive appearance, most of the tribes are well-educated and sophisticated. Their belief in living gently on the land does not prevent them from using the most modern technology, especially if it does not pollute or harm the environment. Paradoxically, the most backward of the S-S people are the pinkskins, who reject all high technology and try to live as Indians did centuries ago.

TIR TAIRNGIRE

When most of what was formerly Oregon and portions of California and Washington States became independent of all but Elven rule, it caused a rift in the Sovereign Tribal Council, whose members either opposed or favored the establishment of a separate nation of metahumans. Meanwhile, the Elves who emerged as the leaders of the nascent state were establishing diplomatic ties throughout the world. When Tir Tairngire was admitted to the United Nations two years later, its sovereignty was established beyond a doubt.

Much of Tir Tairngire's original population was native to the Northwest. Metahumans, mostly Elves and Dwarfs, migrated from their homes to this new promised land, whose rulers

offered a home to metahumans from any nation. This influx of the Awakened strengthened the claim of High Prince Lugh Surehand, Tir Tairngire's ruler, that his was the realm of magic.

The High Prince is an absolute monarch, but he is advised by the Council of Princes, whose members are all absolute rulers of smaller domains within the realm. There are 15 seats in the Council, most of them held by Elves. Two members are Dwarfs and two are Dragons. One Sasquatch and one Ork also have seats.

The borders of Tir Tairngire are closed. Visas are issued occasionally, with favoritism shown toward metahumans, but the realm's boundaries and airspace are heavily patrolled and guarded by technology, magic, and, it is rumored, Dragons. Few who attempt to cross illegally succeed. Most who try are dumped near their point of entry, with little or no memory of their experiences and no desire to return. Immigration is now discouraged, except among those of Elven blood.

OTHER NEIGHBORS

Unconnected, fiercely independent enclaves of Orks and other minority groups inhabit the spectacular mountains ranges of the Northwest. Most of these are malcontents among the metahumans and their "normal" sympathizers. They are so economically weak that they must often resort to stealing from their neighbors.

The Tsimshan nation seceded from the North American Nations in 2035. Its leaders called the move a protest against the Elven secession, but it became known afterward that they had long planned to break from NAN. They had long been at odds with the STC, seeking a stronger stance against technology and advocating the removal of all non-Native influence from Council lands.

A region of the northern Rockies is the site of the domain of the Great Dragon Dunkelzahn. The beast itself lairs in Lake Louise and commands tribute from the surrounding areas, which were once a Canadian parkland. The region's natural wonders still draw tourists by the thousands. They are welcome because their nuyen and credit transfers go mostly into the Dragon's coffers. The style of the place is no longer the rough and ready pioneer atmosphere, nor that of the jetsetter's playground. It is now like a medieval fiefdom out of fantasy, and the lake's world-famous chateau is its centerpiece. Visitors are advised that in this fantasy realm, the Dragons always win.

STATUS OF SEATTLE

The metroplex of Seattle exists in the midst of the Salish-Shidhe Council as an enclave of another sovereign nation. This gives it a status similar to that of Berlin during the Cold War, except that as a major port, it receives goods from all over the Pacific basin. The international ambiance within the metroplex notwithstanding, the city remains relatively isolated from the rest of the continent. All land routes to and from Seattle pass through either Native American or Elven lands. Air travel over those areas is restricted to carefully specified and monitored routes.

TRIBES

THE SALISH

Predominant Race: Human
Land: Most of the region west of Puget Sound
Chief: Harold Gray Bear
Chief Shaman: Leaping Salmon
Principal Commercial Activities: Fishing, power generation, and tourism
Philosophy:

The Salish are, by tradition, traders, seeking only to live off the commercial opportunities provided by the land. At the same time, they carefully monitor the latest technological advances for anything that can be turned to their advantage.

This tribe is the biggest and most influential group within the S-S Council. They are responsible for ensuring that the Seattle enclave adheres to all of the Council's regulations. To this end, they maintain a standing Ranger Force of elite troopers. Regular Coast and Border Patrols supplement high-tech monitor systems.

THE SINSEARACH

Predominant Race: Elf
Land: Southwest of Seattle, including former Mount Rainier National Park
Chief: Lady Gillian Morningsong, a Coyote shaman
Chief Magician: Lord Ryan Highbrow, a mage
Principal Commercial Activities: Natural forest products, crafts, tourism, and animal husbandry
Philosophy:

Yearning for the long-lost days of the primeval forest, the Sinsearach seek to preserve and protect the land as it returns to its natural state. They have little or no use for modern technology, preferring to rely on magic and alliance with other Awakened beings.

The Sinsearach are the largest and most organized grouping of the Elven tribes within the S-S Council. The tribe's strong political and magical power helped preserve its influence after the majority of Elves in the northwest broke away from the Native American Nations and its Sovereign Tribal Council to claim the land of Tir Tairngire as their own.

THE MAKAH

Predominant Race: Human
Land: Olympic Peninsula in the northwestern corner of former Washington State
Chief: George Lodgepole
Chief Shaman: Black Otter
Principal Commercial Activities: Forestry
Philosophy:

The Makah rejoice at the return of the land. They have taken up where the white man left off in utilizing the forested land. Unlike their predecessors, however, they take only what they need in order to ensure the continual availability of their wealth. They will use either technology or magic to get any job done best.

Because of the apportionment of the land, the Makah are powerful despite their small population. Their control of the southern shore of the Juan de Fuca strait gave them several former USN facilities, including the Trident submarine base.

THE CASCADE CROW

Predominant Race: Human
Land: Most of the territory east of Seattle as far as the peaks of the Cascades
Chief: Frederick Eye-Like-Eagle
Chief Shaman: Red Buffalo Woman
Principal Commercial Activities: Livestock (horses and cattle), and agriculture

The Cascade Crow are strong advocates of the removal of Anglo and Asian presence in the Northwest, thus cultivating a strong Plains Revival.

THE CASCADE ORK

Predominant Race: Ork
Land: Small holding in the Cascades just north of the eastern route out of Seattle
Chief: Pawl Shaggy Mountain (Troll)
Chief Shaman: Skink (Ork)
Principal Commercial Activities: Raising sheep, mining, and occasional raiding of traffic using the East road
Philosophy:

The Cascade Orks are a reluctant and troublesome member of the S-S Council who dismiss any illegal activities as the actions of renegades and others not associated with the tribe.

The tribe is involved in smuggling contraband, and has been repeatedly identified as an accomplice in offering rest and refitting for illegal panzer runs through the Cascades.

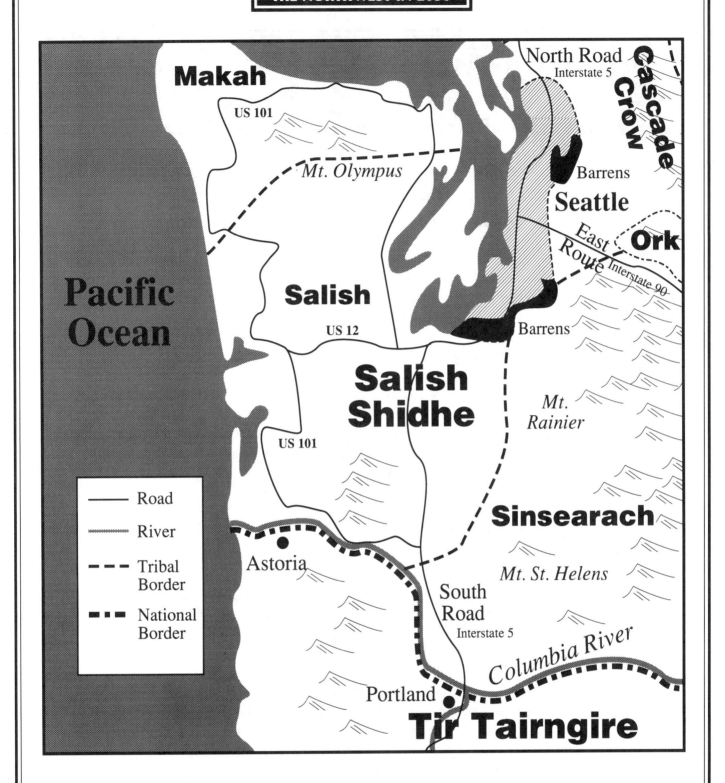

Makah

US 101

Mt. Olympus

Pacific
Ocean

Salish

US 12

Salish
Shidhe

US 101

North Road
Interstate 5

Cascade
Crow

Barrens

Seattle

Ork

East
Route

Interstate 90

Barrens

Mt.
Rainier

Sinsearach

Mt. St. Helens

Road
— Road
River
Tribal
Border
National
Border

Astoria

South
Road
Interstate 5

Columbia River

Portland

Tir Tairngire

Seattle and the
Pacific Northwest

SEATTLE

"We don't have any social problems here that a couple of thousand troops won't solve."
—Marilyn Schultz, Governor of Seattle

he information in this chapter is excerpted from *Fromor's Guide to the Northwestern American Continent: 2049*. The author gratefully acknowledges permission to reprint these sections on Seattle.

Though no longer the fair playground it was in the twentieth century, Seattle is a vital and vigorous city. Today's Seattle sprawls from Everett to Tacoma, encompassing 1,600 square miles along the coast of Puget Sound. It remains an outpost of the United Canadian and American States, so travelers need not concern themselves about passports or duration of stay as long as they remain within the city limits. Hemmed in by the Salish-Shidhe Council Nation, Seattle is an active port city, still very much the gateway to the Orient.

GETTING TO SEATTLE

For the rich or corporate traveler, regularly scheduled flights arrive and depart daily to and from Seattle-Tacoma International Airport. Customs check-in is efficient, and the ordinary traveler should experience only minor delays as his luggage is checked for contraband. Clearing the airport after arrival generally takes about an hour. S-TI boasts a low rating for violent incidents.

S-TI has been capable of handling transorbital flights to other major airports since the Council sanctioned expansion in 2042. Service in this area is not regular, and so the traveler is advised to check with the airport or his licensed transport agent for schedules and availability of seats.

Seattle's harbor handles more than 1,800 ships per year. Travelers wishing to exit the Seaport Commercial Zone are expected to present themselves at the Port of Entry Complex within three hours of arrival at the dock.

The Salish-Shidhe Council has sanctioned three major ground routes, known as the North, South, and East roads into the free city of Seattle. The North and South roads follow the track of old U.S. Interstate Highway 5. The East road is the old I-90 and leads to the Yakima Trading Center Complex at Ellensburg, where it joins with I-82/84.

Alternate transport from California is available via Ressha Corporation's sealed-tube maglev-bullet train that links San Francisco with Seattle. This is the only passenger rail service to the city. The service is regularly scheduled, but the frequent traveler can expect occasional rescheduling due to breaks in the tube. The ride is smooth and fast, taking just over two hours, but none of the scenic vistas of the northwest are on display. Even outside the restricted lands of Tir Tairngire, the tube is opaque for technical reasons.

Travel outside the routes prescribed by the Salish-Shidhe Council is not recommended. The Council reserves sovereignty to restrict access to all lands under its governance. The Council's border and highway patrols are armed and operate on the principle of "reasonable cause."

GOVERNMENT

Seattle's government is democratic. Like the rest of the UCAS, the registered voters of Seattle make their choices known in telecomp elections held on the first Tuesday of November. Seattle is noted for its vigorous, vociferous electoral campaigns.

The Governor holds supreme executive power for a term of four years. There is no limit to the number of terms a Governor can serve. The current Governor, now in her third term, is the Honorable Marilyn Schultz.

The Governor is advised by a bicameral council, composed of the Cabinet and the Congress. Cabinet members serve a six-year term and form an immediate action body. Congressmen serve two-year terms. They promulgate laws with the approval of the Council and the Governor, and serve as a review and ratification board for gubernatorial and special executive orders. All members of the Council, except the non-voting Salish-Shidhe Council representative to the Cabinet, are elected.

All registered voters are subject to a city tax. Travel passes, transit taxes, transient worker taxes, business licensing fees, and donations make up the rest of the city's income base. The city uses these taxes to contract for essential services with independent corporations. Some of the most prominent are:

Police Services – Lone Star Security Services
Fire Control – Franklin Associates, Inc.
Sanitation – Various district contractors
Public Works Maintenance – Shiawase Envirotech
Public Database – Renraku Computer Systems
Grid-Guide System – Sony Tech
Power – Gaeatronics (Salish-Shidhe Council), Shiawase Atomics

---

VITAL STATISTICS
Population: 3,000,000+
Human: 63%
Elvish: 13%
Dwarvish: 2%
Orkan: 19%
Troll: 2%
Other: 1%
Density in Populated Districts: 500+ per square mile
Per Capita Income: 25,000¥
Population Below Poverty Level: 30%
Persons Rated on Fortune's Active Traders List: 1%
Persons of Corporate Affiliation: 50%
Hospitals: 54
Means of Commuting to Work:
Internal Combustion Vehicle: 3%
Grid-Guide Electric Vehicles, Individual: 43%
Grid-Guide Electric Vehicles, Group: 20%
Monorail Ring Riders: 22%
On-site Workers: 10%
Other: 2%
Felonious Crime Rate: 15 per 1,000 per annum
Education:
High School Equivalency: 55%
College Equivalency: 30%
Advanced Studies Certificates: 10%

VISITOR INFORMATION

Any traveler who wishes to go outside the city limits must apply for a transit pass. These "blue tickets" are issued by the Salish-Shidhe Council and are good for a limited time. They can be obtained at the Council Lodge, and must be prominently displayed at all times by someone outside the city limits.

Any visitor seeking gainful employment must apply for a temporary work card at City Hall. The work permits are quite similar to a citizen's red card. They are striped with red and will accept all payments rendered to the visitor, minus deductions of appropriate city taxes.

Corporate cards, either gold or green, are honored at all legitimate establishments throughout the city.

MEDICAL AID

Eight public hospitals serve the Seattle area, all of which are linked through the 912 system. A variety of independent medical corporations operate as well, offering choice of care as well as overflow capability in the event of a major disaster. The roving DocWagon™ is also a common sight.

LEGAL AID

Legal advice and representation is available through the North American Civil Liberties Union (NACLU) at the following numbers:

General Public: 555-5LAW
Special Hotlines:
Orks: 555-ORCS
Elves: 555-ELFS
Native Americans: 555-TRIB

PUBLIC DATANET

Library databanks, time, weather, local news services, and general information are available at a nominal charge from the Public Datanet. Renraku Corporation's friendly and efficient experts guide people through the datanet to whatever public information they desire.

EMERGENCY SERVICES

Seattle's police, fire, and rescue teams all subscribe to the international standard PANICBUTTON system. Any Seiko wrist telecomm puts a person in instant contact with the system's central clearing desk. Anyone not carrying a telecommunicator can use the bright yellow and red PANICBUTTON boxes scattered throughout the city. It is, of course, both a federal and local offense to use the system without demonstrable need.

GETTING AROUND SEATTLE

Despite its isolation from major highway grids, Seattle is served by a fine intracity commuter grid. This computer-controlled, limited-access system allows motorists to join their electric cars and enjoy the freedom and convenience of directed-control travel. The system has the additional benefit of minimal power costs, as the cost of power drawn from the system is included in the motorist's use license. Previous reports in other travel guides notwithstanding, Seattle's first-class, high-speed lanes are well-insulated and its power connections safe. Near the grid, there are power recharging stations at many commercial establishments and all public parking facilities.

SEATTLE'S METROPLEX GUARD

As a city-state of the United Canadian and American States, Seattle is entitled to the military protection of that nation. In practice, the city-state is defended by the Metroplex Guard, the bulk of whom are recruited and trained locally, though the unit is officially part of the UCAS military. Seattle also benefits from its location in the heart of the Salish-Shidhe Council lands, counting on the Council and the NANC states to preserve stability in the region.

The Guard is a mechanized infantry force of three battalions and an attached air defense company. Its soldiers are a mixture of full-time professionals and part-time reservists. They are equipped with antiquated vehicles and weapons that are outclassed by the various corporate security and hireling police forces. Staff and field officers, who are drawn from among UCAS officers, former mercenaries, and political appointees, rotate through the three battalions of the Seattle Guard, though the commanding colonel is a regular UCAS officer. This system results in uneven troop quality and morale, a problem aggravated by the Guard's part-time nature.

The Guard can be activated by either the Governor or by executive order of the City Council, though such action must be ratified by the city-state Congress within 48 hours. Should the Congress disapprove of activation, the law provides for strict sanctions against those responsible for the abuse. A full call-up of UCAS forces would activate the Guard and place the commanding colonel under direct military orders.

Public roads are well-maintained and full of electric cars, bikes, and buses. Petrochem vehicles are also common in the area, but strict anti-pollution standards are in effect, with such vehicles reserved for important business or occasions when high performance is required.

Seattle's famed monorail, once limited to runs between Seattle Center and the downtown district, has recently been refurbished and expanded. It now runs on a ring track and serves the Renraku Arcology and other residential buildings. Visitors may experience some delay in receiving a travel pass, as the monorail is popular with commuters and is often filled to capacity with regular travelers.

The Renraku Arcology, like other corporate structures, maintains its own landing pads for intracity and city-airport service of rotor and tilt-rotor aircraft. Unlike the others, Renraku offers three public pads with full storage, refueling, and repair facilities. Charges are reasonable and service is swift and reliable.

ENTERTAINMENT AND MEDIA

Seattle's popular special events include the summer Seafair Festival, the Gold Cup motorboat races on Lake Washington, and the annual Salish-Shidhe Council's Horse Exposition at the former Longacres Racecourse, south of Seattle in Renton. Travel passes for the latter event, which features auctions, races, and displays of horsemanship unrivaled on the west coast, are available at the Council Lodge beginning three months prior to opening day.

The Kingdome is still the home field of many traditional sports teams, including the baseball Mariners, the football Seahawks, and the basketball SuperSonics. Recent additions to Seattle's sports teams include the Timberwolves combatbike team and the Screamers urbanbrawl team. Information on dates, times, and tickets is available from the public database.

The Omnidome, under the benevolent ownership of Renraku Corporation, has expanded to include the Northwest's largest triscreen theater and live illusionists on metavision. Reserving tickets in advance is recommended.

Along with its service as a sports stadium, the Kingdome also hosts a wide array of popular and classical music programs. The Summer Jazz Festival, in August, is centered at the Dome, but spills over throughout the city as well. As in every city, today's hot clubs are tomorrow's memories, but the ambiance of this bordertown draws the steamiest rockers. Seattle is also the homebase of the eccentric, megapopular Concrete Dreams. C-Dreamers, local and imported, haunt the club circuit in hopes of catching one of the band's legendary "drop-ins." These unscheduled performances have been Concrete Dreams's only public appearances in the past three years.

POINTS OF INTEREST

The Space Needle remains the most distinctive element of the Seattle skyline, and more than ever is worth a visit. The revolving restaurant at the top, the Eye of the Needle, serves five-star cuisine, and its regular patrons include the elite of the magically active. Thus, the sights within are often as spectacular as the view of the city without.

The Aztechnology Pyramid glows on the eastern edge of the city. The building, modeled after the ancient step-pyramids of old Mexico's Aztecs, is stunning even when its image is thrust into the modern age, as when a tilt-wing craft lands on the airpad on the flattened peak. Tours are rarely available.

The Seattle Underground is a prime attraction for the adventurous visitors. Members of the Ork community who reside there offer tours of the small areas of old Seattle on display since the last century, along with the expanding tunnels and quaint village life of the inhabitants. A liability waiver is required.

The latest major addition to Seattle's growing business district is the Renraku Arcology. Even though incomplete, this structure is overwhelming. It contains private homes for a small town. Its public mall on the first five levels, the extensive aquarium and algae-farming facility in the over-the-Sound extension, and the lively Club Quarter on the north face all offer an unforgettable experience. Tours of public Renraku facilities depart hourly from the central information area on Mall 3.

THE BARRENS
—Introduction to Part Four of Woody Bernstein's unfinished "Dreamtime Garbage" series, April 5, 2050

The Governor doesn't want tourists to know it, but all is not so pleasant in the great metroplex of Everett-Seattle-Tacoma. The dirty truth is that urban wilderness grows in the forested Northwest. Yes, Virginia, the same blight that darkens many of the cities of the East flourishes here as well.

The city that brought "skid row" to the world now bids to bring the Barrens to replace it.

Shanty towns sprawl over abandoned neighborhoods, making warrens and mazes that are the homes of the poor, the dispossessed, and those shunned by the corporations. These are the forgotten, the lost, the flesh-and-blood ghosts that clatter through the shells of man's dream of urban plenty.

And the tribes—where is their fabled concern for the

Human condition? They turn these people away from good land that could give them a home, forcing them back in desperation against the corporate concrete, the sealed buildings, and the cutwire barricades. This goes on because it is in the interests of certain powerful people and organizations.

The Barrens serve as testing grounds, dumps, and secret meeting places. Out of the city light and away from the Awakened forests, the concrete rats run with the woodland jackals. They hide in the shadows of the Barrens to do their shadowy business. Among these callous folk, the Barrens is a marketplace to buy and sell Humanity.

Meanwhile, the people of the Barrens have become like animals, seeing ahead only as far as the next meal and a safe place to sleep. Even the cheap vid sets, soy bars, and paper clothing distributed by corporate relief agencies do little to offset the real problems.

Come with me now and meet some of them. Inside, they are people just like us. Come along, and understand…

The Salish-Shidhe Council also offers guided tours of portions of their lands. Weather and other conditions permitting, regularly scheduled runs include the popular tour of Puget Sound, Tillicum Indian Village, Forest Walks, and visits to some of the active volcanoes. (A liability waiver required for the last.) The native guides for these tours are renowned for their wit and urbanity.

TRIBAL HOLDINGS

The impressive Council Lodge is the only formal presence of the Salish-Shidhe Council Nation within the Seattle metroplex's boundaries. Modeled after a traditional Salish lodge on a massive scale, this building serves as both an embassy and a cultural center. Non-tribal visitors are welcome. Tours through the public areas include superb displays of neotribal artifacts.

Tribals own and operate many other businesses and facilities in Seattle as well. Such operations are conducted on an individual or family basis. The Council Lodge maintains a directory of these and can arrange meetings between interested parties both in the city and on Council lands.

CORPORATE HOLDINGS

Profiles of the many national, international, and extranational corporations with offices in Seattle are available in the public database. They include the times, if any, of facility tours. Most corporations maintain public information desks and displays of their products at their main offices.

SEATTLE IN THE SHADOWS

Like all big cities, Seattle has its share of crime, both organized and not. The largest syndicate in the city is a branch of the Yakuza, the Japan-based, international criminal network. Other international organizations have insinuated themselves into this city's underworld as well, including the Triads and various Tongs. Most people have heard of the Mafia, but are not aware of the other rough newcomers, the Seoulpa Rings.

Seattle law enforcement officers' biggest concern is the Yakuza. The early part of the century saw these criminals returning to the cultural influences of their origins in Shogun-ruled Japan. Many of their soldiers carry swords, but they remain constantly open to new techniques, technologies, and criminal opportunities. Yakuza are usually armed with state-of-the-art weaponry. The police's best defense against them is their own clannishness. Since their return to their roots, they have closed the door to outsiders. The expulsion of their Korean soldiers may have been a factor in the rise of the Seoulpa Rings.

The Yakuza represent an association of gangs that work like traditional Japanese society, as a web of obligations and expectations rather than a rigid chain of command. The current *oyabun*, or gang lord, of Seattle owes favors to other *oyabun*, notably those of San Francisco, Hawaii, and Chiba. He is also obliged to the big boss, the *oyabun* of *oyabun*. Despite this, he does not really answer to anyone for his actions. He controls his own gang in Seattle, estimated to number several thousand, but has no direct influence on the numerous other Yakuza gangs in the city. It would seem from this that coordinated actions would be difficult, but the ordered nature of Japanese society makes it possible for these gangs to cooperate with frightening efficiency. Consequently, the Yakuza's infiltration of corporations has given them extensive combat and data assets.

The Mafia's organization was once very similar, but their power base has eroded. The influx of Asians and the Awakened and the resurgence of Amerindian culture have weakened it, forcing a reorganization. The Mafia now resembles a single, extranational corporation often referred to as The Family by members. Though still a powerful factor, it no longer dominates criminal activity in North America.

The Seoulpa Rings organize on a different pattern, modeled on the criminal gangs of late 20th-century Korea, though they are no longer Korean any more than the Mafia is really Sicilian. Each Ring is small and self-contained, but draws on a common cultural pattern of self-reliance, strongarm tactics, and blood ties. Having been burned by racial bigotry in the Yakuza, they have opened up rather than retreated into tiny cells of their own kind, and are the most heterogeneous of the organized criminal groups. The result is a crossbreed that resembles an Old West outlaw gang combined with a family business. A ring forms around a single influential person, and often fragments as soon as he or she is removed. Though the Rings lack the power of the Yakuza, they have influence and an ability to inspire fear disproportionate to their size. Should the Seoulpa Rings ever consolidate, they could challenge the Yakuza's criminal supremacy.

Besides the organized felons, there is also a wild mix of independents, everything from data pirates to shadowrunners buzzing panzers across Council lands.

SEATTLE

- CHINESE DISTRICT
- JAPANESE DISTRICT
- ELVEN DISTRICT
- ORK DISTRICT (UNDERGROUND CITY)
- SAFE DOCK AREAS
- PARKS / PUBLIC RECREATION

HIGHLAND DR.
ALOHA ST.
LAKE UNION
PROSPECT ST.
MERCER ST.
5TH AVE. W.
1ST AVE. N.
MERCER ST.
5TH AVE. N.
BROAD ST.
DENNY WAY
FAIRVIEW AVE.
ELLIOT AVE.
BROAD ST.
ALASKAN WAY
1ST AVE.
4TH AVE.
WESTLAKE AVE.
STEWART ST.
OLIVE WAY
PINE ST.
1ST AVE.
ALASKAN WAY
6TH AVE.
BOREN AVE.
BROADWAY
15TH AVE.
16TH AVE.
MADISON ST.
9TH AVE.
JAMES ST.
CHERRY ST.
YESLER WAY
S. KING ST.
BOREN AVE.
4TH AVE. S.
CHARLES ST.
S. ROYAL BROUGHAM WAY
DENNY PARK
N

SHADOWRUN 201

FIRST RUN

"Shadowrunners are essential to the fabric of modern society"
— *Anonymous Cybermage*

 f you are not gamemastering **Shadowrun** adventures, *stop reading now.* The following information is for the gamemaster's eyes only. You can come back to it later, after playing it, to enjoy the deathless prose without killing the surprises put in to amuse you.

FOOD FIGHT

There's nothin' more embarrasin' than when some squatty punker points a shotgun at ya when ya got a DoubleThick Sloppie-Soy in each hand. I know, 'cause it happened to me once.

We was headin' back into home zone after a run, when Geist pipes up that she's hungry and wants somethin' bad. After she punches out Morgan for some crack that I didn't hear, we decide to stop at the first Stuffer Shack we saw. We pull into the parking lot and natch it was rainin', so we had to run like a bunch of Dapper Kellys, just singin' and splashin' through the stuff. Like the wiz that he is, Skinner trips and nearly lands head first in the biggest puddle on the lot. Yeah, I probably coulda caught him, but the way my 'flexes are wired, I mighta snapped his arm off doing it.

He was the last one into the place, all drippin and cussin' (at me, natch). Geist had locked target acquisition on the Nuke-&-Serve section and Morgan was agonizing again between the Pure Earth section—comes outta the Tribals' turf, guaranteed pure organic and costs a bucket—and his secret vice, Hyperkrunch BerryBomb Sweeteez.

I sashays over to the Ludivenko Lovelies machine to indulge in some Sloppies. The menu construct chirps that they're outta 'most everything. Finally, I end up punchin' Wicked Watermelon, and, 'cause I can't resist, Meltdown Moscow Chocolate. Goin' for broke, I key in the DoubleThick command and slot my credstik. After a couple of bumps and gurgles and something that sounds like Toshi when he's brain-fried, I get my Sloppies.

'Bout then, I hear a big crash behind me, and some tweety, cheap-synth voice jibes me with "Hey Troggy-Troll, looky what I got for ya!" I turn around slowly (neat trick, for me) and see this wild-eyed punker pointin' his twelve-gauge toy at me. He seems quite pleased with my choice of Sloppies. I wonder if he's gonna like 'em so much when they're up his nose.

I jazz my chips, and go off his line of fire with a duck and spin that puts me in his face. Not without regret, I jam the Ludivenkos into his snout and then…

Hoi, chummer, come on in. **Food Fight** has been designed as a fast and furious introduction to the **Shadowrun** combat system. There are no fancy tactics or scams here, so you can just slot it and run it.

Any Archetypes can play in **Food Fight.** The opposition is a mix that is mostly muscle, with a little magic thrown in. If none of the players are up to running a magician yet, null sweat. There's a little equalizer stashed away to help them.

What makes **Food Fight** more interesting than some squalid brawl in an alley is the environment. Imagine half-a-dozen chimpanzees going berserk in your local supermarket. Then give them big guns. *Now* you've got the picture!

GRABBIN' STUFFERS

It used to be called "junk food" or "munchies." Now we call it "stuffers." Running the shadows takes calories, so you gotta grab those stuffers to keep going. They're probably just as good for you as nutrisoy and krill-filler, regardless of those ads from the Nutrition Council.

Food Fight starts innocently enough. Late one night, someone on the team is going to get hungry. Specifically, the biggest, baddest player character is going to get a raging case of the munchies. He wants stuffers and he wants them *now.* Wise gamemasters will secretly arrange this beforehand with the player who runs the biggest, baddest character.

If the roleplaying goes well, getting to the Stuffer Shack with a hunger-crazed Troll in the back seat could be half the fun.

Of course, it's illegal to walk the streets carrying heavy artillery. Even in 2050, it's unlikely that characters will be lugging assault rifles, grenade launchers, or Light Machineguns for a quick run down to the corner store. Sidearms are all right, but if characters looked like they're armed for war, a Lone Star patrol might pull them over to discuss the value of discretion.

STUFFER SHACK™

Stuffer Shack is a chain of supermarkets. They sell everything: Holohayo 3D greeting cards, pneumatic fluid for your bike, cheap fetish trinkets for magical wannabees, soymilk, soykaf, soygrits, and a full line of stuffers with no redeeming nutritional or social value. Stuffer Shack is open 24 hours a day, 365 days a year.

When the team arrives, either by vehicle or on foot, they have to cross the parking lot to get inside. The fact that it's raining ought to discourage loitering. With its half dozen cars and vans, a pair of bikes and an electro-scoot, the lot looks tame enough. No one is hanging around outside in the rain, but if one of the team wants to, that's all right.

When the team gets inside, you may want to read them a sampling of merchandise from the **Map Key** (see below) or make copies of the map and key and let them see it for themselves. If you set up a display, so much the better. Encourage the characters to choose some favorite foodstuff and make a beeline for that section of Stuffer Shack. The map shows, and a display should show, the other people in the store. Their descriptions are given in the following section and there is nothing remarkable about them. A Perception Success Test to spot concealed weapons on any of these guys would be rather difficult (Target Number 8). If the subject noticed it, he would presumably snarl, "Whaddaya scopin' me for, chummer?"

WHO'S IN STUFFER SHACK

Use the Squatter NPC Profile for anyone on the list except the Chiller Thrillers and Sally. Unless otherwise specified, customers will not start trouble with the Chiller Thrillers once the robbery begins. They will be frightened, passive victims.

Wanda, age 22, is the checkout clerk. She is vapidly pretty, with pale skin and orange hair cemented into a single spike, indicating terminal mousse abuse. She reacts to events or comments a few seconds after they occur. She stands behind the checkout counter.

Mr. Nick is the manager, age 43, short and dumpy. He has a Defiance shotgun under his desk. He is working in his office when the robbery begins. Mr. Nick will try to ambush the robbers from his door and will probably get killed.

Johnny, 17, is the stock boy. He is gangly and pimpled, with close-cut blond hair. He wears a Stuffer Shack apron, has a secret lust for Wanda, and is stocking boxes of soup in Aisle Nine.

Mrs. Needles 33, is an obese woman who drags a small child along as she pushes a shopping cart down Aisle Eleven like a finalist in the Destructo Derby. During the robbery, she will hide behind her shopping cart and scream herself hoarse.

Louis Needles, 8, is a streetwise urchin who will make smartmouth cracks all during the robbery.

Timmy Thinners is 29, very tall (over two meters), scrawny, and dressed in tattered black leathers. With his hollow eyes and long, scruffy black hair, he strongly resembles Spike, one of the robbers. Timmy is scoping the audio players in Area E.

Jacky and Angie Scatman are in Aisle Six, buying pet food. Jacky is 32, a would-be rocker king in white leathers and several kilograms of GoodAsGold™ jewelry. He carries a Walther Palm-Pistol in a shoulder holster. Angie Scatman is 27, a would-be rocker queen in a tight black leather jumpsuit with about 42 zippers and draped over with some eight meters of heavy steel chains. She carries a Beretta Model 101T in her shoulder bag. The Scatmans will not start a firefight, and once the shooting does start, will shoot only in self-defense.

The Chiller Thrillers are casing the joint before the robbery.

Slicer Dicer, 22, wears a short, Japanese-style jacket. His hair is dyed blood-red and styled into a samurai topknot. He carries a long sack slung over one shoulder, the shape of which suggests a katana. He is in Aisle Twelve, looking through the personal hygiene displays.

Wendy is a sexy lady of 23, heavily made up, with hair in the latest Nova style and dyed neon blue. She wears an armored duster over a skimpy pair of cutoffs and a halter top. The duster has a gory emblem on its back, a skull with a bloodstained icicle stuck through its left eye. Her shoulder bag contains an Ares Predator. She is in Aisle Eight, near the Aztec-Mex displays.

Static is a big guy of 32 years who carries a large shoulder-bag. He is dressed in baggy fatigues, with an armor coat covered with circuit diagrams. His hair is pure white and cropped close to his skull. His temples are studded with about half-a-dozen jacks. Static stands in Aisle Two conversing animatedly with a motor oil display. He has a Defiance shotgun concealed under his coat.

Last but not least, the equalizer for this adventure:

Sally Tsung was in **Night on the Town**—the gorgeous mage with the sword. She's in the store for a quick munch. She can help the player team if they get into trouble, but will stay clear of the fighting. Use the fighter orientation of the Street Mage Archetype. Her real stats are probably better than the ones listed, but they will do for this scenario.

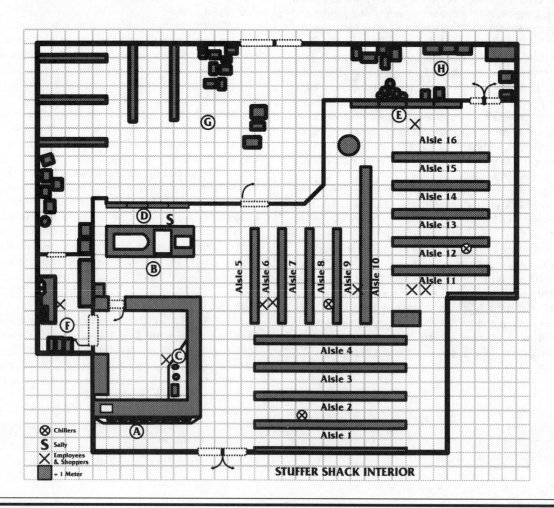

STUFFER SHACK INTERIOR

⊗ Chillers
S Sally
✕ Employees & Shoppers
■ = 1 Meter

STUFFER SHACK MAP KEY

Aisle 1

On the left is a locked display of chips and CDs for purchase or rental. A big display sign in the middle of the shelf hawks the latest "Beauty and Her Beasts" simsense chip.

On the right are snacks to go along with the vids—sodas, soynuts, Slurpee-doos, Zap-corn, and a host of individually wrapped treats.

Aisle 2

On the left are air filters, radon testers, water purifiers, Detoxy™ products ("Clean your Oxy…Use Detoxy!") and other environmental and antipollution products.

On the right are automotive supplies.

Aisle 3

On the left are first aid supplies, along with a big sign reading: "Don't Wait To Get Hit…Stock Your Medkit!" There are also patent medicines, vitamins, and so forth.

On the right are assorted stuffers: chips, dips, crackers, cookies, twitters, choco-slurps, and berry-bombers.

Aisle 4

On the left are soypasta, sauces, ramen noodles, and Cup-O-Soup products.

On the right are baked goodies, such as cakes, donuts, twisters, Sweeteez, and Krak-L-Snaps.

Aisle 5 contains a wide assortment of Nuke & Serve snacks, dinners, and banquets.

Aisle 6

On the left are pet foods and supplies.

On the right are breakfast foods, such as AlmostEgg, BacoSoy, and cold cereals (including Maxiblast Sugar Bombs in three popular flavors, Red, Green, and Purple!).

Aisle 7

On the left are soykaf, teas and herbal teas, Koko chocolate substitute, and beverage mixes.

On the right are plasti-packed fruit dishes and vegetables that are gamma-ray treated to retard spoilage. There are small radiation wrappers on the packaging.

Aisle 8

On the left are candies and other mega-carbohydrate-death stuffers like Boostergum, SucroZoom, and Whomp-Snappers.

On the right are Aztex-Mex cuisine, ranging from mild ("Wussy") to very spicy ("Meltdown"). Most products have the stepped-pyramid logo of Aztechnology on them.

Aisle 9

On the right are soups and stews, both freeze-dry mixes and prepackaged heat-and-serves.

On the left are flour, raw nutrisoy and flavor additives, krill filler, textured vegetable protein, dextro- and levo-sugars and sugar substitutes.

Aisle 10 features Use'N'Lose disposable plastic products, such as clothing, tablecloths, small furniture, umbrellas, and so on.

Aisle 11

On the right is small hardware, household goods, paints and sprays.

On the left, against the wall, are small appliances, such as Zaponuke microwaves, Toast-R-Ovens, coffee makers, and so on.

Aisle 12

On the right are soaps, detergents, bug sprays, roach condos, rat traps, big rat traps, and so forth.

On the left are personal hygiene soaps, sprays, pads, strips, and spritzes, in regular or industrial strength.

Aisle 13 is stocked with health foods, guaranteed organic from the Tribal territories. Prices are very high. Perishables in freezer cases.

Aisle 14 is the freezer section. It features soymilk, neomeats, raw krill, seafood, and other perishables.

Aisles 15 and 16 are being refurbished. There are large stacks of paint cans, plaster, plastics and bonding resins, and other remodeling materials all over the area.

Area A is a tiny, dusty display of books and magazines in hardcopy format. There are also two NewsFax printout terminals and a HoloQuik copy machine.

Area B features four simsense arcade games. (1¥ per minute of play. Just insert a credstik and put on the 'trodes.) Current titles are: "Little Mutant Vik Ninja Cyberboy!", "Orbital Ninja Death Commando", "Ultimate Bike Race Ninja Street Duel," and "Super Mareno Brothers LXXVIII."

Area C is the checkout counter, with a barcode scanner, cash register terminal, credstik receptor, and various counter displays.

Area D contains Dispenser Bars for liquid and viscous products such as Shmoozies, Snorkels, Shakeups, Soykaf, Fizzygoo, and so on. It also features Ludivenko Lovely Soya-Sloppies with the DoubleThick option.

Area E has a locked display of cheap, personal electronics. personal computers, cheap CD and chip players, data readers, and portable simsense rigs.

Area F is the manager's office.

Area G is the stockroom. The door leads to an alley behind the store.

Area H is the employee lounge, featuring the time clock, lockers, a sofa and some chairs.

ENTER SHOOTING

Once the player-characters are inside foraging for sustenance, the Stuffer Shack will be robbed. Come on, aren't you at all surprised? Not even a little?

The robbers are a thrill-gang called the Chiller Thrillers. The trouble with robbery in 2050 is that there is no cash. Credit can't be stolen because no one can use anyone else's credstik. Crooks steal commodities and valuables like food, weapons, or gold fillings instead.

The Chiller Thrillers have a major case of munchies and will load up on stuffers. They will also be looking for anything of value that the customers have. They don't mind if they have to kill or maim someone to get loot because they've got the minds of psychotics who get their kicks out of having their feet on someone else's neck. They kill on a whim, they do not back down, and they fight until killed or incapacitated.

The robbery begins after the player characters are scattered around the store. The Chiller Thrillers inside (Slicer Dicer, Static, and Wendy) signal Catcher that the place is ripe for plucking.

The other gangers jump out of their van in the parking lot. As they enter the store, Spike smashes the PANICBUTTON box outside. If anyone is caught hanging around by the entrance, Spike covers him and orders him inside. When the door is kicked open, the three robbers already inside pull their guns and order anyone they can see to raise their hands.

Until a firefight begins, the Chiller Thrillers behave with casual brutality toward everyone in the place. If they want something, they take it. If anyone objects, they shoot them. They try to goad people into fighting.

The gang becomes more wantonly abusive the longer they remain unopposed. Wendy and Wiley body-search people for valuables, though they do not pick out a player character at first. After that, the gangers start to smash the place up.

At the first sign of trouble, Sally Tsung fades into the stock room (area G). She is in this adventure for safety purposes.

If the player team cannot handle Wiley, Sally blows the Chiller Thrillers' shaman away. Until he is disposed of, Sally maintains Spell Defense and helps player characters who need it. Once Wiley is down, Sally ducks into the storeroom and out the back door. If pursued, she becomes invisible. By the time the fight is over, she is long gone.

SUPERMARKET SWEEP

A supermarket is a dynamic battleground. Things break. Things spill. Colorful substances spurt all over the place. If a shot misses someone, roll 1D6 against the Food Fight Table to see what breaks and how it looks. The glop splashes all over the missed target, along with anyone within two meters of him. The floor in that area becomes Difficult Terrain.

FOOD FIGHT TABLE

Roll 1D6:	Result
1	Nothing Broken
2 – 3	Liquid
4	Powder
5 – 6	Mushy

A Mushy is anything that used to be a recognizable foodstuff before being impacted by a shotgun blast.

Roll another 1D6:

Die Roll	Liquid	Powder	Mushy
1	Green and Gooey	Fine and Blue	Gross and Soft
2	Red and Syrupy	Thick and Green	Spongy and Soft
3	Clear and Smelly	Powdery and Red	Lots O' Pieces
4	Black and Sticky	Lumpy and White	Gross and Smelly
5	Pink and Gross	Sudsy and Blue	Hard Little Chunks
6	Roll twice	Roll twice	Roll twice

Danny Danger ducks to the side as the drooling thrill-ganger pumps a blast of buckshot at him. (The gamemaster Rolls 1D6. It's 3, indicating Liquid. As Danny is in Aisle 9, the shot hits a shelf of soups and stews.) The shelf full of Doggy Moon Zap & Serve soup explodes into a cascading mass of…(The gamemaster rolls 1D6 and gets a 2)… cherry- red, syrupy glop that pours down on Danny. "You drek-faced goon," he howls. "I hate Maraschino Chowder!"

CLEANING UP

There is not much left to say once the shooting stops. The property damage outweighs any gratitude Stuffer Shack, Inc. feels that the robbery was prevented. The Badges are on the way and the shadowrunners feel no urge to explain to Lone Star Security why they were packing all that hardware. Police statements are a permanent record ("Just what is your SIN, citizen?"), which means there is going to be too much light around here for shadows to take.

KARMA

Not much karma is involved in **Food Fight**. Everyone who survives gets a point for staying alive. The Chiller Thrillers are nasty opposition, which is worth an additional point. Thus, Team Karma is 2 points. Anything else must be for individual performance.

THE CHILLER THRILLERS

Lucas "Catcher" Katcherman is 22, is of average height and build, with hair spiked in various lengths and different colors. He is the leader of the Chiller Thrillers, and he is psychotic.

When he not in combat, Catcher keeps up a dangerous, high-speed rap on a number of subjects.
Attributes/Skills: Use Gang Member Archetype. Add Wired Reflexes +1.
Gear: Catcher is armed with a Defiance T-250 Shotgun and carries 3 magazines of ammo. He also has a Ruger Super Warhawk. He wears a lined coat bearing the Chiller Thrillers' emblem, a skull, pierced through the left eye socket with a bloody icicle.

Frank "Slicer Dicer" Pilgrim, 22, is tall and wiry. Fancying himself to be a modern samurai, he wears his hair blood red in a samurai topknot, just like martial arts simsense star Nicky Saitoh.

Slicer Dicer's weapon of choice is his katana. He will not refuse an apparent challenge to single combat. He utters loud *kiai* in combat.
Attributes/Skills: Use Street Samurai Archetype, with Arm Spurs instead of Hand Razors.
Gear: Slicer Dicer's arsenal includes his katana, an Ares Predator, and nine shuriken. He wears an armor jacket tailored into a samurai tunic.

Bill "Static" Pruitt, 32, looks as though he's had major Muscle Replacement. He is both a steroid-abuser and a weight-lifter. A burned-out wirehead with significant brain damage, he is also balding, with hair dyed stark white.

Static is convinced that numerous inanimate objects are his friends. He likes to talk sports with them.
Attributes/Skills: Gang Member Archetype. Reduce Willpower by 2 and increase Strength by 2. Increase Firearms to 6. Optical cyberware is still burned out following overindulgence in the Screaming MeeMee wire. The Hand Razors still work.
Gear: Static wields a Defiance shotgun with three clips of ammo and a Defiance Super-Shock Taser. His lined coat is decorated with numerous circuit diagrams of wires he has jacked.

Wendy (no last name known) is a voluptuous 23-year-old who affects to be the gang's "mom". She has a deep CAS drawl and is prone to play off one ganger against another for her maternal affections. Her current "good boy" is Wiley. They will work together during the robbery.

Attributes/Skills: Use Street Samurai Archetype. Reduce Strength by 1 and add 1 to Quickness.
Gear: Wendy is armed with an H&K 227 SMG with Smartgun circuitry. She wears a lined coat with the gang emblem. Her spike heels make all terrain Difficult Ground for her, with a +5 modifier if she tries to run on really Difficult Ground.

Spike (real name and age unknown) strongly resembles Timmy Thinners, an innocent customer in the Stuffer Shack. Unlike the rest of the gang, Spike does not really like trouble, and will sometimes try to persuade other members not to get too violent. He wants food and loot, but prefers not to have to fight to get it.
Attributes/Skills: Use Gang Member Archetype.
Gear: Spike carries an Ares Predator with three clips of ammo.

Willis "Wiley" Fabrizzi, 19, wears a full-length synth-fur lined coat. His greasy brown hair is done up in a beehive of dirt and mud, feathers, twigs, and small rocks. A bulging leather pouch hangs from his belt and he is festooned with fetishes.

Wiley is a Coyote Shaman. He is manic. During the robbery, he will tag along with Wendy, but follows her by clambering over the tops of displays and shelves. In moments of excitement, he howls.
Attributes/Skills: Use Street Shaman Archetype. Drop Conjuring to 2 and raise Sorcery to 6. He has the 10-point Fighter Spell Package (allocate the 10 points as you see fit), but add +1 to the Force of all his spells, because he uses Fetishes to cast them.
Gear: Wiley has four expendable fetishes for each of his spells and carries a Colt-American L36 pistol.

Name:_____ **Street Name:**_____ **Sex:**_____

Race:_____ **Karma:**_____ **Archetype:**_____ **Lifestyle:**_____ **Money:**_____

SKILLS & LANGUAGES

Skill	Rating
_____	_____
_____	_____
_____	_____
_____	_____
_____	_____
_____	_____
_____	_____
_____	_____
_____	_____
_____	_____
_____	_____
_____	_____
_____	_____
_____	_____

ATTRIBUTES

PHYSICAL   **Rating**

  Body: _____

  Quickness: _____

  Strength: _____

MENTAL

  Charisma: _____

  Intelligence:_____

  Willpower: _____

SPECIAL

  Essence: _____

  (Magic): _____

  Reaction: _____

ALLERGIES

  Substance: _____

  Severity: _____

  Racial Adv: _____

CONDITION MONITOR

PHYSICAL   MENTAL

Unconscious > Possibly dead.   < Unconscious, Further damage causes wounds

Seriously > Wounded.   < Seriously Fatigued.

Moderately > Wounded.   < Moderately Fatigued.

Lightly > Wounded.   < Lightly Fatigued.

Damage Modifiers

Damage	T#	Initiative
None	–	–
Light	+1	-1
Moderate	+2	-2
Serious	+3	-3

CYBERWEAR

Type	Rating
_____	_____
_____	_____
_____	_____
_____	_____
_____	_____
_____	_____
_____	_____
_____	_____
_____	_____
_____	_____
_____	_____
_____	_____
_____	_____

WEAPONS

Type	Short	Medium	Long	Extreme	Dmg. Code
_____	_____	_____	_____	_____	___/___/___
_____	_____	_____	_____	_____	___/___/___
_____	_____	_____	_____	_____	___/___/___

SPELLS

Type	Max Force	Staging	Drain Code
_____	_____	_____	___/___
_____	_____	_____	___/___
_____	_____	_____	___/___
_____	_____	_____	___/___
_____	_____	_____	___/___
_____	_____	_____	___/___
_____	_____	_____	___/___
_____	_____	_____	___/___

Astral Pool _____   **Defense Pool** _____   **Dodge Pool** _____   **Magic Pool** _____

SHADOWRUN is a trademark of FASA Corporation. Copyright 1989. Permission to photocopy for personal use.

CYBERDECK

Type _____

Program Condition Monitor

	Rating
Persona	——
Hardening	——
Memory	——
Storeage	——
Load	——
I/O	——
Response	——
Hitcher Jacks	——
Vidscreen	——

< Deck Crash

< Seriously Wounded.

< Moderately Wounded.

< Lightly Wounded.

Programs in Memory

PROGRAMS

	Rating	Size
Bod	_____	_____
Evasion	_____	_____
Masking	_____	_____
Sensors	_____	_____
	_____	_____
	_____	_____
	_____	_____
	_____	_____
	_____	_____
	_____	_____
	_____	_____
	_____	_____
	_____	_____
	_____	_____

CHARACTER DRAWING

VEHICLE

Type _____

Condition Monitor

	Rating
Handling	___
Speed	___
Body	___
Armor	___
Signature	___
Pilot	___
Firmpoints	___
Hardpoints	___

< Vehicle Destroyed

< Serious Damage

< Moderate Damage

< Light Damage

Other Items

OTHER GEAR

Hacking Pool _____

CHARACTER NOTES

CONTACTS

| Name: | Street Name: | Sex: |

| Race: | Karma: | Archetype: | Lifestyle: | Money: |

SKILLS & LANGUAGES

Skill	Rating
_____	___
_____	___
_____	___
_____	___
_____	___
_____	___
_____	___
_____	___
_____	___
_____	___
_____	___
_____	___
_____	___

ATTRIBUTES

	Rating
PHYSICAL	
Body:	___
Quickness:	___
Strength:	___
MENTAL	
Charisma:	___
Intelligence:	___
Willpower:	___
SPECIAL	
Essence:	___
(Magic):	___
Reaction:	___
ALLERGIES	
Substance:	___
Severity:	___
Racial Adv:	___

CONDITION MONITOR

PHYSICAL   MENTAL

Unconscious > Possibly dead.   < Unconscious, Further damage causes wounds

Seriously > Wounded.   < Seriously Fatigued.

Moderately > Wounded.   < Moderately Fatigued.

Lightly > Wounded.   < Lightly Fatigued.

Damage Modifiers

Damage	T#	Initiative
None	–	–
Light	+1	-1
Moderate	+2	-2
Serious	+3	-3

CYBERWEAR

Type	Rating
_____	___
_____	___
_____	___
_____	___
_____	___
_____	___
_____	___
_____	___
_____	___
_____	___
_____	___
_____	___
_____	___

WEAPONS

Type	Short	Medium	Long	Extreme	Dmg. Code
_____	___	___	___	___	___/___/___
_____	___	___	___	___	___/___/___
_____	___	___	___	___	___/___/___

SPELLS

Type	Max Force	Staging	Drain Code
_____	___	___	___/___
_____	___	___	___/___
_____	___	___	___/___
_____	___	___	___/___
_____	___	___	___/___
_____	___	___	___/___
_____	___	___	___/___
_____	___	___	___/___

Astral Pool _____

Defense Pool _____

Dodge Pool _____

Magic Pool _____

CYBERDECK

Type _____

Program Condition Monitor

	Rating
Persona	_____
Hardening	_____
Memory	_____
Storeage	_____
Load	_____
I/O	_____
Response	_____
Hitcher Jacks	_____
Vidscreen	_____

< Deck Crash

< Seriously Wounded.

< Moderately Wounded.

< Lightly Wounded.

Programs in Memory

PROGRAMS

	Rating	Size
Bod	_____	_____
Evasion	_____	_____
Masking	_____	_____
Sensors	_____	_____
	_____	_____
	_____	_____
	_____	_____
	_____	_____
	_____	_____
	_____	_____
	_____	_____
	_____	_____
	_____	_____
	_____	_____
	_____	_____

CHARACTER DRAWING

VEHICLE

Type _____

Condition Monitor

	Rating
Handling	_____
Speed	_____
Body	_____
Armor	_____
Signature	_____
Pilot	_____
Firmpoints	_____
Hardpoints	_____

< Vehicle Destroyed

< Serious Damage

< Moderate Damage

< Light Damage

Other Items

OTHER GEAR

Hacking Pool _____

CHARACTER NOTES

CONTACTS

NPC RECORD SHEETS

ATTRIBUTES

PHYSICAL   **Rating**

Body: _____

Quickness: _____

Strength: _____

MENTAL

Charisma: _____

Intelligence: _____

Willpower: _____

SPECIAL

Essence: _____

(Magic): _____

Reaction: _____

CONDITION MONITOR

PHYSICAL   **MENTAL**

Unconscious >
Possibly dead.

    < Unconscious,
    Further damage
    causes wounds

Seriously >
Wounded.

    < Seriously
    Fatigued.

Moderately >
Wounded.

    < Moderately
    Fatigued.

Lightly >
Wounded.

    < Lightly
    Fatigued.

Weapons, Spells & Notes

ATTRIBUTES

PHYSICAL   **Rating**

Body: _____

Quickness: _____

Strength: _____

MENTAL

Charisma: _____

Intelligence: _____

Willpower: _____

SPECIAL

Essence: _____

(Magic): _____

Reaction: _____

CONDITION MONITOR

PHYSICAL   **MENTAL**

Unconscious >
Possibly dead.

    < Unconscious,
    Further damage
    causes wounds

Seriously >
Wounded.

    < Seriously
    Fatigued.

Moderately >
Wounded.

    < Moderately
    Fatigued.

Lightly >
Wounded.

    < Lightly
    Fatigued.

Weapons, Spells & Notes

ATTRIBUTES

PHYSICAL   **Rating**

Body: _____

Quickness: _____

Strength: _____

MENTAL

Charisma: _____

Intelligence: _____

Willpower: _____

SPECIAL

Essence: _____

(Magic): _____

Reaction: _____

CONDITION MONITOR

PHYSICAL   **MENTAL**

Unconscious >
Possibly dead.

    < Unconscious,
    Further damage
    causes wounds

Seriously >
Wounded.

    < Seriously
    Fatigued.

Moderately >
Wounded.

    < Moderately
    Fatigued.

Lightly >
Wounded.

    < Lightly
    Fatigued.

Weapons, Spells & Notes

ATTRIBUTES

PHYSICAL   **Rating**

Body: _____

Quickness: _____

Strength: _____

MENTAL

Charisma: _____

Intelligence: _____

Willpower: _____

SPECIAL

Essence: _____

(Magic): _____

Reaction: _____

CONDITION MONITOR

PHYSICAL   **MENTAL**

Unconscious >
Possibly dead.

    < Unconscious,
    Further damage
    causes wounds

Seriously >
Wounded.

    < Seriously
    Fatigued.

Moderately >
Wounded.

    < Moderately
    Fatigued.

Lightly >
Wounded.

    < Lightly
    Fatigued.

Weapons, Spells & Notes

ATTRIBUTES

PHYSICAL   **Rating**

Body: _____

Quickness: _____

Strength: _____

MENTAL

Charisma: _____

Intelligence: _____

Willpower: _____

SPECIAL

Essence: _____

(Magic): _____

Reaction: _____

CONDITION MONITOR

PHYSICAL   **MENTAL**

Unconscious >
Possibly dead.

    < Unconscious,
    Further damage
    causes wounds

Seriously >
Wounded.

    < Seriously
    Fatigued.

Moderately >
Wounded.

    < Moderately
    Fatigued.

Lightly >
Wounded.

    < Lightly
    Fatigued.

Weapons, Spells & Notes

ATTRIBUTES

PHYSICAL   **Rating**

Body: _____

Quickness: _____

Strength: _____

MENTAL

Charisma: _____

Intelligence: _____

Willpower: _____

SPECIAL

Essence: _____

(Magic): _____

Reaction: _____

CONDITION MONITOR

PHYSICAL   **MENTAL**

Unconscious >
Possibly dead.

    < Unconscious,
    Further damage
    causes wounds

Seriously >
Wounded.

    < Seriously
    Fatigued.

Moderately >
Wounded.

    < Moderately
    Fatigued.

Lightly >
Wounded.

    < Lightly
    Fatigued.

Weapons, Spells & Notes

IC MONITORS

IC

Program Condition Monitor

Type _____

Rating _____

Construct

< Program Crash

< Seriously Wounded.

< Moderately Wounded.

< Lightly Wounded.

Notes

IC

Program Condition Monitor

Type _____

Rating _____

Construct

< Program Crash

< Seriously Wounded.

< Moderately Wounded.

< Lightly Wounded.

Notes

IC

Program Condition Monitor

Type _____

Rating _____

Construct

< Program Crash

< Seriously Wounded.

< Moderately Wounded.

< Lightly Wounded.

Notes

IC

Program Condition Monitor

Type _____

Rating _____

Construct

< Program Crash

< Seriously Wounded.

< Moderately Wounded.

< Lightly Wounded.

Notes

IC

Program Condition Monitor

Type _____

Rating _____

Construct

< Program Crash

< Seriously Wounded.

< Moderately Wounded.

< Lightly Wounded.

Notes

IC

Program Condition Monitor

Type _____

Rating _____

Construct

< Program Crash

< Seriously Wounded.

< Moderately Wounded.

< Lightly Wounded.

Notes

VEHICLE MONITORS

VEHICLE

Type _____

Condition Monitor

	Rating
Handling	_____
Speed	_____
Body	_____
Armor	_____
Signature	_____
Pilot	_____
Firmpoints	_____
Hardpoints	_____

< Vehicle Destroyed

< Serious Damage

< Moderate Damage

< Light Damage

Other Items

VEHICLE

Type _____

Condition Monitor

	Rating
Handling	_____
Speed	_____
Body	_____
Armor	_____
Signature	_____
Pilot	_____
Firmpoints	_____
Hardpoints	_____

< Vehicle Destroyed

< Serious Damage

< Moderate Damage

< Light Damage

Other Items

VEHICLE

Type _____

Condition Monitor

	Rating
Handling	_____
Speed	_____
Body	_____
Armor	_____
Signature	_____
Pilot	_____
Firmpoints	_____
Hardpoints	_____

< Vehicle Destroyed

< Serious Damage

< Moderate Damage

< Light Damage

Other Items

FIREARMS

Pistols	Type	Conc.	Ammo	Damage
Streetline Special	Hold-out	8	6 (Clip)	3L1
Walther Palm Pistol	Hold-out	9	2 (Break)	3L1
Colt America L36	Light	6	9 (Clip)	3M2
Beretta Model 101T	Light	5	10 (Clip)	3M2
Fichetti Security 500	Light	6	10 (Clip)	3M2
Fichetti Security 500	Light	8	22 (Clip)	3M2
Ares Predator	Heavy	5	10 (Clip)	4M2
Ares Slivergun	Heavy	6	30 (Clip)	2M3
Browning Max-Power	Heavy	6	8 (Clip)	4M2
Remington Roomsweeper	Heavy	8	6 (Magazine)	3M3
Ruger Super Warhawk	Heavy	4	6 (Cylinder)	4M2

Rifles				
FN HAR	Assault	2	20 (Clip)	5M3
AK-97	Assault	3	22 (Clip)	5M3
AK-98	Assault	NA	22 (Clip)	5M3
Remington 750	Sporting	3	5 (Magazine)	5S2
Remington 950	Sporting	2	5 (Magazine)	6S2
Ranger Arms SM-3	Sniper	NA	6 (Magazine)	6S2
Enfield AS7	Shotgun	3	10 (Clip)	4M3
Defiance T-250	Shotgun	4	5 (Magazine)	3M3

Submachine Guns				
AK-97 SMG/Carbine	SMG	4	22 (Clip)	4M3
Uzi III	SMG	5	16 (Clip)	4M3
Heckler & Koch HK227	SMG	4	20 (Clip)	5M3
Heckler & Koch S variant	SMG	5	16 (Clip)	5M3

Tasers				
Defiance Super Shock	Taser	4	4 (Magazine)	Special

Heavy Weapons				
Ingram Valiant	Light MG	NA	Belt	5S3
Medium MG	Medium MG	NA	40 (Clip)	8S4/4M2*
Heavy MG	Heavy MG	NA	40 (Clip)	12S4/6M2*
Assault Cannon	Cannon	NA	20 (Clip)	10D4/5S2*

WEAPON RANGE

Type Target Number	Short 4	Medium 5	Long 7	Extreme 9
Firearms				
Hold-out Pistol	0–5	6–15	16–30	31–50
Light Pistol	0–5	6–15	16–30	31–50
Heavy Pistol	0–5	6–20	21–40	41–60
Taser	0–5	6–10	11–12	13–15
Shotgun	0–10	11–20	21–50	51–100
Sporting Rifle	0–30	31–60	61–150	151–300
Sniper rifle	0–40	41–80	81–200	201–400
Assault Rifle	0–15	16–40	41–100	101–250
SMG	0–10	11–40	41–80	81–150
Heavy Weapons				
Light MG	0–20	21–40	41–80	81–150
Medium MG	0–40	41–150	151–300	301–500
Heavy MG	0–40	41–150	151–400	401–800
Assault Cannon	0–50	51–150	151–450	451–1300
Grenade Launcher	20–50	51–100	101–150	151–300
Missile Launcher	20–70	71–150	151–450	451–1,500
Impact Projectiles				
Bow	0–5	6–50	51–150	151–300
Light Crossbow	0–10	11–40	41–100	101–200
Medium Crossbow	0–20	21–60	61–150	151–250
Heavy Crossbow	0–30	31–80	81–200	201–300
Thrown Knife	0–3	4–6	7–12	13–20

CLOTHING AND ARMOR

	Ballistic	Impact
Armor Clothing	3	0
Armor Jacket	5	3
Armor Vest	2	1
Vest With Plates	4	3
HEAVY ARMOR		
Partial Suit	6	4
Full Suit	8	6
Helmet	1	1
LEATHER		
Real	0	2
Synthetic	0	1
Lined Coat	4	2
Ordinary Clothing	0	0
Fine Clothing	0	0

REFERENCE TABLES

FIREARM ACCESSORIES

	Mount	Concealability	Rating	Ammo	Effect
Concealable Holster	—	—	—		—
Grenade Launcher	Under	–3	—	6 (Magazine)	—
Laser Sights	Top	–1	—	—	–1 Target Number
Imaging Scopes					
Low-Light	Top	–2	—	—	Special
Thermographic	Top	–2	—	—	Special
Magnification 1	Top	–1	1	—	—
Magnification 2	Top	–1	2	—	—
Magnification 3	Top	–1	3	—	—

Recoil Compensators and Gyros

	Mount	Concealability	Rating
Shock Pads	Stock	—	1
Gas-Vent 2	Barrel	–1	2
Gas-Vent 3	Barrel	–2	3
Gyro Mount	Under	–5	4
Deluxe Gyro Mount	Under	–6	6

Others	Mount	Concealability	Effect
Silencer	Barrel	–1	Special
Smart Goggles	Top	—	–1 Target Number
Smartgun Adapter	Top	–2	—
Smartgun Variant	—	—	–2 Target Number

EXPLOSIVES

	Concealability	Damage
Grenades		
Offensive	6	6M3
Defensive	6	6M3
Concussion	6	4M3 Stun
Gas (neuro-stun VIII)	5	—
Mini	8	—
Smoke	5	—

Explosives, Per Kilo

	Concealability	Rating
Commercial	6	3
Plastic, Compound 4	6	6
Plastic, Compound 12	6	12
Timer	6	—
Radio Detonator	8	—

AMMUNITION

	Damage
Regular Ammo	—
Explosive Rounds	+2 Staging
Flechette Rounds	–1 Power Level, +1 Staging
Gel Rounds	4L1 Stun
Stun Rounds	4M4 Stun
Taser Dart	Special
Taser Cartridge	Special

Missile	Intelligence	Ammo	Damage
AVM	4	4 (Break)	12D8/6D4*
APM	3	4 (Break)	5M3
HEM	2	4 (Break)	4M4

*Vehicle Damage

MELEE WEAPONS

	Conc.	Reach	Damage
Edged Weapons			
Katana	3	+1	(Str)M3
Knife	8	—	(Str+2)L]
Sword	4	+1	(Str)M2
Pole Arms/Staffs			
Pole Arm	2	+2	(Str)S3
Staff	2	+2	(Str)M2 Stun
Clubs			
Club	5	+1	(Str+1)M2 Stun
Sap	8	—	(Str)M2 Stun
Stun Baton	4	+1	L2 + Special
Whips/Flails			
Monofilament Whip	10	+2	6S4
Unarmed	—	—	(Str)M1 Stun.

PROJECTILE WEAPONS

	Conc.	Reach	Damage
Bows			
Bow	3	—	(Str)M2
Arrows	3	—	—
Crossbows			
Light	2	1	4L3
Medium	2	2	5M2
Heavy	NA	2	6S2
Bolts	4	—	—

THROWING WEAPONS

	Conc.	Reach	Damage
Non-Aerodynamic			
Throwing Knife	9	—	(Str+2)L]
Aerodynamic			
Shuriken	8	—	(Str+2)L1

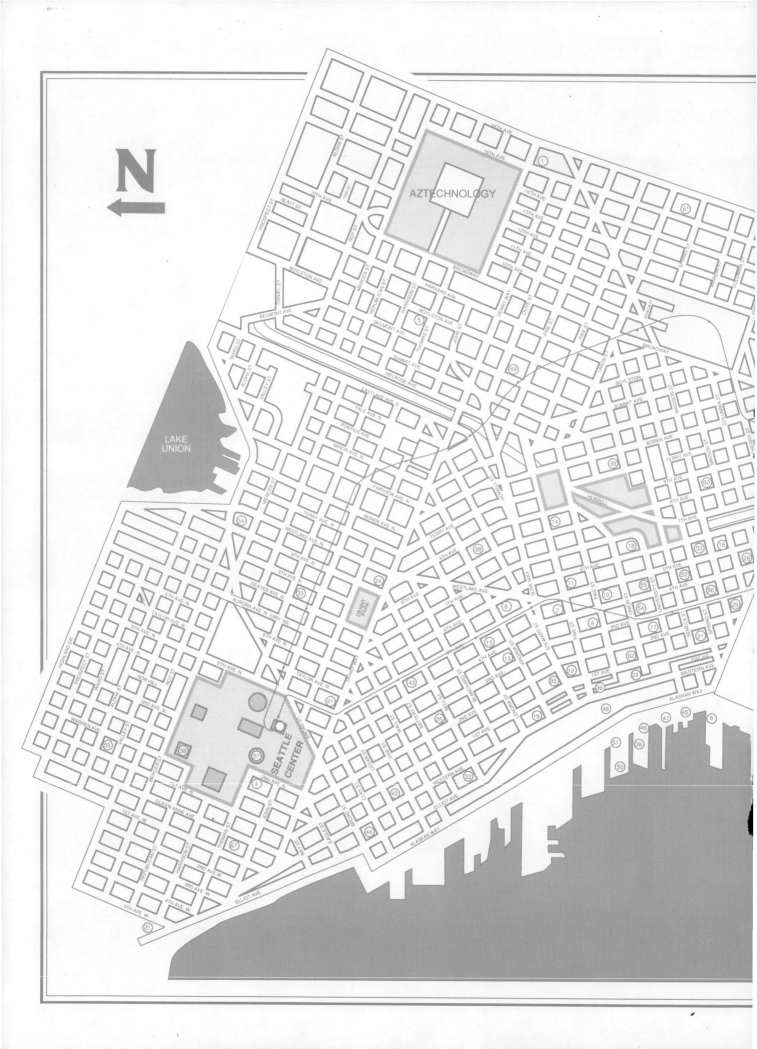